AF443040

CONCURRENT INFORMATION PROCESSING AND COMPUTING

NATO Science Series

A series presenting the results of scientific meetings supported under the NATO Science Programme.

The series is published by IOS Press and Springer Science and Business Media in conjunction with the NATO Public Diplomacy Division.

Sub-Series

I.	Life and Behavioural Sciences	IOS Press
II.	Mathematics, Physics and Chemistry	Springer Science and Business Media
III.	Computer and Systems Sciences	IOS Press
IV.	Earth and Environmental Sciences	Springer Science and Business Media
V.	Science and Technology Policy	IOS Press

The NATO Science Series continues the series of books published formerly as the NATO ASI Series.

The NATO Science Programme offers support for collaboration in civil science between scientists of countries of the Euro-Atlantic Partnership Council. The types of scientific meeting generally supported are "Advanced Study Institutes" and "Advanced Research Workshops", although other types of meeting are supported from time to time. The NATO Science Series collects together the results of these meetings. The meetings are co-organized by scientists from NATO countries and scientists from NATO's Partner countries – countries of the CIS and Central and Eastern Europe.

Advanced Study Institutes are high-level tutorial courses offering in-depth study of latest advances in a field.
Advanced Research Workshops are expert meetings aimed at critical assessment of a field, and identification of directions for future action.

As a consequence of the restructuring of the NATO Science Programme in 1999, the NATO Science Series has been re-organized and there are currently five sub-series as noted above. Please consult the following web sites for information on previous volumes published in the series, as well as details of earlier sub-series:

http://www.nato.int/science
http://www.springeronline.nl
http://www.iospress.nl
http://www.wtv-books.de/nato_pco.htm

Series III: Computer and Systems Sciences - Vol. 195   ISSN 1387-6694

Concurrent Information Processing and Computing

Edited by

Alex Nicolau

Department of Information and Computer Science, University of California, Irvine, USA

and

Dan Grigoraş

Department of Computer Science, University College Cork, Ireland

Press

Amsterdam • Berlin • Oxford • Tokyo • Washington, DC

Published in cooperation with NATO Public Diplomacy Division

Proceedings of the NATO Advanced Research Workshop on
Concurrent Information Processing and Computing
5-10 July 2003
Sinaia, Romania

ISBN 1-58603-502-9
Library of Congress Control Number: 2005923142

Publisher
IOS Press
Nieuwe Hemweg 6B
1013 BG Amsterdam
Netherlands
fax: +31 20 687 0019
e-mail: order@iospress.nl

Distributor in the UK and Ireland
IOS Press/Lavis Marketing
73 Lime Walk
Headington
Oxford OX3 7AD
England
fax: +44 1865 750079

Distributor in the USA and Canada
IOS Press, Inc.
4502 Rachael Manor Drive
Fairfax, VA 22032
USA
fax: +1 703 323 3668
e-mail: iosbooks@iospress.com

Concurrent Information Processing and Computing
D. Grigoras and A. Nicolau (Eds.)
IOS Press, 2005

Preface

It is with great pleasure that we introduce this volume of selected papers from the second NATO-sponsored Advanced Research Workshop (ARW) held in Sinaia, Romania during the summer of 2003. The first NATO Workshop was the International Workshop on Concurrent Computing, held in Mangalia, Romania in July 2001. This current workshop was the third in a series of scientific events devoted to parallel and distributed computing which were organized in Romania (the first in this ongoing series was the International Symposium on Parallel & Distributed Computing in Iasi in 2000).

One of the goals of the current workshop was to provide Ph.D. students from Central and Eastern Europe the possibility to meet leaders in the field from Western Europe, the US and Japan, and to allow for a high degree of interaction and in-depth dialogue between these scientists. Indeed, we hope and expect that this interaction may lead to joint research efforts across these groups in the future. Fifty-nine people from 12 countries attended the workshop (50% more than at the 2001 conference in Mangalia).

The conference included 12 invited talks and a total of 26 papers presented during the workshop, out of the total 31 papers submitted. From these papers and after an additional round of reviews, the organizing committee selected the 16 papers included in this volume.

Our thanks go to the Program Committee members who diligently and promptly handled the review process, to the local Organization Committee for finding the right site for the meeting and dealing with the myriad details surrounding it, and especially to Sabin Buraga and Melanie Sanders, without whose organizational skills the meeting could not have taken place. Last but not least, special thanks are due to our sponsors and the Al. I. Cuza University in Iasi.

For the Program Committee,

Dan Grigoras and Alex Nicolau

NATO ARW Co-Directors

Alex Nicolau
*Department of Information and Computer
Science, University of California, Irvine,
USA*

Ferucio Ţiplea
*Faculty of Computer Science,
"Al. I. Cuza" University of Iaşi,
Romania*

General Chair

Isaac Scherson
*Department of Information and Computer Science,
University of California, Irvine,
USA*

Program Chair

Dan Grigoraş
*Department of Computer Science,
University College Cork,
Ireland*

Program Committee

F. Boian - UBB, Romania
K. Boyanov - Bulgarian Academy of Sciences, Bulgaria
Michel Cosnard - INRIA, France
Valentin Cristea - PUB, Romania
Bertil Folliot - University Paris 6, France
Akira Fukuda - Kyushu University, Japan
Guang Gao - University of Delaware, USA
Wolfgang Gentzsch - SUN Microsystems, USA
Claude Girault - University Paris 6, France
Sergei Gorlatch - TU Berlin, Germany
Lucio Grandinetti - University of Calabria, Italy
Dan Grigoraş (Program Chair) - UCC, Ireland
Hai Jin - Huazhong University of Science and Technology, China
Toader Jucan - UAIC, Romania
H. Kasahara - Waseda University, Japan
C-T. King - National Tsing Hua University, Taiwan
Traian Muntean - University of Marseille, France
Alex Nicolau - UCI, USA
Can Özturan - Bogazici University, Turkey
Constantine Polychronopoulos - University of Illinois, Urbana Champaign, USA
Omer Rana - Cardiff University, UK
Isaac Scherson - UCI, USA
Bernard Toursel - USTL, France
Marek Tudruj - ICS-PAS/PJIIT, Poland
Nicolae Ţăpuş - PUB, Romania

Ferucio Ţiplea - UAIC, Romania
Mateo Valero - Universita Polytechnica di Barcelona, Spain
David Walker - Cardiff University, UK
Harry Wijshoff - Leiden University, The Netherlands
W. Zhou - Deakin University, Australia

International Organizing Committee

Bertil Folliot - University Paris 6, France
Wolfgang Gentzsch - SUN Microsystems, Palo Alto, USA
Dan Grigoraş - University College Cork, Ireland
Alex Nicolau - University of California, Irvine, USA
Isaac Scherson - University of California, Irvine, USA
Bernard Toursel - University of Science and Technology, Lille, France
Ferucio Ţiplea - "Al. I. Cuza" University of Iaşi, Romania

Local Organizing Committee

Sabin Corneliu Buraga - "Al. I. Cuza" University of Iaşi, Romania
Mihaela Brut - "Al. I. Cuza" University of Iaşi, Romania
Cristina Nistor - "Al. I. Cuza" University of Iaşi, Romania

Sponsors

IEEE Romania Section

IFIP WG10.3

Microsoft

Sun Microsystems

ROMSYS

Romaqua Group Borsec

The Coca-Cola Company

Contents

Papers

Invited Papers

Concurrent Information Processing and Computing
D. Grigoras and A. Nicolau (Eds.)
IOS Press, 2005

3

Modeling Resource Management in Concurrent Computing Systems

Isaac D. Scherson[1]   Dinesh Ramanathan[2]
Raghu Subramanian[3]   Piotr Chrząstowski-Wachtel[4]

[1]*Dept. of Computer Science (Systems)*   [2]*Raza Microelectronics, Inc.*
School of Information and Computer Sciences   *3080 N. First Street*
University of California, Irvine   *San Jose, CA 95134*
Irvine, CA 92697-3425 - USA   *USA*

[3]*Juniper Networks*   [4]*Institute of Informatics*
1194 N. Mathilda Ave.   *Warsaw University*
Sunnivale, CA 94089   *Banacha 2, PL02-097 Warszawa*
USA   *Poland*

Abstract.

Efficiently managing resources in very large concurrent computing systems can be viewed as a problem of spatial and temporal allocation of resources to running parallel programs. This basic parallel scheduling problem is considered and a framework is proposed for its definition and analysis. It is assumed that there are multiple parallel jobs executing on a large architecturally MIMD machine. Without loss of generality, each job is assumed to be data parallel, using as many virtual processors as necessary to exploit its inherent parallelism. The notion of virtual processor plays a unifying role in the conceptual design of a scheduler. The basic functions of any scheduler may be viewed as operations on the global set of job's virtual processors. In the context of the above framework, several open problems are identified, and in particular, the twin problems of spatial and temporal scheduling are addressed. Preliminary analysis points to the viability of horizontal spatial schedules and periodic temporal schedules.

1   Introduction

An attempt is made in this paper to provide a framework for the statement, study and analysis of the parallel scheduling problem as a basic function for the efficient resource management of resources in a concurrent computing system. The work is in progress and is presented here as a first approximation to a basic formalism for the study of this important problem.

To write efficient programs in parallel computers, users needs to know architectural details such as the number of processors available, the topology of the interconnection network and the amount of memory on each of the computational nodes. In addition, users often analyze the characteristics of communication delays of the machine and the application's communication patterns in order to speed up programs [2]. Current parallel programs are, therefore, highly machine dependent, and difficult to port across different parallel machines. To alleviate

---

[0]This work was carried out while all the authors were at the University of California, Irvine. [1994-1998]

this situation there is a need for an agreement upon a virtual machine model, i.e. a high level parallel programming paradigm and associated language, for compiler techniques to simulate the virtual machine model on various existing physical machines, and for an operating system to judiciously allocate resources while simulating several virtual machines (multiple users) on the same physical system.

So far there has been little consensus on the issue of a virtual machine model with its associated programming paradigm (language). Several virtual machine models have been proposed in the past and there seems to be a convergence on the data parallel programming model in the form of HPF [7] and Fortran 90 [3]. Sabot [12] mentions that in a survey of 120 parallel algorithms from three ACM Symposia on Theory of Computing (STOC), all were data parallel. Hence the data parallel programming model is assumed in this paper. There are several compiler and operating systems issues to consider. Sample research work on compilers for massively parallel machines can be found in [6]. The compiler discussion is beyond the scope of this paper and will not be addressed.

Operating systems for past and current massively parallel machines are uniprocessor operating systems, which run on a front end or a subset of processors. For example, CM-5's CMost [15] and the CRAY Research T3D's front-end UNICOS [10] are extensions of UNIX^{TM}. Typically, partitions are defined for each user and code is compiled for a particular partition. The resulting code cannot be run on another partition of different size. If a processor idles during the execution of a program, system resources are not properly utilized. This occurs frequently in current parallel systems when some processors are waiting for another processor to update its data so that it can be correctly read by others. Typically, allocated partitions are subsets of available processors and if an incoming job cannot fit into the remaining unallocated partition, it cannot be executed until such time as an appropriate partition is free.

If a parallel machine is viewed as a single, very powerful processor, this processor should be effectively shared among all its potential users. An operating system that performs this task should efficiently manage the systems resources, support program portability by providing a programming model which is architecture independent and masks any idling time that arises in the implementation of the virtual machine model. An operating system for a massively parallel machine should provide a *mainframe*-like behavior with two non-exclusive modes of operation, namely **throughput** and **responsiveness**. In throughput mode, the goal would be to maximize resource utilization by minimizing processor idling time. In responsiveness mode, the goal would be to place an upper limit on the response time for each running job. Furthermore, a parallel OS should provide a uniform parallel programming model conducive to the standardization of parallel programming languages, thereby enabling ease of programming and portability. The model should allow the user to write programs in the problem space, instead of forcing the user to fit the problem to the available machine. The parallel OS is seen as the layer directly below the programming language and above the actual hardware implementation.

We believe that the scheduling problem is at the heart of any improvement in parallel OS implementation. Parallel Scheduling can be basically viewed as the proper allocation of parallel job tasks to physical processors and properly managing when in time each task executes in each physical processor.

Most of the prior work done on scheduling is on the fork-and-join programming model. Scheduling in this model was studied in detail in [4, 5, 8, 9, 11, 13, 14]. These papers suggest that the more the system is loaded, the lower the degree of paralellism that should be allowed. This is achieved by reducing the number of processors allocated to a job.

Some dynamic scheduling policies were studied for the fork-and-join model and they were shown in [4] to work better than the static ones. Moreover, a "run to completion" strategy was proven in [16] to work better than the round robin strategy.

When the programs cannot fit in memory, some paging and caching strategies need to be considered. [9] states that although without memory considerations large degrees of parallelism can be costly, when memory is taken into account, a large degree of parallelism should be achieved to avoid paying for paging and cache penalties. The two main bottlenecks that lead to high penalties and make some scheduling strategies perform poorly in the fork-and-join model are: (a) *Context switch overhead* caused mainly by the time required to save the old context, the time to load the new context, the time to run the scheduler and the time for the low cache hit ratio that is affected during the initialization. (b) *Paging overhead* which trades off the advantages of paralellization, due to a limited I/O speed (usually sequential).

In [1, 5] several strategies for scheduling programs in the fork-and-join model are evaluated experimentally. Some of them include: time slicing, coscheduling, priority synchronization, handsoff scheduling, affinity scheduling, gang scheduling or hardware partitions. Time slicing turns out to be expensive in the analyzed models because of the large overhead time involved in context switching. Similarly, priority synchronization seems to be worse than batch scheduling. The conclusion of these papers is that the best one can do is to hardware partition the processors and not allow jobs to share resources. It is our belief that this conclusion was reached because of the nature of the programming model and the assumption of virtual memory. Our model differs from the fork and join model as shown in [11], as it is assumed that the jobs in the system are loaded into memory and context switching involves writing into local memory and not the disk. Also, [11] mentions that the SPMD model yields better execution efficiency than the fork-and-join model.

2　Preliminaries

The Programming Model

The data parallel programming model is assumed: all processors execute the same program on multiple data sets simultaneously. The user writes only one program, and specifies the number of copies (each copy is a virtual processor) to be executed as a single job.

To provide hardware transparency to the user, the parallel processor topology is defined by the user and implemented by the programming language as a set of linked Virtual Processors (VPs). This model of programming allows the user to exploit the natural parallelism inherent in the application rather than worry about the target architecture.

The Execution Model

A natural way of executing a data parallel program is on a SIMD (Single-Instruction Multiple-Data) machine. However, it is easy to confuse the semantics of the abstract model with the hardware implementation, and equate data parallelism with SIMD. No such thing is implied and it is our belief that a SIMD implementation forces unnecessary synchronization and sequentializes the branches of an `if-then-else` and other similar constructs even though they may not interfere with each other. In contrast, our implementation envisions a scenario in which both branches are executed in parallel if they can be proved to be non-interfeering.

Such an implementation is called Single-Program Multiple-Data (SPMD): all processors execute the same program, even though they may be executing different instructions at any given time. The underlying architecture is hence assumed MIMD.

The Notion of Virtualization

It is assumed that a programmer writes parallel programs in the virtual problem space, utilizing as many VPs as required by the problem. Communication between these VPs is defined by the application. It is the task of the parallel OS to schedule VP execution on the available physical resources and thus *emulate* the user-defined virtual parallel computer. In a multiuser environment, many jobs contribute to a large aggregate of VPs which must share the computer's resources. As a result, the OS manages the emulation of as many virtual parallel computers as there are jobs in the system.

The number of physical PEs available will be typically less than the number of VPs. It is the task of the operating system to allocate VPs of various jobs to the PEs (this is called space sharing [4]) and to schedule VPs for execution within each processor (this is called time sharing [4]).

Some sequentializing may become necessary to fit the program onto the whole machine. If the VPs are allocated over many processors, interprocessor communication over the network increases. Decreasing the allocated processors for a job decreases network access, however, increases the time to completion of the job as all its VPs are now sequentialized. This paper investigates the tradeoffs in the allocation of a job over processors.

The proposed OS paradigm tries to maximize resource utilization by allocating resources between jobs and their VPs. It provides a programming model to the user that is architecture independent and allows the user to exploit the natural parallelism available in the application. The user can now devote more time to extracting parallelism from the problem at hand rather than worry about the implementation on specific architecture. This makes parallel programs portable across machines.

Effects of Virtualization

Some of the problems arising under virtualization include: assigning physical resources to each job (initial partitioning), scheduling the VPs of jobs on available physical resources and a jobs' VPs to run in each one of the PEs (scheduling), balancing work loads as resources are relinquished by terminating tasks (load balancing), designing interconnection networks to facilitate OS emulation of user defined machine topology (network design), and providing system services. This paper addresses the problem of scheduling a large number of VPs on the limited PEs.

Parallelism is used for the concurrent execution of processes and also for the large amounts of memory available. The latter is often missed in evaluating massively parallel machines. Our model assumes that each PE has a large memory capacity and can fit all the jobs scheduled for execution in its memory.

Since I/O is always a bottleneck for shared memory models of computations, the operating system policies should be able to mask I/O. Among the different kinds of I/O, rolling jobs into the sytem causes a very large overhead. Rolling in time can be masked only if multiple jobs are allocated to each processor, so that the I/O for one job can be done while the processor is busy executing VPs of other jobs.

3 The Framework

In this section, a mathematical framework for the study of the scheduling problem on parallel computers is proposed. The thrust is not so much to implement a particular OS but to provide a comprehensive handle on the issues; only then can the tradeoffs between the benefits and drawbacks of various OS policies be properly evaluated.

Model of the System

Let $\mathcal{J} = \{J_1, J_2, \ldots, J_m\}$ denote the set of jobs in the system at some time. For notational convenience, job J_i is identified with its set of VPs $\{P_{i1}, P_{i2}, \ldots, P_{i|J_i|}\}$. Let $\Pi = \{\pi_1, \pi_2, \ldots, \pi_n\}$. denote the set of physical processors or processing elements (PEs). The details of the interconnection network are ignored by assuming that it *guarantees* the completion of all communications within a reasonable time bound (which is not necessarily a constant, as in the PRAM model).

Break time into discrete intervals of equal length. Each interval is a **time slice** for the schedule of jobs. The time slice is assumed to be machine dependent and constant. Within each time slice, every π runs some VP chosen from the VPs allocated to it, or it idles. A PE runs a VP until: (a) The VP issues a communication request which cannot be completed (data to be read is not ready), or (b) The time slice expires. The communication instruction is considered an indivisible instruction and time slices are extended accordingly.

Types of Scheduling

The operating system's scheduling problem can be described as follows: Given a job, J, as a set of $|J|$ VPs, how is this job allocated over the n PEs of the massively parallel computer so that the resources are efficiently utilized? More generally, how are VPs of the same and different jobs, say $J_1, J_2, \ldots, J_m$, allocated over the PEs to efficiently utilize system resources? This is called the problem of spatial scheduling or spatial allocation.

Once an allocation has been made, the problem is more local in nature. Each PE has a list of VPs of the same and/or different jobs that it has to execute. How are these VPs scheduled for execution so that the resouces of the system are efficiently utilized? This is called the problem of temporal scheduling.

Intuitively, a spatial schedule answers the question: "Where to run the VPs of job J?", while a temporal schedule answers the question: "When to run the VPs of job J?".

Definition 1. *A* **spatial schedule**[1] *is an n-tuple allocation function $A : \mathcal{J} \longrightarrow \mathbb{N}^{|\Pi|}$ such that for any job J, $A(J) = (a_1, a_2, \ldots, a_n)$, a_i VPs of J are allocated to processor $\pi_i \in \Pi$,*

$$\left(\sum_{i=1}^{n} a_i = |J| \right).$$

Definition 2. *A* **temporal schedule for a time slice** *t is defined as an n-tuple function, $S(t)$, such that $S(t)[i]$ is the job run by π_i in the time slice t. A* **temporal schedule**, *$\mathcal{S}$, is a time ordered sequence of $S(t)$ for all $t > 0$.*

---

[1]The terms **allocation** and **spatial schedule** will be used interchangeably.

Definition 3. *A **tower** of jobs on any processor $\pi \in \Pi$ is an m-tuple $T : \Pi \longrightarrow \mathbb{N}^{|\mathcal{J}|}$ such that $T(\pi)[k] = b_k$ is the number of VPs of job J_k on π.*

Definition 4. *Define h as the height of the tower of jobs on π: $h(\pi) = \sum_{j=1}^{m} T(\pi)[j]$*

An allocation can be viewed in terms of either the job or the processor:

$$T(\pi_l)[k] = A(J_k)[l]$$

For simplicity of analysis, it is assumed that jobs run indefinitely: when the OS receives a job, the OS does not know when the job is going to terminate. The OS assumes that the job is going to last forever in the system and schedules it. This is not to imply that jobs never end, but is only an assumption reflecting that the time slice of the system is very small (in the order of milliseconds) compared to the execution times of the jobs (in the order of minutes). The assumption of infinite running time might be removed with negligible change to the final results, but with significant complications in the definitions and proofs.

Definition 5. *Define a schedule, $\mathcal{S}$, to be **impartial** if every job $J \in \mathcal{J}$ occurs infinitely many times in $\mathcal{S}$. An impartial schedule ensures that every job in it completes.*

Consider a machine (see Figure 1) with 5 PEs and 5 jobs: J_1 requires 1 VP, J_2 requires 4 VPs, J_3 requires 1 VP, J_4 requires 5 VPs, J_5 requires 1 VP.

One possible allocation function for the jobs is as folllows:

$$A(J_1) = (0,0,0,0,1), A(J_2) = (1,1,1,0,1), A(J_3) = (1,0,0,0,0), A(J_4) = (1,1,0,3,0),$$
$$A(J_5) = (0,0,1,0,0)$$

In Figure 1, each square represents a VP and the number inside represents the VP's job number. Each column represents all VPs allocated to a processor. Since all VPs are assumed identical, it is not required to know which VP is allocated to which processor, just *how many* VPs of each job are allocated to each processor.

Job Execution

A global communication is a communication in which all VPs of a given job participate in. A legal execution of a job is one in which no VP is ahead of any other VP of the same job by more than one global communication step at any time. Hence, a legal scheduling strategy will always choose any trailing VP before any non-trailing VP. As a result, the VPs proceed in lock step.

A **step** begins when all VPs of a job have executed the same number of global communications and it ends at the occurrence of the same condition at a future time slice (after at least one VP of the job has been executed).

<table>
<tr><td>4</td><td></td><td></td><td>4</td><td></td></tr>
<tr><td>3</td><td>4</td><td>5</td><td>4</td><td>2</td></tr>
<tr><td>2</td><td>2</td><td>2</td><td>4</td><td>1</td></tr>
</table>

$\pi_1 \quad \pi_2 \quad \pi_3 \quad \pi_4 \quad \pi_5$

Figure 1. An Allocation

Progress Vectors

In order to keep track of the execution of jobs in the system, the progress of a job in a time slice is defined and then the system progress as a matrix where the rows are progresses of jobs.

Definition 6. *Define a job J's t-schedule vector, $\epsilon(t, J)$ as a 0-1 n-tuple such that,*

$$\epsilon(t, J)[k] = \begin{cases} 1 & \text{if } \pi_k \in \Pi \text{ runs job } J \text{ in time slice } t \\ 0 & \text{otherwise} \end{cases}$$

Definition 7. *Define* **progress of a job** *(at the begining of a time slice t) as an n-tuple function $\mathcal{P} : t \times \mathcal{J} \longrightarrow \mathbb{N}^{\Pi}$ such that:*

1. $\mathcal{P}(t, J) = \vec{0}$ *for $t = 0$,*

2. *If $\mathcal{P}(t - 1, J) + \epsilon(t, J) = A(J)$ then $\mathcal{P}(t, J) = \vec{0}$,*
   else $\mathcal{P}(t, J) = \mathcal{P}(t - 1, J) + \epsilon(t, J)$ (where the addition is componentwise)

3. $\mathcal{P}(t, J) \leq A(J)$ *where the $\leq$ order is applied componentwise.*

The intuition behind the progress vector is as follows: Start at the first step of a job J, let job J proceed on the processor's having 1's on the $\epsilon(t, J)$. If the progress vector reaches $\mathcal{A}(J)$ then another step of job J is complete and progress counters associated with each processor are reset. A new step cannot be started until the previous one is complete. Every job has a progress vector associated with it at the beginning of every time slice.

Consider an allocation on 5 processors (see Figure 1), an example of an arbitrary schedule for job J_4 is given below.

$$
\begin{aligned}
A(J_4) &= (1,1,0,3,0) \\
P(0, J_4) &= (0,0,0,0,0) \\
\epsilon(1, J_4) &= (0,1,0,1,0) \\
P(0, J_4) + \epsilon(1, J_4) = P(1, J_4) &= (0,1,0,1,0) \\
\epsilon(2, J_4) &= (1,0,0,1,0) \\
P(1, J_4) + \epsilon(2, J_4) = P(2, J_4) &= (1,1,0,2,0) \\
\epsilon(3, J_4) &= (0,0,0,1,0) \\
P(2, J_4) + \epsilon(3, J_4) &= (1,1,0,3,0) \\
P(3, J_4) = A(J_4), \; reset\; P(3, J_4) &= (0,0,0,0,0)
\end{aligned}
$$

$\epsilon(1, J_4) = (0,1,0,1,0)$ indicates that processors π_2 and π_4 run job J_4. $\epsilon(1, J_4)$ is added to $P(0, J_4)$ componentwise to give the new progress vector $P(1, J_4)$ for job J_4 and so on.

Definition 8. *Define the* **system progress matrix**, *Q, as a $(n \times m)$-array of progress vectors (columns) of all jobs (rows) in the system.*

Definition 9. *For an allocation A, $\mathcal{S}_p = S(t), S(t+1), \ldots, S(t+p-1)$ is called a* **periodic schedule**, *iff $\exists\, p > 0$ such that $S(t) = S(t + p)$ for all $t > t_s$, where t_s is called the startup time of the schedule. p is the period of the schedule.*

Also for each job J in $\mathcal{S}_p$, $\sum_{1 \le t \le p, 1 \le i \le |\Pi|}[S(t)[i] = J] = k \cdot |J|$ must be satisfied for some positive integer k to ensure that during each period a (positive) integer number of steps (k) of each job is executed (k need not be the same for every job). If π_i does not run any job during a particular time slice t, then $S(t)[i] = 0$. Assume that the startup time, t_s, is relatively small compared to the number of time slices necessary to complete all jobs. Since the periodic part of the schedule will be repeated, every job should be included in $\mathcal{S}$ so that it can progress to completion (impartiality).

3.1   Scheduling Metrics

A parallel OS should be able to satisfy two objectives: minimize processor idling time, and guarantee an upper limit on the system response time to every job. From a single user's point of view, the second objective is of primary importance while from the system's point of view, the first objective is important. It is natural that in a working system, both objectives have to be traded off and each satisfied to varying degrees. Two measures of the quality of a schedule are:

- The **idling ratio** measures quality from the system manager's point of view, who is concerned with the throughput and utilization of the machine.

- The **happiness function** measures quality from the users' point of view. It guarantees that the system will respond within a specific time.

Idling Ratio

Throughput optimization is important from the machine owner's point of view. The owner would like to minimize the idle time of the machine and thereby maximize revenue. Maximizing throughput will also ensure that the users do not incur the cost of idling processors caused by a bad allocation. The idling ratio is a measure of the resource utilization.

Definition 10. *For a schedule S, at time t, define the **idling ratio or throughput** of S as:*

$$\imath_S : \mathbb{N} \to \mathbb{R}, \quad \imath_S(t) = \frac{\displaystyle\sum_{k \le t} \imath_k}{tn}$$

$\imath_t$ *is the total number of idling processors during time slice t.*

The idling ratio is the simplest metric that is considered in all prior work done in scheduling. This ratio gives an estimate on the effective use of the computer at hand. Since, massively parallel computers are quite expensive, it is understandable that the owner of such a computer would like to squeeze out the maximum performance from it.

Happiness Function

The happiness function measures the performance of the OS from the users' point of view by guaranteeing an upper bound on the system's response time.

Definition 11. *Define the* **happiness function,** $\hbar_{\Delta t}(J)$, *of a job J for a time length Δt as,*

$$\hbar_{\Delta t}(J) = \min_{t \geq 0} \left\{ \frac{\displaystyle\sum_{\tau=t}^{t+\Delta t-1} \sum_{\pi \in \Pi} \epsilon(\tau, J)}{|J| \cdot \Delta t} \right\}$$

Intuitively, happiness represents the machine power that a job is given during a time slice. The term in the braces represents the fraction of the full parallel speedup that was achieved by job J in time interval $(t, t + \Delta t - 1)$. Δt represents the expected **impatience latency** of the user. It is the minimum time the user is required to wait before the system responds.

The proposed parallel OS paradigm allows the user to program in a virtual parallel model with no limit on the number of VPs in a job. To get a handle on the maximum parallel speedup that can be achieved for a job given n physical processors, define **virtual happiness,** $v(J) = \min\{1, \frac{n}{|J|}\}$. Virtual happiness of a job J represents the happiness of the job if the entire machine is used by J. Hence, J cannot be happier than $v(J)$.

It is expected that a job (user) will be happier if it acquires more parallel speedup in a given time segment. If the schedule is unable to provide the required happiness for a job, rescheduling with a different allocation which better parallelizes the job J without affecting the happiness of other jobs in the system may have to be considered. If the required happiness for a set of jobs cannot be achieved by any allocation, then some jobs must be queued for later allocation. This paper does not address this problem; it assumes that the happiness for all allocated jobs can be met by some schedule and generates such a schedule. A happy schedule is not necessarily optimal from the throughput point of view. It merely guarantees an upper limit on the response time.

It is assumed that Δt is the same for all jobs and is the time slice under consideration. As a result, each job has a happiness associated with it. A job J, computes its happiness as follows: The programmer assumes a virtual computer on which J has to run. This computer has as many processors as the job has VPs. In reality, these VPs have to be run on a machine with fewer PEs than assumed by the programmer. As a result, the program will slow down. The programmer accepts a fraction of this slow down and this fraction is the happiness of the job.

The next section addresses the problem of spatial scheduling, i.e., Given a collection of VPs of the same or different jobs, each job having some happiness associated with it, how are these VPs allocated on the limited PEs to maximize system utilization and minimize response time?

4　Spatial Scheduling

Assume that m jobs have been selected to run on the computer. How these jobs are selected is a problem that merits an examination in its own right. One criterion for their selection could be that the sum of the happiness of the selected m jobs is less than one. However, this paper does not address this problem. The allocation of VPs to PEs is a static allocation. Once the m jobs are selected for execution, no job enters or leaves the system. Further, it is assumed that the m jobs selected can be allocatd to satisfy the happiness function of each job. For jobs whose sizes are multiples of the number of processors, the necessary and sufficient condidition for an allocation to exist is that the sum of the happiness functions are less than one. However, for jobs whose sizes are not multiples, the above condition becomes a necessary condition, but not a sufficient one. The selection of these jobs remains an open question and is not addressed in this paper.

The problem of spatial allocation can be formulated as follows: Given a parallel computer with n PEs, and $J_1, J_2, \ldots, J_m$ jobs, each job having an associated happiness, how are these jobs (their VPs) to be allocated on the n processors to minimize processor idling and guarantee the required response time? In this section, this problem is formulated as a non-linear programming problem.

Consider $J_1, \ldots, J_m$ jobs and happiness $\hbar_1, \ldots, \hbar_m$, such that $\hbar_i$ is the happiness function of job J_i. An allocation for all the jobs in a system of n PEs, can be represented as a matrix. Call such a matrix, with n (PEs) columns and m (jobs) rows, an allocation matrix and denote it by $\mathbf{A}$. So, $\mathbf{A}(j, p)$ gives the number of VPs of job J_j on processor π_p. Let $\mathbf{H} = (\hbar_1, \ldots, \hbar_m)$ denote the happiness of each job in the system. To satisfy the happiness of all the jobs, every job will have to be replicated in the schedule. Let T be maximum height of all the towers of allocation $\mathbf{A}$ and let $\mathbf{R} = (R_1, \ldots, R_m)$ be the repetition vector of jobs, such that $\mathbf{R}(i)$ is the repetition of job J_i, that satisfy the happiness function. Let $\mathbf{N} = (|J_1|, \ldots, |J_m|)$ be the number of VPs of eah job in the system. $\mathbf{H}$ and $\mathbf{N}$ are the only data available once the jobs have been accepted into the system. $\mathbf{R}$, T and $\mathbf{A}$ have to be computed. The relations between the inputs and outputs are:

$$\sum_j \mathbf{A}(j, p) \left(\frac{\mathbf{R}(j)}{T} \right) \leq 1, \; \frac{\mathbf{R}(j)}{T} \geq \mathbf{H}(j), \text{ and } \sum_p \mathbf{A}(j, p) = \mathbf{N}(j)$$

Now, the idling ratio has to be minimized which is the objective function and is:

$$\min \left(1 - \frac{\sum_p \sum_j \mathbf{A}(j, p) \mathbf{R}(j)}{T \cdot n} \right)$$

This is a non-linear program as equation 2 involves the product of two input variables. Normalizing, with respect to T, the non-linear program that represents the spatial allocation is given by:

$$ll\text{Objective:} \quad \min \left(1 - \frac{\sum_p \sum_j \mathbf{A}(j,p) \mathbf{R}(j)}{n} \right) \tag{1}$$

$$\text{Subject to} \quad \sum_j \mathbf{A}(j, p) \left(\frac{\mathbf{R}(j)}{T} \right) \leq 1 \tag{2}$$

$$\mathbf{R}(j) \geq \mathbf{H}(j) \tag{3}$$

$$\sum_p \mathbf{A}(j, p) = \mathbf{N}(j) \tag{4}$$

Equation 2 says that the maximum number of VPs on any processor cannot exceed T. Equation 3 says that by replicating job J_j, its happiness must not be destroyed.

Solutions to non-linear programs are difficult to implement and involve large overheads. If the front-end of the parallel computer has to solve a non-linear program each time a job enters the system, the operating system overhead will be high. As a result, solving a non-linear program is not a viable option for an OS. However, if the allocation matrix was provided as an input, the non-linear program reduces to a linear program. But, the linear program has output variable R with an integer range. So, the linear program is an integer linear program, which is known to be NP-complete. However, if the domains of H and A are rational, the range R will be rational. If R has a rational range, the tuples of R can be converted into integers by appropriately multiplying them with the least common multiple. Hence, to reduce the problem of generating a static spatial allocation to a linear program, the allocation matrix (which makes the non-linear program linear) should be presented as an input. In remaining part of this section, the merits of some simple allocations are considered, namely, vertical and horizontal allocations.

Definition 12. *An allocation is* **vertical** *if the number of PEs allocated to a job is the minimum number of PEs for which the happiness function of a job can be satisfied.*

Definition 13. *An allocation is* **horizontal** *if the VPs of a job are spread over the maximum number of PEs the job can use in parallel.*

A vertical allocation will not require the solution of a linear program as the repetition vector will be a unit vector. This is the allocation stragey followed in massively parallel machines like the CRAY T3D [10] and the CM-5 [15]. A vertical allocation also trivializes the concept of temporal scheduling as the PE now has to execute only VPs of one job. However, these computers do not have the concept of response time and therefore partitions are not allocated using this concept. Partitions are fixed at boot-time and cannot be changed.

A horizontal allocation requires a solution to the linear program to compute the repetition vector. Once the repetition vector is computed, each PE is provided with the list of VPs it has to run along with the integer repetitions for each job. The method of execution of the VPs by each PE is discussed in section 5 while the next section gives a qualitative comparison between vertical and horizontal allocations.

5　Temporal Scheduling

The problem addressed in this section is: Given a spatial allocation, determine a temporal schedule that minimizes processor idling and maximizes the happiness function of each job in the system. The OS overhead should be minimized for maximum throughput. As a result, the temporal schedule should be simple. It is shown that the simple periodic schedules are the ones that should be used.

In this section, it is assumed that the OS does not know when a job is going to leave the system. The OS, therefore, assumes that the job is going to last forever in the system and schedules it accordingly. This does not imply, in any way, that jobs are infinite. The OS merely assumes that its schedule is going to last forever.

Given an allocation A, and an infinite temporal schedule S for the allocation, the following lemma will be used in proofs of theorems in the next two sections.

Lemma 1. *Let S be an impartial temporal schedule (S need not be periodic). There exists an infinite subsequence $t_{i_1}, t_{i_2}, \ldots$ such that the corresponding system progress matrices $Q_{i_1}, Q_{i_2}, \ldots$ are the same, and each time segment $[t_{i_k}, t_{i_{k+1}}]$ is impartial.*

Proof: The number of different system progress matrices is finite. Since the schedule executes indefinitely, at least one of the system progress matrices, Q, must repeat infinitely many times in the schedule S.

Consider an infinite subsequence $t_{k_1}, t_{k_2}, \ldots$ of time slices for which Q is the system progress matrix. Though it can be the case that between t_{k_j} and $t_{k_{j+1}}$, not all jobs were present in S, we may still choose a subsequence $t_{i_1}, t_{i_2}, \ldots$ from $t_{k_1}, t_{k_2}, \ldots$ satisfying the impartiality requirement by the following procedure.

Choose $i_1 = k_1$. Skip all the subsequent elements $k_2, k_3, \ldots, k_l$ for which the time segment $[k_1..k_l]$ is not impartial for $j = 2, 3, \ldots, l, l \geq 1$. Set $i_2 = k_{l+1}$ for the first k_{l+1} for which the time segment $[k_1, k_{l+1}]$ is impartial in S. Such an index, $l + 1$, will always be found, since the original schedule S is impartial.

Continue the procedure to choose subsequent elements $i_3, i_4, \ldots$ in an analogous way. $\square$

In the following sections, the problem of finding the best schedules is solved: it is shown that it suffices to limit the search for the best schedule to a small, well-behaved class of schedules called **periodic schedules**. It is also shown that the number of candidate periodic schedules is finite (although very large), and hence the best one could be found (at least in principle) by exhaustive search. The best periodic schedule is based on the spatial allocation function and a simple algorithm to determine it is presented in section 4.

Minimizing the Idling Ratio

A temporal schedule should minimize idling ratio, thereby increasing system uitilization. This section shows that periodic schedules minimize idling ratio but cannot guarantee that a job will terminate after entering the system.

Definition 14. *Define $g(S) = lub\{x : \exists t_s : \forall t > t_s, x > i_S(t)\}$ where lub denotes the least upper bound of a set.*

Only the asymptotic behavior of schedules would be of interest to us. For most interesting schedules the limit $\lim_{t \to \infty} i_S(t)$, will exist and will be the same as the least upper bound. However, for the moment the cases for which the limit does not exist are also considered.

Definition 15. *A schedule S' is not worse than S iff, for all $t \geq t_s$, $g(S) \leq g(S')$ holds.*

Hence, g is the measure of how efficiently the VPs are scheduled, or more precisely, how many processors are in use with respect to the maximum number available.

Theorem 1. *If there exists an impartial periodic schedule, S_p, with the least $g(S_p)$ among all impartial periodic schedules, then for all impartial schedules, $S : g(S) \geq g(S_p)$.*

Proof: Proof: Assume the contrary, that for some (non-periodic) impartial schedule, S,

$$g(S) < g(S_p) \tag{5}$$

Let $\varepsilon = \frac{g(S_p) - g(S)}{2}$ and consider a subsequence $t_{k_1}, t_{k_2}, \ldots$ such that $t_{k_j} - g(S) < \varepsilon$ for each $j \geq 1$. Choose a sub-subsequence $t_{k_{j_1}}, t_{k_{j_2}}, \ldots$ such that all the system progress matrices corresponding to $t_{k_{j_1}}, t_{k_{j_2}}, \ldots$ are the same in S and all the time segments are impartial (lemma 1).

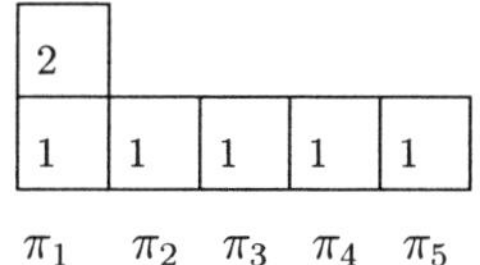

Figure 2. An example with no optimal schedule

Define the idling ratio in the time segment $[t_1..t_2]$ to be the ratio of the number of idling processors to the total number of processors during $[t_1..t_2]$, i.e.,

$$\frac{\sum_{k=t_1}^{t_2} i_k}{(t_2 - t_1 + 1)n}$$

If the idling ratios of all time segments $[t_{k_{j_1}}..t_{k_{j_2}}], [t_{k_{j_2}}..t_{k_{j_3}}], \ldots$ are greater than or equal to $g(\mathcal{S}_p)$ then $g(\mathcal{S}) \geq g(\mathcal{S}_p)$ as well, which contradicts inequality 5. Otherwise, let $[t_{k_{j_l}}..t_{k_{j_{l+1}}}]$ be the time period in which the idling ratio is smaller than $g(\mathcal{S}_p)$. Let this interval be the period of an impartial periodic schedule, $\mathcal{S}_{p'}$, with $g(\mathcal{S}_{p'}) < g(\mathcal{S}_p)$ which contradicts the assumption that $\mathcal{S}_p$ is the best periodic schedule. Since, a contradiction is reached in both cases, $g(\mathcal{S}) \geq g(\mathcal{S}_p)$ must hold. $\qquad\square$

It is not always the case that a periodic schedule that minimizes the idling ratio and guarantees completion of all jobs exists. For the example in Figure 2 (5 PEs, $|J_1| = 5$ and $|J_2| = 1$), every impartial periodic schedule (as well as every impartial non-periodic schedule) can be improved.

If J_1 and J_2 run for one time slice each, the idling ratio is $\frac{2}{5}$. The idling ratio can be improved to $\frac{4}{15}$ by running J_1 for two time slices before running J_2. A periodic schedule where J_1 is run for n time slices will always have a better idling ratio than one where J_1 is run for $n - 1$ time slices before running J_2.

This problem arises due to the fact that the schedule is not assumed to be impartial. When a "bad" job (Job J_2 in Figure 2) enters the system, its execution is delayed as much as possible: the more it is delayed, the better the system performs in terms of throughput. This implies that the system should ensure that all jobs will be serviced regularly by the OS. This was the notion of system response time, the happiness function of job. The next section incorporates happiness into temporal schedules.

Maximizing the Happiness Function

Definition 16. *A job J_1 is **not** Δt-happier than J_2 for the schedule $\mathcal{S}$ iff $\hbar_{\Delta t}(J_1) \leq \hbar_{\Delta t}(J_2)$. Otherwise J_1 is said to be Δt-happier than J_2. A schedule $\mathcal{S}_1$ is **not** Δt-**happier** than $\mathcal{S}_2$ iff the least happy job scheduled by $\mathcal{S}_1$ is at most as happy as the least happy job scheduled by $\mathcal{S}_2$. Otherwise $\mathcal{S}_1$ is said to be Δt-happier than $\mathcal{S}_2$.*

Note that "**not** Δt-**happier**" is a total order.

Hence, the happiness of the least satisfied job in a schedule is considered as a measure of the schedule's happiness.

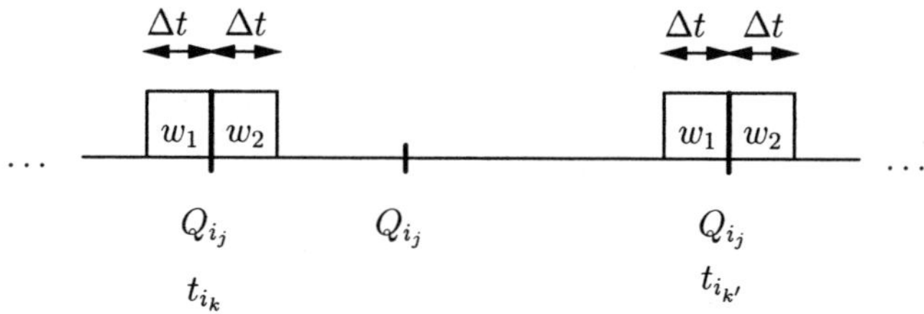

Figure 3. Using the time segment between t_{i_k} and $t_{i_{k'}}$ as a period cannot destroy happiness.

Definition 17. *A job J is $(\lambda, \Delta t)$-happy iff $\hbar_{\Delta t}(J) \geq v(J) \cdot \lambda$ for some real number $0 < \lambda \leq 1$ called the **happiness threshold** of the system. The schedule S is $(\lambda, \Delta t)$-happy iff all jobs are $(\lambda, \Delta t)$-happy in S.*

Hence, when a schedule is $(\lambda, \Delta t)$-happy every job in the system gets at least λ fraction of the machine power during any Δt interval of time. As system parameter, λ, is tunable and reflects the minimum speed expected for each job in the system measured in the units of the maximum speedup possible, $v(J)$.

With each time slice, $t \geq \Delta t$ in S, associate a **configuration**, (Q, w_l, w_r), which is a triple consisting of a system progress matrix, Q, and two temporal schedules, w_l and w_r, for time intervals $t - \Delta t + 1..t$ and $t + 1..t + \Delta t$, respectively. Intuitively, a configuration at time t represents the progress of the system together with schedules in windows of length Δt on the left and right hand side of t. This leads to the following lemma which will be used in the proof of the periodicity theorem.

Lemma 2. *The number of configurations for a given $(\lambda, \Delta t)$-happy schedule is finite.*

Proof: Since the number of system progress matrices and the number of Δt long sequences of temporal schedules of single time slices are finite, the number of triples formed from them is finite. □

It is shown that it is sufficient to consider periodic schedules when maximizing happiness (parallel speedup).

Theorem 2. *For every impartial schedule S and every $\Delta t > 0$ there exists an impartial periodic schedule S_p such that S is not Δt-happier than S_p.*

Proof: Consider an infinite subsequence $t_{i_1}, t_{i_2}, \ldots$ such that the system progress matrices $Q_{i_1}, Q_{i_2}, \ldots$ for $t_{i_1}, t_{i_2}, \ldots$ are the same, and each time segment $[t_{i_k}, t_{i_{k+1}}]$ is impartial. The existence of such a sequence is guaranteed by lemma 1.

Consider the set of configurations associated with all the above t_{i_j}s. Since there are only a finite number of configurations (lemma 2) and an infinite number of t_{i_j}s, a pair of configurations must repeat for some t_{i_k} and $t_{i_{k'}}$, $k \neq k'$ (See Figure 3).

Pick the time segment $[t_{i_k}..t_{i_{k'}}]$ as the period interval of the periodic impartial schedule S_p. Within the time segment of the period the happiness cannot fall below the happiness of S as it did not do so in S.

The two intervals of size Δt at the end of the first period and the beginning of the second occurred in the same order in S. Hence, in the time interval between the two consecutive periods, the happiness cannot fall below the happiness of S since the configurations at the beginning and at the end of the period are the same. $\quad\square$

Theorem 2 says that while looking for the best among happy schedules, the domain of search can be restricted to periodic schedules. In fact, it follows from the proof that this domain is finite.

A Theorem on Periodic Schedules

Using the results of the previous section, this section's theorem proves that the search for happy schedules with the least idling ration can be restricted to the class of periodic schedules. This class is finite, well-behaved. Intuitively, if every job is guaranteed a happiness threshold in some Δt, its execution cannot be delayed indefinitely. As a result, a periodic schedule with the minimum idling time will always exist:

Theorem 3. *Consider the class $\mathcal{S}^{(\lambda,\Delta t)}$ of $(\lambda, \Delta t)$-happy schedules for some $\lambda > 0$ and $\Delta t > 0$. There exists a periodic schedule $\mathcal{S}_p^{\lambda}$ such that for any other schedule $\mathcal{S}$ in $\mathcal{S}^{(\lambda,\Delta t)}$: $g(\mathcal{S}) \geq g(\mathcal{S}_p^{\lambda})$.*

Proof: The set of $(\lambda, \Delta t)$-happy schedules is restricted to one with a specific property. Without loss of generality, it is assumed that periodic schedules have no startup time and all of them start at the zero system progress matrix, since for the asymptotic behavior the startup time is negligible.

The set of configurations for every schedule is finite (lemma 2). Let C be the number of configurations. It is shown that for every periodic schedule, $\mathcal{S}_p$, in $\mathcal{S}^{(\lambda,\Delta t)}$ there exists a schedule with period at most $C \cdot \Delta t$ which has an idling ratio no worse than $\mathcal{S}_p$.

Consider any periodic schedule $\mathcal{S}_p \in \mathcal{S}^{(\lambda,\Delta t)}$. Suppose its period, p, is greater than $C \cdot \Delta t$. Within each time segment Δt, all jobs make some progress. Eventually, some configuration must repeat at t_k and $t_{k'}$ in $\mathcal{S}_p$, where $t_k, t_{k'} < p$.

If the idling ratio of the time segment $[t_k..t_{k'}]$ is less than or equal to the idling ratio of $[0..p]$, then choose the schedule in time segment $[t_k..t_{k'}]$ as the periodic schedule whose idling ratio is no worse than that of $\mathcal{S}$, and whose period is less than $C \cdot \Delta t$. This will be a $(\lambda, \Delta t)$-happy schedule with idling ratio no worse than $\mathcal{S}_p$.

If the idling ratio of the time segment $[t_k..t_{k'}]$ is greater than the idling ratio of $[0..p]$ then removing $[t_k..t_{k'}]$ from $\mathcal{S}_p$ results in a schedule $\mathcal{S}_p' \in \mathcal{S}^{(\lambda,\Delta t)}$ with a smaller idling ratio. If the period of $\mathcal{S}_p'$ is still larger than $C \cdot \Delta t$, then continue this procedure until either a time segment $[t_j..t_{j'}]$, whose idling ratio is not worse, is found or the length of the period is less than or equal to $C \cdot \Delta t$.

Hence for every periodic schedule $\mathcal{S}_p \in \mathcal{S}^{(\lambda,\Delta t)}$ there exists a schedule $\hat{\mathcal{S}}_p \in \mathcal{S}^{(\lambda,\Delta t)}$ such that $\hat{\mathcal{S}}_p$ has no worse idling ratio than $\mathcal{S}_p$ and the period of $\hat{\mathcal{S}}_p$ is at most $C \cdot \Delta t$. Since there are finitely many periods of length at most $C \cdot \Delta t$, the one with minimum idling ratio, $\mathcal{S}_p^{\lambda}$, can be picked.

Theorem 1 concludes that for all schedules $\mathcal{S} \in \mathcal{S}^{(\lambda,\Delta t)} : g(\mathcal{S}) \geq g(\mathcal{S}_p^{\lambda})$. $\quad\square$

Observe that without the assumption of happiness the proof fails, because the time segment $[t_k..t_{k'}]$ need not be impartial. In fact, $(\lambda, \Delta t)$-happiness implies impartiality.

Theorem 3 implies that while looking for a happy schedule with the least idling ratio, the domain of search can be restricted to periodic schedules. In fact, it follows from the proof that this domain is finite.

In section 4, the problem of finding the static schedule that gives the periodic schedule matrix was addressed. It was shown that this problem can be formulated as a linear programming problem. In this section, it was shown that a periodic execution strategy should be followed by each PE. Each PE has a list of VPs of the same or different jobs that it has to execute and the number of times a job has to be executed in each period. The PE schedules them in the following manner: Each jobs VPs are run bunched together, until one pass is made over all the jobs. Then all the jobs that need to get repeated are run again, until all the jobs have been run as many times as they need to in one period. The PE then restarts this process. If a VP cannot run during a time slice, some other VP of either the same or different job is run during that time slice.

References

[1] A. Tucker A. Gupta and S. Urushibara. The impact of operating system scheduling policies and synchronization methods on the performance of parallel applications. In *Performance Evaluation Review*, pages 120–132, May, 1991.

[2] Tom Blank. Personal communications, 1993. MasPar Computer Corporation, Sunnyvale, CA.

[3] Walter S. Brainerd, Charles H. Goldberg, and Jeanne C. Adams. *Programmer's guide to Fortran 90*. McGraw-Hill Book Co., 1990.

[4] R. Vaswani C. McCann and J. Zahorjan. A dynamic processor allocation policy for multiprogrammed shared-memory multiprocessors. *ACM Transactions on Computer Systems*, 11(2):146–178, 1993.

[5] M. Crovella et al. Multiprogramming on multiprocessors. In *Proceedings of the Third IEEE Symposium on Parallel and Distributed Processing*, pages 590–597, Dec, 1991.

[6] P. Hatcher, M. Quinn, A. Lapadula, B. Seevers, R. Anderson, and R. Jones. Data-Parallel Programming on MIMD Computers. *IEEE Transactions on Parallel and Distributed Systems*, 2(3):383–388, July 1991.

[7] David B. Loveman. High Performance Fortran. *IEEE Parallel and Distributed Technology*, 1(1):25–42, 1993.

[8] S.T. Luetenegger and M.K. Vernon. The performance of multiprogrammed multiprocessor scheduling policy. In *Performance Evaluation Review*, pages 226–236, May, 1990.

[9] C. McCann and J. Zoharjan. Processor allocation policies for message-passing parallel computers. In *Performance Evaluation Review*, pages 19–32, May, 1994.

[10] Wilfried Oed. The Cray Research Massively Parallel Processor System CRAY T3D. available by anonymous ftp from ftp.cray.com, November 1993.

[11] J. Lipkis R. Cytron and E. Schonberg. A computer-assisted approach to spmd execution. In *Proceedings of Supercomputing '90*, pages 398–406, Nov, 1990.

[12] Gary Sabot. *The Paralation Model: Architecture-Independent Parallel Programming*. MIT Press, Cambridge, MA, 1988.

[13] Sanjeev Setia and Satish Tripathi. Analysis of processor allocation in multiprogrammed, distributed-memory parallel processing system. *IEEE Transaction on Parallel and Distributed Systems*, 5(4):401–430, April, 1994.

[14] K. C. Sevcik. Characterization of parallelism in applications and their use in scheduling. In *Performance Evaluation Review*, pages 171–180, May, 1989.

[15] Thinking Machines Corporation, Cambridge, MA. *The Connection Machine CM-5 Technical Summary*, October 1991.

[16] J. Zoharjan and C. McCann. Processor scheduling in shared memory multiprocessors. In *Performance Evaluation Review*, pages 214–225, May, 1990.

Concurrent Information Processing and Computing
D. Grigoras and A. Nicolau (Eds.)
IOS Press, 2005

19

Application-Level Concurrency Management

Frederic Ogel   Gael Thomas   Bertil Folliot   Ian Piumarta

Regal Group
INRIA Rocquencourt
Domaine de Voluceau 78153 Le Chesnay, France
&
Laboratoire d'Informatique de Paris VI, CNRS,
Université Pierre et Marie Curie,
4, place Jussieu, 75252 Paris Cedex 05, France
`http://www-sor.inria.fr/projects/vvm`

Abstract. Traditionally an execution environment faces a trade-off between providing high-level or low-level concurrency mechanisms. The former trades flexibility for ease-of-use, while the latter results in a concurrency management closer to applications needs at the cost of an increase in the complexity of the applications code. Thus, one way or another, an application programmer has to match his application's semantic to the set of abstractions exported by the target execution environment.

Most execution environments, such as Java or Corba, are still rigid and closed and thus export high-level and general purpose abstractions that prevent application programmers from having any control or knowledge on the way their applications behave. Because concurrency concerns are closely related to applications semantics, a "one-size-fits-all" approach does hardly work.

Hence, we propose a flexible and minimal execution environment[1] that allows dynamic construction of dedicated execution environments and dynamic reconfiguration at both the execution environment and the application level. We present its architecture and its utilization to construct a dynamically adaptable Java runtime that exploits this flexibility to overcome some limitations of traditional Java environments.
Keywords: dynamic flexibility, adaptable concurrency, virtual machine.

1   Introduction

Writing concurrent applications is not a trivial task. Developers must prevent deadlocks and inconsistencies, while preserving parallelism. Since this trade-off between performance and consistency is closely related to an application's semantic, the suitability of the abstractions exported by the execution environment is critical.

The problem lies in the limited flexibility of traditional execution environments. While flexible operating systems only offer service replacement in a controlled way, most often for security concerns, language-based extensible systems, such as Java or Corba, are still monolithic and closed execution environments. This lack of flexibility results in a "one-size-fits-all" approach to system and language abstractions, which leads programmers to concentrate on

---

[1]This work is partially funded by the European IST project COACH (2001-34445).

the adaptation of their application to the exported abstractions, rather than on their application's internal problems.

Indeed, as limitations of existing environments are identified, ad-hoc solutions are proposed, most often to solve a particular problem or limitation. Those solutions are thus as rigid and closed as the original environments they are based on. Most of the research projects focusing on solving a limitation in Java end up with a modified version of an otherwise standard Java Virtual Machine (JVM). For example, to introduce reflection in Java, like MetaXa [17], object persistence, as in PJama [19], real-time (RT-Java [13]) or compilation optimizations, like Marmot [18], it was necessary to develop a new Java runtime, because the original was not flexible enough to be dynamically adapted. What about a Java runtime offering object persistence and compilation optimizations? It has to be another dedicated Java runtime.

In particular, the continuous emergence of novel application domains and computing models have led to a significant proliferation of scheduling algorithms. This increasing diversity demonstrates that no single scheduling policy is adequate for meeting the requirements of all applications.

In response to traditional environments lack of flexibility, the Virtual Virtual Machine (VVM) [4] is a project to build open and flexible execution environments including both system and language aspects. Its objectives are: (i) to allow dynamic adaptation of the execution environment to match any application-specific semantics; (ii) to provide a common language substrate on which to achieve interoperability between different languages or application domains. Whereas traditional execution environments are still closed and rigid, the VVM's complete flexibility lets developers concentrate on their application's internal problems rather than on the problem of adapting their application to the limitations of the target execution environment.

We propose in this paper the architecture of a minimal execution environment, composed of a Hardware Abstraction Layer (HAL) and a flexible dynamic compiler. Because there are no predefined and imposed abstractions, any execution environment can be dynamically instantiated upon it. Moreover, by combining the dynamism and the reflexivity inherent in the dynamic compiler, every piece of code can be dynamically reconfigured.

The paper is organized as follows. The next section describes the architecture of our minimal yet flexible execution environment. Section 3 presents the construction of a dynamically adaptable Java runtime and some evaluations. Then, section 5 examines related work and section 6 summarizes and concludes.

2 A flexible execution environment

In order to provide complete application flexibility, the execution environment must be completely open and free of predefined abstractions (hence following the Exokernel approach). Therefore, our architecture relies on a minimal execution environment composed of a HAL and a dynamic compiler, as illustrated in Figure 1.

The HAL is in charge of hardware initialization at boot-time. It reifies hardware resources through a set of functions in a policy-neutral way, that is, without adding any semantics to them. The only abstraction needed by the dynamic compiler is a memory allocator, therefore the HAL only defines a basic flat memory allocator, through malloc/free functions. Drivers for network cards, frame-buffer, or irqs can be defined later, using the dynamic code generator.

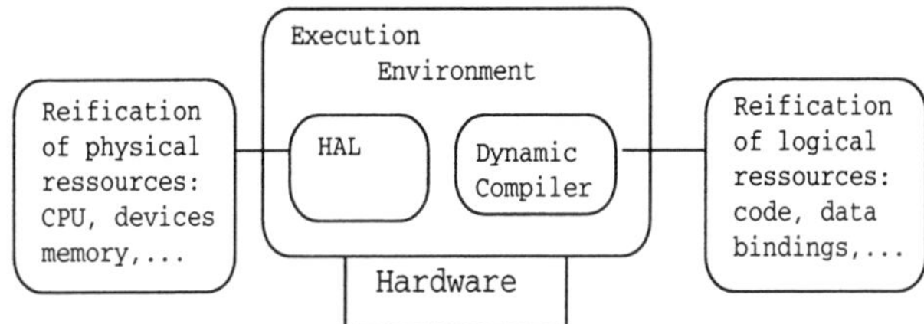

Figure 1. Architecture of the minimal execution environment.

Whereas our current prototype use the THINK[2] [6] nano-kernel as a HAL (developed by France Telecom R&D), the dynamic compiler also runs as a standard Linux application or embedded in a Linux kernel module.

The centerpiece of our execution environment is the dynamic compiler we have realized, called the YNVM.[3] It provides a complete reflexive language, and an execution environment for both applications and specifications of domain-specific execution environments. It has been developed in the context of the VVM project [28] in order to dynamically instantiate application-domain specific virtual machines.

The YNVM is structured as a set of components and interfaces based on the ODP Reference Model [20–22], such as lexer, parser, tree optimizer, tree compiler or code generator, as illustrated in Figure 2. Components implementing those interfaces can be dynamically (re-)composed to form any dedicated chain of compilation. Since the execution model is similar to that of C, applications in different execution format, from native ELF binaries to any bytc-codcd languagcs, can bc loaded and executed.

Moreover, having a single execution engine, which acts as a common language substrate, allows to achieve complete interoperability and data sharing at both the execution environments and applications level.

The dynamic compiler relies on a garbage-collected object memory, used to store metadata. An optional parser converts text, obtained by any input method, into an Abstract Syntax Tree (AST) stored in this object memory. A "tree compiler" then converts ASTs into instructions for an abstract stack machine, whose semantics and execution model are those of C. The tree compiler also provides meta-data reflecting the state of compiled code and applies transformation rules supplied at the application level, if any. Meta-data are organized into hierarchical namespaces called *modules*. Using two abstraction levels (AST and stack machine) allows two independent and specific optimization processes. Finally, a code generator (containing a platform-specific dynamic assembler) converts the intermediate representation into concrete machine instructions. The generated instructions are not stored in the internal object memory, but rather in the application's memory.

Although most expressions are read, compiled and then executed, a mechanism (called *syntax*) provides for the definition of AST nodes that are executed during the dynamic compilation process, allowing dynamic code verification and arbitrary dynamic transformation/rewriting of tree structures.

Upon the YNVM, entire execution environments are dynamically constructed, from low-

---

[2]for THINK Is Not a Kernel
[3]for YNVM is Not a Virtual Machine.

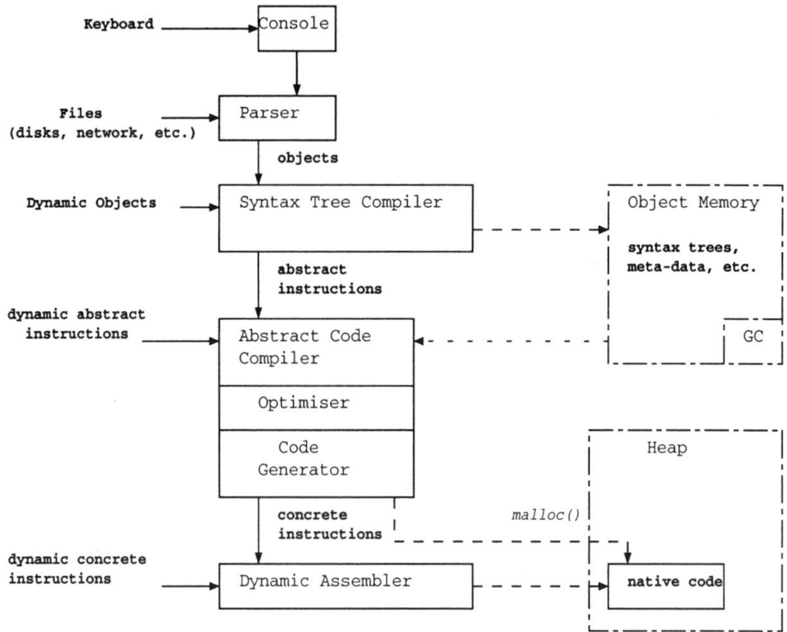

Figure 2. Structure of the YNVM.

level I/O drivers (keyboard, network cards or hard disk) to more sophisticated abstractions such as schedulers, TCP/IP network stacks or complete mobile agent environment. The predefined flat memory allocator, required by the YNVM, can then be replaced by a more complex one, in order to provide isolation between applications or simply to keep track of resources consumption. Likewise, the loading and compiling mechanisms can be adapted to enforce some peculiar security policy (based on code verification).

Such description of a complete virtual machine or execution environment is called a VMlet. Since they are implemented over the YNVM, VMlets are portable.

3　Application-level concurrency management in Java

Although Java has become a de-facto standard for distributed and concurrent programming, it is still a good illustration of the inherent problems of rigid and monolithic execution environments. It defines a small set of high-level abstractions, basically threads, wait/notify synchronization and an object-level locking mechanism (i.e. synchronized methods). Because the Java runtime is built on top of an operating system, those abstractions are bound to the concurrency model exported by the underlying kernel. In the name of portability, these abstractions need to be generic and high level enough to hide the particularities of those underlying kernels. As a result, programmers have no control or knowledge of the underlying concurrency management upon which their application has to be built. For example, object-level locking, while providing basic mutual exclusion between simple method call, forbids atomic acquire of locks from multiple objects in a synchronized block [1]. Limitations of Java's concurrency

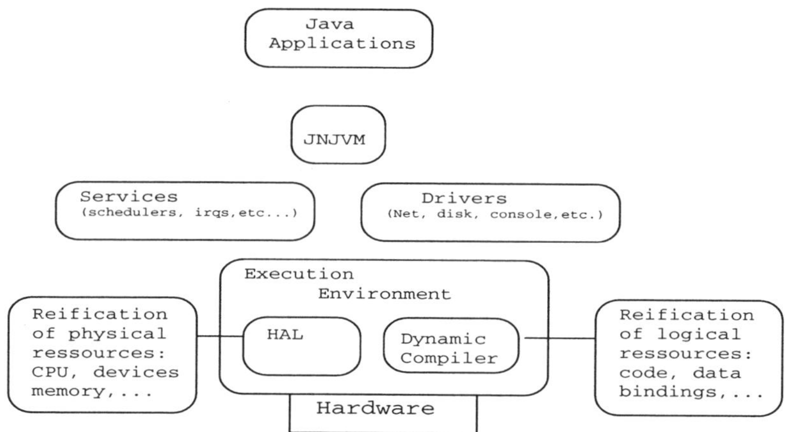

Figure 3. Architecture of a dynamically adaptable Java runtime.

control mechanisms are further discussed in [2].

[7] identifies concurrency limitations related to excessive locking. Their multi-threaded web crawler spent 20% of its time in synchronization-related operations and only 1.5% after removing the "useless" locks from the Java core classes. This comes directly from a very conservative conception choice that is imposed on developers because of the rigidity of the system. As a result, converting an IP address into a string, with InetAddress.getHostAddress(), requires 27 lock acquisitions, most of which are unnecessary!

In addition, even the interactions between threads and memory have to be considered as indeterminate, since specifications for the memory model remain hard to interpret, are poorly understood, and thus are violated in most JVMs [23].

To illustrate the potential benefits of the VVM approach, we have implemented a Java VMLet, called JNJVM, on top of our minimal execution environment. The resulting Java runtime, while being still totally compliant with standard Java applications, is dynamically reconfigurable at both system and language levels. This includes the possibility to adapt concurrency control mechanisms at the application level or directly at the execution-environement level, in a completely transparent way for running applications.

3.1 JNJVM: a dynamically adaptable Java runtime

As illustrated in Figure 3, our Java environment, called JNJVM[4], relies on the YNVM and some basic services for thread creation/destruction or class loading. The JNJVM is compliant with the second edition of SUN's specifications [10,11]. Actually, it relies on three main components that are dynamically integrated into the YNVM: a class loader, a bytecode compiler, and an exception manager.

The generic class description, as its name indicates, describes the content of the class without any hypothesis on the higher level VMlet. It is a structure that enumerates the fields and the methods of the class. Both fields and methods have a symbol and a signature. Also,

---

[4]for JNJVM is Not a Java Virtual Machine.

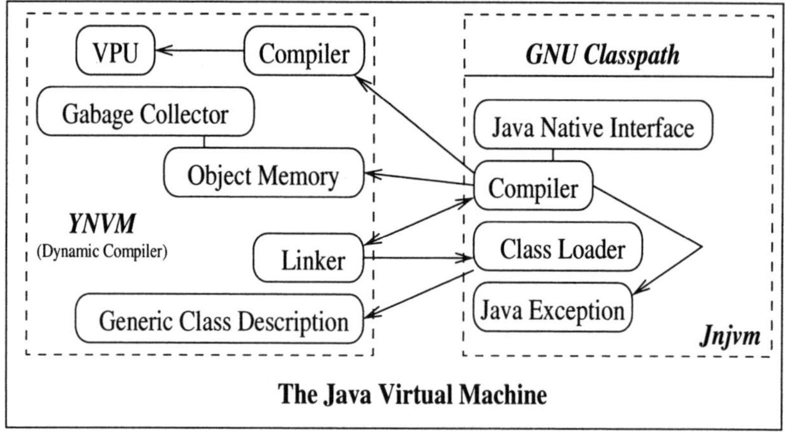

Figure 4. The JNJVM architecture

fields have an associated offset and methods have both a bytecode and an associated VMlet
to compile this bytecode.

Using those two abstractions, the JNJVM implements a Java compiler, a Java Exception
Manager and a Java Class Loader. Its internal architecture is represented in Figure 4. Some
startup java classes come from the GNU Classpath Project [8].

3.2 The Java class loader

When the YNVM finds a class that is not already loaded (like the main class), it delegates the
loading processes to the appropriate VMlet. The JNJVM then loads the Java class and fills
the generic class description. The JNJVM possesses its own class description (the Java Class
Description). This structure contains the java constant pool, which is the mapping between
java symbols and numbers, and the java version of the class. The bytecode of a method is
then stored in the YNVM's method description. Using the YNVM structures results in a very
small Java Loader.

3.3 The compiler

The compiler is used when the JNJVM executes a method that has not yet been compiled. It
transforms the bytecodes into an equivalent syntax-tree representation. For example, the opcode iload 22 is compiled in the syntax-tree (:vpu.ldi vpu 22). This representation corresponds
to the default front-end language of the YNVM. Thus, the compiler uses the YNVM's internal
code-generator to complete the transformation of bytecodes into native-code. Moreover, as
stated before, VMlets using the YNVM's code generator are entirely platform-independent,
thus portable.

Every opcode is compiled by a function and the resulting native code is inserted into a
table of function pointers. Therefore, the modification of an opcode's behavior is equivalent
to changing the contents of this vector of function pointers. For example, ignoring all the

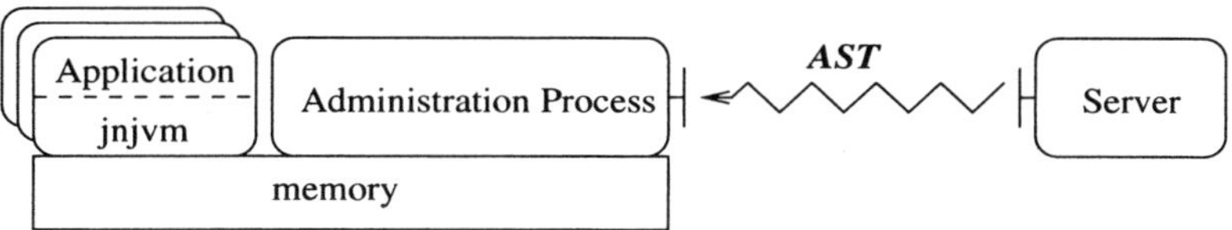

Figure 5. Remote administration of a Java runtime.

monitors opcodes (194 and 195) only implies replacing the entries 194 and 195 of the table by an empty function.

3.4 The language interface

The Java VMlet is implemented according to the VVM's approach. First, we built an environement dedicated to the constrtuction of Java environment (the Java VMlet itself), then we implement a dynamically flexible Java environment uppon this Java VMlet (called the JNJVM).

The Java VMlet is structured as a set of primitives, such as **define-opcode** to define how a given Java bytecode has to be compiled 3.3 or **define-component** to define a structure holding meta-data related to an element of the JNJVM (classes, attributes, methods,...). The JNJVM uses thoses primitives to implement a Java virtual machine. This acrhitecture allows an application to perform "in-depth" modification to the JNJVM.

3.5 The reflexive layer

The JNJVM exports a complete reflexive layer: any Java symbol is mapped to a YNVM symbol, which is used to call Java methods or inspect the value of any fields of classe or object from a YNVM script. Moreover, this mapping is used to modify any method's implementation: by dynamically re-binding the YNVM symbol to some code, we dynamically change the implementation of the associated method. For example, redefining the java.lang.Object.toString() java method is done by simply modifying a pointer in the method's structure associated with the :jnjvm.classes.java.lang.toString_signature VVM symbol.

This reflexive layer is directly accessible from within the YNVM, but it is going to be exported to Java applications through a Java class, encaspulating access to the underlying JNJVM via JNI.

3.6 Adaptability

Thanks to the language interface and the reflexive layer, the JNJVM achieves a high level of flexibility. A java application is embedded in a YNVM script, which we called an active script. This active script is responsible for loading and configuring a JNJVM, through the Java VMlet's primitives, according to the application's needs or constraints. Then, the script can open a "back-door" destined to receive, from an administrator, reconfiguration scripts.

As illustrated in Figure 5, the active script starts a thread listening for serialized ASTs from any input (file, network, keyboard, etc.). Those ASTs are then executed by the YNVM,

```
class YNVM {
    static public native int
        readEvalPrint(String);
};
```

Figure 6. A simple Java class reifying access to the YNVM through JNI

which allows remote administration of the Java runtime : such scripts can use the Java VM-let's primitives to reconfigure the JNJVM and the reflexive layer to modify the state of an application.

The main interest of this approach is to achieve dynamic flexibility without sacrifying performances: it allows a Java application to apply "in-depth" reconfigurations to its execution environment to match its needs, without prohibitive peformance overheads.

3.6.1   Performances

In order to evaluate our prototype, we compared it with two optimized JVM: SUN's JVM 1.3.1 (without jit compiler) and IBM's JVM 1.4.1 (with dynamic compilation). We used a G4 PowerPC, running a standard Linux distribution (Yellow Dog). Most of the benchmarks we used, shows that the JNJVM is nearly 3 times slower than it's IBM counterpart and 3 times faster than SUN's.

We found that most of the overhead induced by the JNJVM came from memory allocation and exception handling code, which are probably way too simple to compare with IBM optimized JVM. Garbage collecting, for example, is particularly inefficient (about 20 times slower than IBM's): since the YNVM's object memory is also used for storing Java classes, objects and meta-data, every garbage-collection involves a useless checking of the YNVM's internal objects (about 50.000 objects). Hence spliting the garbage collecting according to object's life cycle (and usage pattern) would considerably improve overall performance: YNVM's objects are created and destroyed only during dynamic compilation and loading phases, whereas Java objects life cycle is restricted to an application's execution.

Indeed, the JNJVM is entirely compiled by the YNVM, which produces native code as fast as optimized C. Moreover, the hooks used to modify the JNJVM are based uppon raw pointers to dynamic loading and dynamic compilation functions. The reflexive layer uses only meta-data structures related to the Java appplication, and thus does not introduce any indirection. Hence, our approach seems not to introduce severe performance penalties, but only an "in-depth" optimization work of our prototype would confirm it.

4   Application-level concurrency management

In order to demonstrates the interest of the VVM approach, we have used our flexible Java environment to illustrate how limitations of traditional Java environments can be overcome thanks to dynamic flexibility.

The dynamic adaptation of the JNJVM internals mechanisms, and in particular the concurrency management, can be achieved either by the execution of an external script at the YNVM level, or at the application level, through a Java package exporting the YNVM's interface.

```
import YNVM;
class Foo {
    void Foo() {
        YNVM.readEvalPrint
            ("(set! :jnjvm.debug 255)");
    }
};
```

Figure 7. Using the YNVM to dynamically enable the debug mode

Since the YNVM allows the dynamic adaptation of anything built upon it, the simplest way to reconfigure a JNJVM, and thus a Java application, is to execute a script inside the YNVM. Depending on what kind of inputs are available on the host, the reconfiguration is either performed by loading a file (from a local disk or a remote filesystem), reading from the keyboard or executing a mobile agent. Thus, the reconfiguration of legacy applications is handled in a completely transparent way.

When the required adaptations are closely tied to the application's semantics, and hence embedded into it, reconfigurations need to be driven by the application and often imply application-level extensions. For those cases, we used the JNI (Java Native Interface) [9]. Since the YNVM produces C-compliant code, the JNI permits to interface any YNVM-level code with Java classes, thus to define a YNVM class that encapsulate the YNVM's interface, as illustrated in Figure 6. Thus any application can import this class and use it to adapt its execution environment through the underlying YNVM, while still being fully compliant with any Java compiler. Figure 7 represents a class using the previously defined YNVM class to dynamically turn the Java runtime into a debug mode.

As stated before, due to a very conservative concurrency management, many classes exhibit synchronized methods and thus excessive locking. To implement synchronization, every Java object has an associated lock. As with any object, a lock has a table of virtual methods (with two entries, lock and unlock). Hence, with the YNVM class that provides access to the underlying YNVM, any class can dynamically replace the virtual method table of any object's lock when no synchronization is needed. This reconfiguration can be undone the same way, by switching back to the old table. Further, this operation can be made recursive to really suppress any locking along the invocation path of a method.

Since it is designed to be independent of the underlying scheduler, the Java runtime does not manage concurrency. It relies on a pthread-like interface to create and destroy threads whose management is then left to the underlying system's scheduler. Hence developers have very poor control and knowledge about the way their application behave.

Through the YNVM class, an application can replace the thread-related functions used by the JNJVM by its own version, and then change the underlying scheduler, for example, by defining a new scheduling function and registering it in the Interruption Vector with the registerTrap primitive of the underlying minimal execution environment. We have experienced a simple multi-threaded application that replaces the default scheduler (a round-robin time-sharing) by a progress-based scheduling function. Basic thread creation and destruction functions are then encapsulated in new functions responsible to create and destroy per-thread additional data-structures (as the progress-metrics) and the scheduling function is just a loop to allocate some CPU time to the "slower" process, based on its average progression-speed.

Thus, the progression-gap between the threads can be confined to a given threshold. This kind of scheduling is especially useful in multimedia systems to synchronize threads with different progression rate, such as audio and video codecs.

While the administrator can reconfigure, at any time, every aspect of the entire system, it may not be desirable to let any application do the same. Such security issues are handled in a flexible way too, as part of the configuration of the execution environment. By (re)configuring the loading mechanism, the administrator defines security rules to apply to applications. As opposed to a fixed set of predefined static and dynamic checks, the reflexivity of the YNVM allows to dynamically adapt the set of static checks to be performed when an application is loaded, for example to take into account a trust-level in its source, and to use the results of those static checks to determine and inline the dynamic checks that really have to be performed. Therefore, it is possible to restrict the possibilities offered to any applications, hence preventing misbehaving code to damage the system, in a completely flexible way.

5 Related Work

Dynamic adaptation is an active research area. Several flexible operating systems have been proposed, such as SPIN [24], VINO [5] or Exokernel [3], to allow application-based resource management. Therefore, they focus only on system aspects and most often mechanisms supporting dynamic adaptation are still fixed and rigid, as well as the security policies.

XVM [16] proposes a component-based extensible virtual machine that uses a dedicated language to describe a virtual machine's internals. Applications provide their extensions, as with the Exokernel approach, and the underlying virtual machine uses call-backs to replace an internal policy, such as garbage collector, by an application's extension. Although the virtual machine is extensible, its lack of reflexivity limits the flexibility to a predefined set of aspects.

Vanilla [15] uses a DSL-based approach for the construction of dedicated virtual machines. Elements such as parsers, type checkers and interpreters are described using a dedicated language. A Language Definition File identifies the components that need to be combined to obtain the desired virtual machine. While being well-adapted to the construction of dedicated/specialized virtual machines, it remains a static approach and the resulting environments are rigid and closed and thus lack flexibility.

Harissa [14] is a another DSL-based project. Its goal is Java program specialization through program transformation and especially partial evaluation, hence it focuses on adatation of an application to a specific context of utilization rather than on the definition of a flexible execution environment. A dedicated language is used to define specializations of "generic" classes and the specialization parameters, which can be static (evaluated at compile-time) or dynamic (evaluated at run-time). The result is an equivalent specialized C-program that can be compiled with gcc. This approach is obviously orthogonal and may be applied to the construction a specialized execution environment, matching some given application domain semantics.

Concerning Java, several projects of Java-based operating systems have been proposed to address traditional limitations of JVMs (resources control, isolation, etc.), such as GVM [25], a monolithic Java-based kernel providing complete resources isolation between processes, Alta [26], a micro-kernel based JVM extended to support hierarchical scheduling, J-Kernel, a Java-based kernel, using device drivers to account resources usage, SUN's JavaOS, a Java runtime based on the Chorus micro-kernel to provide some realtime support to applications or

JX-Kernel [12]. Their objective remains adding some features to overcome some limitations, thus it is still an "ad-hoc" and rigid solution to a dedicated problem, since those features, as well as the entire resulting system, are not meant to be flexible. Hence, applications are stuck again in a rigid "one-size-fits-all" based execution environment.

Bossa [29] rely on a domain-specific-language (DSL) based approach and thus proposes a language for describing new scheduling policies. Specialized schedulers are then generated and can be loaded through a (Linux-)kernel module. This work is obviously orthogonal with ours and certainly very complementary.

6 Conclusions and perspectives

This paper presented the architecture of a flexible execution environment, based on a HAL and a flexible dynamic compiler, free of any predefined, imposed abstraction. This high-level of dynamic flexibility allows dynamic construction of dedicated execution environments as well as their dynamic reconfiguration. To demonstrate the benefits of this approach, we used this minimal execution environment to build the JNJVM, a dynamically adaptable Java runtime.

The inherent flexibility of the JNJVM allows to address some of the limitations of traditional rigid Java runtimes, in particular concurrency management and concurrent programming support.

With the VVM projects we continue to investigate a systematic approach for building flexible, adaptable and interoperable execution environments, to free applications from the artificial limitations on reconfiguration imposed by programming environments.

The HAL part of the minimal execution environment is currently being embedded in a Linux kernel-module so that our flexible Java runtime can be used on top of a traditional operating system, as a standard JVM, while preserving a maximum of flexibility.

Concerning the JNJVM, we plan to develop further our flexible Java environment toward a complete flexible Java-OS and also to integrate it in the context of component based middleware, as the Corba Component model, to illustrate the adequacy of our approach to the needs of moderns distributed applications.

References

[1] P. Felber and M. Reiter. *Advanced concurrency control in java*, Technical report, Bell Labs Research, Jan. 2002. http://citeseer.nj.nec.com/felber02advanced.html

[2] D. Lea. *Concurrent Programming in Java*, Second Edition. Addison Wesley Longman, November 2000.

[3] M.F. Kaashoek, D.R. Engler, J. O'Toole. *Exokernel: an operating system architecture for application-level resource management* Proceedings of the 15th ACM Symposium on Operating System Principles, Copper Mountain, Colorado, December 1995.

[4] B. Folliot. *The Virtual Virtual Machine Project*, Proceedings of IFIP Symposium on Computer Architecture and High Performance Computing, Sao Paulo, Brasil,October 2000.

[5] M. Seltzer, Y. Endo, C. Small and K.A. Smith. *Dealing with Disaster: Surviving Misbehaved Kernel Extensions*, in Proceedings of the 2nd Symposium on Operating Systems Design and Implementation, Seattle, Washington, pp 213–227, 1996. citeseer.nj.nec.com/seltzer96dealing.html

[6] J.P. Fassino and J.B. Stephani. *THINK : un noyau d'infrastructure répartie adaptable*, Proceedings of CFSE 2, Paris, France, April 2001.

[7] A. Heydon and M. Najork. *Performance limitations of the Java core libraries*, in Concurrency: Practice and Experience, vol. 12, number 6, pp 363–373, 2000. http://citeseer.nj.nec.com/heydon00performance.html

[8] GNU Classpath Project, www.gnu.org/software/classpath/classpath.html

[9] JNI Spec version 1.4, http://java.sun.com/j2se/1.4/docs/guide/jni/index.html

[10] J. Gosling, B. Joy, G. Steele and G. Bracha. *The Java(TM) Language Specification, Second Edition*, Paperback, 1996.

[11] : T. Lindholm and F. Yellin. *The Java(TM) Virtual Machine Specification (2nd Edition)*, Paperback.

[12] M. Golm, M. Felser C. Wawersich, and J. Kleinder. *The JX Operating System*, 2002 USENIX Annual Technical Conference, June 10-15, 2002, Monterey, CA, pp. 45-58

[13] The RealTime for Java Expert Group. jcp.org/jsr/detail/1.jsp

[14] G. Muller and U.P. Schultz, *Harissa: A Hybrid Approach to Java Execution*, in IEEE Software, March/April 1999.

[15] S. Dobson, P. Nixon, V. Wade, S. Terzis and John Fuller, *Vanilla: An Open Language Framework*, in Lecture Notes in Computer Science, Volume 1799, 2000.

[16] T. Harris, *An extensible virtual machine*, in Proceedings of the Simplicity, Performance and Portability in Virtual Machine Design Workshop (OOPSLA), Denver, Colorado, November 1999.

[17] M. Golm, *Design and implementation of a meta architecture for Java*, Master's thesis, University of Erlang, January 1997.

[18] R. Fitzgerald, T.B. Knoblock, E. Ruf, B. Steensgaard and D. Tarditi, *Marmot: An optimizing compiler for Java*, in Software Practices and Experiences 30(3), March 2000.

[19] M.P. Atkinson, L. Daynes, M.J. Jordan, T. Printezis and S. Spence, *An Orthogonally Persistent Java*, in ACM Sigmod Record, Volume 25, Number 4, December 1996.

[20] ISO/IEC. "Open Distributed Processing - Reference Model, Part 2 : Fundations". ITU-T Recommendation X.902 International Standard 10746-2, ISO/IEC, 1995.

[21] ISO/IEC. "Open Distributed Processing - Reference Model, Part 3 : Architecture". ITU-T Recommendation X.903 International Standard 10746-3, ISO/IEC, 1995.

[22] ISO/IEC. "Open Distributed Processing - Reference Model, Part 1 : Overview". ITU-T Recommendation X.901 International Standard 10746-1, ISO/IEC, 1998.

[23] W.Pugh. *The Java Memory Model is Fataly Flawed*, in Proceedings of ACM Java Grande Conference 1999, San Francisco, California, June 12-14, 1999

[24] B. Bershad, S. Savage, P. Pardyack, E. Gun Sirer, D. Becker, M. Fiuczynski, C. Chambers and S. Eggers. *Extensibility, Safety and Performance in the SPIN Operating System* in Proceedings of the 15th ACM Symposium on Operating System Principles, Copper Mountain, Colorado, December 1995.

[25] G. Back, P. Tullman, L. Stoller, W. Hsieh, J. Lepreau. Java Operating Systems: Design and Implementation, University of Utah Technical Report, UUCS-98-015, August 1998.

[26] P. Tullmann and J. Lepreau. *Nested Java Processes: OS Structure for Mobile Code*, in Proceedings of the Eighth ACM SIGOPS European Workshop, Sintra, Portugal, September 1998.

[27] C. Hawblitzel, C. Chang, G. Czajkowski, D. Hu, and T. von Eicken. *Implementing Multiple Protection Domains in Java*, in Proceedings of the 1998 Usenix Annual Technical Conference.

[28] B. Folliot, I. Piumarta, L. Seinturier, C. Baillarguet, C. Khoury, A. Lger, F. Ogel. *Beyond flexibility and reflection: the virtual virtual machine approach*. NATO Advanced Research Workshop, Environments, Tools and Applications for Cluster Computing. LNCS 2326, Springer-Verlag, pp. 17-26, 2002

[29] J. Lawall, G. Muller, L.P. Barreto. *Capturing OS expertise in an Event Type System: the Bossa experience*, in Proceedings of the ACM SIGOPS European Workshop 2002 (EW'2002), Saint-Emillion, France, September 2002.

Concurrent Information Processing and Computing
D. Grigoras and A. Nicolau (Eds.)
IOS Press, 2005

Optimizing Object Oriented Programs based on the Byte Code-Defined Data Dependence Graphs

Violeta Felea[1]   Eryk Laskowski[2]   Bernard Toursel[1]   Marek Tudruj[2]

[1] *Université des Sciences et Technologies de Lille, France*
Laboratoire d'Informatique Fondamentale de Lille (LIFL UMR CNRS 8022)
`{felea,toursel}@lifl.fr`
[2] *Institute of Computer Science Polish Academy of Sciences, Warsaw, Poland*
`{laskowsk,tudruj}@ipipan.waw.pl`

Abstract. The paper is concerned with scheduling of the byte code generated for parallel object oriented programs written in Java, in order to reach efficiency through optimal distribution of objects. Two static optimization methods based on byte code analysis and one complementary dynamic approach to adjust object distribution in unpredictable situations, are proposed. These optimization methods are based on the use of several levels of program graph representation which show intensity of mutual references between potentially parallel elements of programs. The first static optimization method uses such graphs to provide locality of intra-threads method calls and to reduce the number of remote object method calls. The second optimization algorithm applies a clustering algorithm to an extended macro data flow graph generated on the basis of the byte code compiled for a program. This graph depicts data and control dependencies between sequential code macro data flow nodes identified in threads and methods of a program. The algorithm defines distribution of nodes and objects on processors, so as to minimize the total execution time of programs. In the third approach, a complementary dynamic adjustment is achieved through program execution monitoring combined with a general load balancing mechanism, developed in the ADAJ project.

1 Introduction

Object-oriented programs are defined by a programmer in a way to include classes and their methods whose selection reflects the prospective desires of a programmer in respect to the general shape of the computational problem. Classes are instantiated into objects that in some parallel object oriented environments (JavaParty [10]) can be placed on parallel virtual machines. In this way a parallel program is based on initial image of the problem seen by a programmer. Placement of the objects on processors (Java Virtual Machines – JVMs) should be done aiming at maximal performance of the parallel program. Unfortunately this is not the case in the current practice of object oriented computing. In the case of irregular parallel object oriented programs, an analysis of relations between objects, which would support good parallel distribution, is rarely used. Objects are usually placed using completely ad hoc assignments, only the number of the available processors is observed.

This work tries to optimize placement of objects and methods on processors aiming at minimization of the program execution time. For this, a more detailed picture of the program is generated, based on the analysis of the byte code generated by the compiler. An analysis of the byte code identifies control dependencies and data dependencies among methods in the program. Based on these dependencies, control flow and data dependencies between the byte code instructions can be discovered and represented in the form of relevant graphs [1–3]. The first presented heuristics tries to make method calls inside threads local to the JVMs. This is done by clustering of nodes in a call dependence graph of the program. By optimized placement of threads on available JVMs, the reduction of RMI (Remote Method Invocation) calls to remote objects is obtained. In the second presented heuristics an analysis of byte code instructions can produce a macro control/dataflow graph of a program where in which we have nodes that are created by agglomeration of sequential instructions that appear between instructions that can potentially produce parallelism in program execution: inter-method calls, thread spawning and inter-object data references. We can next analyze the macro/dataflow graph of the program and try to optimally assign the macro nodes to processors so as to reduce inter-processor communication overheads. This optimized placement may be subject to redistribution when dynamic modifications of resource availability appear during program execution or when the program behavior is particularly different from the predictable execution. The third proposed heuristics provides a complementary program execution monitoring which builds a dynamic relation graph of a program by observation of the effective method calls. It is next used by a load balancing mechanism which applies object migration as proposed in the ADAJ (Adaptive Distributed Applications in Java) project [8].

The paper is composed of two parts. In first part, two static pre-optimization methods are explained. In the second part, the dynamic load balancing approach is presented.

2   Static pre-optimization algorithms

The system is based on many JVMs that can work in parallel. A distributed program is a program written in Java language, which is executed with the use of several JVMs. The communication is done through Remote Method Invocations and direct access to objects' fields. A *distributed class* is a Java class whose objects can reside on more than one JVM. Objects of such a class are called *remote objects*. Data exchange between objects located in different JVMs can be done through execution of RMI both for method calls and for access of remote object fields. Execution of an RMI can read a remote object field at a different JVM and return the value of the field to the calling method. Communication between objects via RMI is included in the JavaParty environment [10]. Before a Java program is executed, we will perform a pre-optimization algorithm, which will determine an introductory placement of objects on virtual machines in the system. Taking a sequential (i.e. meant for execution in a single JVM) multithreaded version of a Java program as input information, the aim of the parallel program optimization is to determine which of the classes should be distributed and what should be the distribution of objects of remote classes on different JVMs so as to balance loads of the virtual machines (equivalent to minimization of the total execution time of a parallel program) and to decrease direct inter-object communication. In this pre-optimization step we will use two graph representations of the program: method dependence graph and method call graph.

Based on the static analysis of a Java program and the program byte code, we create a

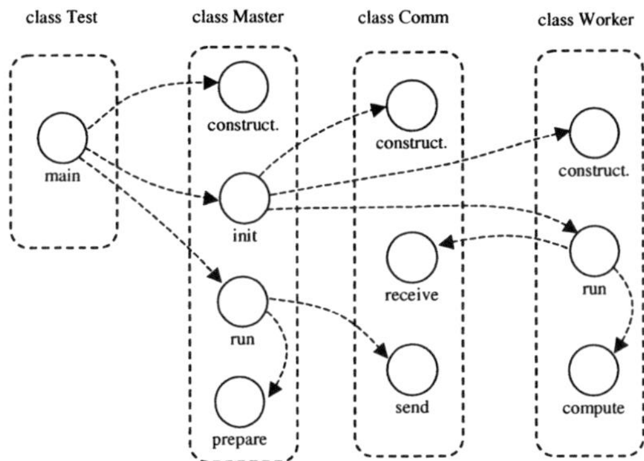

Figure 1. An MDG graph of a program.

program Method Dependence Graph (MDG) which shows mutual calls of methods in the program. A MDG is a directed graph $MDG = (U, A)$, in which node $u_i \in U$ represents a method. Edge $a_{i,j} \in A$ depicts call of method u_j from method u_i. Nodes are grouped according to class membership. The MDG graph is constructed by static analysis of program representations. An example of MDG is shown in Fig. 1.

We execute programs for some representative data for which the optimization will be done. During execution, we carry out measurements of the number of mutual method calls and thread spawns using the mechanism, which is similar to that used in ADAJ. The execution results are stored in a trace file in which method calls and their observed quantities are registered. The trace file should contain information on identification of all created objects in each class, identification of all methods called in each method of each object and identification of all threads that were spawned. We create a Method Call Graph of the program.

A Method Call Graph (MCG) is a directed graph $MCG = (V, E, W, T)$, in which a nodes $v_i \in V$ represent methods or spawned threads identified based on the trace file and the MDG. Edges correspond to method calls or thread spawns. A label $t_{i,j} \in T$ of edge $e_{i,j}$ connecting nodes v_i and v_j has value 1 if v_j is a thread spawned by v_i or value 0 if v_j is a method called by v_i. A weight of edge $e_{i,j}$ with the label $t_{i,j} = 0$ is pair $w_{i,j} = \langle num, atime \rangle$, $w_{i,j} \in W$, where *num* is a number of method calls and *atime* is an average method execution time. As opposed to MDG, nodes are grouped according to objects on which methods are invoked.

An example of MCG is shown in Fig. 2, method calls which effectively spawn new threads are shown as dotted lines, normal calls are depicted as solid lines. We should note that by thread spawn we mean an explicit thread creation by the programmer (not an implicit as in JavaParty during remote object method call).

Next phase of the optimization algorithm is clustering. It can be done at two levels:

- clustering at the method call graph level,
- clustering at the level of a macro data flow graph of a program.

2.1 Clustering of the method call graph

Clustering at the method level aims in determining which classes should remain distributed and how the objects generated should be placed on a final set of JVMs. In the clustering algo-

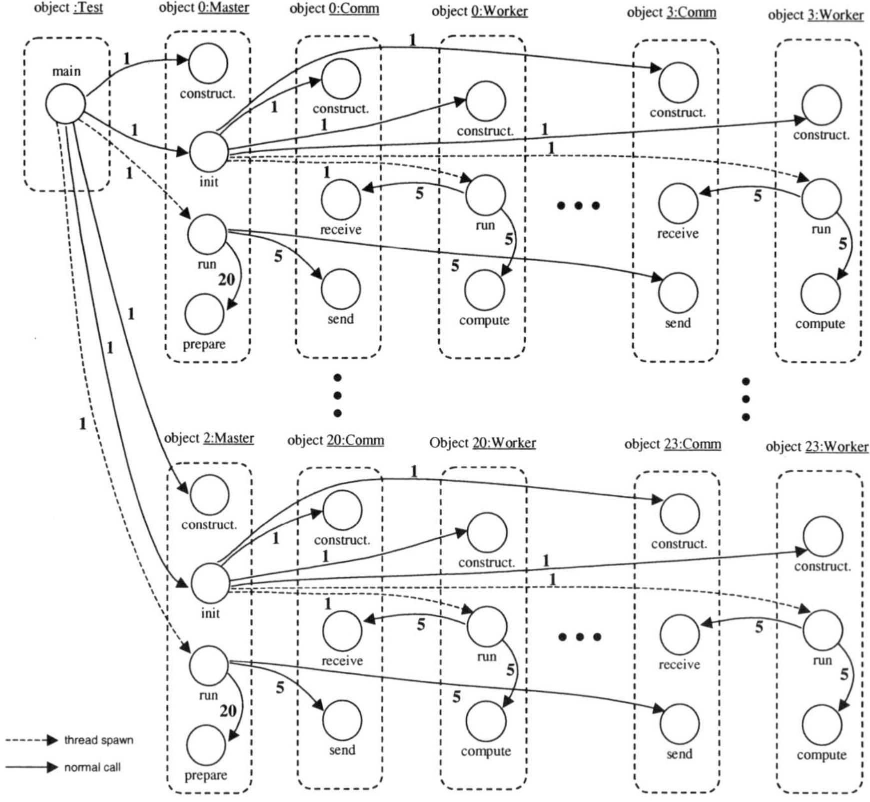

Figure 2. An example of MCD graph for program from Fig. 1.

rithm, we treat all objects as remote objects (respectively all classes are distributed classes). The heuristics we use is as follows:

- method call locality inside each thread should be as strong as possible; to obtain this effect we designate the calls inside a single thread to the same JVM,

- the number of the inter-thread calls, which cross the boundaries of JVMs should be reduced as much as possible, this is accomplished by suitable distribution of threads across available JVMs.

The algorithm has two phases. In the first phase the MCG graph is traversed in the DFS (Deep-First-Search) manner to agglomerate method calls executed in a single thread. In this step, the algorithm finds MCG subgraphs, which are constructed of vertices connected by solid edges (i.e. calls inside threads). We assume that each subgraph is executed in a dedicated JVM. Subgraphs are built at the level of single objects. In case when an object belongs to different subgraphs, the new subgraph is constructed and a unique JVM number is assigned to it. We expect that, in most cases, at the end of this phase the number of found subgraphs is far bigger than the number of available JVMs in the system.

Algorithm MCG_Clustering
Input:
aMCG - MCG of a program, aJVM - the number of available JVMs
{Phase I}
S := Traverse aMCG using DFS algorithm to find subgraphs s $\in$ S,
        s $\subset$ aMCG, of aMCG, which represent threads
{Phase II}
Vars:
M : matrix of size $|S| \times |S|$
L : int   *{the number of JVMs used}*
J : vector of size $|S|$ *{J[i] is JVM number assigned to subgraph s_i}*
{initialize M}
<u>for</u> m = 1 <u>to</u> $|S|$
   <u>for</u> n = 1 <u>to</u> $|S|$
      M[m][n] := $\sum c_{i,j} : v_i \in s_m,\ v_j \in s_n$
{initialize J and L}
<u>for</u> i = 1 <u>to</u> $|S|$
   J[i] := i
L := $|S|$
{main loop}
<u>while</u> L > aJVM
   Select M[m][n] with the biggest value and for which J[m] <> J[n]
   k := Select JVM with smallest number of assigned threads
   J[n] := J[m] := k   *{assign S_m and S_n to the same JVM_k}*
   L := the number of JVM used by threads
<u>end</u>

Figure 3. General outline of clustering at the method call graph level.

In the second phase of the algorithm we cluster the subgraphs obtained in the previous phase until the number of clusters is equal to the number of JVMs. The general outline of this phase is similar to Sarkar's [6] edge-zeroing clustering heuristics. At each clustering step, the algorithm finds the sub-graphs, which are connected by edges with the biggest weight value and which connect nodes placed on different JVMs. All nodes of those sub-graphs are assigned to the same JVM while the total number of remote calls decreases. The algorithm stops when the number of clusters is equal to the assumed number of JVMs.

The first phase of the algorithm makes method calls inside programmer-declared threads local to the JVM. This allows exploiting thread level parallelism without introducing large inter-JVM communication overheads. The gain of the second step of the heuristics lies in reduction of RMI calls to remote objects. Fig. 3 shows the algorithm outline.

Using the presented algorithm, we prepared optimized distribution of remote objects for an exemplary Java application program whose MDG and MCG were shown in Fig. 1 and Fig. 2. A class diagram for the program is shown in Fig. 4 (the actual program Java source code is not shown due to its size). Program performs hypothetical scientific calculations by partitioning problem domain into several sub-domains. Each sub-domain is computed in master/slave manner in `tstMaster` class by invoking `computeData` method of `tstWorker` class. Data between `tstMaster` and `tstWorker` classes are exchanged using `tstCommMedium` class.

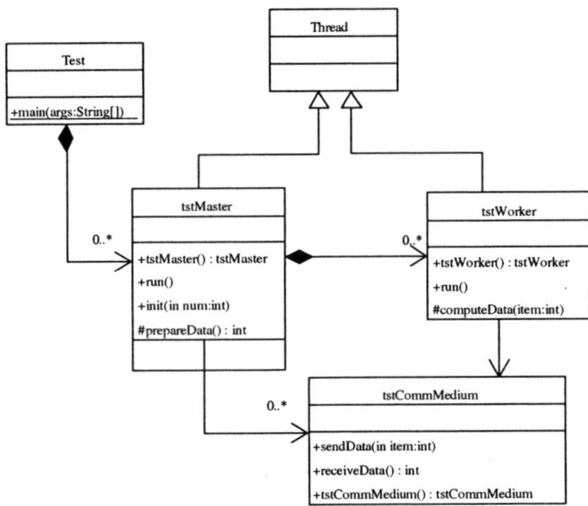

Figure 4. UML class diagram of exemplary Java application.

The result of the first phase of the algorithm is shown in Fig. 5. A MCD has been partitioned into sub-graphs and objects, which belong to more than one sub-graph, are assigned to unique JVM. The total number of JVM used after this phase is equal to 28 (in fact, each object is assigned to a unique JVM). During clustering phase, objects that frequently invoke methods in different objects are moved to the called object's JVM. Since most calls in this exemplary program take place between `tstMaster` and `tstCommMedium` classes (also between `tstWorker` and `tstCommMedium`) clustering algorithm moves objects x:`tstMaster`, xy:`tstWorker`, xy:`tstCommMedium` to the same JVM. Final distribution of program objects across JVMs is shown in Fig. 6.

2.2 Clustering of the macro data flow graph

We take the method call graph of a Java program generated after program execution for a specially selected set of data. In the method call graph we have labels of edges, which determine if the edge represents a standard method call (0) or a spawned thread call (1). We have also call edge weights, which are numbers of performed method calls. We can imagine that each called method and each spawned thread has its own method control/data dependence graph – MCDG determined on the basis of the byte code of the program produced by the compiler. The nodes in the MCDG graphs are the byte code instructions that appear inside a method (thread) byte code. The edges correspond to control flow and data dependencies between byte code instructions of a method (thread). Between the control graphs of methods (threads) related to different objects there can be data dependence and control edges. Data dependence edges connect byte code instructions, which result in data exchange between threads (methods) defined by thread spawning. They can transfer input parameters passed in method invocations (threads), returns of the results of invoked methods and direct accesses to remote object fields. Control edges between method (thread) graphs can connect byte code instructions, which result in invocations of complete methods (by thread spawning) from inside other methods (threads). By connecting method (thread) control/data dependence graphs

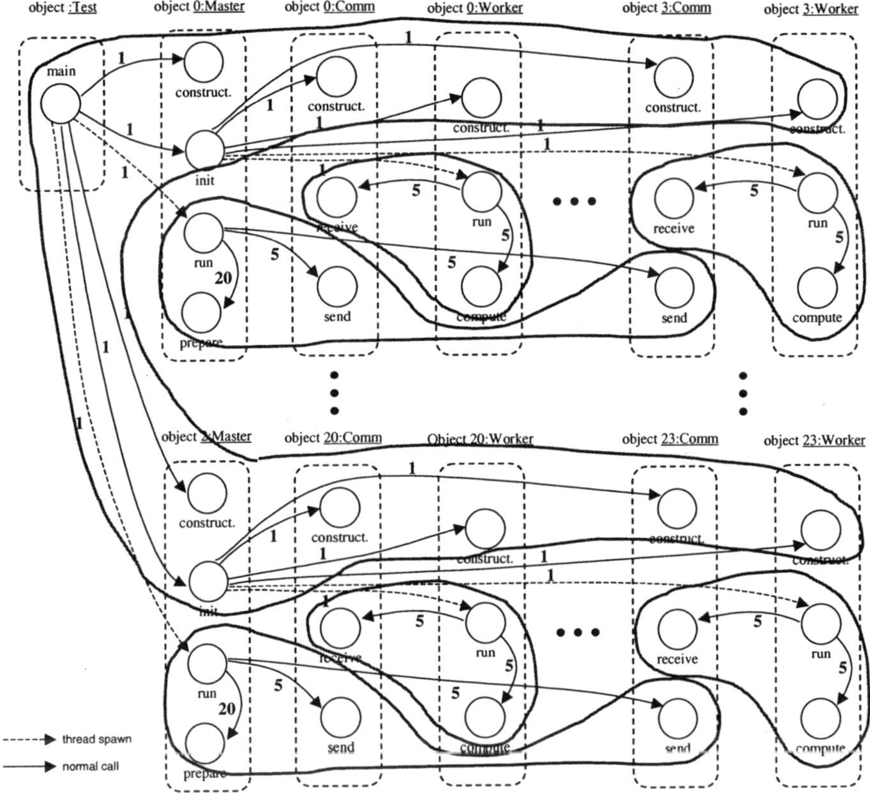

Figure 5. A MCD for Java program from Fig. 4 with threads' sub-graphs shown.

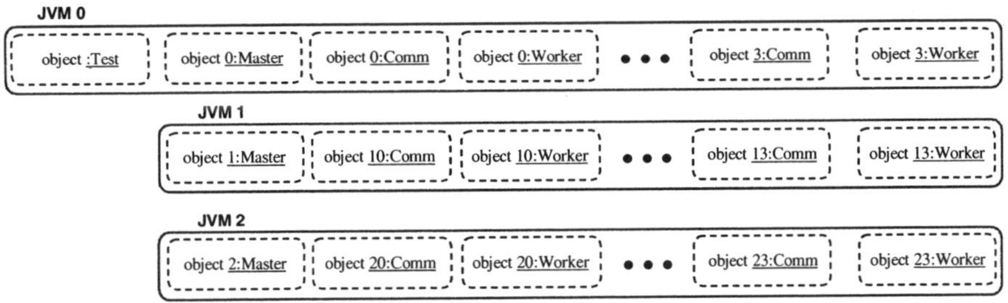

Figure 6. Final distribution of application objects across JVMs.

by additional control/data dependence edges between threads (remote methods) we create the second level of the program graph representation composed of interconnected method control/data dependency graphs of methods and threads (MCDGs), Fig. 7.

In the MCDG graphs, we can unroll all iterative method invocations, with the number of iterations known from the execution trace or the byte-code, to obtain the acyclic data

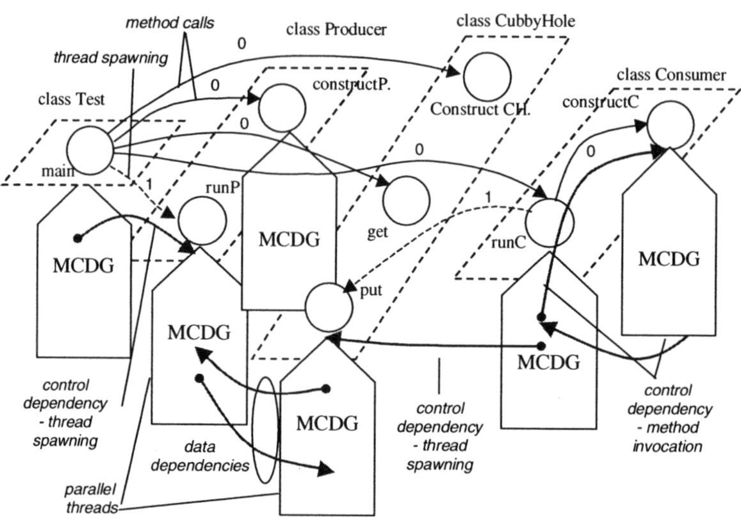

Figure 7. Interdependencies of control and data dependency graph of methods (threads).

dependency graph of the program. The iterations with unknown iteration numbers are left unrolled. We can transform the unrolled control/data dependency graph into a macro data flow graph by agglomerating in macro nodes all sequential byte code instructions, which are separated by method calls, thread spawning or accesses to remote object data fields. Control and data dependence edges between boundary byte code instructions in adjacent macro nodes (connected by control dependence edges) are replaced by data dependence edges between macro nodes. Thus, all control dependence edges in all macro nodes are eliminated and the only edges that remain are the data dependence edges. Consecutive byte code instructions in the control scope of conditional instructions (branches) are placed in the same macro nodes, unless they do not represent method calls, thread spawning or accesses to remote objects. In the contrary case, the instructions are divided into separate macro nodes with the above mentioned instructions and some extra control instructions at the boundaries. To each macro node a weight is assigned, which correspond to the execution time of the node. To each data dependence edge entering a macro node a weight is assigned, which corresponds to the time of serialization and transfer of all data from the edge source macro node, which are necessary to activate and execute the edge target node on a different virtual machine. That will depict time of preparation and transfers of all global or shared data that are used by macro instruction nodes. The edge weights correspond to the cost overhead that would appear if the adjacent macro instruction nodes were assigned to different virtual machines. The weights are obtained by execution of the byte code modified by insertions at the boundaries of the macro data nodes of the code blocks, which perform data serialization and data communication volume estimations. Code insertions are performed using available tools such as BCEL [5]. In case of conditionally executed graph elements, the weights are computed using probability weighted constituent execution times.

To the macro data dependency graph of the program we can apply all known static program graph optimization methods that lead to minimization of the total program execution

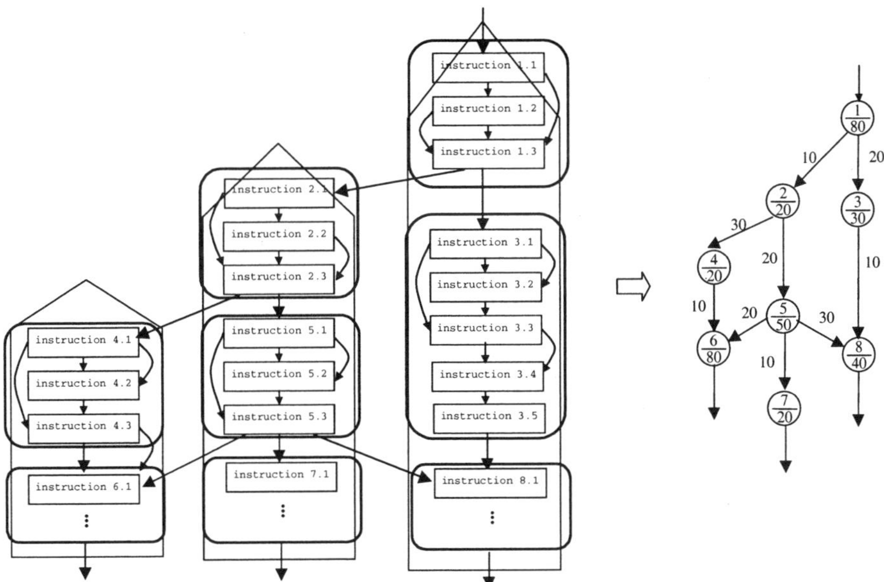

Figure 8. Constructing macro dataflow graph from MCDG.

time. The optimization methods can first do clustering of macro nodes on unlimited number of processors (logical JVMs) in a way to reduce the execution time of the clustered nodes (placing nodes on the same processor eliminates costly external communication, we assume the internal data passing to be done with zero cost), Fig. 9. Next, merging of the assigned clusters has to be performed to reduce the number of logical JVMs to the number of real processors with simultaneous load balancing. The optimization algorithm is similar to that used in the PYRROS static optimization tool [4] based on the Dominant Sequence Clustering (where a dominant sequence DS is a dynamic critical path in the program graph). The applied clustering technique places the consecutive heaviest macro nodes of methods of different remote objects on different processors (JVMs) if it leads to the reduction of the total program execution time, otherwise they are placed on the same JVM. After clustering of each two nodes, a new dominant sequence is determined.

In the clusterized macro data flow graph some single nodes and clusterized nodes will be executed on different virtual machines. The clusterized nodes of the macro data flow graph whose execution has to be migrated to different virtual machines have to be transformed in distributed threads. In this we would break the standard assignment practice of placing an object and all the body of its attributed methods on the same virtual (or real) processor. The distributed threads are constructed using statically a similar technique as is applied in the Brakes tool [11–13] for dynamic thread distribution among virtual machines.

The distribution of threads is done exclusively by modification of the byte code i.e. without modifications of the virtual machines. On each virtual machine, which is to execute a distributed thread, the code of the thread and a static copy of the object the thread belongs to, are placed. On each virtual machine, a thread manager object is installed, which has a special supervisor method to implement static object updating and thread activation in response to

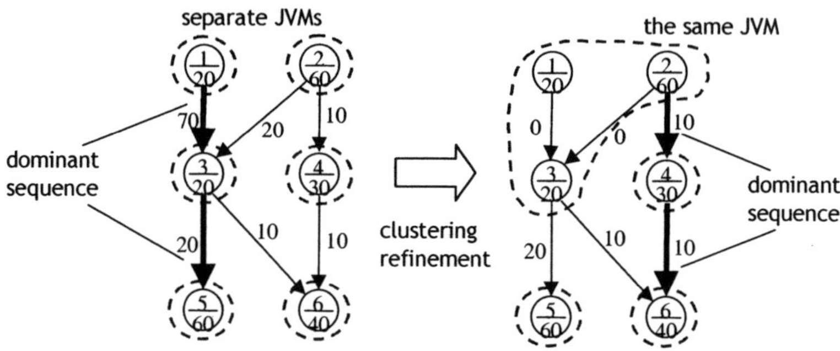

Figure 9. Clustering of macro data flow nodes.

method invocations coming from other virtual machines. Updating of the object context and thread activation is done using the serialized data that are brought with the remote supervisor method invocation. The created distributed threads obtain unique identification inside a system of all virtual machines. The supervisor method invocations are done by insertions of appropriate remote method call instructions in the program byte code. They result in remote thread activations on determined virtual machines. The context of the remote thread is re-established on a remote machine by using the transferred data. While the migrated thread is executed, the parent thread can be executed on the parent virtual machine. After execution of the remote method (in the form of the distributed thread), the return to the parent thread can be performed with the re-migration of the serialized object data to the parent virtual machine.

3   Dynamic optimization of program execution

Optimization of object placements may be achieved through the use of method call graph. This optimization is based on observation of computing time and communications. However, dynamic modifications of resource availability or some dependence from the initial data set can lead to modifications of object distribution, concurrently with object placement. Some optimization can be achieved based on the use of another type of graph representation of programs, which measures dynamic object interactions and activity. A heuristic is proposed in ADAJ that aims at identification of unbalanced load situations and their corrections, based on such graph representations.

Previously defined graphs, used in section 2.1, are either constructed by static analysis of the Java byte code (MDG) or on basis of measurements from trace files, created during program execution (MCG). Another possible graph program representation of a program is the dynamic relation graph (DRG), Fig. 10, generated during program execution, as in the ADAJ environment [9]. The nodes of this graph are remote objects (as those in JavaParty), and edges between nodes represent object interactions, in terms of method invocations. Edges are weighted with the numbers of method invocations.

Counting method invocations between objects gives an approximation of the object interactions and of the object own activity. ADAJ has chosen this solution because of the type of asynchronous applications it is meant for. Asynchronism makes difficult the estimation of the execution time of method invocations. At the same time, computation in an object-oriented

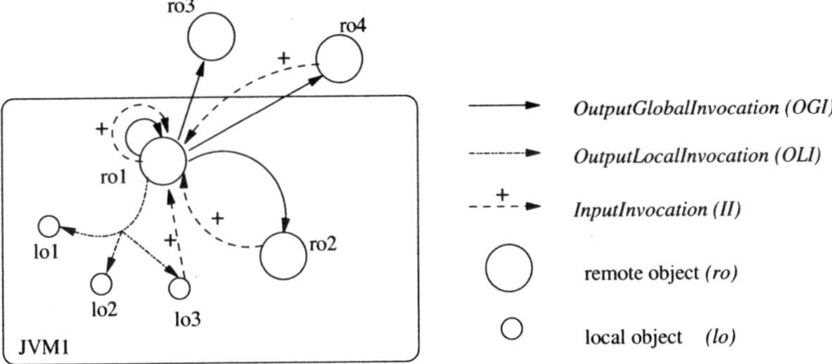

Figure 10. Relations between ADAJ objects in the DRG

language is generated by invocations of objects and the computation intensity depends on the number of method invocations. The remote objects which are observed are called global objects.

Three kinds of object interactions are identified (Fig. 10):

- if a method of a remote object is invoking a method of another remote object, this is counted by an directed edge connecting two remote objects, as an output global invocation,

- if a method of a remote object is invoked by itself or another (global or local) object, this is counted as an input invocation,

- if a method of a remote object is invoking a method on a Java local object, this is counted as an output local invocation.

The image of the program graph representation at a particular moment does not reflect evolution in time. In order to include this kind of information, values are smoothed, so that weights on edges represent a history of execution [8].

The MDG and the MCG graphs allow static optimizations of remote object placements over JVMs. The corresponding decisions are taken, based on execution for given sets of input program data. This static approach may not be enough for dynamic and irregular applications, or for executions in the context of machine load variation. A DRG – dynamic relation graph – as in ADAJ, enables good redistribution of objects by dynamic load balancing [9].

The redistribution algorithm is composed of two phases. In the first phase, the detection of an imbalance is achieved, on the basis of the dynamic relation graph. An imbalance exists is there is at least one overloaded and one underloaded machine. This classification is done depending on the double threshold of the load metric. A JVM load depends on the number of threads and on the workload of all remote objects is contains. The workload of an object is generated by all input invocations and by all local invocations towards Java local objects. The two metrics are combined in order to capture the difference between active and blocked threads, information, which cannot be obtained from Java tools. In the second phase, if an imbalance is detected, correction is achieved in a distributed manner, choosing the best candidates from the overloaded machine which will be transferred to the underloaded one(s). Objects which do not have important communication links to other remote objects of the machine, and which have a mean workload will be preferred. Their new locations depend on the workload and communication intensity with the objects on the destination machine.

Redistribution of objects in ADAJ is based on information on the behaviour of the application, captured concurrently with its execution. Exploiting this information dynamically during execution may be costly, due to the distributed character of the graph, but it gives historical and continuous view of execution, no matter what the input data sets are, or how the computation evolves.

Experimental results [14] have shown gains in execution times up to 30%, compared to a version without the interference of the load balancing mechanism. Initial distributions were voluntarily unbalanced, which tested the capacity of the dynamic load balancing algorithm to adapt distribution to unbalanced situations. The test of an ideal and perfectly distributed program shows that the cost overhead of the monitoring does not exceed 1%.

4 Conclusions

In this paper we have proposed some optimization algorithms for distributed Java programs. The algorithms use control and data dependencies that can be identified in Java programs. These dependencies are described by graphs and depict main relationship between potentially parallel elements of programs. Dependency graphs are constructed by static analysis of Java programs, program byte code and then extended by information obtained from traced program runs. This approach allows to perform optimizations of remote objects placement over JVMs (including data and distributed code) for execution with representative sets of input program data. The optimization explores both static and dynamic dependencies between objects and their constituent elements.

A dynamic load balancing mechanism may be supported by three kinds of information: information about the computer load and performance, information about dynamic relation between objects and information deduced from code analysis. The proposed static pre-optimization introduces a byte code analysis, which can be used in synergy with dynamic load balancing strategies (which, in most cases, do not exploit static information coming from Java source code or compiled byte code). Further use of dynamic load balancing may limit the load imbalance due to unexpected situations or the use of non-regular program input data. Compile-time optimizations do not introduce any penalty in execution time programs and thus, they can use more sophisticated and time-consuming heuristics, which give better results.

References

[1]   J. Zhao *"Multithreaded Dependence Graphs for Concurrent Java Programs"*, Int. Symp. Software Engineering for Parallel and Distributed Systems, May 1999, pp.13-23, IEEE CS.

[2]   J. Zhao *"Dependency Analysis of the Java Byte code"* Proceedings of the 24 IEEE Annual Int. Computer Software and Application Conference, Taipei, October 2000, pp. 486-491.

[3]   J. Zhao, L. Xiang, K. Nishimi, and T. Harada, *"Understanding Java Byte code Using Kafer"*, 20th IASTED Int. Conf. on Applied Informatics, Innsbruck, Feb. 2002

[4]   T. Yang, A. Gerasoulis, *"PYRROS: Static scheduling and code generation for message passing multiprocessors"*, Proc. of 6th ACM Int. Conf. on Supercomputing, Washington D.C., July 1992, pp. 428-437

[5]   M. Dahm, *"Byte-Code Engineering"*, Proceedings JIT'99, ed. Clemens Cap., Freie Universitat Berlin.

[6]　V. Sarkar *"Partitioning and Scheduling Parallel Programs for Execution on Multiprocessors"*, The MIT Press, 1989.

[7]　V. Felea *"Méthodologie de conception et exécution efficace de programmes Java distribués"*, PhD Thèsis, Université des Sciences et Technologies de Lille, May 2003.

[8]　A. Bouchi, R. Olejnik and B. Toursel *"A New Estimation Method for Distributed Java Object Activity"*, IPDPS – Workshop on Java for Parallel and Distributed Computing, Fort Lauderdale, USA, 2002.

[9]　V. Felea *"Exploiting Runtime Information in Load Balancing Strategies"*, Proc. Distributed and Parallel Systems – Cluster and Grid Computing, Kluwer Academy Publishers, Linz, 2002, pp. 21-29.

[10]　M. Philippsen, M. Zenger *"JavaParty – Transparent Remote Objects in Java"*, ACM Workshop on Java for Science and Engineering Computation, Las Vegas, USA, 1997.

[11]　E. Truyen, B. Robben et al., *"Portable Support for Transparent Thread Migration in Java"*, KU Leuven, Dept of Comp. Science, 2000.

[12]　D. Weyns, E. Truyen, P. Verbaeten, *"Distributed Threads in Java"*, Proceedings of the International Symposium on Parallel and Distributed Computing, July, 2002, Iasi, Romania, in: Informatica, Vol. 11, 2002, Alexandru Ioan Cuza University, pp. 94-109.

[13]　Runtime Repartitioning with DistibutedBrakes, Background Information and Prototype,
`http://www.cs.ku-leuven.ac.be/~danny/DistributedBrakes.html`

[14]　V. Felea, B. Toursel, *"Middleware-Based Load Balancing for Communicating Java Objects"*, Proc. of the NATO Advanced Research Workshop on Concurrent Information Processing and Computing, July, 2003, Sinaia, Romania, IOS Press.

Concurrent Information Processing and Computing
D. Grigoras and A. Nicolau (Eds.)
IOS Press, 2005

Power-Aware Multimedia Streaming in Heterogeneous Multi-User Environments

Radu Cornea   Shivajit Mohapatra   Nikil Dutt
Alex Nicolau   Nalini Venkatasubramanian

Dept. of Information & Computer Science
University of California, Irvine, CA 92697-3425
`{radu,mopy,dutt,nicolau,nalini}@ics.uci.edu`

Abstract. Streaming multimedia content to heterogeneous handheld devices is a significant research challenge, due to the diverse computation capabilities and battery lifetimes of these devices. A unified framework that integrates low level architectural optimizations (CPU, memory), OS power-saving mechanisms (Dynamic Voltage Scaling) and adaptive middleware techniques (admission control, transcoding, network traffic regulation) can provide significant improvements in both the system performance and user experience. In this paper, we present such an integrated framework and investigate the trade-offs involved in serving distributed clients simultaneously, while maintaining acceptable QoS levels for each client. We show that the power savings attained at both CPU/memory and network levels can be aggregated for increased overall performance. Based on this, we demonstrate how an integrated framework, that supports tight coupling of inter-level parameters can enhance user experience on handheld devices.

1   Introduction

Advances in processor and wireless networking technology are generating a new class of multimedia applications (e.g. video streaming) for mobile handheld devices. Typically, these devices have limited resources - lower processing power, memory, display capabilities, storage and limited battery lifetime as compared to desktop/laptop systems. On the other hand, multimedia applications have higher Quality of Service(QoS) and processing requirements which tend to make them extremely resource-hungry. In addition, human perception of multimedia quality is significantly influenced by the device specific attributes (e.g form factor) [7]. Therefore, delivering high quality multimedia content to mobile handheld devices, while preserving their service lifetimes remain competing design requirements. This introduces key research challenges in the design of multimedia applications, intermediate adaptations and low-level architectural improvements of the device. Moreover, distributed environments where heterogeneous devices perform simultaneous streaming pose an important challenge for the system designer. The distribution poses new problems related to mobility, shared resources, and QoS trade-offs for accommodating an increased number of users.

Recent years have witnessed researchers aggressively trying to propose and optimize techniques for power and performance trade-offs for realtime applications. Different solutions have been proposed at various computational levels: architecture (hardware) – caches/memory optimizations [17], dynamic voltage scaling(DVS) [10], dynamic power management (DPM) of system components (disks, network interfaces), efficient compilers techniques – and application/middleware based adaptations [13]. However, an interesting disconnect is observed in the research initiatives undertaken at each level. Power optimization techniques developed at each computational level have remained seemingly independent of the other abstraction hierarchy levels, potentially missing opportunities for substantial improvements achievable through cross-level integration. The cumulative power gains observed by aggregating techniques at each stage can be potentially significant; however, it also requires a study of the trade-offs involved and the customizations required for unified operation. For example, decisive middleware/OS based adaptations are possible if low-level information(e.g optimal register file sizes & cache configurations) is made available; similarly low level architectural components (e.g CPU registers, caches etc.) can be optimized if the architecture is cognizant of higher-level details such as specific video encoding. The interaction between different layers is even more important in distributed applications where a combination of local and global information helps and improves the control decisions (power, performance and QoS trade-offs) made at runtime. Fig. 1 presents the different computation levels in a typical handheld computer and the cross layer interactions for optimal power and performance deliverance.

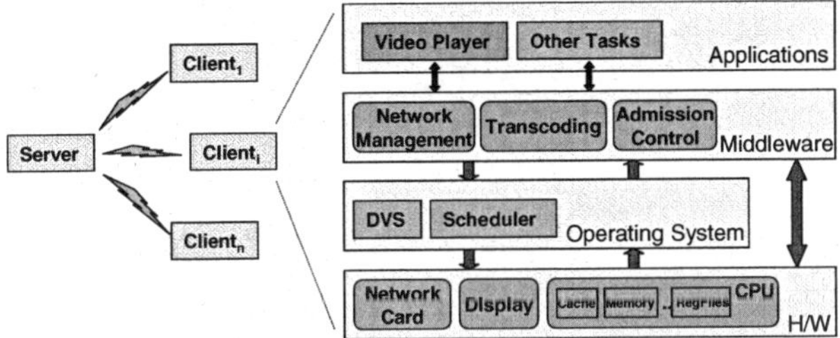

Figure 1. Abstraction layers in a distributed multimedia streaming application

The purpose of our study is to develop and integrate hardware based architectural optimization techniques with high level operating system and middleware approaches (Fig. 1), for improvements in power savings and the overall user experience, in the context of video streaming in a distributed environment of heterogeneous low-power handheld devices.

Multimedia applications heavily utilize the biggest power consumers in modern computers: the CPU, the $network$ and the $display$. Therefore, we aggregate hardware and software techniques that induce power savings for these resources.

To address the challenge of integrating techniques at different levels (hardware, OS, middleware, user) we have adopted a multi-phase approach. First, low-level architectural tuning knobs are identified and combined with compilation techniques for optimized CPU performance; then, ideal operating points are determined for video streams of specific quality levels using these knobs; we then study the trade-offs involved in performing DVS along with our low-level optimization methods and evaluate the power gains of the wireless network interface using an adaptive middleware technique for a typical network with multiple users (noise). In this paper we start by summarizing these previous results. Next, the effect of multiple users on system resources is estimated, to drive our integrated framework. We then present a feedback-based middleware for multi-user power-aware admission control, quality and power-supported video transcoding; we study power vs. quality tradeoffs in the context of a distributed network of handheld computers. Finally, experiments with the integrated approach are presented, withe the final goal of improving the overall user experience (satisfaction) in the context of streaming video to handheld computers in a distributed environment.

By integrating the above techniques we are able to enhance the individual user experience and dynamically perform adaptation to also provide an improved overall system performance (among all users). Our previous results [7] have shown that architectural optimizations can give as much as 57% energy savings for the CPU and memory and middleware techniques up to 78% savings in the power consumption of the network interface card. Based on these combined results, our framework is able to accommodate a larger number of users in the system and serve clients with an increased level of video quality (even for devices that were unable to stream a video clip to completion initially, due to low battery life).

2   System Architecture

We assume the system model depicted in Fig. 2. The system entities include a multimedia server, a proxy server that utilizes a directory service, a rule base for specific devices and a video transcoder, an ethernet switch, the wireless access point (AP) and users with low-power wireless devices. The circles represent the noise at the access point due to network traffic introduced by "other" users. The multimedia servers store the multimedia content and stream videos to clients upon receipt of a request. The users issue requests for video streams on their handheld devices. All communication between the handheld device and the servers is routed through the proxy server, that can transcode the video stream in real time.

The middleware executes on both the handheld devices and the proxy, and performs two important functions. On the devices, it obtains residual energy availability information from the underlying architecture and feeds it back to the proxy and relates the video stream parameters and network related control information to lower abstraction layers. On the proxy, it performs a feedback based multi-user power aware admission control and realtime transcoding of the video stream, based on the feedback from the device. It also regulates the video transmission over the network based on the noise level and the video stream quality. Additionally, the middleware exploits dynamic global state information(e.g mobility info, noise level etc.) available at the directory service and static device specific knowledge (architecture, OS, video quality levels) from the static rule base, to optimally perform its functions. The rate at which feedbacks are sent by the device is dictated by administrative policies like periodic feedback etc.. Moreover we assume that network connectivity is maintained at all times.

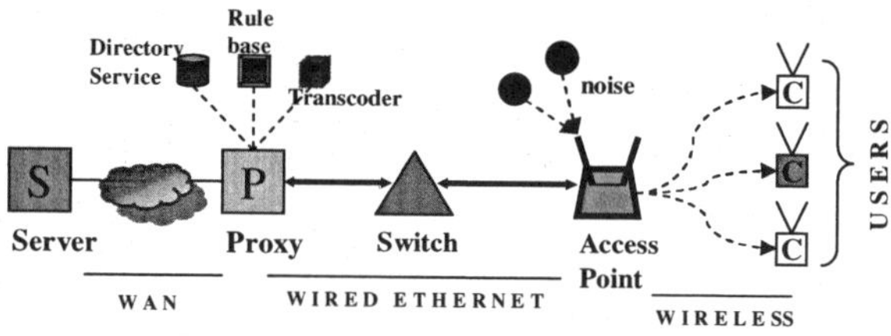

Figure 2. System Model

Our goal is to provide an optimal user experience and maintain an acceptable utility factor for the system. We define an "acceptable utility factor" to be obtained when the system can stream the highest possible quality of video to the user such that time, acceptable quality and power constraints are satisfied (i.e the video clip runs to completion, at a quality level above or equal to the one the user specified). To accomplish this it is important to understand the notion of video quality for a handheld device and its implications on power consumption. Video applications introduce the notion of human perception of video quality as an important measure of performance. Moreover, user perception of quality is significantly influenced by the environment and the viewing device(e.g PDA) [1]. For example, most people are able to differentiate between close video quality levels on laptop/desktop systems; however only few are able to differentiate between close quality levels on a handheld device. It is hard to programmatically identify video quality parameters(a combination of *bit rate, frame rate and video resolution*) that produce a user perceptible change in video quality and/or a noticeable shift in power consumption.

In previous work [7] we established that users can only distinguish between mostly eight different levels of quality on a handheld device. Based on this, we selected eight quality levels, between Q1 (very high, like original) to Q8 (very low), chosen such that there is a perceptible video degradation and power variation between different adjacent levels. We identified transformation parameters (*bit rate, frame rate and video resolution*) for our proxy-based realtime transcoding, in order to generate the different quality level videos (transcoding is a process of decoding the original clip and re-encoding it at different parameters). Profiled average power consumption values were used to perform a high-level (coarse) power aware admission control for the system (this controls how users are accepted into the system and how resources are allocated to them in order to maintain a desired QoS). Similar device specific transformations can be made for other portable computers. More importantly, we also optimize our low-level architecture based on these discrete video quality levels. This approach provides us with two significant advantages: (i) Real time stream quality transformations can be performed with no overheads of dynamically determining quality degradation parameters, (ii) using the architectural tuning, optimized operating points can be pre-determined for a particular video stream quality. With the knowledge of the stream qualities, low-level cpu voltage scaling can also be improved. The following sections summarizes the architectural and middleware optimizations that are integrated into our system, followed by the system level optimizations and final integration.

3   Optimizations for Multimedia Streaming

Managing a distributed multimedia streaming system is a complex task and requires coordination at different levels of abstractions. We start by focusing on a single client model and identifying areas where power and performance optimizations can be performed, with the end result of an improved user experience. This section contains a summary of our previous work, in the context of the current endeavor. For more details on these techniques, see [7].

3.1   Hardware-level Adaptation

Hardware design techniques that identify multiple modes of operation and dynamic reconfiguration can be employed to attain high power and performance gains at the CPU architecture level. In order to optimize the architecture for delivering optimal energy performance, we first studied the low level functional units that have maximal impact on power consumption.

We identified "knobs" for these components that can be made available to the higher abstraction levels for dynamically tuning the hardware for MPEG video applications.

Previous work has shown that there are three major sources of power consumption in a handheld device, like iPaq (Fig. 3): display (around 1W for full backlight), network hardware (1.4W) and CPU/memory (1-3W, with the additional board circuits). Each of these subsystems expose ways for controlling the power dissipation. In case of the display (LCD), the main energy drain comes from the backlight, which is a predefined user setting and therefore has a limited degree of controllability by the system (without affecting the final utility). The network interface allows for efficient power savings if cognizant of the higher level protocol's behavior and will be explored in a subsequent section. Out of the three components mentioned above, the CPU coupled with the memory subsystem poses the biggest challenge. Its intrinsic high dependence on the input data to be processed, the quality of the code generated by the compiler and the organization of its internal architecture make predicting its power consumption profile very hard in general; nevertheless, very good power saving results can be obtained by utilizing the knowledge of the application running on it and through extensive profiling of a representative data input set from the application's domain. Therefore, we focused our attention on the possible optimizations at the CPU level for a multimedia streaming application (MPEG).

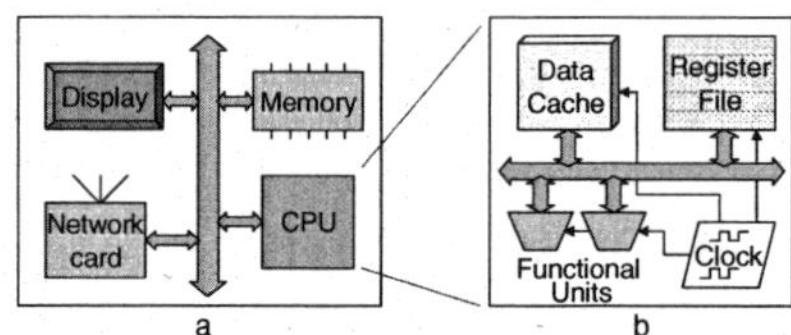

Figure 3. Main Components of a Handheld Device

3.1.1   Quality-driven Cache Reconfiguration

Through extensive simulation, we identified the subcomponents of the CPU that consume the most power and observed the power distribution inside the CPU for MPEG decoding. It follows that internal CPU caches account for the largest part of the energy consumed by the processor. Moreover, the relative power contribution of the internal units of the CPU does not vary significantly with the nature or quality of the video played.

There are various techniques pertinent to cache optimizations. Power consumption for the cache depends on the runtime access counts: while hits result in only a cache access, misses add the penalty of accessing the main memory (external). Fortunately, in most applications the inherent locality of data means that cache miss rate is relatively low and so are accesses to external memory. However, MPEG decoding exhibits a relatively poor data locality, which, when combined with the large data sets exercised by the algorithm, leads to an increase in the cache memory-traffic.

Our cache reconfiguration goal is optimizing energy consumption for a particular video quality level Q_k. In general, cache power consumption for a particular configuration and video quality is dependent on cache size and associativity. By profiling this function for the entire search space of available cache configurations, we determine the optimized operating point for that video quality.

We found out that for all video qualities such an operating point exists and it improves cache power consumption by up to 10-20% (as opposed to a suboptimized configuration). This technique effectively fine-tunes the organization of the cache so that it perfectly matches the application and the data sets to be processed, yielding important power savings.

We should mention that while current processors (including the ARM core on iPaq) in general do not exhibit such aggressive architectural reconfigurations, except for special purposes, there are many research projects on this and eventually the techniques will be incorporated into more future processors.

3.1.2 Integrated Dynamic Voltage Scaling

A different knob for controlling power drawn by the processor is dynamic voltage scaling (DVS) [10]. Voltage scaling is a method for trading-off processor speed against power, by lowering both voltage and operating frequency (power consumption when running at a high speed and voltage is much larger than when running at low speed and voltage). This technique provides significant savings for MPEG streaming as it allows tradeoffs for transforming the frame decoding slack time (CPU idle time) into important power savings.

In MPEG, frames are decoded in a fraction of the frame delay ($F_d = 1/frame\_rate$). The actual value for the frame decoding time D depends on the type of MPEG frame being processed (**I** – intra-coded, **P** – predicted and **B** – bidirectionally predicted frames) and also on the cache configuration (size, associativity) and DVS setting (frequency, voltage). In our study, we assumed a buffered based decoding, where the decoded frames are placed in a temporary buffer and are only read when the frame is displayed. This allowed us to decouple the decoder from the displaying; decoding time was still different for different frames, but we could assume an average D for a particular video stream/quality. The difference between the average frame delay and actual frame decoding time gave us the slack time $\theta = F_d - D$. When we performed DVS, we slowed down the CPU so as to decrease the slack time to a minimum, so we computed an operating frequency and voltage that minimized the slack θ.

Having the best DVS setting for each cache configuration and quality level, we looked at the effect of the integrated approach on the power consumption. The DVS is not totally independent of the cache reconfiguration technique (cache configurations with a largest slack time allow for higher DVS based power reductions) and as a result it effectively reshaped the total power consumption. Through simulation, we found the best operating points for the DVS/cache reconfiguration combined approach.

3.2 Architecture-Aware Middleware Adaptation

The gains obtained from the lower levels (architecture) can be further amplified if combined with techniques on higher levels (middleware). An adaptive middleware framework at the proxy can dynamically intercept and doctor a video stream to exactly match the video characteristics for which the target architecture has been optimized. Additionally, it can regulate the network traffic to induce maximal power savings in a network interface.

3.2.1 Network Traffic Regulation

We developed a proxy-based traffic regulation mechanism to reduce energy consumption by the device network interface. Our mechanism is able to dynamically adapt to changing conditions in the network and specific attributes of the wireless transmission (bandwidth, access point buffering). The packets are transmitted into optimized bursts of video by the proxy, along with control information. Since wireless network cards typically consume significantly more power in active vs sleep mode (about one order of magnitude [9]), our goal was to optimize the video burst sizes in order to maximize energy savings without performance costs.

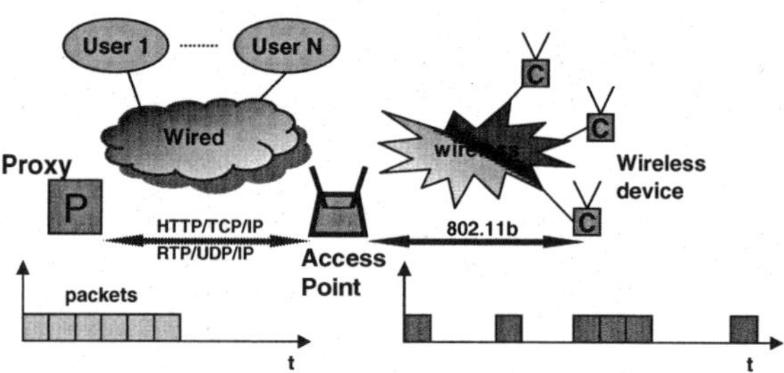

Figure 4. Wireless Network

The analysis for the above power saving approach was performed using a realistic network framework(Fig. 4), in the presence of noise and AP limitations. The proxy middleware buffers the transcoded video and transmits several frames of video in a single burst along with the time for the next transmission as control information. The device then uses this control information to switch the interface between active/idle mode and sleep mode. A queueing theory analysis was used to predict packet loss rates at the access point due to limited buffering capacity, in the presence of multiple users (packets introduced by other users were modeled as exernal noise). We observed that large values of the burst length can result in packet losses at the access point and/or buffer overflows at the device. We acknowledged that a QoS aware preferential service algorithm at the access point can impact power management significantly. The above analysis could be used by an adaptive middleware to calculate an optimal burst length for any given video stream and noise level.

4   System-level Optimizations

In the previous sections we studied multimedia streaming/adaptation in a scenario where a single client was served by the proxy node. While this allowed us to concentrate on the server-proxy-client interaction, a real system would encompass multiple heterogeneous client devices being served simultaneously by one or more proxy nodes. Today's handheld devices exhibit a large variation in terms of multimedia playing capabilities. This includes processing power, display size, battery life, factors that in our approach drive multimedia adaptation on the proxy. In order to provide the best user experience at the device and be able to accommodate an increased number of clients at the same time, the proxy/middleware level must be cognizant of architecture level characteristics of each of the devices being served. This allows the transcoder on the proxy to better shape the streaming traffic to the devices so that a maximum number of clients can be served with a QoS above the requested threshold.

Extending our system architecture to multiple users unfolds new problems, like network congestion, proxy node resource exhaustion, etc. We address these problems and present possible solutions in the next sections.

4.1 Transcoding Multiple Streams

When performing transcoding for multiple users, the proxy node can soon become saturated, as this process is a very CPU intensive, especially if real-time is a requirement. *Transcoding a video stream typically involves two steps (Fig. 5):*

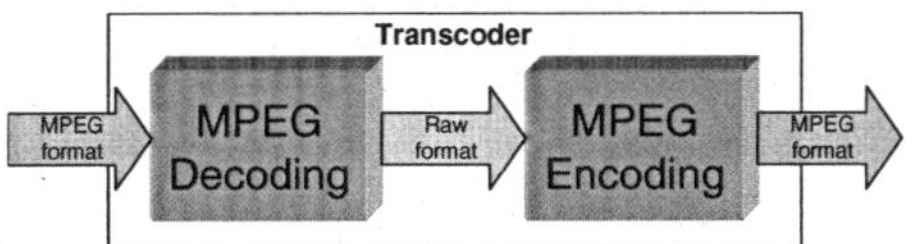

Figure 5. Transcoder Phases

- *decode* MPEG stream into a raw format (YUV, YV12, PPM, etc)
- *encode* the raw format back into MPEG video, at the new encoding parameters, after an initial processing (adjust frame size, change frame rate, bitrate)

The encoding step demands most processing power (in general about 3-4 time more than decoding, for the same encoding) and is heavily dependent on the encoding parameters (e.g. frame size). [14]

If we denote by L the average CPU processing power (percentage load) for performing a task, then the requirement for transcoding from initial format f_i to final format f_f is :

$L_{trans}(f_i, f_f) = L_{dec}(f_i) + L_{enc}(f_f)$, where fs, fr, br specify frame size, frame rate and bit rate respectively of the MPEG encoding format and $L <= 1$. L_{dec} and L_{enc} denote the proxy load for the decoding and encoding (intermediary steps) in real time.

The middleware continuously monitors the system and ensures that enough resources are available to serve all clients. For example, when n users are connected to a proxy, the total load on the proxy node should not exceed the available computing resources: $\sum_n L^i_{trans} <= 1$, where L^i_{trans} represents the load required for user i (in the case of a cluster of N_P proxies, total load should be less than N_P).

4.2 Network Bandwidth Limitation

As the wireless network bandwidth is limited, a large number of users performing simultaneous video streaming may lead to network congestion and the inability to provide the users with an acceptable quality video stream (above the user defined threshold).

Network traffic regulation was discussed before for a single user case and is revisited here in a multi-user context.

Each individual client requires a burst transmission of length P_b bits every I seconds. It follows that the bandwidth consumption per user is given by:

$BW^i = P_b^i / I^i$ (in *bps*), for client C^i.

If the total wireless bandwidth available at the access point AP is BW_{total}, then the condition for avoiding network congestion is: $\sum_n BW^i <= BW_{total}$.

Note that we are considering the average network bandwidth, local communication spikes should be handled by AP, as long as the local buffering allows.

4.3   Multi-User Energy-Aware Admission Control & Stream Transformations

The middleware on the proxy utilizes the feedback from the devices, to continuously monitor the overall state of the system. Initially, for each client device under its control, it performs an energy aware admission control to identify whether a request can be scheduled (the video can be streamed at the user requested quality level for the entire length of the video). Subsequently, it monitors the residual energy at the device and streams the highest quality video (performing realtime video transcoding) that meets the energy budget at the device and maintains an acceptable QoS.

As this is a heterogeneous multi-user environment, with large diversity among various client devices, an information record is maintained that lists the device capabilities (in terms of power consumption, hardware characteristics, power management, battery information, etc). Moreover, to assist the control process, a configuration/mode table is created for each client device C_i which, for each video quality Q_k, lists information available from the client, network and proxy level:

- architecture: optimal knob configuration (cache parameters, DVS mode) and average CPU power consumption at the architecture level for this configuration
- network: ideal burst length and corresponding network level power consumption
- proxy: load required for converting from initial stream to quality Q_i
- access point: bandwidth for streaming video at quality Q_k

Part of the information is sent by the actual device when it registers and the rest is precomputed by the proxy node middleware level. This table predicts the effect of streaming video quality Q_k to client C_i for all the involved components (client architecture - CPU and network card configuration and power consumption, proxy node - load, access point - bandwidth).

The system level admission control algorithm is presented in Fig 6. When a new client request or a feedback from a client is received, the proxy first tries to determine if it can accommodate the existing users at a minimum acceptable quality level (as specified by the users themselves). If not, the client is denied the request. Otherwise, starting from the minimum quality level, the middleware gradually increases the quality levels for all clients as long as all the constraints related to proxy load, AP bandwidth and available residual power on the individual devices are satisfied. When an optimized operating point for the system is determined as a result of this process, the new configuration is updated on the control system and the clients are notified about the changes (where changes exist).

The order in which clients are chosen by the algorithm as candidates for increasing quality levels is important for providing

```
WHILE (TRUE)
{
    IF (R_i OR F received)
    {
        FOR each client
        {
            Determine k, such that Q_k=Qa
            IF ((T - (T_cur - T_start))* P_k <= E_res          (1)
                Compute L_trans, BW_AP for video quality Q_k
            ELSE
                REJECT the request OR (Negociate video quality)
    }

        IF ( ∑ L^i_trans <= 1 && ∑ BW^i_AP <= BW_total)        (2)
        {
            WHILE (at least one change in the client configurations)
            {
                FOR each client C_i (use heuristic to select)
                {
                    Increase quality by 1: Q_k <- Q_k + 1
                    IF (Inequalities (1) and updated (2) hold)
                        CHANGE quality to Q_k for client C_i
                }
            }
            UPDATE system with new client configurations
        } ELSE
            REJECT the request OR (Negociate video quality)
    }
}
```

Figure 6. Multi-user Admission Control

an overall improved user experience for all users. One possible heuristic would favor clients with a lower current quality, so that the system tends toward a uniform quality level coverage. When more clients are at the same quality level, the heuristic would select the one which incurs less delta change in proxy load and bandwidth as a result of a increase in the video quality by one level. In this way, possibly other users could be further served and the number of users for which a higher quality level is provided is maximized.

5 Performance Evaluation

We adopted a multi-phase methodology to achieve our results. First, through extensive experimentation and profiling we identified eight determinate video quality levels for a handheld. This determined our dynamic video transcoding parameters. Next, we optimized the low-level architecture to perform optimally with the above video streams. We also identified the best network transmission characteristics for video streams encoded at the above quality levels. Moving to a multi-user environment, we performed experiments to estimate the CPU load for transcoding between different formats. Using the operating points for architecture and network transmission, combined with the results from transcoding we used our proxy admission control algorithm to guide streaming videos to the iPAQ, and evaluate the performance for the system.

5.1 Experimental Setup

All our measurements for video quality measurements were made for a Compaq iPAQ 3650, with a 206Mhz Intel StrongArm processor, with 16MB ROM, 32MB SDRAM. The iPAQ used a Cisco 350 Series Aironet 11Mbps wireless PCMCIA network interface card for communication. The batteries were removed from the iPAQ during the experiment and we measured power drawn by the device during MPEG streaming.

The CPU architecture simulation was implemented using the Wattch/SimpleScalar [3] power simulator. We configured our simulated CPU to resemble a typical Intel XScale processor (widely used in today's mobile devices, mostly due to their excellent MIPS/Watt performance): ARM core, 400 MHz, 1.3V, 0.18um, 32k instruction cache, 32k data cache, single issue. The MPEG decoder from Berkeley MPEG Tools [15] was used. Video transcoding was done using the commercially available TMPGEnc transcoder [18]. As input video for the decoding, we used traces from various video clips from low action(e.g. "news") like content to high action (e.g. GTA) fast scene changing streams. For each of these clips, we extract a sequence to be simulated and we encode it at noticeable different levels of quality . Level 1 corresponds to the best possible quality: 320x240 frame size, 30fps framerate, 650kbps bitrate. From 1 to 8, each level differs from the previous one by at least one parameter (frame size, frame rate or bitrate). This way, we have a clear (observable) degradation in quality between each quality level.

The decoding program is then simulated through Wattch and statistics are extracted from the simulator output.

Video Quality	Cache Size	Cache Associativity	Clock Frequency	Voltage	Original Energy	Optimized Energy	Savings
Q1	8	8	100	1	1.29	0.76	47.5%
Q2	8	8	100	1	1.09	0.64	47.8%
Q3	8	8	100	1	0.95	0.56	48.0%
Q4	32	2	66	0.9	0.54	0.26	57.6%
Q5	32	2	66	0.9	0.48	0.23	57.8%
Q6	32	2	33	0.9	0.42	0.20	58.0%
Q7	8	8	33	0.9	0.29	0.14	57.3%
Q8	8	8	33	0.9	0.24	0.11	57.5%

Table 1. Architectural Configurations for Ideal Energy and Performance Gains (*Action* Clip)

5.2 Experimental Results

In this section, we first present the performance of our architectural and middleware optimizations, obtained in prior work. Our integrated framework is based on top of these individual results. Later, we present the improvements in the overall utility of the system achieved in the system with the integrated approach, in a distributed environment.

5.2.1 Architectural Optimizations

By profiling short (10sec) video clips through our power simulator, for all combinations of cache parameters (size: 4Kb to 64Kb, associativity: 1 to 32) we collected the total energy consumption for the entire duration of each video clip (with quality from 1 to 8)

For all video quality levels, we were able to determine a cache configuration that minimizes energy consumption. Moreover, through cache reconfiguration, we obtained power savings in the range 10-15%, depending on the nature of the video.

We made the following observations:

- Cache associativity produces the largest shift in energy consumption, extreme values proving very inefficient(especially for direct mapped caches).

- The best cache configurations reflect the internal storage requirements for different frame sizes and organization of the decoding algorithm.

5.2.2 Optimized Knobs after Applying DVS

We combined dynamic voltage scaling technique with cache reconfiguration for an increased overall effect on power consumption. The combined approach gave us up to 60% in energy savings as compared with the initial architecture. We repeated the same procedure for all the video quality levels.

In most of the cases we were able to run the CPU at a significant lower voltage, mainly due to the initial high speed of the simulated XScale processor (400MHz) and the quality of the code (highly optimized).

The overall energy savings we obtained after both above techniques and the knob values for the optimized configuration are summarized in Table 1, for an *action* video clip. These numbers serve as input of our integrated framework.

5.2.3   Middleware Optimization for Video Bursts

For each video quality (1-8), we varied the video burst time, the network noise level and the network packet size. The wired and wireless ethernet bandwidths were set to 10Mbps and 8Mbps(effective B/W, 802.11b is capable of higher throughput) and γ was set to a 0.85. The transmission delay of the wireless access point was also fixed at $400\mu s$ per packet.

As expected the highest quality video had a very small burst time compared to the lowest quality video. The ideal burst times were ascertained such that none of the frames missed deadlines at the device.

Table 2 shows the ideal burst times and the corresponding power savings for the same video stream encoded at the eight quality levels. We can observe that the power saved at the NIC, is the least for the highest quality video and the most for the lowest quality video. Also, as expected the power gains diminish with noise. Clearly, very small burst times yield no gains. Interestingly, for every additional user in the system, a new optimal burst time exists. The numbers we gathered are used to drive our integrated approach.

Quality Lev.	Burst Len (N=1, sec)	Power Saved (N=1,Watt)	Burst Len (N=3, sec)	Power Saved (N=3,Watt)	Burst Len (N=5, sec)	Power Saved (N=5, Watt)
Q1	2.3	.925	2.0	0.89	1.8	0.87
Q2	3.5	1.0	3.05	0.98	2.76	0.96
Q3	4.6	1.04	4.05	1.02	3.68	1.0
Q4	4.85	1.05	4.2	1.03	3.85	1.02
Q5	6.8	1.08	6.25	1.07	5.75	1.06
Q6	14.5	1.12	12.5	1.11	11.5	1.11
Q7	17.5	1.13	15.0	1.12	13.5	1.11
Q8	17.0	1.12	15.4	1.12	14.0	1.11

Table 2. Optimal network video burst lengths(in secs) and corresponding power gains for different quality and noise levels for the Grand Theft Auto action video, assuming sufficient buffer available at client and network packet size of 500KB

5.2.4   Transcoding Results

We perform transcoding experiments with the TMPGEnc transcoder. The original action type movie clip was converted using different parameters (frame size, bitrate, frame rate). By measuring the time required to perform the transcoding on a Intel P4 2.4Ghz, 512Mb internal memory, we make the following observations:

- Frame size (followed by frame rate) has the largest influence in transcoding time and hence, proxy load. This is expected, as the amount of processing required increases with the size of the frame to be processed.

- The bitrate does not change transcoding time significantly. Bitrate values control the quantization step in MPEG encoding, which is not computationally intensive.

- The nature of the video stream (action vs news type) slightly affects the total transcoding time, as seen in Fig 7, where we measured the transcoding time as a function frame size (relative to original clip) and video type

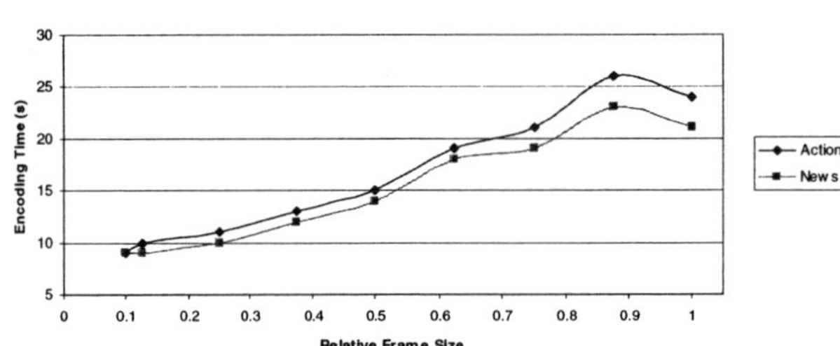

Figure 7. Transcoding time for different frame sizes

Video	Proxy Load	
	Action	News
Q1	0.40	0.35
Q2	0.40	0.35
Q3	0.40	0.35
Q4	0.30	0.28
Q5	0.30	0.28
Q6	0.30	0.28
Q7	0.20	0.18
Q8	0.20	0.18

Figure 8. Proxy loads for videos

The transcoding time was used to compute the proxy load: if the total transcoding time when using 100% CPU utilization (single user mode) is t_{trans} (in seconds), the CPU load on the proxy system in a multi-user, real time transcoder is determined as: $L_{trans} = t_{trans}/60$. Proxy loads for converting from the original format to our defined quality levels (Q1 through Q8) are presented in Fig 8 (for a 60 second video sequence).

5.2.5 The Integrated Framework

We finally evaluate the performance of the integrated framework with the architectural and middleware optimizations in place in Fig 9.

In order to generate a scenario that captures some of the problems in real environments we chose a set of constraints that make the system very sensitive to changes in the user configuration and performs a new adaptation on any important event (new user joins, power change feedback, MPEG stream finishes). Therefore we assume a system with one proxy node and a 1Mbps bandwidth available wireless network bandwidth. Each user specifies an acceptable video quality (Q_a) of 7 or 8 (very low quality), to allow for a larger range of possible operating points.

Initially (T=0) there are 3 users in the system. Based on the available residual energy, the system decides on an initial video quality and device configuration for each user. At time T_1 a new user request to join the system controlled by our proxy. In order to accommodate the new client, the middleware decides

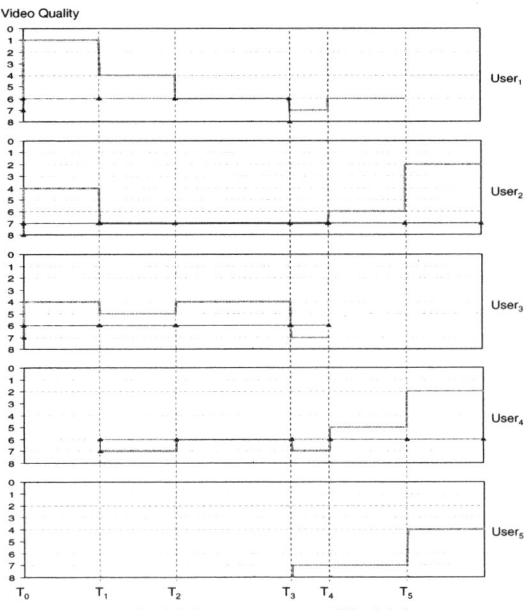

Figure 9. Multi-user Scenario

on lowering the video quality for the rest of the users in the network, as seen in the graphs. Note that all video qualities are still above or equal to the acceptable (threshold) video levels.

Due to unforseen circumstances user 1 is consuming energy at a higher rate than anticipated (for example, a new process was started on the actual device). As a result, at T_2 the system lowers the quality to stream to client 1 and is able to increase the quality level for a different user (3 in our example).

At time T_3, a fifth user joins the group. In order to accept the new user, the system is lowering the quality for all the user to decrease proxy node load and bandwidth usage. When user 3 finishes execution, the newly freed resources (proxy load, bandwidth) allow the system to improve on video quality for the other nodes.

Finally, when streaming finishes on client 1, more resources are released and the clients that are left can experience their video streaming at even higher levels.

As seen on the graph, without our optimizations and system adaptation, only 4 clients could be served simultaneously by the system. Moreover, due to the increased power consumption from other tasks, user 1 would not have been able to stream the entire video to completion. Even for the rest of the users, the possible video quality to be streamed was very low (between 6 and 8), while the dynamic adaptation could deliver quality above that most of the time. Note that there are situations where the system chose to lower the quality for some users to allow for a better overall global function.

Our integrated approach brings a significant improvement in the power consumption, which translates in a higher video quality that can be streamed and hence substantially improves the user experience at the client end. More users can be served and our dynamic adaptation is able to adjust the streams to meet the current state of the system.

6 Related Work

To provide acceptable video performance at the hardware level, efforts have concentrated on analyzing the behavior of the decoder software and devising either architectural enhancements or software improvements for the decoding algorithm. Until recently it was believed that caches can bring no potential benefit in the context of MPEG (video) decoding. In fact, due to the poor locality of the data stream, many MPEG implementations viewed video data as "un-cacheable" and completely disabled the internal caches during playback. However, Soderquist and Leeser [17] show that video data has sufficient locality that can be exploited to reduce cache-memory traffic by 50 percent or more through simple architectural changes. Dynamic Voltage Scaling [6, 12] for MPEG streams have been widely researched. At the application and middleware levels, the primary focus has been to optimize network interface power consumption [4, 5, 8]. A thorough analysis of power consumption of wireless network interfaces has been presented in [8]. In [16], Shenoy suggests performing power friendly proxy based video transformations to reduce video quality in real-time for energy savings. They also suggest an intelligent network streaming strategy for saving power on the network interface. The GRACE project [21] professes the use of cross-layer adaptations for maximizing system utility. They suggest both coarse grained and fine grained tuning of parameters for optimal gains. In [20], a resource aware admission control and adaptation is suggested for multimedia applications for optimal CPU gains. Dynamic transcoding techniques have been studied in [2] and objective video quality assessment has been studied in [11, 19].

7 Conclusions & Future Work

In this paper, we integrated low-level hardware optimizations with high level middleware adaptations for enhancing the user experience when streaming video onto handheld computers in a distributed environment. First we identified and fine tuned low level hardware to best perform with video streams at discrete quality levels. We then used a higher level middleware approach to intercept and transform the stream to compliment the architectural optimizations. A proxy based adaptive network transmission mechanism was developed to minimize the power consumption of the network interface card. The impact of handling multiple users on system resources was studied next. Finally, all the above techniques were integrated into a system, and the overall system functionality was tested for a realistic scenario. Significant improvements were observed in the requested video stream quality, enhancing the user experience substantially. We are currently exploring further architectural, middleware and system level adaptations for improving the power consumption of displays, storage devices etc. and integrating them into the framework.

8 Acknowledgement

This work was partially supported by NSF award ACI-0204028.

References

[1] "ITU-R Recommendation BT-500.7, Methodology for the subjective assessment of the quality of television pictures". In *ITU Geneva Switzerland*, 1995.

[2] S. Acharia and B.C.Smith. Compressed Domain Transcoding of MPEG. In *ICMCS*, 1998.

[3] David Brooks, Vivek Tiwari, and Margaret Martonosi. Wattch: A framework for architectural-level power analysis and optimizations. In *ISCA*, June 2000.

[4] Surendar Chandra. Wireless Network Interface Energy Consumption Implications of Popular Streaming Formats. In *MMCN*, January 2002.

[5] Surendar Chandra and A. Vahdat. Application-specific Network Management for Energy-aware Streaming of Popular Multimedia Formats. In *Usenix Annual Technical Conference*, June 2002.

[6] Kihwan Choi, Karthik Dantu, Wei-Chung Chen, and Massoud Pedram. Frame-Based Dynamic Voltage and Frequency Scaling for a MPEG Decoder. In *ICCAD 2000*, 2002.

[7] Radu Cornea, Shivajit Mohapatra, Nikil Dutt, Alex Nicolau, and Nalini Venkatasubramanian. Integrated power management for video streaming to mobile handheld devices. Technical Report 03-19, University of California, Irvine, 2003.

[8] L.M. Feeney and M Nilsson. Investigating the Energy Consumption of a Wireless Network Interface in an ad hoc Networking Environment. In *IEEE Infocom*, April 2001.

[9] Paul J. M. Havinga. *Mobile Multimedia Systems*. PhD thesis, University of Twente, Feb 2000.

[10] Chung-Hsing Hsu, Ulrich Kremer, and Michael Hsiao. Compiler-directed dynamic frequency and voltage scheduling. *Lecture Notes in Computer Science*, 2008:65–??, 2001.

[11] Jan Jansen, Toon Coppens, and Danny De Vleeschauwer. Quality Assessment of Video Streaming in the Broadband Era. In *ACIVS*, 2002.

[12] M. Mesarina and Y. Turner. A Reduced Energy Decoding of MPEG Streams. In *MMCN*, January 2002.

[13] Shivajit Mohapatra and Nalini Venkatasubramanian. PARM: Power-Aware Reconfigurable Middleware. In *ICDCS-23*, 2003.

[14] Darsan Patel and Wansik Oh. Performance profile of MPEG-2 transcoding with motion vector reuse mechanism. Technical report, Kent State University, 2001.

[15] Ketan Patel, Brian C. Smith, and Lawrence A. Rowe. Performance of a software mpeg video decoder. In *ACM Multimedia*, 1993.

[16] Prashant Shenoy and Peter Radkov. Proxy-Assisted Power-Friendly Streaming to Mobile Devices. In *MMCN*, 2003.

[17] Peter Soderquist and Miriam Leeser. Optimizing the data cache performance of a software MPEG-2 video decoder. In *ACM Multimedia*, pages 291–301, 1997.

[18] TMPGEnc. http://www.tmpgenc.net.

[19] S. Winkler. Issues in vision modeling for perceptual video quality assessment. In *Signal Processing 78(2), 1999.*, 1999.

[20] W. Yuan and K. Nahrstedt. A Middleware Framework Coordinating Processor/Power Resource Management for Multimedia Applications. In *IEEE Globecom*, Nov 2001.

[21] W. Yuan, K. Nahrstedt, S. Adve, Doug. Jones, and Robin Kravets. Design and Evaluation of a Cross-Layer Adaptation Framework for Mobile Multimedia Systems. In *MMCN*, January 2003.

Concurrent Information Processing and Computing
D. Grigoras and A. Nicolau (Eds.)
IOS Press, 2005

Service-Oriented Naming Scheme for Wireless Ad Hoc Networks

Dan Grigoraş

Computer Science Department
University College Cork
Ireland
`d.grigoras@cs.ucc.ie`

Abstract. Wireless ad hoc networks are created by mobile devices that contact each other while on the move. Within an ad hoc wireless network, a name service that allows nodes to discover services and resources is essential. This paper introduces a service-oriented attribute-based naming system for ad hoc wireless networks. An attribute-based name has the power of expressing the capabilities and current state of a service or resource of a node. The discovery process is governed by what the initiator wants and not by a location. All levels of indirection imposed by binding names to IPs are eliminated. The name system we propose is expressive, responsive and robust.

1   Introduction

Recent years encountered tremendous developments in mobile computing technologies. Personal devices like laptops, PDAs, palmtops, tablet PCs and even sensors are wireless enabled, making them part of a larger Internet. While on the move, wireless devices can contact each other and create ad hoc networks. Mobility of code, devices and users, heterogeneity, feeble communication links, large differences in communication latency and bandwidth among separate segments are some of the features of wireless networks. To be effective, an ad hoc wireless network needs means for resource and service discovery. In a highly dynamic environment where mobile devices come and go, all involved parties have to be able to advertise for their capabilities, to discover potential partners' offers and, possibly, make use of them. Basic services like naming, discovery, or routing well-established in wired networks have to be re-designed in order to take into account wireless networks' properties. To achieve this goal, one of the first steps is to devise a naming system that allows heterogeneous mobile devices to address each other. Most of current work focused on designing mobile IP solutions that assign temporary care-of address IP to mobile devices [12, 14, 15]. That approach assumes quasi-permanent attachment of mobile devices to wired networks by access points (AP). However, in many situations there is no accessible AP, or wireless devices cannot benefit of any support service, including DHCP for assigning an IP address. In these circumstances, a service-oriented attribute-based naming system offers necessary information for the discovery, selection and use of services running on mobile devices, without the support of APs. Using a different naming system as an alternative to the host name/IP scheme becomes even more important in the context of Internet current trends towards increasing the number of wireless mobile nodes.

The large adoption of mobile wireless devices makes Internet gradually change from static topology to a more dynamic one, where some regions are occasionally covered by networked wireless devices. Currently, there are three classes of computer networks in use. Purely wired networks are still the dominant technology[1]. Mixed wired-wireless networks extend the OSI stack protocol over wireless devices connected to APs. In this way, client-server applications already in use can be ported to the mixed wired-wireless network. Mobile IP, IP Paging, IPv6, TCP-F and TCP-BuS make possible end-to-end communication in this case [14]. Purely wireless networks are generally created in an ad hoc manner for solving temporary tasks. The high interest in mobile ad hoc networks (MANET) led to the creation of the MANET IETF [18] and many research groups.

Regarding the current applications running on mobile ad hoc networks, the vast majority are either of content delivery type, like in the health care system, or of peer to peer class as multiple player games [17]. These applications make use of very simple naming/addressing schemes that are not scalable. When mobile devices will become dominant and once the appropriate protocols for heterogeneous mobile nodes will be deployed, complex applications will be possible. For example, a user with a camera-enabled mobile phone will be able to send a picture to a laptop for image processing and demand the result be forwarded to an image repository on the wired side of the net – user's desktop computer or a data server. In contrast to the static Internet topology where the processing chain and the destination of the result are well known, as every node is identified by a name/IP address, in the case of mobile wireless devices these are difficult problems to manage. For example, if a device starts some processing involving nodes recognised as members of its current ad hoc network but leaves shortly that network itself, where should the result (if produced) be delivered ? The result may be stored locally, sent to a different destination commonly agreed, or dropped. The cost of processing and especially communication in terms of power consumption would suggest the choice of the first or second solution. The consistency and reliability of the processing chain is a major concern for mobile ad hoc networks. One basic service for providing consistency and reliability is the name service.

In this paper, we investigate the features and merits of an attribute based naming scheme for services and resources available in ad hoc wireless networks. Nodes are recognised by the names of services and resources they make available publicly instead of an IP address. In our system, a name is a set of attribute-values pairs that express the type of service or resource, the capabilities of the device and its ownership. Each node stores the set of names for the services and resources it makes available to other nodes. The system allows nodes to initiate a distributed search in their proximity for what they need and not for logical locations of other nodes in the network. The initiator broadcasts the request and each node that receives it executes a pattern matching. For any match, the result is returned to the requestor. Any node can act as a router and forward the query message further on up to a limited number of hops, coded by the message. This system eliminates any need for name binding as is the case for DNS and offers a quick reply to the requestor. The IP concept proves its effectiveness for stationary devices as it expresses their topological position in wired networks. In order to preserve the routing protocols for wired-wireless networks, variants of mobile IP were proposed for mobile devices. However, there is a contradiction in using such addresses for mobile devices whose main feature is mobility. All current mobile IP solutions increase system complexity, by introducing more indirection, and the possibility for errors. Many researchers recognised that and proposed attribute-based naming scheme, on top of an overlay IP network [1, 2], or

---

[1]A purely wired network may include radio and/or satellite links as well. The network topology is however, static.

as a feature of sensor networks [6]. This paper proposes a naming system for purely wireless networks that can, however, be used for wired-wireless and wired networks as well. It is based on the expressive power of the attribute-value concept that exposes the features of the services and resources of a mobile device.

This paper is organised as follows. Section 2 describes the mobile ad hoc network architecture for which the new naming system is devised. Section 3 presents current work. Section 4 compares our system to similar systems that include the name and discovery services, or just one of them. Finally, Section 5 presents our conclusions at this stage of the project.

2   System Architecture

Mobile ad hoc networks are highly dynamic architectures that can physically restrict themselves to an area of several tens of square meters, like in the case of Bluetooth enabled devices (piconets), or cover a larger, however limited area, as a building or a national park. The communication technology determines the area dimensions. Mobile devices enter and leave the area, forming ad hoc networks without knowing each other's identity. Nodes connect to each other using wireless network technology such as Bluetooth or IEEE 802.11b (wireless Ethernet). All nodes are peers, sharing the same rights (except for Bluetooth where the initiator becomes the master). There is no central authority or manager, and any node can belong to one or more ad hoc networks simultaneously. Wireless ad hoc networks can overlap when at least one node belongs to more networks.

The time a mobile device belongs to a certain ad hoc network is unpredictable, but we can assume that some of them have a longer membership than others. Each device runs some services that may want to be made available or not to other interested parties - clients. If a service is made available, it will get the attribute *public*. Otherwise, it will be *private*. This distinction is important as devices belonging to the same user can access private services of each other, forming a private network. This can be the case for the PDA, mobile phone and the laptop of a user. While they are not accessible from outside, they can use the services within the private network, and search for public services outside. The user can change the nature of a service, public or private, at any time. Each node advertises its services in the form of attribute-value expressions when it joins a network. A client can request a service using a query expression.

The minimal service any node should provide to the network is message routing. This is important for several reasons. First of all, some nodes may not be able to reach other nodes in the network and cannot benefit of their services. In some situations, the number of nodes inside an area can sharply decrease, consequently reducing the links' bandwidth. The routing potential of all existing nodes is valuable in such circumstances.

Once an ad hoc network is formed, a *network id* will be created and received by all its nodes. The network id is randomly selected by the initiator of the network. Each new node joining the network will receive the network id. This id is part of the *soft state* stored by the node. It is refreshed by any new message received from a node in the network. If one node belongs to several ad hoc networks, it will store each network id. When a network ceases to exist, there will be no messages exchanged among its nodes and, as a consequence, that id will be cancelled as a result of a timeout event. Leaving the network results in cancelling the network id after a time as well. A new network id will signal that the node is moving, and the rate of id changes can be considered as a relative measure of its moving speed. A

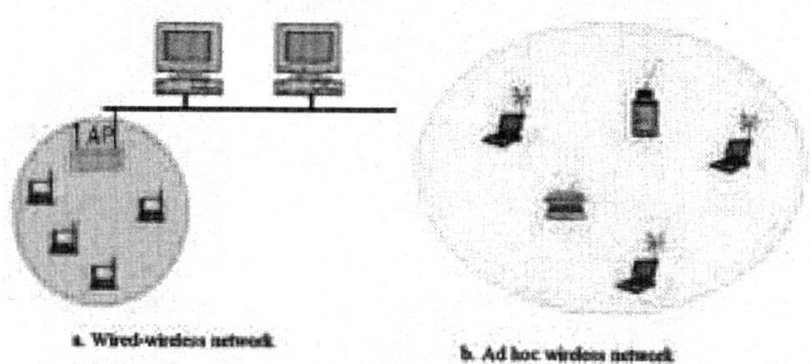

Figure 1. Examples of wireless networks

high rate of network id changes can be associated with a device on the move that can join a network for a very short time. On the other hand, if the rate is low, the device can be considered as a (quasi-)permanent member of the network and its services are reliable. The rate of network id changes is used to compute the estimation for the "time to live" attribute of any service or resource advertised by the node. The rate of network id changes is relative as what it really shows is how many networks the node joined and left for a given time interval, possible without any move. The network id is also used to make distinction among messages travelling within overlapping networks.

Power is of major concern for mobile wireless devices, and all protocols in use need to minimise power consumption. Processing thousands of instructions has the same cost of sending 1 bit 100 m by radio [10]. For that reason, computation should be used to reduce communication. One common approach to saving battery power is to allow wireless nodes switch from the *active state* to the *parked state* (power-saving state). While in the parked state, nodes sample from time to time new messages or advertise for their capabilities.

2.1 Name description

Mobile devices' membership to an ad hoc network is volatile property. Even for a short membership time interval, one node must have the possibility to address the other nodes and to be addressed. The most natural way of doing it is by using a name that presents its capabilities and makes it globally unique in the same time. More important for an ad hoc network is the set of services and resources one node can contribute with, and not a flat, useless identification number. Following this idea, a node can advertise one, more, or no name. For example, a PDA can offer an agenda service, a mobile phone, a camera and an internet access service, and a laptop beside a plethora of services can also offer some resources (CPU cycles, memory, etc.). Referring to a service, it is important to mention its version, if it is public or private and if it is in use (booked) or available. A multi-threaded service requires a load balancing strategy that has to use a load attribute. The "time to live" attribute is important for deciding if and how to select one candidate. A relative short time to live of the service in respect to the search requirement may lead to a failure in selecting it.

Different devices can run similar services (for example, same function but with different resolution, or precision). Therefore, it is important to include the device type or class attribute in the name. Service and device attributes can be the same for many nodes, but the ownership makes the distinction among them. The name of reference we adopted concatenates three

```
<service> camera
<version>1.0</version>
  <type format="jpg" mime="image/jpeg">picture</type>
  <nature>public</nature>
  <availability>yes</availability>
  <time_to_live>999</time_to_live>
</service>
<device> canon
  <market>PS-A70</market>
</device>
<owner>990-1881-8771-4428</owner>
```

Figure 2. Name representation of a camera service

categories of information, like below.

```
service.device.owner
```

Each category consists of a set of attribute-value pairs that characterise it from the application perspective. An attribute represents a classification criterion, for example its 'version'. A value corresponds to an attribute and shows the classification according to that criterion, for example '1.02' for the version. Attributes and values are represented as strings defined by applications. There is no restriction in the number of attribute-value pairs for each category of the name.

The service category is a set of attribute-value pairs that may include name, version, type, availability and lifetime of that service. The device category is a similar set of attribute-value pairs that include its manufacturer name and numeric id or its marketing name. Other attributes may be considered as well. Finally, the owner attribute has the value, a universally unique number. A central authority offers unique keys to attributes.

Names have a representation that is used when they are advertised or included in a message as in Figure 2. A name description can include several levels of nesting.

In the same time, name descriptions of services and resources are stored by their device as part of the state information (local registry). Any change of a value may cause different effects. For example, the nature of a service can change from 'public' to 'private', making it unavailable to other devices but to those owned by the same user. Or, if a service is booked, it cannot be offered to any new requestor until it is released. As another example, a laptop CPU may become overloaded and that resource becomes unavailable.

The proposed name scheme is expressive enough to handle a wide variety of services, resources and devices. The three categories of information used to define a name cover all the aspects that are of interest for a client and for the network management. The uniqueness of the name is provided by the presence of the owner's universally unique number.

The name system is responsive to any changes in the state of a service or resource. The state information includes the accessibility, public or private, the availability and the time to live attributes of the entity. If a reply was already sent and there is a local decision to change the value of a state's attribute, this decision will be postponed until the service is "released". In reality, the service may not be selected for use. In order to preserve the consistency of the information about the entity, a time delay has to be introduced before any change in the state values can take place.

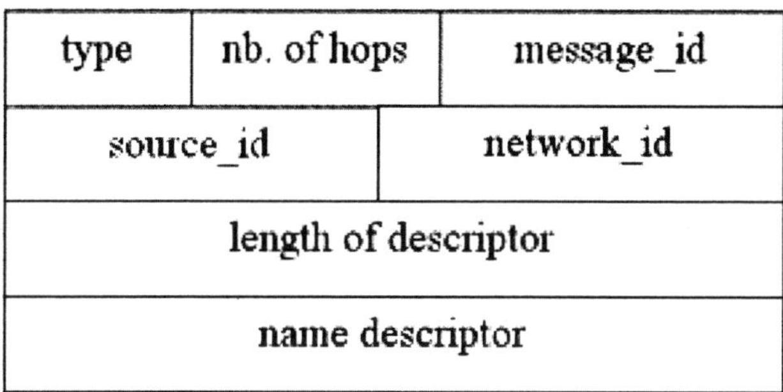

Figure 3. The format of the service/resource query message

2.2 Discovery

Each device holds the names for the services and resources it advertises. Whenever it joins an ad hoc network, it broadcasts the set of names of its public services and resources, and listens for others' advertisements. The nodes store all the names they get in the cache if this is available. As some devices may have a limited radio range, their advertisements can be forwarded further on by devices that got the messages. The number of retransmissions is limited to small numbers, like 2 or 3. Because of mobility, the cache can become out of date soon, but cache information can be a quick indicator if some services or resources of interest exist in the network or not.

The discovery process consists in broadcasting the query, followed by pattern matching at every node that received the query. The name can be fully or partially specified. A wild-card token (*) can be placed instead of a value. For example, all camera services can be looked up irrespective of the manufacturer if the value 'canon' is replaced by '*'.

The format of the query message is presented in Figure 3. The *type* field shows if it is a query, a reply to a query or any other type of message (join network, etc). A query message is stamped at the source with a *message id*. That id will be included in all reply messages to let the requestor detect replies addressed to it. Its existence is associated with only one query and corresponding reply messages, and will no longer be used in other communication.

The *number of hops* limits the propagation of the query within certain limits. The *source id* allows for reply messages to be routed back by the same router. The network id is included in each message. Each node will use it to refresh the corresponding soft state field. As the name descriptor has a variable size, it is necessary to indicate its length in number of bytes. It follows the name descriptor for the service or resource.

When a query message is issued, a timer is started. If it timeouts and no answer was received, the service or resource does not exist in the network or is not available. However, it is possible that new devices advertising that service or resource will join the network or they will become available from the existing network's nodes. For this reason, a discovery failure will not prevent the node in repeating the query after some time. Successive failures will affect the repeat time that will get longer and longer. It is the application decision to cancel the query after a certain number of failures.

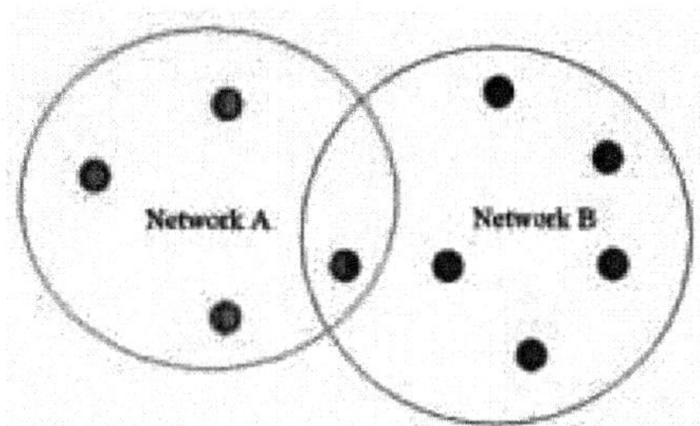

Figure 4. Two ad hoc networks are created. One device is a member node of both

3   Protocols

As the naming scheme is so tightly connected to the mobile ad hoc network where it is used, we introduce here a basic set of protocols that can be used starting with the creation of such a network until it ceases to exist.

3.1   Creating a mobile ad hoc network

Before a mobile ad hoc network can be used, it has to be created. This operation assumes that at least two devices can communicate and agree to join a common network. If we consider, for the beginning, this simple case, the first node sending a join message starts the process. The other device that has no network membership listens and will acknowledge the operation by sending a join message without any network id. The initiator will receive only one answer. The lack of network id signals that in fact creates a new network. Consequently, it will choose an id and send it to the partner. From that moment, both devices are nodes of the same ad hoc network. While the first two messages exchanged were join without any network id, the third join message will include the network id (join-id message). The initiator assumes that the second device adopts the id and will advertise for its services and resources.

If several devices start the creation procedure about the same time, there will be only join messages sent during the initial period of time. All parties will notice that, and after an auto-imposed delay of random value one of them will send the network id it chose to all the others. We can assume that all devices hear all the others and, therefore, the first join-id message will be received and adopted by all of them. Otherwise, it is possible that some devices will get more than one join-id message and, if they accept, can belong to more than one newly created ad hoc network. These nodes belong to the overlapping region. In Figure 4, one node that started the join procedure simultaneously with all the others receives two join-id messages, and agrees to join both ad hoc networks.

When a new device enters an area, its intention of joining an existing mobile ad hoc network is signalled by broadcasting a join message. Any active node reacts to the join message by sending an acknowledgment message (join) that includes the network id. In order to save energy, after one join-id answer, all the active nodes learn that the newly arrived one received the network id. If there are several answers with different network ids, the requestor has the option to join one or all networks. Finally, if there is no network id, the requestor will create its own ad hoc network, by choosing a network id and sending it in join-id messages to all the correspondents. If they wish, they will acknowledge the membership to the new ad hoc network and store that id.

```
Join:
    start join_timer
    send join message
    while (not timeout) {
            receive join message
            check for net id and store}
    if (one net id)
            adopt it
    if (more net ids)
            decide to adopt one or more
    if (no net id) {
            start delay_timer
            while (not timeout) {
                receive join message with net id
                adopt net id }}
    if (no net id adopted) {
            choose net id randomly
            send join message with net id}
    exit
```

Figure 5. The join mobile ad hoc network procedure

Only an active node can start the join procedure. It uses two timers, the join timer and the delay timer. The join timer allows the node to wait a reasonable time for replies. If there is no reply it exits. The delay timer has a randomly chosen interval of time. The first node that timeouts selects a network id and sends it to all the other nodes that will adopt it. The two time intervals associated with the join and delay timers basically determine the time consumed for setting up a network.

An active node that has no network membership listens to join messages and decides to join or not.

3.2   Search for services and routing

Services and resources are self-identifying making the search for them as simple as a pattern matching. The node looking for a service or resource creates the query message and broadcasts it. All nodes that get the message store it, check the number of hops field, decrement it and send it again, if not zero. Before forwarding the message, the node will store the message id and source id in a routing table and will replace the source id in the message field with its own id. Afterwards, the node executes the search by pattern matching. It compares the name it got with all the names it manages. If there is a match, it creates a reply message and sends it. Otherwise, it will continue to act as a router for messages to/from remote nodes. When it receives a reply message with its id, it knows it has to forward it back to the node that initially sent the query. It will check the routing table, extract the source id and use it to replace existing source id (its own). Then, it will send the message. Routing is hop by hop controlled by message id, number of hops and source id on the reverse path.

Figure 6 illustrates the search process initiated by node A. As the number of hops is 2, the query message will reach B, C, D and E. However, the return paths stop at B and D as A is out of their radio range. This example shows that in wireless ad hoc networks there is no guarantee for using the same path in both directions. Either one link (or more) is missing, or the return path traverses different nodes that may have no data stored about that search – no recollection of that message id and source id. In this case, the node will simply broadcast the message with the assumption that it will reach its destination eventually.

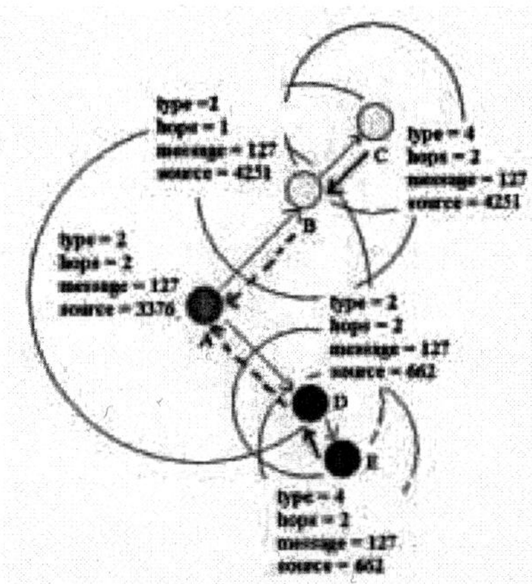

Figure 6. Node A (id = 3376) broadcasts query message 127. The message is received by node B (id = 4251) and node D (id = 662). Both nodes broadcast the message as hops number is 2. Nodes C (id = 22) and E (id = 34) receive the query, process it and send reply messages (type 4) to previous hops, B and D respectively. B and D will forward the messages towards the destination, node A. In this example, A is out of the radio range of both B and D.

If a node receives the same message from different sources, it will process the first and drop all subsequent messages. All these messages will be of the same type, have identical message id but different sources.

In the most favourable case, the time for a successful search is expressed by the following equation.

$$\text{time}_{search} = k * \text{time}_{broadcast} + \text{time}_{local\_search},$$

where k is the number of hops on the path that starts with the initiator, includes the node that offers the service/resource, and ends with the initiator, $\text{time}_{broadcast}$ includes radio transmission time and the time spent for message header processing, and $\text{time}_{local\_search}$ includes time spent on local search and for creating the reply answer, if there is a match. The timeout interval chosen by the initiator has to be greater than an estimation of the search time.

Figure 7 presents the search and forward procedure run by all nodes.

There is no guarantee that a reply will arrive at the node that initiated the search. This result does not mean the service is not present within the reachable proximity. It may be there but it is not public, or there is no return path. As the network evolves dynamically, new devices may bring that service or create the return path. For these reasons, a search failure is not interpreted as the final result.

3.3 The lifetime of an ad hoc network

An ad hoc network exists as long as at least two devices are active and exchange messages. It will cease to exist when there is no message carrying its id reaching the member nodes within each node timeout interval. Its only purpose is to provide services and resources. If this is

```
Search and Forward:
  While (true) {
    receive message
    refresh network_id
    if (type = 2) {
      if (this message already received)
        drop this message
      decrement number_of_hops
      if (number_of_hops >= 1)
        send message
        store (message_id, source_id) pair in routing table
        search the service locally
        if (service found) {
          create reply message
          send message }}
    if (type = 4) {
      if (this message already received)
        drop this message
      if (message_id stored in routing table)
        replace the message source_id with source_id in table
      send the message}
  }
```

Figure 7. Each node executes search and acts like a router

not possible, after a short time of message activity, there will be no reason in exchanging messages.

An interesting observation is that an ad hoc network can be mobile itself. It is the case of personal ad hoc networks, but any network whose nodes are still connected while on the move is mobile itself.

4 Similar work

4.1 Name services

The most successful name service is the Internet DNS that maps host names to IP addresses, using a predefined hierarchical naming scheme. Implemented as a distributed collection of servers for scalability, it proves its effectiveness in locating stationary hosts according to their IP addresses. An IP address is unique and denotes the membership of the node to a certain network. It lacks any provision for mobility.

A name service can be extended with a directory service (i.e. X.500, LDAP [17]). Such services include attributes for each named entity. The lookup process may start with a name and produce the entity reference and attributes, or, alternatively, start with a set of attributes and find out entities. For example, X.500 has a tree structure where each node stores a wide range of attributes for each name. In this way, the search may use a combination of attributes. Our system use the attribute-value concept, allowing for imprecise queries as well. However, it includes state information regarding the service or resource and it makes no reference to a certain location – no binding.

UDDI (Universal Description, Discovery and Integration) registry is a logically centralized, physically distributed service with multiple root nodes that replicate data with each other on a regular basis for scalability purposes [19]. It is a client-server architecture designed for wired networks. It has no provision for mobility.

JNDI (Java Naming and Directory Interface) is an API that provides naming and directory functions to Java applications [9]. One of its interesting features is that it is independent of any specific directory service implementation. JNDI is in fact an interface. This means that it can integrate easily into an environment where there is an established naming service. When a server starts, it will register its location with the Naming Service through JNDI. This provides the Naming Service with an object reference to the server, which will be the server's IP address. This reference can then be used to locate the server if the server's IP address is needed. The JNDI idea is interesting, can be implemented by our system by using a level of indirection if the target network architecture is wired-wireless.

The mobile IP approach [14, 15] is the most important effort for hiding the mobility feature. The mobile device is registered with a home network from which receives an IP. A Home Agent (HA), present in the home network, acts on its behalf and forward all messages to its current (foreign) network. While on the move, the mobile device contacts the Foreign Agent (FA), present in the foreign network, and receives a care-of address, IP. FA informs the HA of the new address. All correspondents' messages are, at least initially, sent to the HA which forwards them to the FA. FA delivers the messages to the mobile host. Afterwards, the mobile host can directly contact any correspondent, using its care-of address or home network address. This approach tries to hide the mobility feature by introducing the agent concept and several levels of indirection. It is error-prone and if the node has a high degree of mobility it might not work at all. In our view, mobile IP is a temporary solution that will not be acceptable when the vast majority of networked devices will be mobile.

IP Paging [12] typically includes transmitting a request for a mobile host to a set of locations, in one of which the mobile host is expected to be. The set of locations is called a *paging area*, and consists of a set of neighbour base stations. A network that supports paging allows the mobile host to operate in two distinct states: an *active state* for which the mobile host is tracked at the finest granularity possible such as its current base station, and a *standby state* – the host is tracked at a much coarser granularity such as a paging area. The mobile host updates the network less frequently in standby than in active states. This approach introduces more flexibility than mobile IP, but, basically, it uses the same concepts of IP addressing, HA and FA.

In a Bluetooth environment, up to eight Bluetooth-enabled devices, one master and seven slaves, can form a network, called piconet [14]. The device establishing the piconet becomes the master, all the others will be slaves. The limit of eight is dictated by the Bluetooth choice of three bit addresses for active nodes (the so called active member address). Two additional types of devices are the parked devices and the stand-by devices. Although the parked devices are not active, any one of them can replace a slave that switches to the park state. The parked devices use an eight bit address (parked member address) and, consequently, their number can exceed 200. Bluetooth nodes can discover each other's services. Devices offering services have to run a Service Discovery Protocol server that stores a record for each service. The record is a list of service attributes and is identified by a 32-bit service record handle. A service attribute consists of an attribute id and a value. The client sends an SDP request to an SDP server using unicast. The server returns a response message to the client. If the client wants to use the service, it must open a separate connection to the service provider. Bluetooth has a very simple addressing scheme that imposes limits on the number of nodes. A 3- or 8-bit address says nothing about the services of a node. The discovery service is distinct from the name one and complies with the classical client-server architecture. By combining naming and discovery, our system eliminates the need for any server and indirection.

The intentional naming system (INS) [1, 2] uses a distributed network of resolvers (application-level overlay network) over the Internet to discover names and route messages. Each service attaches to a resolver and advertises an attribute-value-based service description and an application-controlled metric. Each client connects to a resolver and can request a service using a query expression. The resolver looks up the name and if it has no match it disseminates the query in the overlay network. A match will return the IP of the host where the service is available. While the motivation of INS is identical to ours, INS relies on the Internet infrastructure. Our system is targeted at mobile ad hoc networks, the search is simpler and there is no need for load balancing.

4.2 Service discovery

The discovery service is new to networks. Its necessity was triggered by dynamic network/cluster architectures. In such an environment, new applications need to discover services they can use. Most of current discovery services use the client-server model, appropriate for wired networks. In a wireless ad hoc networking environment the peer-to-peer model applies: any peer can interrogate and other peer and use its services. Following, some of the most popular discovery services are reviewed.

JINI [5, 8] uses a look up service and two protocols, discovery and join, for allowing services to join or leave a cluster, dynamically. The events of join and leave are triggering signals to interested parties. This way, they are informed that new services are available or old services cease to be active. The main goal of JINI is to share services, but the system itself offers no guarantee of gaining performances. JINI Mobile Edition version [20] was proposed for limited resource wireless devices that work independently of any fixed infrastructure. Clients can search for a service according to a service identifier or attributes.

The Service Location Protocol (SLP) was designed for intranets' resources discovery and management [21]. Resources are collected together into administrative domains called scopes that reflect geographic proximity or network topology. User agents are typically configured with the name of the administrative scopes where they belong. The directory service can be located by static configuration, DHCP and directory advertisements (IP multicast). In the active mode, the user agent sends a request message of the service together with the attributes it is interested in. The reply message consists of a URL pointing to the service. URLs contain the service host IP or the name that can be solved by the DNS. In the passive mode, service and user agents listen for multicast announcements from directory agents. In the absence of directory agents, the user's agents multicast requests for services and receive responses directly from the service agents.

The Universal Plug and Play (UPnP) is an industry project designed to enable connectivity among PCs and stand-alone devices from different vendors. For that reason, it focuses on the use of proprietary protocols. The UpnP descriptions for services and resources are published within a UpnP forum, such that other members can connect and make use of them. UpnP has no central service registry. Service discovery is implemented by the Simple Service Discovery Protocol (SSDP) [4]. It uses HTTP over multicast and unicast. A joining device advertises its services by multicasting to control points, which are the potential clients. The advertised message includes the type, name and location of the service. The location is a URL that identifies the advertising service and points to an XML file that describes the service. The client sends a HTTPMU (HTTP over multicast) request and any matching devices that hear the multicast will respond by unicast messages. The reply contains the URL to a XML description of the service.

In another development, service offers and demands can be compared for match by a kind of brokers, sometimes called matchmakers [11]. Each resource sends an asynchronous message, tagged with the resource type, to a predefined matchmaking service, to advertise its availability. The matchmaking service responds with another message, time stamped, that includes its IP and some queries concerning dynamic attributes of that resource. The resource manager fills in the document, in XML format, time stamps it and sends back to the matchmaking service. The device is now registered and is a suitable candidate for any assignment. Once registered, if the resource changes, in terms of capability or availability, its manager issues a revised document to the matchmaker. A similar protocol is involved between the user and the broker. The application requirements of resources are coded in XML on a document, and sent to the matchmaking service. The service answers by a set of documents, one for each task of the application. The user fills in those documents, time stamps them and sends back. The matchmaking service tries now to match the requirements with the availabilities, based on some predefined criteria. If a match is found, both parties are informed and start a separate protocol. If the allocation process is successful, the resource manager removes it from the service, or submits a revisited document reflecting the change. The matchmaking services are federated and hence if a request cannot be met by one service, it is forwarded to another one. A broker system is built on top of existing directory services, offering a higher degree of abstraction.

5 Conclusions

Wireless ad hoc networks need simple and effective services that are designed according to their features. In this respect, the concept of IP address and the Domain Name Service cannot meet the requirements of a dynamic and mobile network system. Several attribute-based name schemes were proposed for wireless ad hoc networks but they ultimately make use of the IP infrastructure. In our opinion any such scheme can be just a temporary solution.

The name scheme proposed in this paper makes use of a natural description, attribute-based, of services and resources available in a wireless ad hoc network. The name includes attributes referring to the service features, device properties and ownership. It is the base for services like discovery and routing.

Acknowledgments

I would like to thank Cormac Sreenan for many useful discussions.

References

[1] W. Adjie-Winoto, E. Schwartz, H. Blakrishnan, J. Lilley, *The design and implementation of an intentional naming system*, Operating Systems Review, 34(5), Dec 1999, p.186-201.

[2] M.Balazinska, H. Balakrishnan, D. Karger, *INS/Twine: a scalable peer-to-peer architecture for intentional resource discovery*, Pervasive 2002 - International Conference on Pervasive Computing, Zurich, Switzerland, August 2002, Springer-Verlag 2002.

[3] P. Bellavista, A. Corradi, R. Montanari, C. Stefanelli, *Dynamic binding in mobile applications. A middleware approach*, IEEE Internet Computing, March-April 2003, p.34-42.

[4] Y. Goland, T. Cai, P. Leach, Y. Gu, S. Albright, *Simple Service Description Protocol*, http://www.ietf.org/internet-drafts/draft-cai-ssdp-v1-03.txt.

[5] R. Gupta, S. Talwar, D.P. Agrawal, *Jini home networking: a step toward pervasive computing*, IEEE Computer, Aug. 2002, p.34-40.

[6] J. Heidemann, F. Silva, C. Intanagonwiwat, R. Govindan, D. Estrin, D. Ganesan, *Building efficient wireless sensor networks with low-level naming*, in Proc. Of ACM Symp of OS principles, Oct. 2001.

[7] T. Kanter, *Attaching context-aware services to moving locations*, IEEE Internet Computing, March-April 2003, p.43-51.

[8] W. Keith Edwards, *Core JINI*, Prentice Hall, 1999.

[9] R. Lee, S. Selgman, *JNDI API Tutorial and Reference. Building Directory-Enabled Java Applications*, Addison-Wesley, 2000.

[10] G. Pottie, W. Kaiser, *Embedding the internet: wireless integrated network sensors*, Comm. Of the ACM, Vol. 43. No. 5, May 2000, pp. 51-58.

[11] R. Raman, M. Livny, M. Solomon, *Matchmaking: Distributed Resource Management for High Throughput Computing*. In: Proceedings of the 7th IEEE Symposium on High Performance Distributed Computing, 1998.

[12] R. Ramjee, L. Li, T. La Porta, S. Kasera, *IP paging service for mobile hosts*, Wireless Networks 8, 2002, p.427-441.

[13] O.F. Rana, D.W. Walker, M. Addis, M. Surridge, K. Hawick, *Resource Discovery for Dynamic Clusters in Computational Grids*. In: Proceedings of the 15th International Parallel and Distributed Processing Symposium, San Francisco, April 23 – 27, 2001.

[14] J. Schiller, *Mobile Communications*, Addison-Wesley, 2003.

[15] Y-C Tseng, C-C Shen, W-T Chen, *Integrating Mobile IP with ad hoc networks*, IEEE Computer, May 2003, p.48-55.

[16] P. Wyçkoff, *TSpaces,* IBM Systems Journal, August 1998.

[17] Lightweight Directory Access Protocol (LDAP), 2001
      `http://www.umich.edu/~dirsvcs/ldap/doc/`.

[18] IETF MANET, `http://www.ietf.org/html.charters/manet-charter.html`

[19] Universal Description, Discovery and Integration (UDDI), 2001, `http://www.uddi.org`.

[20] JINI, `http://java.sun.com/products/jini`.

[21] SLP, 2002, `http://playground.sun.com/srvloc/slp_white_paper.html`.

[22] Berkeley OceanSore, `http://oceanstore.cs.berkeley.edu/`

[23] Microsoft Pastry, `http://www.research.microsoft.com/~antr/PAST`

[24] Sun JXTA, `http://www.sun.com/jxta`.

Concurrent Information Processing and Computing
D. Grigoras and A. Nicolau (Eds.)
IOS Press, 2005

A Proposal and Evaluation of the Fast Reconnect Ad-Hoc Network Routing Protocol

Kazuhiro Mizoguchi   Shinichi Furusho   Teruaki Kitasuka
Tsuneo Nakanishi   Akira Fukuda

Graduate School of Information Science and Electrical Engineering, Kyushu University
Kasuga-koen 6–1, Kasuga-shi, Fukuoka, 816–8580, Japan

Abstract. An ad-hoc network works without any infrastructures. It consists of wireless mobile nodes. In this paper, we propose an ad-hoc network routing protocol, called FR-DSR (Fast Reconnect Dynamic Source Routing), which is an improved DSR. When a route is disconnected, FR-DSR can reconnect fast by using prepared spare routes. During communication, spare routes are prepared by sending route check packets through routes in a cache, and an additional route request packet is sent if a spare route is broken. We show that FR-DSR gives better performance than DSR through simulation experiments.

1 Introduction

Today, communication service form has been changing with rapid progress of information and communication technology. These services must have infrastructure such as base stations and a backborn network. Therefore the technology called ad-hoc network has been researched. The ad-hoc network is a collection of wireless mobile nodes dynamically forming a temporary network without the use of any existing network infrastructure. In the ad-hoc network, if there is a long distance between a source node and a destination node, nodes between them must relay packets for them to communicate. Each mobile node in the ad-hoc network operates not only as a host but also as a router.

Since the ad-hoc network consists of mobile nodes, the communication route is frequently changed. Since the route change takes time, it causes deterioration of quality in real-time communication such as voice or video communication. In this paper, we propose FR-DSR (Fast Reconnect Dynamic Source Routing) which is an improved DSR so that reconnection time at the route change is short.

2 DSR and Its Issues

2.1 DSR

DSR [1–3] is one of the typical ad-hoc network routing protocols and has the features of both on-demand routing protocol and source routing protocol. In on-demand routing, looking for a route starts when a source node wants to send packets. In source routing, only a source node controls a route for relay nodes to send packets according to this route information. DSR consists of two mechanisms; route discovery and route maintenance.

2.2   Route Discovery

At first, a node looks for a route when it wants to send packets. Each node has a route cache. The route cache contains routes to the node which has communicated before. If the source node has routes to the destination node, these routes are contained in data packets to send them. If there is no route in the cache, the source node broadcasts a RREQ (Route Request) packet. A RREQ packet includes the source node ID, the destination node ID, the request ID, the list of passed nodes, and so on. Receiving a RREQ packet, each relay node adds the own ID to the list in the RREQ packet and re-broadcasts it. In this way, a RREQ packet is spread over network and reaches the destination node. The destination node returns a RREP (Route Reply) packet to the source node when it received a RREQ packet. In this way, a route is established and communication between the source node and the destination one can start.

2.3   Route Maintenance

Each node does not have to periodically broadcast update packets because DSR is an on-demand routing protocol. Only source node maintains the route.

Consider that the source node S and the destination node D are communicating through the route S-A-B-D. When the link A-B is down, the following action is done. After the node A transfers a packet to the node B, it tries to confirm that the node B receives the packet. This confirmation is used by a standard part of the MAC protocol. The node A decides that the link A-B is down if the node A can not confirm it. The node A deletes this route from the route cache. Then the node A sends a RERR (Route Error) packet to the source node S. The RERR packet includes the information that the link A-B is down. After receiving the RERR packet, the node S deletes the route including the link A-B from the route cache. The node S sends packets to the node D through other routes in the route cache, if there are other routes. If there is no route to the node D in the route cache, the node S looks for new route.

2.4   Issues of DSR

In the ad-hoc network, a route is cut in the case of node movement, *etc* and communication becomes impossible in many cases. When a route is cut, a source node tries to reconnect by using route maintenance and route discovery mechanism described in Sec. 2.2 and 2.3. Then the source node looks up a route to the destination node from the route cache. However the reliability of cached routes is low since the routes in the route cache may be old. When the current route is broken, a possibility that the cached routes are valid may be low.

We consider the case where the routes in the route cache entirely becomes invalid. The source node tries to send packets through a route in the route cache when the current route is broken. When the source node decides the link-down by using route maintenance, it looks for a route from the route cache again. If there are no routes to the destination node, the source node broadcasts the RREQ packets. This process wastes the time. In other words, it takes long time to reconnect a route in this case.

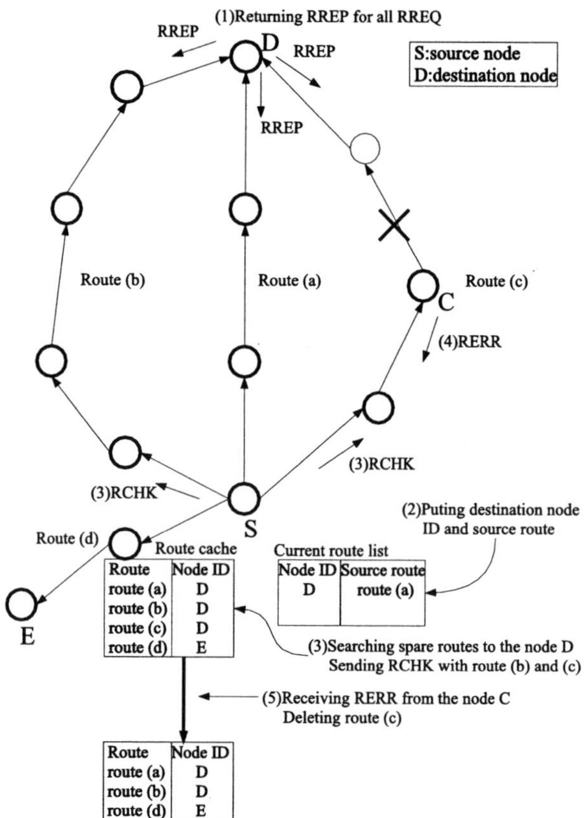

Figure 1. FR-DSR

3 FR-DSR Protocol

3.1 FR-DSR

The cause of the problem described in Sec. 2.4 is low reliable routes in a route cache. If a reliability of routes in a route cache is high, communication will be able to immediately restart even when a current route is broken. Of course, the source node does not have to look for a route.

From the discussions above, we propose an improved DSR, called FR-DSR, so that a source node prepares highly reliable spare routes in the route cache by deleting invalid routes from the route cache and getting new routes into the cache. Therefore communication can immediately restart by using these spare routes.

An outline of FR-DSR is shown in Figure 1. We consider the case where the source node S sends packets to the destination node D. It is supposed that the node S does not know a route to the node D at first and the route (c) becomes impossible to use during communication.

Each node has a current route list to put the destination node and the route into it. FR-DSR works as follows.

1. The source node S broadcasts a RREQ packet to find a route to the destination node D. The destination node D receives RREQ packets and returns RREP packets for all RREQ packets.

2. When the source node S receives RREP packets, it starts communication to the node D with the route (a). At that time, the node S stores the route (a) into the route cache and sends the data packets through this route. When the node S sends the data packets, the node S puts ID of the destination node D and the source route (a) into the current route list.

3. The source node S periodically checks the current route list. Then the source node S takes a pair of the destination node ID and its route from the current route list. Then the node S searches spare routes to the destination node from the route cache. The node S finds the routes (b) and (c) to send RCHK(Route Check) packets to the destination node D through these routes.

4. The RCHK packet sent through the route (b) arrives at the destination node D. The other side, the RCHK packet sent through the route (c) can not arrive at the destination node D due to down of the route (c). After finding this, the node C returns a RERR packet to the source node S.

5. When the source node S receiving the RERR packet finds the route (c) is broken, it deletes the route (c) from the route cache. If the number of spare routes to the destination node becomes below a fixed number, the source node S tries to get spare routes by broadcasting a RREQ packet.

FR-DSR consists of three main mechanisms. They are explained below.

3.2 Getting Spare Routes

As described in Sec. 2.2, with DSR, each node broadcasts a RREQ packet when it looks for a route. With original DSR, a destination node returns only one RREP packet for a RREQ packet which is received first. That is, the destination node ignores existing other routes. With FR-DSR we propose in this paper, the destination node returns RREP packets for all received RREQ packets as in the same way of [5].

3.3 Current Route List

The goal of this paper is to have reconnecting time short by improving on-demand routing DSR. With on-demand routing, a source node does not have to send any periodic packets. Route check that will be described in Sec. 3.4 later is only done during communication. Therefore its advantage keeps.

In this paper, each node has a current route list to keep above advantage. When the source node sends data packets, it puts the destination node ID and the source route which are included in data packets into the current route list. Each node periodically checks the current route list. If there are the destination node ID and the source route in it, each node dose route check described in Sec. 3.4 for a pair of the node ID and its route. They clear the current route list after route check.

3.4　Route Check

Confirmation of spare routes in a route cache is done as follows.

Each node periodically checks the current route list. In the case where there are some routes in the current route list, the source node searches other routes to the destination node from the route cache. Then it sends RCHK (Route Check) packets through these routes. When the destination node receives a RCHK packet, this route can be used and the source node keeps it as a spare route. In the case where the route used by a RCHK packet is broken, a relay node finding link-down returns a RERR packet. When the source node receives this RERR packet, it deletes this route from the route cache. This action is the same as an original RERR packet of data packets. After that, the source node counts the number of spare routes to the destination node. It is the number of sending RCHK packets. If the number of spare routes is below the fixed number, the source node broadcasts a RREQ packet to discover spare routes.

4　Evaluation through the Simulation

We performed two simulation experiments using the ns-2 network simulator [4]. In these simulations, flow control which is an option of DSR is disabled.

4.1　Experiment-1

A situation that FR-DSR works most efficiently is as follows, where Experiment-1 is performed. We use Figure 1 to explain it. The source node S communicates with the destination node D. First routes discovered by route discovery are only the route (a) and (c). The source node S communicates through the route (a). After that, the route (b) can be used and the route (c) cannot be used due to node movement. The route (a) is broken at the time of the state that the route (b) is valid and the route (c) is broken. We measure packet delay and compare FR-DSR with DSR. The number of spare routes which the source node prepares for each destination node is set to be two.

Original DSR acts as follows. After the route (a) is broken, the source node S receives a RERR packet. The source node S sends data packets through the route (c) in the route cache. Since the route (c) is already broken, a node on the route (c) returns a RERR packet to the source node S. The source node S starts the route discovery process because there is no route to the node D in the route cache. It gets the route (b) by using route discovery, and sends data packets through route (b).

On the other side, FR-DSR proposed in this paper acts as follows. The source node S sends a RCHK packet to the spare route (c). Then the source node S starts the route discovery process because the number of spare routes is one below two. This action is repeated during communication. After that, the node S finds the route (b) by using route discovery. The node S stops route discovery because there are two spare routes, but the route check is continued. After that, the node S finds that the route (c) is broken by using route check. Then the node S restarts the route discovery process because it has only one spare route. The node S receives

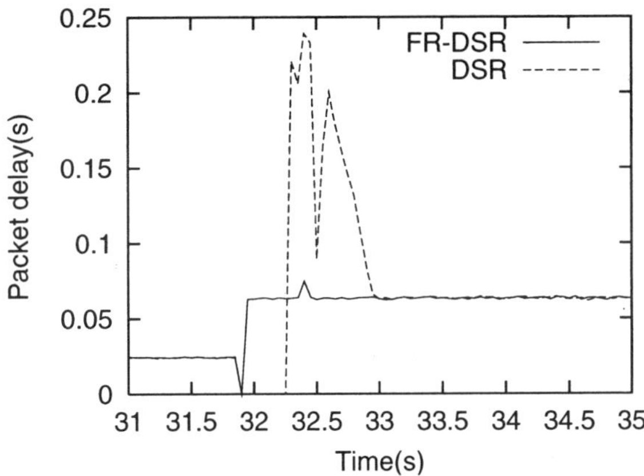

Figure 2. Delay of each packet around the time when the route (a) is broken

a RERR packet after the route (a) is broken. The source node S uses route (b) to send data packets.

An environment of Experiment-1 is described below.

- Transport layer protocol:UDP

- Interval of sending packets:0.05s

- Interval of route check:1.0–1.1s

- Simulation time:60s

4.2　Result of Experiment-1

Figures 2 and 3 show delay of each packet around the time when the route (a) is broken and the time before the route (a) is broken, respectively. The horizontal axis is the time when packets were sent, and the vertical axis is the delay until a sent packet reaches a destination node. Dropped packets are counted as no delay packet in Figure 2.

The route (b) is broken at 31.9 seconds. We can see certainly dropped packets and the rapid rise of delay. With DSR, packets are dropped and the delay rises rapidly. It takes about 1.1 seconds to converge on the stable state. On the other side, with FR-DSR one packet drops but next packet can reach. It takes about 0.1 seconds to converge on the stable state. This reason is that with FR-DSR the communication restarts through route (b) immediately after the route (a) is broken. Converging on the stable state means a communicating route is not broken.

As shown in Figure 3, with DSR the packet delay is almost fixed in the stable state. With FR-DSR, the delay periodically increases. This cycle is the same as the cycle (1.0–1.1 seconds) of route check and route discovery. In the other word, RCHK and RREQ packets are periodically sent and they make delay of data packets a little long. Therefore the packet delay increases. The packet delay before the route (a) is broken is different from that after.

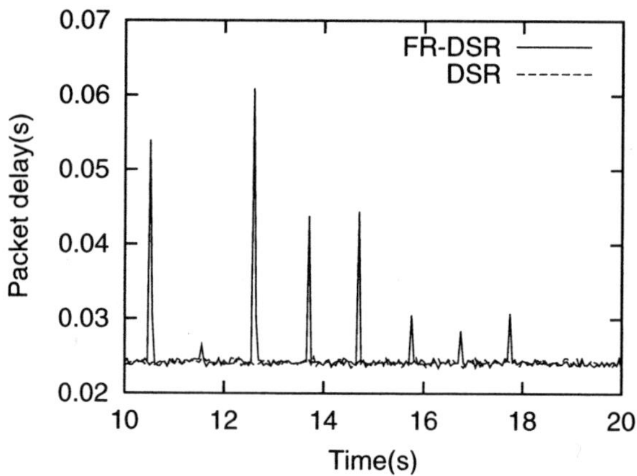

Figure 3. Delay of each packet before the route (a) is broken

This reason is the difference of routes. The route (a) before down is 4 hops and the route (b) after down is 10 hops.

This packet delay in the stable state is less than the reconnecting time by changing a route. Although the maximum delay with DSR is 0.239 seconds due to reconnection, with FR-DSR, it is 0.075 seconds.

From these results, FR-DSR is better than DSR since the packet delay is short when a route is broken and the communication can be immediately restarted.

4.3   Experiment-2

Experiment-2 is performed in the state where each node moves at random. A source node and a destination node are placed on the points (200, 200) and (800, 800) in the simulation field (1000m × 1000m), respectively. We suppose that these two nodes do not move. In addition, there are 100 mobile nodes in this field. The transmitting radius of each mobile node is 250m. The source node communicate with the destination node using these nodes. Mobile nodes move at random where pause time is 0 second and moving speed is 0–5m/s. The simulation is performed 10 times, and we take the average of them. Simulation time is 200 seconds. The other parameters are the same as those in Experiment-1.

4.4   Result of Experiment-2

Figure 4 shows the histogram of the packet delay. The horizontal axis is the packet delay, and the vertical axis is the rate of the number of packets at this packet delay. Packets of which delay is greater than 0.2 seconds are shown as one of 0.2 seconds in Figure 4. The QoS restriction time in this paper is decided to be 0.2 seconds. Packets of which delay are over 0.2 seconds are treated as invalid. This reason is that packets which reached over fixed time may cause deterioration of QoS of real-time restriction.

As shown in Figure 4, the rate of packets of which delay are over 0.2 seconds are 46.7% with FR-DSR, and 52.9% with DSR. These packets include packets of which delay increases

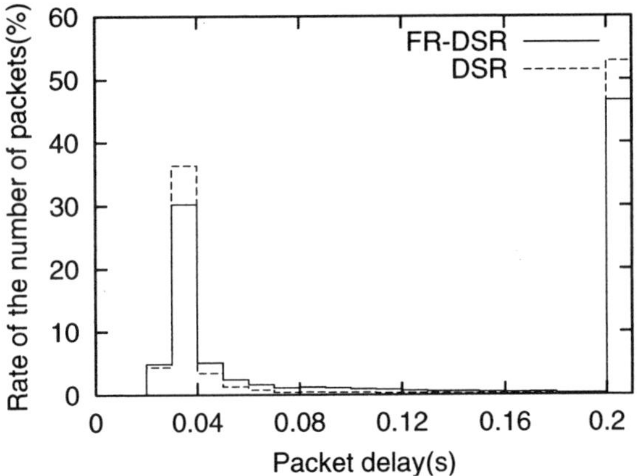

Figure 4. Histogram of the packet delay

Table 1. Rate of invalid packets

QoS restriction[s]	FR-DSR[%]	DSR[%]
0.20	46.71	52.91
0.15	49.24	54.00
0.10	53.37	55.65
0.05	64.76	61.92

due to reconnection or collisions, dropped packets, and packets left in the queues of relay nodes. Packets left in the queues of relay nodes are packets which are not sent by relay nodes despite that there are routes to the destination node. This is a fault of ns-2 network simulator used in this paper. For this fault, there are packets left in the queues until the end of simulation and of which delay is over 100 seconds. Therefore packets delayed over the QoS restriction 0.2 seconds increase. As shown in Figure 4, the rate of these bad packets with FR-DSR becomes less than one with DSR, from about 53% to about 47%.

Table 1 shows the rate of invalid packets when the QoS restriction time is changed between 0.05 and 0.20 seconds. The short is thought as more severe communication in real-time restriction. As shown in Table 1, DSR becomes better than FR-DSR when the QoS restriction time is 0.05 seconds. FR-DSR is better than DSR when the QoS restriction time is 0.10 seconds.

With DSR, when a route is changed, packets drop continuously and the packet delaying over the QoS restriction time increases. However with FR-DSR, this bad event does not arise. On the other side with FR-DSR, delay increases periodically due to route check and route discovery, but it is below the QoS restriction time. Delay at reconnecting is longer than delay at route check and route discovery. Therefore a performance of FR-DSR becomes lower than one of DSR if the real-time restriction becomes severe. The diverging time is 0.07 seconds in this simulation.

5 Conclusion

We have proposed FR-DSR which improves the reconnecting delay. With FR-DSR, each node has the spare routes in advance. Through simulation experiment using the ns-2 network simulator, we have shown that with DSR the reconnecting time by route change becomes 1.1 seconds and one with FR-DSR becomes 0.1 seconds. Moreover we have shown that a performance of FR-DSR is better than one of DSR in the case the QoS restriction time is over 0.07 seconds. Future works include the following:

- Congestion of network by RCHK packets and RREQ packets

- Power consumption

- Selection of spare routes

Acknowledgment

This research has been partially supported by MPHPT Strategic Information and Communications R&D Promotion Scheme, JPSP Grant-in Aid for Young Scientists (B) (KAKENHI 15700062), and NTT.

References

[1] J. Broch, D. A. Maltz, D. B. Johnson, Y.-C. Hu, and J. Jetcheva, "A Performance Comparison of Multi-Hic Wireless Ad Hoc Network Routing Protocols," *Mobicom'98* (1998) 85–97.

[2] X.-Y. Hong, K.-X. Xu, and M. Gerla, "Scalable Routing Protocols for Mobile Ad Hoc Networks," *IEEE Network*, Vol.16, Issue 14 (2002) 11–21.

[3] C. E. Perkins *et al.*, *Ad Hoc Networking*, Addison-Wesley (2001).

[4] K. Fall and K. Varadhan (Eds.), *ns notes and documentation*, The VINT Project, UC Berkeley, LBL, USC/ISI, and Xerox PARC (2002).

[5] S. Furusho, K. Moriwaka, T. Kitasuka, T. Nakanishi, and A. Fukuda, "Load Balancing Routing for Wireless Ad-hoc Network," *IPSJ DICOMO2002* (2002) 413–416 (in Japanese).

Concurrent Information Processing and Computing
D. Grigoras and A. Nicolau (Eds.)
IOS Press, 2005

Resource Bartering in Grids

Can Özturan

Department of Computer Engineering
Bogazici University, Istanbul, Turkey

Abstract. Grids will allow various resources to be shared among many users. This sharing however will definitely not mean that everyone will have unrestricted use of the resources. Some mechanism such as pricing or quotas can be employed in order to enforce controlled sharing of resources. In this work, we propose a barter model for resource sharing whereby users or computer centers can get something in return for letting their resources to be used by others. We utilize directed hypergraphs to develop a barter model in which multiple resources can be traded. We prove that the decision version of the multi-resource bartering problem is NP-complete. We present an integer programming formulation for the bartering problem. We also present a linear time algorithm to compute components that may contain feasible bartering solutions. Finally, we present various computational results from our software that makes use of LP_SOLVE and CPLEX mixed integer programming libraries to solve example bartering problems.

1   Introduction

Grids will allow various resources such as cpu cycles, storage, licensed software executions and data to be shared among many users. For small academic and research communities that know and trust each other free unrestricted sharing of resources may not pose a big problem since people in these communities will be courteous and avoid abuse of resources. On the other, when we move to larger scale grids and in particular to commercial platforms, sharing, however, will definitely not mean that everyone will have unrestricted use of the resources. Some mechanism such as pricing or quotas would have to be employed in order to enforce controlled sharing of resources. The best example of what may happen if resources are provided free of charge is the spam mail problem on the Internet. If grids are to be successfully deployed on a large scale, then mechanisms must be devised to manage resources. Buyya et al. [1] discusses several economic models that can be used for resource management in grids. These are commodity market, posted price, bargaining, spot market, tendering, auction, coalition, bartering, monopoly and oligopoly models. Since prices of grid resources such as cpu cycles, storage and data can be too subjective and dynamic, we believe that pricing based schemes such as auctions may have disadvantages. In this paper, we propose the use of bartering for grid resource management and provide a formal mathematical model that enables us to develop scheduling algorithms for bartering problems. Recently complementary auction and double auction markets have received a lot of attention among researchers. These markets have purchase/sell prices as a fundamental component in their problem formulation. We believe that in its most general form involving multiple resources and multiple resource instances, bartering offers a much more general and stronger combinatorial market and that it probably contains complementary auction and double auction markets as special cases. On the Internet, several sites that offer bartering services can be found. These sites, however, utilize barter units in place of money. In this paper, we focus on a market that allows *direct bartering*. In direct bartering, multiple resources can be traded *directly* without involvement of money by traders. However, unlike the auctions, the bids in the barter market are made in terms of resource(s) offered and resource(s) requested. In our barter market, we want to choose a feasible set of bids that can be satisfied and that optimizes some objective. We will call this problem multi-resource bartering problem.

This paper is a follow-up of our earlier paper [11] which we review in Section 2. In Section 3, we present a graph theoric model for multi-resource bartering problem that arises in our barter market. In Section 4 we prove that multi-resource bartering problem is NP-complete. We give an integer programming formulation of our problem in Section 5 which enables us to use widely available integer programming packages to solve our problem. We also look into the problems of eliminating unnecessary resources and decomposing the problem into smaller subproblems. We present a linear time algorithm to do this in Section 6. Finally, the last two sections present timings from various tests and a discussion of results.

2 Previous Work

The difficulty of finding "double coincidence of wants" in direct bartering was formally stated by Jevons [8]. Since then a lot of studies have been carried on the analysis of bartering and monetary issues from economists' perspectives using various models [4, 9, 14].

Depending on the number of distinct resources and the number of instances (units) of these resources that can appear in a bid, we can classify the bartering problems into four categories: (i) Single instance single resource, (ii) Multiple instance single resource, (iii) Single instance multiple resource, (iv) Multiple instance multiple resource problems. The subject matter of this paper is bartering problems of type (iii). We have addressed in particular problems of type (i) and (ii) in our earlier work [11, 12]. These two problems have polynomial time solution. Problems of type (i) in which we maximize the number of resources bartered is in fact the graph theoric maximum vertex disjoint cycles problem that is addressed in Gutin *et al.* [6]. Gutin *et al.* solves this problem by $O(n^3)$ algorithm. In our paper [11], we tried to generalize the solution technique that utilizes cycle finding on directed graphs to hypercycle finding in directed hypergraphs for type (iii) problems. This hypercycle formulation implied that in order to get all the resources requested in a bid, we must give *all* the resources offered in the bid. Therefore, in order to facilitate the cases in which a *subset* of offered resources could be used to satisfy a bid, an ad-hoc solution was proposed in which extra (dummy) bids were injected into the original set of bids. The extra bid insertion scheme given in [11] injected at most $O(|B|^2)$ bids where $|B|$ is the number of bids. However, if all subsets of offered resources are allowed to be inserted, the number of bids inserted can become exponential. In this paper, we propose a new formulation : if a bid is satisfied then *all, some or none at all* of offered resources can be given and *all* of the requested resources *must* be assigned to the barterer. By this relaxed formulation, we are able to avoid extra bid insertion process to enable subsets of resources to be given. We also note that in [11], we claimed that hypercycles which are the feasible solutions appear in hyper-strongly connected components. This claim, however, is erroneous and it is possible to construct examples which disprove it. An example is given in Section 3.1.

Double auction mechanisms [7, 10, 16] in which simultaneous buy and sell bids may be placed may look similar to bartering mechanisms. Pricing, however, is a major component in the formulation of the double auction problems. Double auction mechanisms can be used in barter exchanges in which barter units are employed to value (price) resources. However, in this paper, we address direct barter exchange, in which resources are not priced by barter units.

3   Multi-Item Bartering Model

Our multi-resource barter exchange is a synchronous market which consists of two main components:

- Resources: Each barterer puts forward a set of distinct (i.e. single instance) resources that he owns and combinations of which he may want to trade away for resource(s). The set of all resources of all the barterers is denoted by R.

- Bids: Each barterer makes a number of bids. A bid consists of a set of owned resources of the barterer that is offered for another set of resources owned by other barterers. The following example illustrates the form of a bid:

```
{ resource1, resource2 } => { resource3, resource4, resource5 }
```

We will call the offered (requested) set of resources on the the left (right) hand side as the tail (head) set of a bid. The bid simply declares that the barterer can give away resources in the tail set provided he can get the resources in the head set. We will let B denote the set of all bids by all barterers.

Having collected these bids over a period of time, we can then close the market (hence the name synchronous) and then solve the bartering problem which in the simplest case may have the objective of maximizing the number of bids that can be satisfied. In this way, we may be able to directly trade away grid resources for other grid resources without involvement of money. We put forward a few rules that must be satisfied by a bartering solution:

- Rule 1: If a bid is selected (satisfied) in a bartering solution, then *all* the resources in the head set must be given to the barterer owning the satisfied bid.

- Rule 2: In a bartering solution produced, it is possible that a subset of (i.e. none, some, or all) of resources in the tail set may be given in order to get all the resources in the head set in a satisfied bid. What this means is that it is possible that we can give fewer resources than what appears in the declared tail set and yet be able to get all the resources requested. This also implies that it is possible to get something simply as free without giving away anything at all.

- Rule 3: the third rule simply says that in a bartering solution, a resource can appear in the head set of only one satisfied bid. Violating this rule may mean giving the same resource to more than one barterer which is unacceptable. We also enforce this rule even if the bids satisfied belong to the same barterer.

Directed hypergraphs are generalizations of directed graphs. Whereas single vertices appear at the tail and head of arcs in directed graphs, arbitrary sized sets of vertices appear at the tail and head of *hyperarcs* in directed hypergraphs. Hence in our bartering problem,

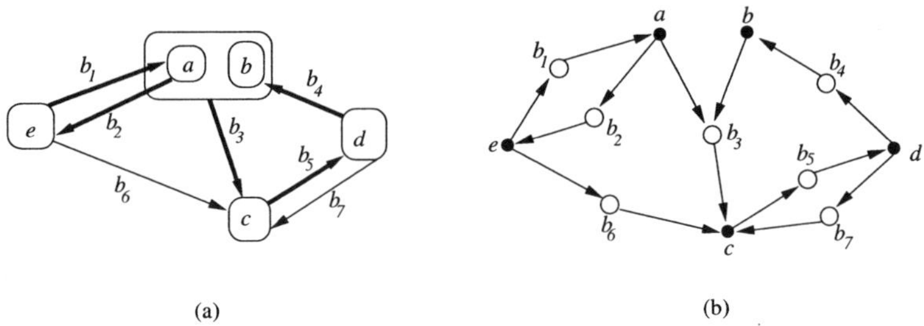

Figure 1. An example showing bartering bids (a) and its AND/OR graph representation (b)

bids can be represented by hyperarcs and resources as vertices in directed hypergraphs. In the rest of the paper, we use the notation R for the set of vertices and B for the set of hyperarcs since these coincide respectively with resources and bids in our problem. We now give formal directed hypergraph definitions that we will utilize while formulating a solution technique for the bartering problem. A *directed hypergraph* $D(R, B)$ consists of two sets R and B where R is a set of vertices and B is a set of hyperarcs. Each hyperarc $b = <R_t, R_h>$ is an ordered pair of non-empty disjoint subsets R_t and R_h of R. Here, R_t and R_h are the sets of vertices that appear respectively in the *tail* and *head* of the hyperarc b . For the example shown in Figure 1(a), $R = \{a, b, c, d, e\}$ is the set of vertices (resources), $B = \{b_1, b_2, b_3, b_4, b_5, b_6, b_7\}$ is the set of hyperarcs (bids) with $b_1 = <\{e\}, \{a\}>$, $b_2 = <\{a\}, \{e\} >$, $b_3 = <\{a, b\}, \{c\}>$, $b_4 = <\{d\}, \{b\}>$, $b_5 = <\{c\}, \{d\}>$ $b_6 = <\{e\}, \{c\} >$ and $b_7 = <\{d\}, \{c\}>$. The *indegree(r)* of vertex r is defined to be the number of times vertex r appears in the heads of hyperarcs. Similarly, the *outdegree(r)* of vertex r is the number of times vertex r appears in the tails of hyperarcs. The set of vertices that appear in the tail or head of a hyperarc is called a *hypernode*. A $B' \subseteq B$ induced *directed subhypergraph* $D'(R', B')$ of $D(R, B)$ is defined as a directed hypergraph with $R' = (\bigcup_{b \in B'} head(b)) \bigcup (\bigcup_{b \in B'} tail(b))$.

Directed hypergraphs are also known as AND/OR graphs [13, p. 21]. In the *AND/OR graph representation*, a directed graph is constructed with two types of nodes: AND nodes which represent hyperarcs (bids) and OR nodes which represent vertices (resources). Figure 1(b) shows the AND/OR graph representation of the example in Figure 1(a). In the figure, the white nodes represent the AND nodes and the black nodes represent the OR nodes.

For the example in Figure 1, the possible maximal (maximal in the sense that the set cannot be grown bigger) bartering solutions are $S_1 = \{b_1, b_2, b_3, b_4, b_5\}$ and $S_2 = \{b_1, b_2, b_5, b_7\}$. If our objective is to maximize the number of bids satisfied, we choose S_1 as our maximum solution. The bold edges in the Figure 1 (a) show this optimal solution.

In summary, the resources and the bids in our multi-resource bartering problem can be represented by a directed hypergraph. The feasible solutions of the bartering problem are bids, B', that have their head sets disjoint (because of Rule #3) and whose induced subhypergraphs, $D'(R', B')$, have $outdegree(r) \geq indegree(r)$ for each vertex $r \in R'$ (because of Rules #1 and #2).

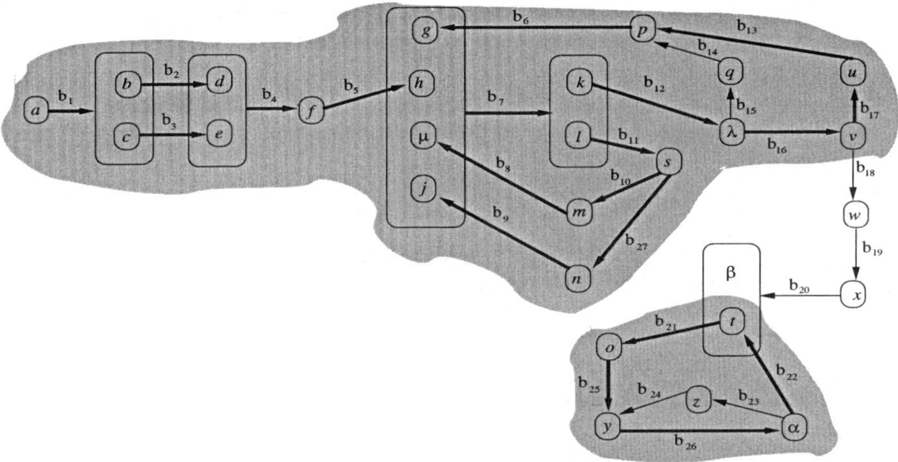

Figure 2. An example showing bartering bids and the two bc-components present in the directed hypergraph

3.1 Another Example Illustrating Problem Reduction

We give another more complicated example in Figure 2 to illustrate how some of the unsatisfiable bids and unnecessary resource nodes can be removed. The bold edges in this figure again give the solution that maximizes the number of bids satisfied. We remark the following about this solution:

- The owner of resource a is able to get the resources b and c for free without giving away his resource.

- Some of the bids and resources cannot appear in a feasible solution: These are resources β, x, w and bids b_{18}, b_{19}, b_{20}. It is clear that the resource β cannot appear in a solution, since it does not appear in the tail set of any bid. If we remove β, then the head set of bid b_{20} cannot be satisfied. Hence bid b_{20} cannot be satisfied and must be removed. This removal may propagate. Bids b_{18} and b_{19} and resources w and x are removed because of propagation. Having removed all these resources and the bids that can never be part of a solution, what we are left with is a reduced directed graph which possibly contains disconnected components. In Figure 2, there are two such components shown in the shaded regions. We will call a connected maximal subset of hyperarcs such that its induced directed subhypergraph has all its vertices, r, with $outdegree(r) > 0$ as a *barter-candidate (bc) component*. Here by connected, we mean the connected underlying undirected AND/OR graph with the directions on the arcs removed. We present the details of a linear time algorithm to compute the bc-components in Section 6.

- If we look at resource s, we see that it was used to satisfy tail sets of two bids of the same barterer. Just like getting something for free is possible, it is also possible to get multiple bids satisfied with the same resource(s). In the next subsection (3.2), we cover the details of this objective in more detail and also introduce another model in which a resource can only appear exclusively in the tail set of one satisfied bid.

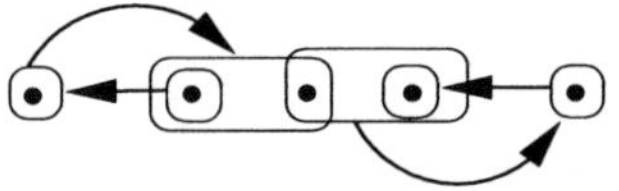

Figure 3. Example disproving problem decomposition by computing hyper-strongly connected components

Finally we note that as remarked in Section 2, in the treatment of [11], we claimed that hypercycles are located in the so-called hyperstrongly connected components and that we could perform problem decomposition by computing the hyperstrongly connected components. This is an incorrect result. The example that disproves this is given in Figure 3.

3.2 Other Objectives and Tail Inclusive and Exclusive Problem Cases

So far, we assumed we had the objective of maximizing the number of bids satified. Alternatively, in order to give the barterers a chance of dictating the priority (importance) of their bids, we can perhaps let the barterers state what fee they are willing to pay if their bid is satisfied. This can be done by associating a fee f_b with each bid b. Our multi-resource problem then becomes that of coming up with a set of bids that maximize total fees. If we do this, then it is possible that a barterer may not want his resources to appear in the tail set of more than one satisfied bid even if it means that he is able to get more of his bids satisfied. Figure 4 exemplifies these two different objectives. The bold hyperarcs indicate the bids that are satisfied. Note that in this particular problem, all the bids can be satisfied as shown in Figure 4(a) and we can collect a total of $235 in fees. But let's say the owner of resource c is willing to pay $100 to only one satisfied bid involving c. Then the solution that can be returned is shown in Figure 4(b). In this case, the total fees that will be collected is $135.

Motivated by the terms inclusive-OR and exclusive-OR, we call the solution objective exemplified by Figure 4(a) as the *inclusive case* and and that of Figure 4(b) as the *exclusive case*. Because of bartering Rule #3, it is clear that in a feasible solution the *head* sets of satisfied bids are disjoint. The exclusive (inclusive) case puts (does not put) similar restrictions on the *tail* sets. In other words, in the exclusive case, tail sets of satisfied bids are disjoint in a feasible solution.

4 Complexity of the Multi-Resource Bartering

The following theorem establishes the complexity of the multi-resource bartering problem.

Theorem 4. *The decision version of the multi-resource bartering problem is NP-complete.*

Proof. Given a directed hyper-strongly connected hypergraph $D(R, B)$ which represents multi-resource bartering bids and a positive integer $K_B \leq |B|$, we ask the decision question: Does B contain a multi-resource bartering solution with at least K_B hyperarcs (bids) ? Clearly multi-resource bartering problem is in NP, since we can guess a set of K_B directed hyperarcs and check in polynomial time whether the vertices (in the subhypergraph induced by guessed hyperarcs) have (i) indegree either 0 or 1 and (ii) outdegree greater than or equal to the indegree.

We transform the maximum independent set problem [5, p. 53] to the multi-resource bartering problem. An independent set in an undirected graph $G(V, E)$ is a subset $V' \subseteq$

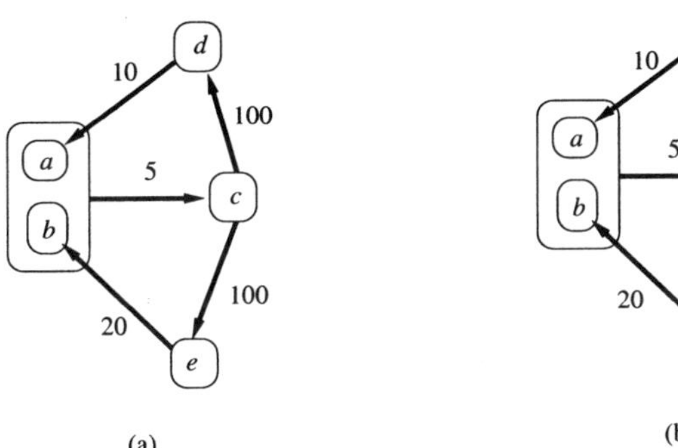

(a)   (b)

Figure 4. Example illustrating inclusive solution (a) and exclusive solution (b) for the same problem instance

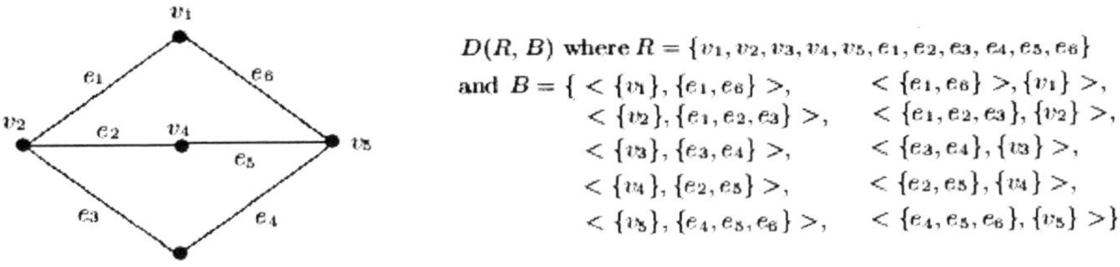

Figure 5. Transformation of independent set problem on graph $G(V, E)$ to the bartering problem $D(R, B)$

V such that for all $u, v \in V'$, the edge $\{u, v\}$ is *not* in E. The decision version of the independent set problem asks whether there exists an independent set of size at least K_G in the graph G. We perform a polynomial transformation of the independent set problem to the multi-resource bartering problem as follows: Let $adjedges(v)$ denote the set of edges that are incident on vertex v in graph G. A directed hypergraph $D(R, B)$ is constructed from the graph $G(V, E)$ by letting $R = V \cup E$ and $B = \{<\{v\}, adjedges(v)> : v \in V\} \cup \{<adjedges(v), \{v\}> : v \in V\}$. Clearly this construction takes polynomial time. We illustrate this construction by the example graph given in Figure 5. Here, an undirected graph with 5 vertices and 6 edges are given. The corresponding directed hypergraph with vertices and hyperarcs that will be constructed are also given on the right.

The independent set problem on $G(V, E)$ can then be stated as a bartering problem on $D(R, B)$: Does B contain a multi-resource bartering solution with at least $2K_G$ hyperarcs ? To show that solution of the multi-resource bartering problem will give an independent set of size K_G, we note that K_G of these bids will be the $<\{v\}, adjedges(v)>$ hyperarcs and the other K_G will be the corresponding $<adjedges(v), \{v\}>$ hyperarcs. The bartering solution guarantees that the head sets of satisfied bids are disjoint (because of Rule #3). Hence, the head sets of $<\{v\}, adjedges(v)>$ hyperarcs are disjoint, meaning the set of all incident edges , i.e. , $adjedges(v)$ of each of the K_G vertices will be disjoint. Since, each vertex v in an independent set of a graph also has $adjedges(v)$ disjoint, then it is clear that the K_G vertices in the tail of $<\{v\}, adjedges(v)>$ hyperarcs form an independent set for the graph $G(V, E)$. Conversely, a solution to the independent set problem induces a solution to the bartering problem: Corresponding to each vertex v that appears in the independent set, bids $<\{v\}, adjedges(v)>$ and $<adjedges(v), \{v\}>$ appear in the solution of the bartering problem.   □

5   Integer Programming Formulation

We solve the inclusive and exclusive case multi-resource bartering problems by formulating them as integer programming problems. Let us define an $|R| \times |B|$ hypergraph matrix T as follows:

$$T_{r,b} = \begin{cases} 1 & \text{if resource } r \in tail(b) \\ 0 & \text{otherwise} \end{cases}$$

and similarly the H matrix as:

$$H_{r,b} = \begin{cases} 1 & \text{if resource } r \in head(b) \\ 0 & \text{otherwise} \end{cases}$$

For the example in Figure 1(a), nonzero entries of matrices T and H are as follows:

T	b_1	b_2	b_3	b_4	b_5	b_6	b_7
a		1	1				
b			1				
c					1		
d				1			1
e	1					1	

H	b_1	b_2	b_3	b_4	b_5	b_6	b_7
a	1						
b				1			
c			1			1	1
d					1		
e		1					

Let us denote $\bar{0}$ as vector of 0's and $\bar{1}$ as a vector of 1's (both of which are of size $|R|$). We also define a fee (or weight) vector f of size $|B|$ which has each component set to the fee (or weight) amount f_b that we would like to maximize.

5.1   Inclusive Case

We can now express the inclusive multi-resource bartering problem as the following integer programming problem:

$$Maximize \ f^T x \tag{1}$$

subject to constraints :

$$Hx \leq \bar{1} \tag{2}$$

$$(T - H)x \geq \bar{0} \tag{3}$$

$$x_b \in \{0, 1\} \quad with \quad b \in B. \tag{4}$$

Note that if the variable x_b is 1 in the solution, then this means bid b is satisfied. Constraints of type (2) basically enforce our rule which says that a resource can be in the head set of only one satisfied bid. Constraints of type (3) simply says that the outdegree of a resource must be greater than or equal to the indegree the feasible solution. The objective function maximizes the total fee (weight). If we want to maximize the number of bids satisfied, then we can set $f = \bar{1}$.

5.2 Exclusive Case

In order to get a formulation for the exclusive multi-resource bartering problem, we simply add the constraint set $Tx \leq \bar{1}$ to the inclusive multi-resource bartering problem in order to enforce the restriction that a resource can only appear in the tail set of one satisfied bid. However, by substituting this new constraint set into (3), we now see that the $Hx \leq \bar{1}$ constraints become redundant and hence can be removed. As a result, we get the following formulation of the exclusive multi-resource bartering problem:

$$Maximize \ f^T x \tag{5}$$

subject to constraints :

$$Tx \leq \bar{1} \tag{6}$$

$$(T - H)x \geq \bar{0} \tag{7}$$

$$x_b \in \{0, 1\} \quad with \quad b \in B. \tag{8}$$

5.3 Redundant Constraints

We also remark that redundant constraints may be generated in (2), (3), (6), and (7). To identify these, let $t_b = tail(b)$ and $h_b = head(b)$. Let also $S_t = \{t_1, \ldots, t_{|B|}\}$ and $S_h = \{h_1, \ldots, h_{|B|}\}$. We will define $conset(S, i)$ as the set of members of S that contain resource r, i.e.: $conset(S, r) = \{s \in S \ | \ r \in s\}$. In constraints of type (2), resources which have $conset(S_h, r)$ identical will have the same row values. Hence, we can delete the redundant constraints of type (2) by finding two or more resources that have identical $consets$. We can repeat the same process for constraints of type (6) this time by considering $conset(S_t, r)$. Similarly, for constraints of type (3) and (7), resources which have both $conset(S_t, i)$ and $conset(S_h, i)$ identical will have the same row values. The redundant constraints that result in this way can also be removed.

6 Finding BC-Components in Directed Hypergraphs

Let $G(V, E)$ be the AND/OR graph representation of the hypergraph $D(R, B)$. A linear, $(|V| + |E|)$, algorithm for finding the bc-components of the directed hypergraph can be implemented by a two-phase procedure as follows:

(i) Remove all the resource (OR) nodes that have outdegree equal to 0 either initially or as a result of propagation. Remove also all the bid (AND) nodes that have one or more removed resource nodes in their head sets.

(ii) Find the connected components on the underlying undirected graph (i.e. graph obtained by removing directions on the arcs) by depth first traversal. The connected components obtained are the bc-components.

It is clear that step (ii) takes $O(|V| + |E|)$. Step (i) functions very similar to the topological sorting algorithm [15, p. 286]. Algorithm for phase (i) is given in Figure 6 using C++/STL (Standard Template Library) syntax. Here, V is the adjacency linked list data structure containing both the resource and the bid nodes as shown in Figure 7. Both forward arc list (i.e. all u such that $<v, u> \in E$) as well as back arc list (i.e. all u such that

```
remove_nodes(V,Nr)
{
 for(r=0 ; r < Nr ; r++) {
     V[r].outdegree = V[r].forward.size() ;
     if (V[r].outdegree == 0) Q.enqueue(r) ;
 }

 while ( Q.size() > 0 ) {
     r = Q.dequeue() ;
     V[r].label = REMOVED ;
     for(j=0 ; j < V[r].back.size() ; j++) {
         b = V[r].back[j] ;
         if (V[b].label == REMOVED)
             continue ; /* to next j iteration */
         V[b].label = REMOVED ;
         for(k=0 ; k < V[b].back.size() ; k++) {
             V[V[b].back[k]].outdegree-- ;
             if (V[V[b].back[k]].outdegree == 0)
                 Q.enqueue(V[b].back[k]);
         }
     }
 }
}
```

Figure 6. Procedure for the removal of unsatisfiable bids and resources

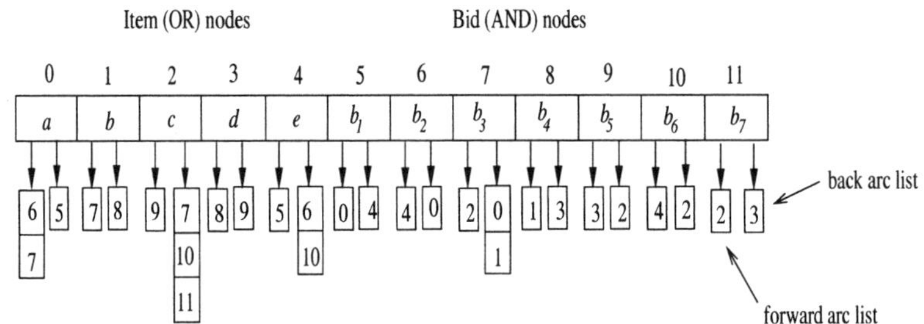

Figure 7. Adjacency linked data structures for the directed hypergraph in Figure 1

$<u, v> \in E$) are stored for each node v. The `size` method (function) returns the cardinality of the lists or arrays. The variable `Nr` is the number of resources (i.e. it is equal to $|R|$). The `remove_nodes` procedure starts by first setting the outdegree field for each resource node and putting those that have outdegree equal to 0 into the queue Q. In the body of the while loop, a resource node with outdegree 0 is removed from the queue and marked as REMOVED. All the bid nodes that point to it are also removed (since the resource in the head set of these bid nodes cannot be obtained). For each removed bid node, we also update (decrease by one) the outdegree of resource nodes that appear in its tail set. If outdegree of a resource node becomes 0, it is entered into the queue. The while loop repeats until the queue is empty. It should be clear that this removal process takes $O(|V| + |E|)$.

7 Implementation and Tests

We have developed code which solves the multi-resource bartering problem by making use of existing mixed integer programming (MIP) packages. We have used two MIP solvers. The first is the LP_SOLVE [3] which is a linear programming solver that is freely distributed under GNU Lesser license. LP_SOLVE also contains a MIP solver that employs branch and bound technique. The second is the CPLEX MIP Solver [2] which is a commercial package and has a sophisticated MIP solver. We have generated various test cases by randomly generating bids. We have used 4 parameters while generating the test cases. These are:

- β : denotes the number of barterers.

- ω : denotes the bound on the number of resources owned by each barterer. The actual number of resources for each barterer is generated randomly in the range $1, \ldots, \omega$.

- ρ : denotes the bound on the number of bids made by each barterer. The actual number of bids for each barterer is generated randomly in the range $1, \ldots, \rho$.

- ϕ : denotes the bound on the number of resources in the head set of a bid. The actual number of resources for each bid is generated randomly in the range $1, \ldots, \phi$.

Note that the number of resources in the tail set of each bid is also generated randomly in the range $1, \ldots, \omega$. Finally, the resources that will appear on the head and tail sets are also generated. The `rand()` function was used on the Solaris operating system as random number generator. The characteristics of a number of tests generated are shown in Table 1.

Table 1. *Characteristics of tests generated*

Test	β	ω	ρ	ϕ	No. of Resources($|R|$)		No. of bids($|B|$)		No. of bc-components
					original	after bc	original	after bc	
(a)	25	10	10	4	153	141	110	89	1
(b)	25	10	10	5	139	133	146	126	1
(c)	35	5	10	3	103	95	212	172	1
(d)	40	10	10	4	217	206	248	216	1
(e)	100	10	10	4	541	513	623	543	1
(f)	400	10	10	4	2727	2360	2632	1861	1

The tests were carried out on a SUN HPC 4500 server with 400Mhz processors and 3 GBytes of memory. The execution times for the tests described in Table 1 are given in Table 2. The test runs that have >24 hrs. as their solution times were terminated because they

Table 2. *Solution times (in seconds) for the various tests given in Table 1*

Test	Inclusive Case		Exclusive Case	
	LP_SOLVE	CPLEX	LP_SOLVE	CPLEX
(a)	0.7	0.2	0.9	0.8
(b)	24.7	0.1	98.6	2.6
(c)	6.6	0.4	387.9	2.8
(d)	124	2.06	>24hrs.	18.9
(e)	>24hrs.	1.8	>24hrs.	1334
(f)	>24hrs.	45318	>24hrs.	>24hrs.

took very long and did not produce any answer after 24 hours. These tests are not meant to be comprehensive performance evaluation of the LP_SOLVE and CPLEX packages. Rather, they were used to test the developed models and routines. The tests, however, do give us some feeling about execution times. We also ran other tests and our observations are the following:

- LP_SOLVE execution times exploded when the number of bids reached above 200.

- The exclusive case always took longer time than the inclusive case. If we look at the constraints for both problems, we see that in the inclusive case, only the head sets of bids in the solution should be disjoint. But in the exclusive case, not only the head sets but also the tail sets should be disjoint. This is probably making the problem computationally harder.

- CPLEX MIP solver worked fast until around 1000 bids. After that it also started to take longer. We had test cases with around 1800 bids which did not terminate within 24 hours even for the inclusive case.

8   Discussion and Conclusion

In this paper, we have proposed the use of direct bartering techniques for managing resources in grids. We believe that bartering techniques offer advantages since they make it possible to have more complex resource trading patterns. This, for example, may help us to get rid of liquidation problems and may make trading possible in cases where due to subjective pricing a solution may not exist. We have presented a new mathematical model for the multi-resource bartering problem by representing it as a directed hypergraph problem. We have also presented the notion of bc-components in directed hypergraphs which help us to remove unnecessary resources and bids from the original problem. We have implemented programs that make use of existing integer programming solvers. We have performed a number of tests. However, in order to determine suitability of the MIP packages for real life use, more computational experiments need to be done.

References

[1] R. Buyya, D. Abramson, J. Giddy, H. Stockinger, Economic Models for Resource Management and Scheduling in Grid Computing. *J. of Concurrency and Computation: Practice and Experience*, (14:13-15), 2002.

[2] CPLEX. http://www.ilog.com.

[3] M. Berkelaar. LP_SOLVE, Linear programming code. ftp://ftp.es.ele.tue.nl/pub/lp_solve.

[4] M. Engineer, Bargains, barter and money. *Review of Economic Dynamics*, 4 (2001) 188–209.

[5] M. Garey and D. S. Johnson. *Computers and Intractability, A Guide to the Theory of NP-Completeness.* W. H. Freeman and Company, 1979.

[6] G. Gutin. Finding a longest path in a complete multipartite digraph. *SIAM J. Discrete Math.*, (6):270–273, 1993.

[7] J. Hu. *Learning in Dynamic Non-Cooperative Multi-agent Systems.* PhD thesis, 1999.

[8] W. S. Jevons. *Theory of Political Economy.* MacMillan and Co., New York, 1888.

[9] R. Jones. The origin and development of Media of Exchange. *J. of Political Economy*, 84 (1976) 757–776.

[10] J. R. Kalagnanam, A. Davenport, and H. S. Lee. Computational aspects of clearing continuous call double auctions with assignment constraints and indivisible demand. *Electronic Commerce Research Journal*, 1:221–238, 2001.

[11] C. Ozturan. Network flow models for electronic barter exchanges. To appear in *J. of Organizational Computing and Electronic Commerce.*

[12] C. Ozturan. Used car salesman problem: A differential auction-barter market. Technical Report, Dept. of Computer Engineering, Bogazici University, Istanbul, Dec. 2003. Submitted to *Annals of Math. and Artificial Intelligence.*

[13] J. Pearl. *Heuristics.* Addison Wesley, 1984.

[14] S. Shinohara, Y. P. Gunji. Emergence and collapse of money through reciprocity. *Applied Math. and Computation*, 117 (2001) 131–150.

[15] M. A. Weiss. *Data Structures and Algorithm Analysis in C.* Addison Wesley, 1997.

[16] P. R. Wurman, W. E. Walsh, and M. P. Wellman. Flexible double auctions for electronic commerce. *Decision Support Systems*, (24):17–27, 1998.

Concurrent Information Processing and Computing
D. Grigoras and A. Nicolau (Eds.)
IOS Press, 2005

Dynamic SMP Clusters as the Architectural Solution for Fine–Grain Numerical Computations

Marek Tudruj[1,2]   Lukasz Masko[1]

[1]*Institute of Computer Science of the Polish Academy of Sciences*
01–237 Warsaw, ul. Ordona 21, Poland
[2]*Polish–Japanese Institute of Information Technology*
02–008 Warsaw, ul. Koszykowa 86, Poland
{tudruj, masko}@ipipan.waw.pl

Abstract. New architectural solutions for cluster–based shared memory systems are presented in the paper. Dynamic SMP clusters assume switching processors between locally shared memory modules at program run–time. A new inter–cluster data exchange mechanism called communication on the fly is used. It is a synergy of switching processors with data in their data caches and parallel reads of data by many processors on the fly – when written into cluster memory. A cache–controlled macro data flow program execution model is assumed. It requires such task composition in programs which enables static behavior of data caches i.e. eliminates re–loading and thrashing of data during task execution. A special macro–data flow graph representation of programs is used to define structuring requested by the proposed architecture. It includes graph morphological elements adequate for modeling program execution control including parallel task assignment, data cache functioning, data bus arbiters, switching processors between clusters, parallel reads of data on the fly and synchronization. The proposed graph representation enables symbolic execution of program graphs, based on decomposition of parallel processes onto dynamic SMP clusters, reads on the fly and communication on the fly. Simulation results for a fine grain parallel numerical example are presented in the paper.

1   Introduction

Massive application of shared memory systems with large number of processors is conditioned by effective solutions for data exchange networks between processors and memory modules. Currently available solutions limit scalability of shared memory systems for execution of fine grain parallel programs. Scalability of shared memory systems can be much improved by cluster–based approach. Shared memory processor (SMP) clusters with inter– cluster communication done by some global networks are popular system implementations [1–7, 9–11]. To compensate slower inter–cluster communication, program organization should be adjusted to system structure. Regions of intensive inter–process communication in programs have to be allocated to shared memory clusters. In current implementations the size of clusters is fixed. Incompatibility of the size of processor clusters and the size of program regions with intensive communication can much decrease program execution efficiency.

This paper discusses program execution and data exchange efficiency provided by special cluster–based architectural solutions of shared memory systems when applied to fine–grained parallel numerical problems. Essential concepts of the proposed architecture were described in [18–20]. One of its basic features consists in the use of dynamically reconfigurable shared memory processor clusters which fit computation and communication features of application programs. Dynamic SMP clusters mean that during program execution, processors can be switched among local data exchange networks which connect processors with memory modules thus forming SMP clusters. Switched processors remain in clusters for a program defined time, usually longer than for a single memory bus transaction. It gives to this architecture a flavor of a dynamically reconfigurable embedded system.

Standard inter–cluster communication in the system is done by data moves between cluster memory modules through a global data exchange network shared by all processors. A new method for data exchange is proposed that is dynamic switching of processors with data cache contents, between SMP clusters. Thus, data transmissions through a global network are replaced by cluster reconfiguration with data transfers, brought in processor's data caches. The proposed architecture is further equipped with multiple parallel reads of data by many processors to their data caches while a processor writes data from its cache to the cluster memory module. We call it read on the fly. It works in a similar way as cache injection proposed in [17]. To enable such feature, data exchange networks should have special "collective" communication properties: such as observability and parallel fetching of data while exposed in the network. Processor shared memory bus is a common network that has these features. Therefore, memory busses are applied in the proposed architecture, without loss of generality of the proposed approach. Reads on the fly can eliminate many data fetch transactions on busses, thus decreasing the overall bus traffic. This mechanism combined with processor switching provides a very fast way of data exchange between processor clusters. We call it communication on the fly. It is shown in the paper, that in numerical parallel programs, communication on the fly can give much better results than cache injection or processor dynamic switching between clusters applied separately.

Processor data cache functionality is another specific feature of the proposed architecture. A task can be executed in a processor only if all data required for its execution are loaded to the processor's data cache. It defines a data cache–controlled macro–data flow program execution paradigm. Due to such data caching strategy, data reloading and thrashing in processor caches are eliminated during computations. In this respect, the proposed strategy provides incomparably better behavior as compared to other caching solutions like cache pre– fetching, data–forwarding and cache injection [15–17].

The proposed architectural paradigms have been verified by simulation experiments performed using a new graph representation of parallel programs. This representation enabled realistic representation of program execution control and program graph structuring required by the proposed architecture. Special attention has been paid to the analysis of fine grain parallel implementation of typical numerical problems. The analysis shows that the proposed architecture is an important step on a way to massively parallel shared memory systems oriented to fine grain parallel computations.

The paper is composed of three parts. In the first part, new system architectural features are discussed. In the second part, a new graph representation for program execution control in the proposed architecture is discussed. In the third part, a numerical program execution control is shown and studied taking as an example of a fine–grained parallel versions of recursive matrix multiplication. Results of simulation experiments are presented.

2   The architecture of a system based on dynamic shared memory clusters

The fundamental features included in the system architecture we propose are the following.
• efficient large scale parallelism due to run–time program execution decomposition into dynamic SMP clusters (optimal decomposition of computations between processors and of communication between clusters organized around memory modules),
• efficient inter–cluster communication based on switching processors with produced data between clusters (elimination of many data transactions on global inter–cluster network),
• efficient intra–cluster communication based on multiple data reads on the fly (elimination of many data transactions on local intra-cluster networks),
• inter–cluster communication–on–the–fly which implements a synergy of processor switching and reads–on–the–fly (elimination of many data transactions simultaneously on global and local system communication networks),
• macro data–flow cache controlled program execution model which imposes a discipline on program design (elimination of unproductive moves of data in caches).

These features require a special system architecture. In a single bus and single memory module SMP system (shared memory system, UMA) only one processor connected to the memory at a time. There is no exchange of data between memory modules. The scalability is very poor due to the saturation effect on the bus and technology limitations (signal propagation time dependency on the number of bus customers). Such systems have coherence problem in data caches. Sharing of data between many processors is logically simple but practically time consuming due to multiple reads from a memory module of shared data. A multiple memory module SMP system includes many processors connected to many memory modules at the same time by a crossbar switch. It provides much better scalability and memory bandwidth but doesn't solve coherence problem in data caches. However there is no collective exchange of data between memory modules and broadcast (multicast) between processors is difficult. Sharing data between many processors is not improved due to necessary multiple reads from a memory module of shared data.

In distributed shared memory system – NUMA (cc–NUMA) processors are connected to local and distant memory modules through data exchange network, which can be: a bus, a mesh, a torus, a ring, a fat tree. Data caches supporting processors reduce traffic over the data exchange network, so there is a very good scalability and memory bandwidth. However, the coherence problem in data caches exists. There is a practical problem with sharing data between many processors due to multiple reads of shared data by many processors. There is weak use of the advantage of faster access to local memory for parallel computations – in this sense local and remote memories are treated in a similar way.

The alternative solution is based on many shared memory clusters connected by a global data exchange network. In such systems, separate processors from NUMA architectural paradigm are replaced by processor clusters organized around memory modules with the use of local data exchange network. Such system structure provides the following features:
• program areas which carry parallel computations with intensive data exchange can be mapped to be executed inside clusters which share local memory modules,
•overall inter–processor communication can be decomposed onto many local sub–networks with distributed control,
• data pre–fetching into caches – cache injection and data forwarding are possible.

Systems with similar general structures exist in many editions. In the category of parallel

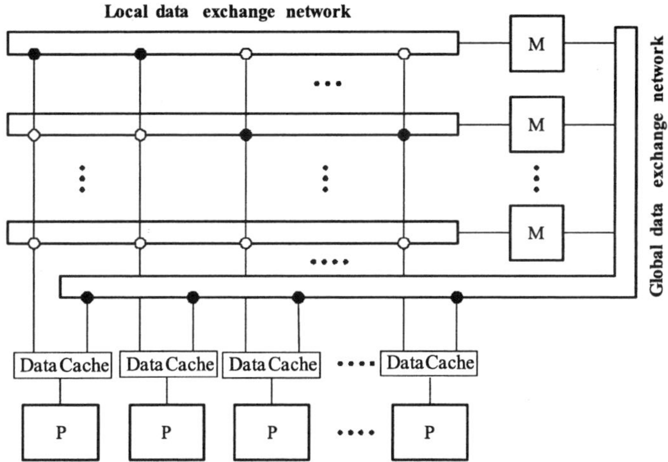

Figure 1. General system structure

systems of SMPs we can enumerate: GigaMax system of Encore Computer Corporation [11] with busses as local and global networks; Stanford DASH [12] with busses as local networks and two–dimensional meshes as the global network, Convex Exemplar [13] where crossbar switches are local networks and multiple rings constitute the global network; SGI Altix [14] with local networks in the form of crossbar switches and a fat tree as a global network. Another kind of such networks are multi SMP cluster networks. We have here many commodity SMP cluster systems connected by inter–cluster networks based on Ethernet, Fast Ethernet, Giga Ethernet, Myrinet, Quadrics, Infiniband protocols [8–10].

All multi–cluster systems we know have fixed cluster sizes and fixed compositions of processors. We propose systems of dynamic SMP clusters of processors, where:
● a processor can be attached to a memory module interface for a longer (program controlled) period of time, than just a single memory transaction,
● a processor can be switched to/from a memory module interface at program run–time,
● many processors attached to a memory module interface can do simultaneous reads of data that are sent to/from a memory module.

Processor clusters should have variable size since it enables such important features as
● adjusting the sizes of co–operative parts of the system to program needs which enables tuning program execution for fine grain parallelism,
● replacing standard inter–cluster communication by processor switching with reads on the fly – a new communication paradigm – communication on the fly.

The general structure of such systems is shown in Fig.1. In this figure: P– are processors, M– memory modules and black points are connections of processors to data exchange networks.

The network inside each processor cluster should be fast. It should work in parallel for many data transfers. It should enable simultaneous reads of data for many processors. It should enable simultaneous writes of data to many processors. Among candidates for internal networks such as crossbar switches (multi–stage networks), memory busses, multi–busses we can select memory busses (busses), which are the commonly available networks with collective communication capabilities. The problem of poor scalability of the bus can be resolved in a natural way by limiting the number of processors that can be connected to the bus. In many practical computational (numerical) problems, this limitation will be automatically met by the algorithm which optimizes the distribution of program between clusters with the minimum execution time as the optimization criterion since it will favor for small size of clusters. Other new "collective communication" fabrics are welcome if designed.

The network, which connects processor clusters can be a potential bottleneck in the system. Regarding optimality of communication between processors, global communication functions should be replaced as much as possible by local communication. Regarding the scalability requirement it could be a crossbar enabling direct non–blocking connections. Regarding the collective communication tuning, it could be a bus or a multi–bus. For the moment we have done applicative research assuming a bus as a global communication network. Next research stage will be other global networks like crossbars or fat trees.

The general structure of the system that uses memory busses as local and global data exchange networks is shown in Fig.2. The constituent elements of the system include a number of processors (Pij), a set of instruction memory modules (Mem ij), a set of data memory modules (Mi), a set of caches and a set of busses that connect processors with memory modules. The processors attached to the Intra–Cluster Bus of a memory module are considered a processor cluster. A processor can only belong to a single cluster at a time and so, can be attached only to one Intra–Cluster Bus. All data memory modules have linear address sub–spaces that belong to an address space shared by all the processors. Dynamical connections of processors with memory busses support an essential feature of the system that is run–time reconfigurability of processor clusters under program control. All processors are also connected to the Inter–Cluster bus. This bus is used only for data reads performed to a memory module of a cluster a processor belongs to. Data words in memory modules are provided with availability bits (with Ready/Empty values) to enable synchronization of reads and writes to the memory.

We introduce 3 special operations which are used to control program activities in clusters:
- reads on the fly (similar to cache injection),
- processor switching between clusters,
- communication on the fly.

A read on the fly is performed by a group of processors connected to a bus and enables avoiding multiple reads of the same data through a bus. It consists in capturing data, which are being written by one processor on a bus, by other processors. To optimize efficiency, synchronization of reading processors with the writing one is required. Processor switching between clusters can be performed for different reasons:
- there can be one more processor needed to perform some work in a cluster,
- a processor is supposed to carry data from one cluster memory to a different cluster,
- a processor has to read data on the fly in a new cluster.

Processor switching consists in disconnecting a processor from a cluster bus, which it is connected to and connecting it to the local bus of another cluster. Both disconnect and connect operations are performed by bus arbiters on requests from a processor. Switching of a processor to a cluster can be done after data cache contents have been written to a memory module, before a write from a cache to the memory or after a read has been done to the cache.

If a processor switched to a cluster brings new data in its cache useful for the target cluster, other processors (existing in the target cluster) can read data (using the read on the fly mechanism) that the switched processor writes to the cluster memory module. In this way the processor performs communication of data from one cluster to processors in another cluster by a mechanism which is a synergy of processor switching and reads on the fly. We call this

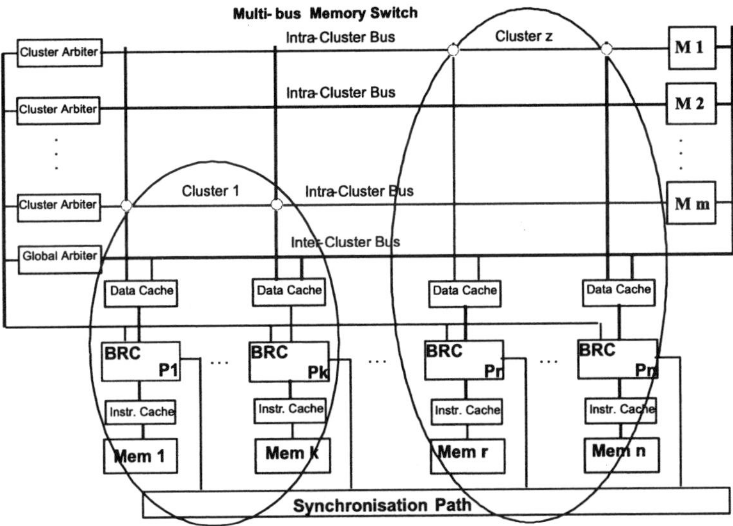

Figure 2. General structure of the bus–based system

mechanism communication on the fly. Communication on–the–fly is composed of:

- switching a processor into a cluster with data in its cache,
- synchronization of all reads with the write to be performed in the target cluster,
- multiple reads on the fly in the cluster during a write to the memory.

Programs are divided into executable tasks whose contents does not require data cache reloading during task execution. A processor data cache has to be filled with all necessary data before a task can start being executed. Some space can be reserved for new computation results. Data are loaded into caches by special cache pre–fetch instructions that execute block transfers from memory modules. Some blocks can be marked as temporarily resident. Cache pre–fetch instructions should never over pass available free cache space. Current computation results are written to data caches. Data can be sent back to memory module of the cluster only after task completion. This data cache read/write strategy avoids data cache thrashing. Special write–block instructions uses old or new target addresses and data lengths expressed in cache blocks. New addresses are used when data modified by a task will be used by other parallel tasks. These single assignment rules together with the specific caching strategy avoids the memory and cache consistency problem. It implements program execution paradigm according to the cache–controlled macro data–flow principle.

In the proposed architecture all data bus transfers result from bus access requests issued by read/ write instructions in application programs. In each processor, a program can issue a write request and 3 types of read requests: standard, standard/on the fly and synchronized. The requests are collected by Bus Request Controllers (BRCs). There are separate queues in a BRC for write requests, standard read requests and standard/on the fly read requests through the local intra–cluster bus and separate queues for standard read requests and standard/on the fly read requests through the global inter–cluster bus. Each bus in the system has an arbiter. It synchronizes memory read and write accesses from processors for standard read/write requests. The inter–cluster bus arbiter co–ordinates only read requests. The intra–cluster bus arbiter schedules the write and read requests. Data bus access instructions have priorities assigned by a programmer or a compiler. The priorities depend on the data volume (larger data have smaller priorities). Writes have higher priority than reads. The queuing is done with the decreasing priorities. BRCs of all connected processors send to arbiters priorities of requests from the top(s) of respective queue(s). The highest priority level request is selected by each arbiter (first write requests are examined, then reads) and the relevant processors are granted the rights to perform communication. The BRCs of the processors perform the transmission.

Read on the fly and synchronized read requests are performed by a technique similar to the cache injection [17] without arbiter control. They consist in reading data on the fly from a bus whose address lines are snooped by a BRC. Separate bus snooping tables are used for storing in the BRC of standard/on the fly read requests and synchronized read requests. When a BRC discovers that the source address on a bus is equal to the source address of a move or cache–pre–fetch request stored in a snooping table, data from the bus are sent to the data cache and to the memory module if requested by a move target address. A "shadow" data cache should be provided in processors for simultaneous reads from inter– and intra–cluster busses. When a read request is completed, it is removed from the table and the respective task (thread) execution control is notified. A completed standard/on the fly read request is additionally removed from the standard request queue. If a read request from the snooping table can not be completed since the snooped transfer on a bus was shorter than needed, the BRC modifies the request in the table and in the queue to enable the rest of data to be read.

Deposing read on the fly requests in the bus snooping tables must be followed by execution of synchronization of the writing process with all reading processes (barrier). Efficient synchronization of states of processes performed in processors is therefore very important for the proposed architecture. A special inter–processor synchronization path has to be included in the system to enable parallel execution of many synchronization operations for the program. The synchronization path can be composed of a set of hardware synchronization lines used by synchronization–based instructions. It can also constitute a tree-like synchronization network as in the CRAY T3E system.

3   Extended macro–data–flow graph representation

To describe program structuring for execution in the proposed architecture, we have introduced an extended macro data flow graph representation of programs. We have introduced special kinds of nodes in the program graph: intra–cluster memory bus arbiter nodes (CA), the inter–cluster global memory bus arbiter node (GA), read nodes (R) from memory to processor's data cache, write nodes (W) from data cache to memory, processor switch nodes (Mi) and barriers (Bi).

An example of the extended macro–data flow program graph (EMDFG) for a macro–data flow graph (MDFG) of two processor clusters that transfer data through an Intra–Cluster Bus and the Inter–Cluster is shown in Fig.3. We have two cluster arbiter nodes CA_1, CA_2 and the global arbiter GA in the graph. An arbiter node can be connected by edges (bi–directional) with many memory read and write nodes. It scans the nodes and activates the one which is ready to be executed (all its incoming edges are activated) and has the highest priority according to the assumed selection strategy. The selected node executes and sends the token back to the arbiter. Nodes in the graph have weights, which correspond to their latencies.

An exemplary graph representation of a read on the fly is shown in Fig.4a. We assume that reads on the fly can be done if all involved processors have introduced the respective memory

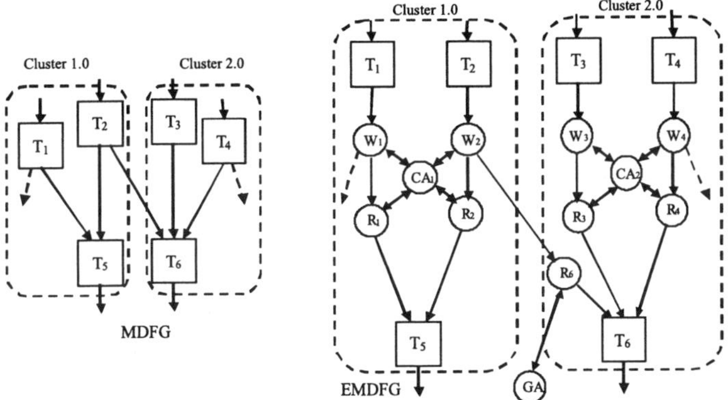

Figure 3. An extended macro–data flow graph

read requests to the bus snooping table in their BRCs. To control that, all the processors (including the one that writes data) are synchronized by a barrier. After fulfillment of the barrier, the write from the data cache to a memory module takes place through the bus. All involved processors can read sent data (all or their portions) to their data caches. We will use bold read node notation for reads synchronized by a barrier (reads on the fly).

Task T4 which is executed after the write node W_1, receives data from T_1 transferred through processor's P_1 data cache (no read node appears in such case). To be able to estimate the execution time of the program on the basis of the graph, we introduce labeling of the read execution nodes that determines the starting times of the transmission performed by the given nodes (in terms of the total data volume).

A section in a program graph is executed by a fixed subset of processors connected to the same memory module bus i.e. belonging to the same processor cluster. Sections are activated after each switching of a processor into (out of) a cluster. At section activation, all initial nodes of new threads are introduced to the active thread queues in all processors. Processors are notified by respective arbiters when a change of section appears.

A schematic of the communication on the fly can be represented as it is shown in Fig.4b.

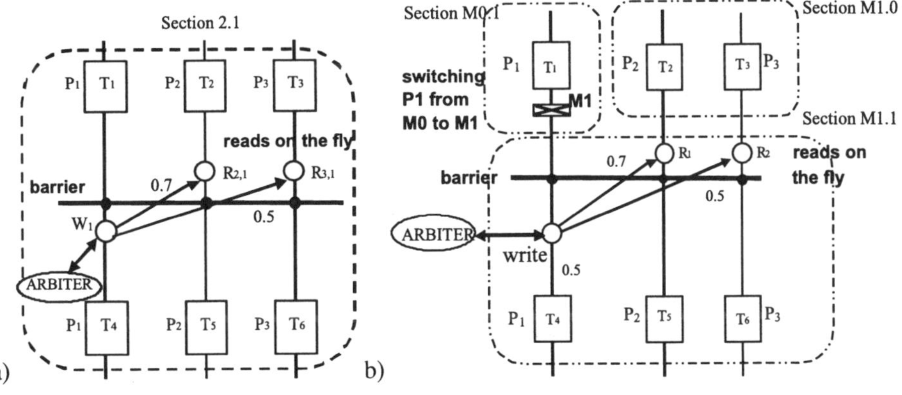

Figure 4. Reads on the fly a), communication on the fly b)

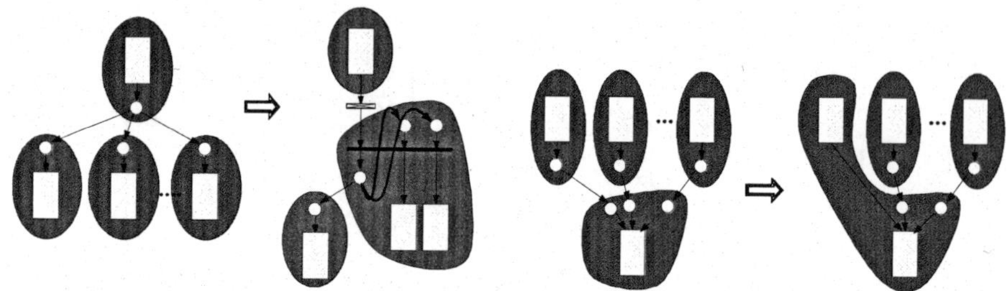

Figure 5. Structuring of program graphs

A special node (a crossed rectangle) represents switching of processor P1 from the cluster of the memory module M0 to the new processor cluster. It is labelled with the target memory module identifier M1. Switching node belongs to the section M0.1 of the graph. After switching of P_1, a new section M1.1 is activated in the graph which corresponds to the cluster of processors P_1, P_2, P_3 sharing the memory module M1. When a switched processor writes data to the memory under a new address, the data are also copied back to the data cache using the "shadow" data cache accordingly to the target address.

Read on the fly and communication on the fly do not require bus assignment control by bus arbiter. Therefore, the read on the fly nodes are not connected with arbiter nodes in the program graph. The write node, which participates in these operations is of course controlled by an arbiter.

To structure a program for execution in dynamic shared memory processor clusters we should perform the following actions:
- build an extended macro data flow graph of the algorithm,
- map all compute nodes with adjacent read and write nodes into separate single–processor SMP clusters,
- introduce reads on the fly inside clusters if it shortens execution time,
- introduce communication on the fly for inter–cluster communication if it shortens execution time,
- unify nodes inside clusters to transfer data through caches.

Communication on the fly between clusters is introduced into program sub–graphs which show features of data communication "one–to–many". In this case, the graph is transformed in the way as shown in left part of Fig.5. If barrier synchronisation delays the write excessively, some reads may be implemented in the standard way. Sections unifications are introduced in the program sub–graphs which show features of the data communication of the type "many–to–one". Graph transformation consists in merging consecutive sections, which enables data transfers through the data cache of the same processor – data write and read nodes to/from memory are eliminated, see right part of Fig.5.

4　Simulation experiments with recursive matrix multiplication

We will illustrate the way how to use the proposed system architecture on an example of square matrix multiplication $A \times B = C$ based on the recursive decomposition of matrices into quarters ($A_{i,j}$, $B_{i,j}$, $C_{i,j}$, $i, j \in \{0, 1\}$). The EMDFGs of the algorithm with 1st and 2nd recursion levels are shown in Fig.6. At the 1st recursion level we have:
- 8 multiplications, which furnish: $M_1 = A_{00} \times B_{00}$, $M_2 = A_{01} \times B_{10}$, $M_3 = A_{00} \times B_{01}$,

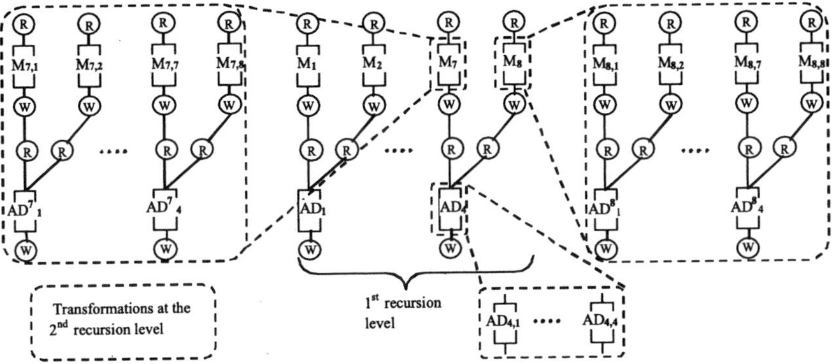

Figure 6. EMDFG of matrix multiplication.

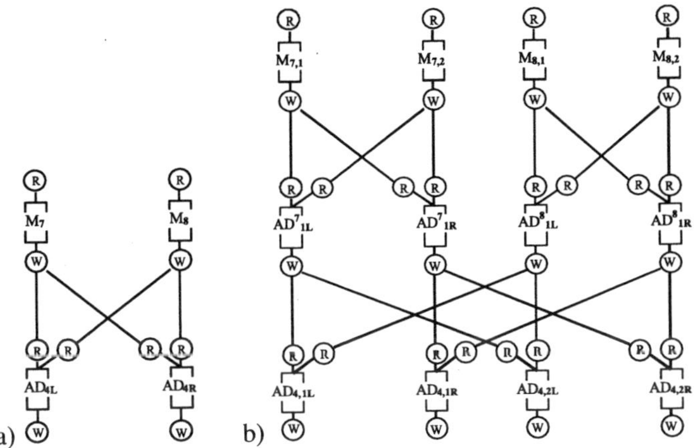

Figure 7. Initial elementary EMDFG: a) 1st recursion level, b) 2nd recursion level

$M_4 = A_{01} \times B_{11}$, $M_5 = A_{10} \times B_{00}$, $M_6 = A_{11} \times B_{10}$, $M_7 = A_{10} \times B_{01}$, $M_8 = A_{11} \times B_{11}$.

• 4 additions $AD_i = M_{2i--1} + M_{2i}$, $i = 1, \ldots, 4$, to produce quarters of C: C_{00}, C_{01}, C_{10}, C_{11}.

At the 1st recursion level each matrix quarter is further divided into 4 quarters and multiply nodes are replaced by entire graphs from the 1st recursion level. At the 1st recursion level:

• each computed matrix M_i is divided into two half–matrices M_{iL} (left) and M_{iR} (right). Half–matrices Ms_{2iL}, M_{2i-1L} and M_{2iR}, M_{2i-1R} are added in parallel using AD_{iL}, AD_{iR},

• sequential nodes, such as (M_{2i-1L}, AD_{iL}), (M_{2iR}, AD_{iR}) are assigned to the same processor, so that half of data for addition are transferred through data cache,

• computation and communication times are reduced by a factor of two.

At the 2nd recursion level multiplication results are divided into halves and are added in parallel (upper level of addition nodes). Their results are further divided into halves to enable parallel addition of respective matrix parts, which further reduces addition time. The complete algorithm graph of matrix multiplication at the 2nd recursion level contains 16 separate elementary sub–graphs, such as shown in Fig.7b.

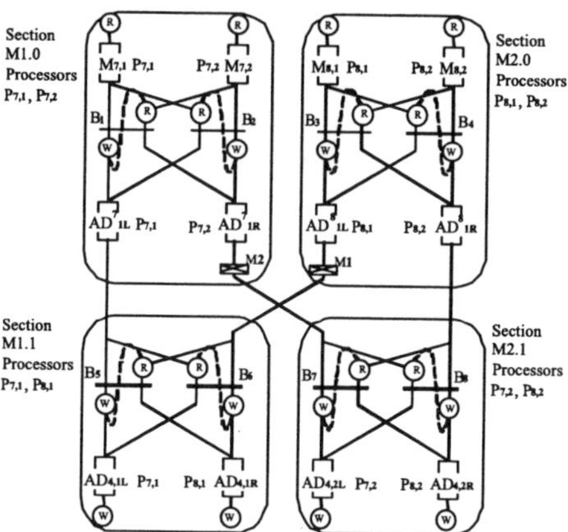

Figure 8. Elementary sub–graph at 2nd recursion level) with communication on the fly

The transformed complete elementary sub–graph from Fig.7b, is shown in Fig.8. The sub–graph has been structured to the use of 2 memory modules (M_1, M_2) that are a basis for two dynamically reconfigurable processor clusters. After execution of sections M_{10} and M_{20}, processors $P_{7,2}$ and $P_{8,1}$ are switched to opposite clusters to bring in their caches results used for further computations by other processors already existing in these clusters. There are 32 dynamic clusters each composed of 2 processors organized for execution of the total matrix multiplication graph. There are no data reads through busses, except for initial data reads and final writes. All data communication is done by reads on the fly, communication on the fly or data transfers through caches. It eliminates 60% of bus transactions – only writes remain.

In Tables 1 and 2 we present results of symbolic execution of the discussed algorithm graphs in the set of 32 2–processor clusters for different configurations of programs (reads on the fly – ROF, processor switching – PS, communication on the fly – COF). Three values of relations between computation speed/communication speed were examined: 6:1, 3:1 and 1:1. For the relation 6:1 (600 MFLOPS processors connected with memory modules via 100 MHz busses) the operation execution times were: 1 for floating point 8–byte scalar addition and multiplication, 6 for transmission of the scalar between data cache and memory.

Table 1 presents communication speedup evaluated against execution on a single 64–processor cluster i.e. using a single bus. It is evaluated for different matrix sizes, which determines the parallelism grain. For the matrix size 32, an elementary sub–matrix at the second recursion level has 8×8 bytes (the smallest communication volume in the algorithm is 384 bytes). With the matrix 1024×1024, an elementary sub–matrix size is 256×256 (the communication volume is 64 Kbytes).

Execution on 32 2–processor clusters without ROF and PS gave communication speedup of 13.4 – 14.7. With ROF but without PS the speedup was only 13.5 to 10. It resulted from small profit of ROF in the presence of high inter–cluster traffic through the global bus. The situation was much better when PS without ROF was applied, communication speedup much improved – to 37 – 27. When both PS and ROF – i.e. communication on the fly were applied. the obtained speedup was the highest 39.5 to 29, was obtained. Communication speedup was the best for the finest grain of computations (34–37% better comparing computation with the coarsest grain). It confirms suitability of communication on the fly and processor switching for communication in very fine grain computations.

Table 2 presents program execution speedup with 32 2–processor clusters versus execution on a single processor. Execution without ROF and PS gave speedup from 9.3 to 51.6, the highest for coarse grain computations. Application of ROF without PS speedup from 9 to 50. When PS without ROF is applied the speedup was from 20.8 to 58.8 due to elimination of the use of the global bus. When both ROF and PS is used i.e. communication on the fly is applied, the speedup is the highest, between 21.8 and 59.2. In this case, the speedup for coarse grain computations was 2.7 times higher than that for the finest grain. This resulted from the assumed high processor computational speed comparing communication speed – 6:1. Slow communication reduced in the case of fine grain computations the total speedup coming from communication on the fly. The speedup went much up when we increased communication speed against processor speed. The speedup values for different system time characteristics and communication on the fly are shown in Table 3. When communication speed increased 2 times the speedup for the finest computation grain was 30. It reached 45 when communication speed and computation speed were equal (6–times increase of the communication speed). With these changes, the coarse grain computation speedup was approaching 64.

The analysis of the time schedules of execution of computational nodes in the graph shows that reads of initial data have strong negative impact on synchronous behavior of the algorithms. It results in idle time of processors and increased delays on barriers introduced to the program graph. We introduced improvements to the graph structuring which decreased the grain of initial data reads for computational nodes and the grain of these nodes as well. The fine grain decomposition of nodes was introduced at program level to balance bus use with computations in processors sharing a bus. The basic graph transformations are shown in Fig.9a. The improvements have been also done at architecture level as "dummy reads" of computational result locations into caches. Real data reads have been replaced by block reservations in caches.

The communication speedup after improvements for different relations of processor speed vs. communication speed (configurations) in 32 2–processor clusters, is shown in Table 9b. COF improved means experiment results with communication on the fly and "dummy reads" alone. In this case communication speedup for the finest grain is slightly improved. COF fine– grained means experiments after both "dummy reads" and finer node decomposition were introduced. In this case communication speedup for the finest grain reaches 52.

The execution speedup after improvements for different relations of processor speed against communication speed in 32 2–processor clusters, are shown in Table 4. COF improved and COF fine–grained have the same meaning as in Fig.9b. SMP means execution in a single cluster of 64 processors, which is very inefficient. For the finest parallelism grain,

Table 1. Communication speedup for matrix multiplication (6:1)

Configuration				Matrix size					
Clusters	Processors per cluster	Reads on–the–fly	Processor switching	32	64	128	256	512	1024
32	2	No	No	1.00	13.39	14.77	14.77	14.77	14.77
32	2	Yes	No	13.50	13.39	13.16	12.71	11.80	9.99
32	2	No	Yes	37.33	37.02	36.40	35.14	32.63	27.61
32	2	Yes	Yes	39.59	39.32	38.66	37.34	34.67	29.34

Table 2. Execution speedup for recursive matrix multiplication (6:1)

Configuration				Matrix size					
Clusters	Processors per cluster	Reads on–the–fly	Processor switching	32	64	128	256	512	1024
32	2	No	No	9.36	14.94	23.04	33.21	43.43	51.63
32	2	Yes	No	8.88	13.99	21.80	31.85	42.22	50.76
32	2	No	Yes	20.85	29.19	38.90	47.89	54.61	58.88
32	2	Yes	Yes	21.80	30.29	39.94	48.70	55.15	59.20

Configuration (6:1)	Matrix size					
	32	64	128	256	512	1024
COF improved	42.12	41.76	40.89	39.12	35.56	28.45
COF fine-grained	45.81	52.38	55.96	55.98	52.09	42.17
Configuration (3:1)	Matrix size					
	32	64	128	256	512	1024
COF improved	41.58	40.85	39.11	35.57	28.46	21.62
COF fine-grained	51.77	55.53	55.77	52.00	42.14	32.23
Configuration (1:1)	Matrix size					
	32	64	128	256	512	1024
COF improved	39.43	37.23	32.01	21.54	21.54	21.54
COF fine-grained	52.30	52.48	46.54	31.80	32.06	32.19

Figure 9. Improvements in fine grain node decomposition a), communication speedup b)

the execution speedup is improved up to 28.4, 35.5 and 52.7 for configurations (6:1), (3:1) and (1:1) respectively. These are very good results, which show that the proposed architecture after careful fine grain structuring of programs is very useful for numerical applications. For coarse grain, the speedup is very close to the maximal possible.

5   Conclusions

The paper has presented a new architecture of a multi–processor system based on dynamic shared memory processor clusters and a new approach to inter–cluster communication. The architecture enables dynamic fitting cluster composition to current program needs. Commu-

Table 3. Execution speedup for COF with different system characteristics

Computation speed /communication speed	Matrix size					
	32	64	128	256	512	1024
6 : 1	21.80	30.29	39.94	48.70	55.15	59.20
3 : 1	30.12	39.88	48.68	55.14	59.20	61.49
1 : 1	44.96	52.70	57.75	60.70	62.30	63.14

Table 4. Execution speedup after fine grain improvements

Configuration (6:1)	Matrix size					
	32	64	128	256	512	1024
SMP	0.91	1.57	2.91	3.57	10.91	21.57
COF improved	26.85	35.65	44.75	52.27	57.42	60.49
COF fine–grained	28.44	40.03	49.57	55.98	59.76	61.82

Configuration (3:1)	Matrix size					
	32	64	128	256	512	1024
SMP	1.56	2.90	5.56	10.90	21.56	35.56
COF improved	35.46	44.68	52.25	57.41	60.49	62.19
COF fine–grained	39.63	49.41	55.93	59.74	61.81	62.89

Configuration (1:1)	Matrix size					
	32	64	128	256	512	1024
SMP	4.19	8.19	16.19	32.06	42.68	51.20
COF improved	49.08	55.49	59.41	61.61	62.78	63.38
COF fine–grained	52.69	58.18	61.05	62.51	63.25	63.63

nication through a global data exchange network can be distributed between local cluster data networks, so that a balanced use of the entire set of networks can be obtained. Adaptability of the system structure enabled a new architectural mechanism – communication on the fly. It is based on synergy of three elements: switching processors between shared memory clusters, data transfers stored in the hardware of switched processors and reads on the fly of data by processors in a target cluster. It enables transformation of data exchange transactions on global networks into communication inside local cluster networks. Further, it improves data exchange inside processor clusters by parallel execution of many transactions on local network. As a result, a very high communication efficiency by elimination of many data transactions on global and local data exchange networks can be achieved.

Simulation experiments were performed with the graph of matrix multiplication with recursive data decomposition. The experiments are based on the use of a new program graph representation. It enables modeling program execution by symbolic execution of the program graph annotated with node weights which correspond to time characteristics of a real system. The representation has adequate means to describe processor switching between clusters, data transfers on the fly and communication on the fly.

The experiments have shown that for the examined program graphs, communication on the fly gives better results than processor switching and reads on the fly applied separately. The biggest communication speedup was obtained for computations with the finest grain of parallelism. In the studied examples, all communication through global data exchange network could be transformed into processor switching with data between clusters and into local communication inside clusters. The experiments have shown that for the matrix multiplication, the best results are obtained with very small sizes of dynamic processor clusters, however, with the inter–cluster data exchange performed with the use of communication on the fly. Communication speedup turned out to be the highest for very fine grain of parallel computations. With the suitably high speed of communication of 64 processors with shared memory modules, the total program execution speedup was about 40 and 53 for the finest grain of parallel computations and the relations of processor speed/memory speed equal 3:1 and 1:1, respectively. The experiments confirmed suitability of the proposed architecture for very fine–grained typical parallel numerical computations.

Further works on the proposed architecture and program execution paradigms will concern automatic program graph structuring and scheduling, based on heuristic approach.

This work has been partially sponsored by the KBN Grant N. 4T11C 007 22.

References

[1]   J. Protic, M. Tomasevic, V. Milutinovic, A Survey of Shared Memory Systems, Proc of the 28th Annual Hawaii International Conference of System Sciences, Maui, Hawai, Jan. 1995, pp. 74 – 84

[2]   D. Sima, T. Fountain, P. Kacsuk, Advanced Computer Architectures; A Design Space Approach, Addison–Wesley, 1997.

[3]   Y. Kanaka, M. Matsuda, M.Ando, K. Kazuto, M.Sato, "COMPaS": A Pentium Pro PC– based SMP Cluster and its Experience, IPPS Workshop on Personal Computer Based Networks of Workstations, LNCS 1388, pp. 486–497. 1998.

[4]   Y. Kanaka, M. Matsuda, M.Ando, K. Kazuto, M.Sato, "Performance Improvement by Overlapping Computation and Communication on SMP Clusters", INT'l Conference on PDPTA '98, Vol. 1, 1998, pp. 275–282.

[5]   "Pentium Pro Cluster Workshop", http://www.scl.ameslab.gov/workshops/

[6]   T. Ikedo, J. Yamada, Y. Nonoyama, J. Kimura, M. Yoshida, An Architecture based on the Memory Mapped Node Addressing in Reconfigurable Interconnection Network, 2nd Aizu Int'l Symposium on Parallel Algorithms/Architecture Synthesis, , Aizu–Wakamatsu, Japan, March 1997, pp. 50–57.

[7]   "Scalable Clusters of Commodity Computers", http://www.csag.cs.uiuc.edu/projects/clusters.html

[8]   N.J.Boden, D.Cohen et al. "Myrinet – Gigabit–per–second Local–Area Network", IEEE MICRO, Vol. 15, No.1, 1996, pp. 29–36.

[9]   Gigabit Ethernet accelerating the standard for speed, Gigabit Ethernet Alliance, http://www.10gea.org/GEA–Accel1999_rev–wp.pdf

[10] J. Liu et al., Micro–Benchmark Level Performance Comparison of High–Speed Cluster Interconnects, Hot Interconnects 11, (HotI'03), Stanford University. August 2003.

[11] Multimax Technical Summary, Encore Computer Summary, March 1987.

[12] D. Lenoski et al. The Stanford Dash multi–processor, IEEE Computer, Vol. 25, N. 3, 1992, pp. 63–79.

[13] Convex Exemplar Architecture, Convex Press, 1994, p. 239.

[14] SGI Altix 3000 Screams on Upcoming Itanium 2 'Madison' Processor Running 64–bit Techn. Applications, http://www.sgi.com/newsroom/press_releases/2003/may/madison.html

[15] D.M. Tullsen, S.J.Eggers, Effective Cache Pre–fetching on Bus Based Multi–processors, ACM Trans. on Computer Systems, Vol.13, N.1 Feb. 1995, pp. 57–88

[16] D.A. Koufaty et al. Data Forwarding in Scaleable Shared Memory Multi–Processors, IEEE Trans. on Parallel and Distr. Technology, Vol. 7, N. 12, 1996, pp. 1250–1264.

[17] A. Milenkovic, V. Milutinovic, Cache Injection: A Novel Technique for Tolerating Memory Latency in Bus–Based SMPs, Proceedings of the Euro–Par 2000, LNCS 1900, 2000, pp. 558–566.

[18] M. Tudruj, L. Masko, A Parallel System Architecture Based on Dynamically Configurable Shared Memory Clusters, PPAM 2001 – Parallel Processing and Applied Mathematics 2001, LNCS 2328, Springer–Verlag, pp. 51 – 64.

[19] M. Tudruj, L. Masko, An Architecture and Task Scheduling Algorithm for Systems Based on Dynamically Reconfigurable Shared Memory Clusters, NATO Advanced Research Workshop, Advanced Environments, Tools and Applications for Cluster Computing 2002, LNCS 2326, Springer–Verlag, pp. 197–206.

[20] M. Tudruj, L. Masko, Communication on the Fly and Program Execution Control in a System of Dynamically Configurable SMP Clusters, 11–th Euromicro Conference on Parallel Distributed and Network based Processing, February, 2003, Genova, Italy, IEEE Computer Society Press, pp. 67–74.

Diffusing Mobile Processes

Traian Muntean

University " Méditerranée" – Marseille
Parc Scientifique de Luminy – Case 925 ESIL
F-13288 Marseille (France)
`muntean@esil.univ-mrs.fr`

Abstract. This paper presents a diffusion-based model for the design of correct distributed systems of communicating mobile objects. It first makes a proposal for a new *diffusion computation*-model, based on broadcasting communications for mobile processes instead of, basically used, point-to-point communication schemes. For this model we have developed a process calculus for reconfigurable communicating systems based on mobile processes, which has broadcast as unique basic exchange mechanism, bπ-calculus introduced initially in [5,6]. We have provided a full operational semantics for this calculus and we have illustrated its expressiveness through some examples taken from complementary classes of applications (built correct exchange mechanisms for messages in reconfigurable networks, checking for inconsistencies of transactions between mobile distributed processes). We have proposed three behavioral equivalencies for reasoning about such systems, namely, barbed equivalence, step-equivalence and labeled bisimilarity. An important result [6] is that all these relations coincide, providing different ways to study the equivalence/non-equivalence of two systems and also a further refinement model for broadcasting systems. [1]

Then, we use a restricted diffusion scheme for constructing correct routing functions for mobile processes in general interconnected networks. We present a new model of routing messages in ad-hoc networks that allow mobile processes to communicate without explicit knowledge of their actual location. The management of the process location is done at routing level, and we present for this new model routing functions that are proved correct and valid for any connected (reconfigurable) network. We also prove that these functions verify two important correction criteria: validity and deadlock avoidance for any network interconnection topology. We demonstrate a good trade off between the length of resulting communication paths and the number of nodes that are to be notified for each process migration. We also provide a way to represent routing information to drastically reduce the overhead of memory space required when the routing model is implemented with a deterministic or an adaptive routing approach.

1 Introduction

For more than fifty years, fundamental exchange schemes in programming languages, distributed computing and parallel programming, networking and open systems design, have inherited from principles behind point-to-point communication which are today well-established. On the other hand more complex and higher level communication schemes, like for instance multicast or broadcast, group communications, reconfigurable multi-exchanges, adaptive interconnects, etc., are encountered in many applications and systems design models, but they remain nevertheless poorly represented in tools and standards for distributed systems. We emphasize here that such interactions shall be considered as a more appropriate exchange

---

[1]This paper presents work partially supported by the IST-1999-11435 Project "MATISSE" (`http://www.matisse.qinetiq.com`) and done in collaboration with Cristian Ene, Javier Garmendia, Léon Mugwaneza and Stéphane Rivas.

scheme for modeling and reasoning about many communicating systems and networking applications. Communicating systems are already integrated in many devices and machines, and the technology looks set for major growth together with new application areas (e.g. mobile computing and wireless networking, multimedia, data and knowledge structuring, ad-hoc and embedded networking systems, information and services dissemination, etc.). More abstract and higher level concepts of interaction in distributed computing than the commonly used point-to-point based schemes, usually expressed by handshaking message-passing primitives or by remote invocations of located processes, are often required. Therefore multi-exchange communication schemes are fundamental for the design of communicating systems as a basis of interaction between their components and well as their inter-operability.

Broadcast, multicast, replication, dissemination or other (asynchronous) multi-exchange communications are often naturally required by existing or future classes of applications. We emphasize that multi-exchange can be considered as a basic paradigm (rule) for the development of new classes of networking applications in the future; point-to-point will be there only the unavoidable exception!

Though, the need of multi-way communications appeared as design requirement for many applications or computing systems, it was not often considered as a basic paradigm for computer science. Multicast/broadcast media have often been used to support computer communications, even on wired networks. The multicast nature of the medium, though, has not been fully exploited for a long time, because of the difficulty in extending this feature to wide area networks media, and also because of the (relative) lack of technological support. The situation has changed in recent years, because of the increasing amount of information available (e.g. through the Web), the widespread use of digital techniques in audio/video processing, and the advances in mobile and wireless network technology for large-scale applications.

These technological developments have increased enormously the number of machines connected to wired or wireless network, thus able to access multimedia information. This in turn has created many new potential users of information services, making the use of multicast transport protocols an attractive approach for the distribution of popular data objects. Several open problems still exist though, related to the correctness and scalability of the techniques used for multicast applications, especially those critical applications requiring reliable data delivery. For instance reliable multicast protocols are often in charge of distributing the same data object (generally split into a number of component modules) to a set of receivers, with some kind of guarantee on the delivery process. Depending on the application, the protocol might be required to deliver packets in a certain order, or ordering constraint. Such a guarantee is suitable for a large class of applications where receivers are independent, so they do not need mutual synchronization. Reliable multicast protocols must face two distinct problems: provide reliable data delivery, and accommodate more than one receiver. Reliable data delivery is a typical problem also in unicast communication, and it is generally solved by having the receiver, explicitly (by means of negative acknowledgements) or implicitly (using positive acknowledgements and timeouts), requests the retransmission of missing packets. This technique is largely used in communication protocols on wired networks; unfortunately, it scales very badly to large sets of receivers.

This approach is clearly not applicable in a wireless/mobile environment where communication is highly asymmetric and receivers can move frequently. In a wireless environment, a second major disadvantage can arise from the requirement of a bi-directional communication link. On most wired networks the feedback channel comes for free, but on wireless networks this is not necessarily true.

Applications development and correctness using diffusion of messages as a basic exchange paradigm shall be considered in a programming model where the above characteristics of the network can be considered independently from the correctness of the application programs.

2   A model for broadcasting mobile systems

Communication between processes is the main aspect of concurrency when dealing with distributed and/or parallel computing. One can specify basic communications from several points of view; primitive interactions can be, for instance, synchronous or asynchronous, associated to point-to-point or broadcast (one-to-many) message exchange protocols. The theory behind point-to-point communication is today well established in process algebra [1]. On the other hand more complex and higher-level communication schemes, like broadcast or multicast are encountered in many applications and programming models. They remain nevertheless poorly represented in the algebraic theory of distributed computing.

We emphasized [5,6] that group interactions shall be considered as a more appropriate exchange scheme for modelling and reasoning about many today's communicating systems and networking applications (e.g. mobile computing, multimedia, data and knowledge mining). Group communications between mobile processes are, in our opinion, a more abstract and higher level concept of interaction in distributed computing than the commonly used point-to-point communications, usually expressed by handshaking message-passing primitives or by remote invocations of located processes. Primitives for broadcast programming offer several advantages: processes may interact without having explicit knowledge of each other, receivers may be dynamically added or deleted without modifying the emitter's behaviour, and activity of a process can be monitored without modifying the behaviour of the observed process (this is clearly not the case with the classical "rendezvous" exchange schemes). Moreover, from a theoretical point of view, it appears difficult to encode broadcast in calculi based on point-to-point communications, as we have demonstrated in [6] for a conjecture often expressed for the last ten years.

Developing an algebraic theory for models of computing based on broadcast communication has its own interest. Hoare's CSP [12, 26] is based on a multi-way synchronisation mechanism, but it does not make any difference between input and output. Or, in a broadcast setting the anti-symmetry between these two kinds of actions is particularly important (in a broadcast communication there is one sender, and an unbounded or possibly empty set of receivers; this is well represented in the I/O automata [14]) where outputs are non-blocking and locally controlled, whereas inputs are externally controlled and can not be refused). Therefore a general theory of communicating systems based on multi-exchange instead of "rendezvous" has an intrinsic interest for future networking applications and interactions modelling. Broadcast communication also permits a very natural introduction of selective priorities and time in a set of communicating processes.

Recent work has been developed some way towards this general goal. At Chalmers University, Prasad first introduces [23] and develops [21,25] a primitive calculus of broadcasting systems, namely CBS implemented as a set of coordination combinators on top of the host sequential language Haskell. His calculus, inspired by Milner's CCS [16] and π-calculus [17], had a main goal to provide a formal model for packets broadcast in Ethernet-like communication media. It is based on broadcast, but its main limitation is that it does not allow to model reconfigurable finer topologies of networks of processes that communicate by broadcast, as for instance dynamic group communications. It is up to the receiver to use the received value or to discard it. Hennessy and Rathke [10] present a process calculus based on broadcast with a more restrictive input primitive, but the continuation process after the input, do not change dynamically his restrictions on further inputs; so their calculus is quite limited for modelling reconfigurable systems based on broadcast.

To summarise, it clearly appeared to us when developing this approach (mainly from 1997), that there is not a general framework which try to analyse (at least at theoretical level) what happens if we combine mobility and broadcasting in a new theory of communicating systems. Independently, recent work by Prasad and his colleagues at Chalmers has gone also towards this general goal (HOBS [25]). Their higher order calculus of broadcasting systems does for broadcast what Thomsen's Calculus of Higher Order Communicating Systems (CHOCS [29]) did for rendezvous. HOBS [21] extends the λ-calculus with the striking constraint that it has a unique entity, processes, and no channel names for modelling exchange in the usual way.

With the rendezvous communication primitives, used in many process calculi and inspired from general programming models developed for the last fifty years, all autonomous actions are observable only when program stops to interact. The impression that handshake is essential to process calculi is widespread as expressed recently for instance in [1]. This view can dissuade potential users when communication in the application model is not naturally expressed by handshake.

Together with others we strongly believe that a theory of communicating systems shall be further developed on the basis of observable interactions between diffusion based components.

In [5], we have introduced a new process calculus, bπ-calculus, as a framework, which combine mobility and broadcast (as it is the case for processes which use group communications, buses-based reconfigurable architectures or Packet Radio Networks). We developed for bπ-calculus a theory of co-inductive equivalences and congruencies. Bisimulations have been successfully used in processes algebra to compare two systems according to their operational ability to simulate each other. Bisimulations are appropriate for distributed reactive systems, which often have infinite behaviour, and make actions as answers to external stimuli. In addition, bisimulations seem well adapted for point-to-point systems, since the execution of such a system is entirely controlled by the environment (or an observer external to the system components). In a broadcast calculus, only the inputs can be controlled by the environment, whilst outputs are controlled by the system itself. For example, when watching TV a "process p", after listening the news can choose between having to watch the "pub" or switch for a movie, $p = news.(pub + movie)$, and the process $q = news.pub + news.movie$ are distinguished by bisimulations. In a point-to-point model, an observer could put them apart: initially, it provides a "news" action, and then, depending on the evolution of q, it provide "pub" or "movie", thus exhibiting a difference between p and q. In a broadcasting model (where outputs are non-blocking), these two processes cannot be distinguished, since the actions of p and q do not depend any more of an external observer (all what we can, is listening and trying to send messages; the system itself, will be forced to accept a message only if it could not continue to evolve autonomously). Intuitively, if we watch TV, we cannot know (nor influence) before (or during) the "news", the decision of the editor to send afterwards the "pub" or the "movie". This example justifies why bisimulations are too restrictive (at least as they are defined) for broadcasting systems in many applications.

We have also proposed a theory of testing for broadcasting systems. Such studies were made before only in the framework of point-to-point processes algebra. Two systems are equivalent whenever they satisfy the same set of tests from observers. Depending on the choice for the universe of observers or for the notion of satisfaction, we obtain several preorders induced by tests. Let S be a system defined over a set of actions A; an observer for the system S is a process O defined over the set of actions $A \cup \{\bar{o}\}$, where $\bar{o}$ is a new action used by the observer O to report the success of its observation. For an observer O, a system S must satisfy it (denoted S *must* O), if any execution in parallel of S and O pass by a state such that O can report a success (can made an output $\bar{o}$); a system S may satisfy an observer O (S *may* O), if there is at least an execution in parallel of S and O that pass by a state such that O can report a success (can made an output $\bar{o}$). The relations *must* and *may* induce two preorders on the set of systems denoted $\angle_{must}$ and $\angle_{may}$. These preorders play a significant role in the methodologies used for the description and verification of systems: they allow establishing the conformance of an implementation with respect to a specification. For a specification *Spec*, the set of behaviours that an implementation must enjoy is modelled by the set of observers that *Spec must* satisfy. The set of erroneous behaviours is modelled by the set of observers that *Spec may* not satisfy. Hence, an implementation *Impl* is correct with respect a specification *Spec* iff *Spec* $\angle_{must}$ *Impl* and *Impl* $\angle_{may}$ *Spec*.

2.1 Asynchrony in broadcasting systems

The communication scheme is modelled by messages, events, which have been produced but not yet received. In any implementation model they have to be buffered, considered as lost for the application, or refined as parallel composition of connectors. HOBS adopt this feature, the buffered values are themselves processes and compositions of processes with their exchanges are also processes.

In our work on bπ-calculus (see also [8]), and future developments we emphasise that the complete theory can be further developed without explicitly representing buffering of messages.

A communication between processes is performed through un-buffered broadcast. Compared to π-calculus, outputs are non-blocking, i.e. there is no need of a receiving process. One of the processes broadcasts an output and the remaining processes either receive or ignore the sending, according to whether they are "listening'" or not on the channel used as support for the output. A process that "listens" on a channel cannot ignore any value sent on this channel. The operational semantics is an early one, i.e. the bound names of an input are instantiated as soon as possible, in the rule for input. See also Ene's PhD thesis [7].

2.2 Case study: detecting inconsistencies in systems of mobile processes

We are interested here in an example of systems where is need for same data items to be replicated over a network (for reliability, dependability or efficiency reasons) and where a distributed transaction can affect several data items located anywhere in the network. In such a system broadcasting to "listeners" is a quite natural exchange primitive. In the same time, we will show how mobility of specific processes (transaction managers) is required and can be fully used in this (quite large) class of applications area.

In a replicated database, there exist several copies of each data item, with copies located at distinct sites in the system. We suppose that the database becomes partitioned (partitions p_j with $j = 1,\ldots,n$). We allow transactions to continue to execute, but when the network is reconnected (simulated by a broadcast on the channel *unif*), we have to check for inconsistencies. The idea is to construct a precedence graph that captures the temporal partial order between transactions. Then, the database is consistent iff the precedence graph contains no cycle. The vertices of the graph are all the transactions. An edge $\langle t, p \rangle \rightarrow \langle t_1, p_1 \rangle$ indicates that transaction t occurred before transaction t_1, where p, p_1 indicate the partition in which the transactions were executed. Such an edge exists iff one of the following holds:

1. t reads a data item i that was later written by t_1 and $p = p_1$

2. t writes a data item i that was later read or written by t_1 and $p = p_1$

3. t reads a data item i that was written by t_1 and $p \neq p_1$

An item manager waits for transactions; for each new transaction, it forks a new transaction manager, and serves the user that was making the request. A transaction for a data item i, is an output on the channel i_1, and contains the transaction identifier t_1,the type (read or write), the partition affected, the return channel, and a value (which make sense for a write transaction). A transaction manager generates a new edge manager for each new ongoing transaction that affects the same data item on the same partition (cases 1. or 2.). Once the network reconnected, transaction managers change their behaviour, trying to detect edges of the third kind. In addition, if there are two transactions, which have written the same data item in two distinct partitions, then an error is detected (two contrary edges between two vertices).

We note that this example uses the entire expressiveness power of our calculus. The same data item can be replicated (for reliability or efficiency reasons) and a transaction t can affect several data items; in this case broadcast is a quite natural communication primitive. In the same time, the ability to send and receive channel names across channels is used by item managers to fork new transaction managers corresponding to the received identifier.

In [5] we explicitly develop the calculus together with three equivalent bisimulation relations that allow comparing or refining systems of broadcasting communicating processes.

In the following sections we show how broadcasting can also be used for building correct and efficient routing algorithms in general network of mobile processes. In this way diffusion can also be applied to efficiently solve the routing problem in ad-hoc networks with mobility.

3　Routing for diffusing mobile processes

Actual distributed applications for ad-hoc and mobile networks rely on the mobile code paradigm which supposes changes in processes locations in order to achieve new functionalities, better performances, or to create new Internet-based services (such as distributed database search agents, e-commerce negotiation, mobile telecommunications......). Several distributed systems have been developed in the last decade to support process mobility (e.g. Charlotte, Sprite, Mosix, Parx, etc.), or to offer mobile agents frameworks (e.g. Telescript, Aglets, ARA).

The management of the communications has proved to be one of the most complex issues for the design of such systems. The routing techniques used on traditional networks suppose that processes are to be executed on the node where they have been created, which allows to implement functions for routing messages processes according to hosts addresses. The introduction of mobility raises the problem of managing the localization of sender and receiver processes dynamically by the routing function.

Most of the approaches followed for the design of systems that support process mobility rely on the use of two techniques. The first one consists in a mechanism introduced in order to let the sender know the localization of the receiver at the moment when the message is produced, either by broadcasting its address to the entire network each time a process migrates, or by the use of a global naming service (which can be centralized or distributed). The main disadvantage of this technique is the overhead introduced by the control messages. This method also lacks support for messages that are already in transit in the network at the moment when a migration occurs. The second technique consists of routing messages to the node where the destination process was created. This approach needs a lightweight process that will forward all messages to the new location of the process. This technique has the drawback of drastically increasing the communication paths lengths, and also could make an application dependent of nodes from where all its processes have left long time ago (and often for ever!).

In [9, 19] we introduce a new model of routing messages in ad-hoc networks that allows mobile processes to communicate, through a new scheme for diffusion routing, without explicit knowledge of their actual location. The management of the process location is done at routing level, and we present for this new model two routing functions which are proved correct and valid for any connected (reconfigurable) network. We also prove that these functions verify two important correction criteria: validity and deadlock avoidance for any network interconnection topology. We demonstrate in most cases a good trade-off between the length of resulting communication paths and the number of nodes that are to be notified for each process migration. This still holds when several processes migrate several times each. We also provide a way to represent routing information to drastically reduce the overhead of memory space required, thanks to the introduction of the processes localization in the implementation of the routing function. The routing model can be implemented with a deterministic or an adaptive routing approach. The routing algorithms are not dependent of any given network topology, they are particularly well suited for large scale ad-hoc networks, also they show to be quite efficient when compared to other existing techniques used for several regular interconnection networks.

3.1　Principles of the mobi-routing model

The mobi-routing model is proposed in order to construct correct routing functions that take into account process mobility at the routing level of a communication system. To achieve this, we focus on four main issues:

- define new routing functions based on process identifications instead of hosts addresses,

- introduce a localization function at the routing level which associates to each process of the system the physical node where it's being executed,

- represent this localization function with partial information in each node, while verifying some correctness criteria for the routing functions as describe hereafter,

- correctly deal with multiple migrations of a set of processes.

In this section we define the diffusion routing functions, which are based on classical node-address based routing functions. We also describe which correction criteria we address, and prove that the routing functions are correct according to these criteria.

Let us represent the network as a symmetrical undirected graph $G = (N, L)$, where N is the set of nodes, and $L \subset N^2$ the set of directed links. We define L_I (respectively L_D) to be the union of L and the set of injection links (respectively delivery links) within a node (local channels[2]).

A classical node-address based routing function may be defined as an application $\mathcal{R}:L_I \times N \to P(L_D)$ where for every couple (l_i, d), $\mathcal{R}(l_i, d)$ is the set of output links that are accepted for messages coming into a node by link l_i and which destination is node d. If there exists a set $\mathcal{R}(l_i, d)$ which is not a singleton, then $\mathcal{R}$ is said *adaptive*; otherwise, $\mathcal{R}$ is said *deterministic* [18]. In the adaptive case, a selection function must choose among the accepted output links, the one that the message will effectively use.

A path between a source n_s and a destination n_d is a tuple of links:

$$\gamma = ((n_s, n_1), (n_1, n_2, \ldots, (n_{k-1}, n_k), (n_k, n_d))$$

The set of paths from n_s to n_d that are accepted by a routing function $\mathcal{R}$ will be noted $\Gamma_{\mathcal{R}}^{ns \to nd}$.

In order to support transparent process mobility, our routing model introduces new routing functions that are applications from $L_I \times P \to P(L_D)$ where P is the set of processes. These functions can be used to route messages based on process identifications rather than hosts addresses and we will call them "mobile or Π-routing functions". Let us consider the localization function $L : P \to N$, that associates to each process the node where it is being executed at a given time.

We focus on routing functions defined by:
$$\forall (l_i, p) \in L_I \times P, \Pi(l_i, p) = \mathcal{R}(l_i, L(p)).$$

Two correction properties are suitable for routing functions (whether $\mathcal{R}$ or Π): validity and deadlock avoidance. Validity ensures that any isolated message reaches its destination in a finite amount of time, while deadlock avoidance ensures that no cyclic requests of already reserved physical resources can exist.

If the routing function is deterministic, validity is guaranteed by the existence of an acyclic path between the source and the destination of each message. This definition of validity can also be used in an adaptive context. Here we will consider a stronger constraint that is to say for every message which has already followed a fraction of the path, there is some acyclic path which leads to destination.

For the deterministic functions, deadlock avoidance is guaranteed if and only if there is no cycle in the dependency graph of the routing function. This condition is sufficient for adaptive functions, and some authors have adopted it. Further research has been done to propose necessary and sufficient conditions for deadlock avoidance that are dependent of the switching technique used by the physical router [4].

Let us first consider that function L is constant during the routing of each message. It is then easy to prove that if $\mathcal{R}$ is valid and deadlock-free, then Π is also correct.

As each node of the network actually computes the routing function for all messages reaching that node, we have to locally implement both $\mathcal{R}$ and L functions. Furthermore, in the mobi-routing model, after each migration, only a restricted subset of the nodes need to be

---

[2] These additional links, which send or collect messages in a node n, can be considered as (n,n) edges.

informed that migration occurred. Knowledge of the localization of the processes can thus be different from one node to another. Nevertheless, as shown in [9], the global routing function is kept correct.

Let us define the localization functions as seen by each node n, as applications $L_n: P \rightarrow N$. L_n can differ from L if node n was not informed of some migrations. Hence, the global routing function Π is:

$$\forall l_i = (n', n) \in L_I, \forall p \in P, \Pi(l_i, p) = \mathcal{R}(l_i, L_n(p))$$

L_n functions change as processes migrate, therefore Π also varies in time and changes occur during the routing of some messages. In order to prove the correction of Π, we first have to look at how L_n functions are updated.

When a process migrates, only a subset of nodes is notified of its migration. All other nodes will keep routing their messages as if the process was still running at its original node. We will focus later on several ways of determining such subsets so that the global routing remains correct. We first consider that a process p migrates only once. We call V^p the set of nodes that are aware of this migration.

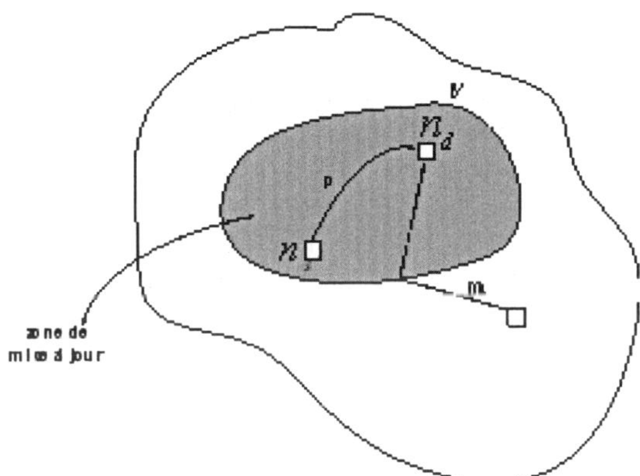

Figure 1. Message routing using Π functions

The figure 3.1 shows message routing using Π functions leads both to a limited number of control messages needed to inform other nodes of the migration, and to a reduced path length when compared to a classical "forwarding" mechanism. This is particularly obvious if we consider a process that migrates several times.

Let us call "localizers", $V^{p,i}$ the set of nodes that have been informed of the ith migration of process p. The localization function in a node which belongs both to $V^{p,i}$ and $V^{p,j}$, i $\neq$ j keeps the information of the most recent migration that it has knowledge of. In the rest of this paper, and when this is not subject to ambiguity, we will use V instead of $V^{p,i}$.

3.2 Definition of the localizers sets

In this section, we present a method to build the $V^{p,i}$ subsets. We will illustrate it with one technique used to evaluate the Π routing functions obtained.

Let p be a process which migrates for the ith time, from a node n_s to a node n_d. During network initialization, on every node n, $L_n = L$. When process p migrates, as $V^{p,i}$ is the set of nodes to be informed of the migration, nodes $n \in V^{p,i}$ update their localization function L_n so that $L_n(p) = n_d$.

Definition 1. *In a node n, the localization function L_n is said to be $\mathcal{R}$-equivalent to L for process p, and we note $L_n \equiv^{\mathcal{R},p} L$ if and only if $\forall l_i, \in L_I \exists n_x, l_i = (n_x, n)$ and $\mathcal{R}(l_i, L_n(p)) = R(l_i, L(p))$.*

In order to construct the localization set V, we use two sets V_T and V_E, such that $V_T \cap V_E = \emptyset$, and $V = V_T \cup V_E$. Let us call $V^{--} = N - V$. An iterative way of building the V set is:

1. Set first $V_E = \emptyset$ and $V_T = \{n_s\}$, where $\{n_s\}$ is the source of the migration.
2. Construct W the set of nodes $n \in V^{--}$ such that:

(i) a neighbor of n belongs to V_T or

(ii) there exists a neighbor $n' \in V$ of node n so that $\exists l_i$ an incoming link of n', $n \in \mathcal{R}(l_i, n_d)$. (i.e. n belongs to a path from a node of V to n_d, the destination node of the migrating process).

3. If $n \in W$ and $L_n(p) \neq L(p)$ and $L_n \equiv^{R,p} L$, then $n \in V_E$.
4. If $n \in W$ and $L_n(p) \neq L(p)$ and $\neg(L_n \equiv^{R,p} L)$, then $n \in V_T$.
5. Repeat steps 2 to 4 until the set V is stable by iteration.

This construction starts at node n_s and makes V grow until it reaches nodes that have a routing function which is R-equivalent to the routing that is expected after the update. Condition (ii) of step 2 guarantees that V will grow enough to reach node n_d. The set V_E represents a frontier between the nodes which have been updated and those who haven't. The main reason to stop when we reach a node with R-equivalent routing functions before and after the update, is to keep the validity of the final global routing. This will be made clear in the proof below. In the next section we will present an algorithm to broadcast the update information to nodes of V without explicitly computing the set V at any single node.

Let us prove now that, when R is a valid and deadlock-free routing function, the resulting Π routing function is correct when all the nodes in V have updated their localization function L_n. Following the construction algorithm, one can easily prove the following results:

Lemma 3. *All nodes in the neighbourhood of a given node $n \in V_T$ belong to V.*

Lemma 4. *Let $n \in V_E$; the node directly connected to n by an output link l_o so that $\exists l_i$ incoming link of n, $l_o \in \Pi(l_i, p)$, belongs to V.*

From the lemmas we can deduce the following:

Proposition 1. *Let m be a message to destination p; if m has arrived by a link $l_i, \in L_I$ into a node $n \in V$ then $\forall l_o = (n, n') \in \Pi(l_i, p)$, $n' \in V$. Furthermore, if m is in a node $n' \in V^{--}$ then $\forall l_o = (n, n') \in \Pi(l_i, p)$, $n' \in V^{--} \cup V_E$.*

We can hence verify that the set V_E represents a "frontier" between V and V_T. An example of such sets is illustrated by the figure 3.2 for a grid network.

One can also prove the following propositions [19]:

Proposition 2. *Let m be a message with destination p being sent by a process located in node $n' \in V^{--}$. The message m will necessarily go through a node $n' \in V_E$.*

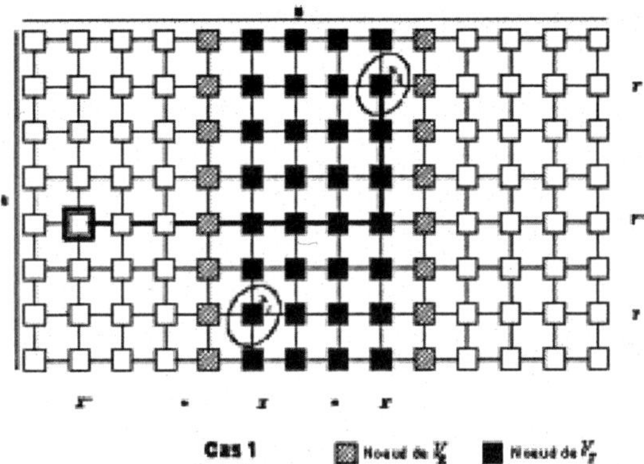

Figure 2. A grid network

Proposition 3. *Let m be a message with destination p being routed at a node $n \in V_E$ such that $\gamma = ((n_0, n_1), (n_1, n_2), ..., (n_{k-1}, n_k), (n_k, n))$ is the path that m has already gone through, and $\forall i \in [0,k]$, $n_i \in V^{--}$. At node n there exists at least one output link accepted by the routing function Π for m.*

Proposition 4. *: Let $n \in V$. $\Gamma_R^{n \to nd} \neq \emptyset$ and all the nodes on any path of $\Gamma_R^{n \to nd}$ belong to V.*

Using the propositions 2 to 4, we can prove that each message, at any stage of its routing, can go forward to the next node towards its destination. Therefore, the Π function is both progressive and dead-end free. Moreover, once a message reaches a node of V, it is always routed towards its destination n_d. Since $\mathcal{R}$ is valid, the message does not indefinitely cycle. Hence, the Π routing function is also valid.

Proposition 5. *If $\mathcal{R}$ is deadlock free, then Π is deadlock free.*

Indeed, Π is defined at each node by: $\forall p \in P, \Pi(l_i, p) = \mathcal{R}(l_i, L_n(p))$. All the dependencies between input and output links of the routes accepted by Π are part of the dependencies generated by $\mathcal{R}$. As the function Π does not introduce any new dependency, if $\mathcal{R}$ is deadlock free, the routing obtained by Π will also be deadlock-free.

When used as a criterion for defining the set of nodes to update after a given migration, the $\mathcal{R}$-equivalence has proved to be quite efficient when used both on regular and general network topologies. However, if the function $\mathcal{R}$ is adaptive, we can obtain another correct function while reducing even further the number of nodes in V. We define the *R-weak equivalence* as: $\forall l_i, \in L_I, \exists n_x, l_i = (n_x, n)$ and $\mathcal{R}(l_i, L_n(p) \cap \mathcal{R}(l_i, L(p)) \neq \emptyset$.

The condition for a node to belong to the frontier is weaker than that of the $\mathcal{R}$-equivalence, so the set V has less nodes. We can easily adapt the propositions that we have given before to this new relation, and prove that the resulting Π routing function is correct.

In order to obtain minimal path lengths while using the mobi-routing model (Π functions) for transparent process localization, it is possible to have $V = N$ and then, at each process migration, completely broadcast to all the network nodes. Even if the control communications overhead (due to intensively broadcasting) is very high, and makes it probably very inefficient in this limit case, we can use it for evaluation purposes.

3.3 Implementation Issues

In this section, we focus on implementation aspects of the mobi-routing model. First, we show how to update the nodes in the set V described in the previous section, without explicitly computing it in any single node. We then discuss how to implement the L_n function on each node, and several ways to reduce the memory space required locally at each node for the localization function.

3.3.1 Dynamic construction of the V set

In order to update the L_n function after a migration has taken place, the node from which the process has migrated starts a partial broadcast using control messages. Those control messages carry the following information: the identification of the migrated process, the destination of the migration, and the number of migrations that this process has performed. This last information is needed in order to allow the recipients of the control messages to be able to keep trace of the most recent localization. The broadcast algorithm for the construction of the V set in the context of the $\mathcal{R}$-equivalence is the following:

- node n_s from which the process has migrated sends a control message to all of its immediate neighbours;

- when a node receives a control message, it verifies if it has been informed of a later migration of the same process, in which case it discards the control message and stops the algorithm;

- if this is not the case, it compares the value of its localization $L_n(p)$ to the destination of the migration announced by the control message;

- if the two values are the same $L_n(p) = L(p)$, the message is discarded and the algorithm stops;

- if $\neg(L_n \equiv^{R,p} L)$, the node updates its localization function, stores the number of times the p process has migrated, and broadcasts the control message to all its neighbours;

- if $L_n(p) \neq L(p)$ but $L_n \equiv^{R,p} L$, the node updates its localization function, stores the number of times the p process has migrated, and broadcasts the control message only through the output links l_o that verify $\exists l_i, \in L_I, l_o \in \mathcal{R}(l_i, n_d)$ where n_d is the destination node of the migration contained in the control message (i.e. all the output links that are accepted by the $\mathcal{R}$ function for destination n_d).

It is easy to verify that the broadcast finishes and then, the set of nodes which have broadcasted the control message to all their neighbours is the V_T set, and the set of nodes which have only broadcasted through some output links is the V_E set.

The implementation of the update by such a partial broadcast of control messages is not immediate. It may be possible that another process wants to communicate with process p while the update takes place. If we look at the correction criteria of the routing function during the broadcast, we observe that there can be situations where the validity is temporally not guaranteed. This is due to the fact that *Lemma 1* may not be verified: a node n has just received the control message and belongs to V_T, but one of its neighbors n' has not already

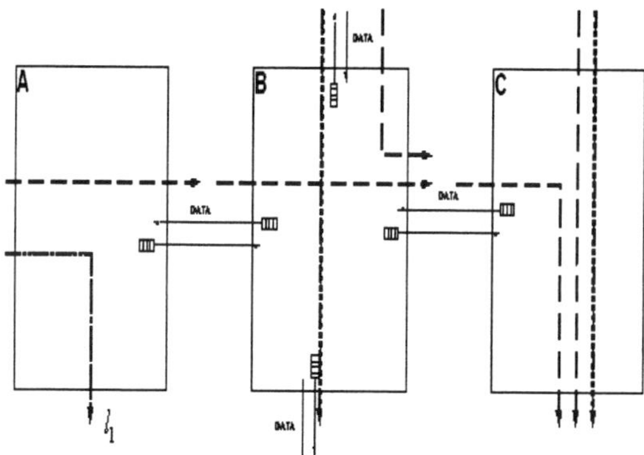

Figure 3.

been notified, and sends messages which cannot be routed at n because $\neg(L_n \equiv^{R,p} L)$ $(L_n(p) = L(p))$ $(R(l_i, L_n(p))) = $ g, with $l_i = (n', n)$. This situation is shown on the following figures. Let's consider the function $\mathcal{R}$ represented by the arrows though the nodes (dashed lines represent authorised routes to n_d and n_s).

The following figures represent the situation while the diffusion is performed.

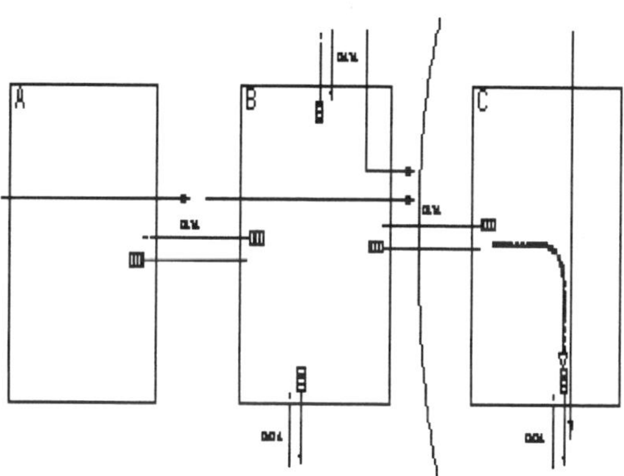

Figure 4.

In order to guarantee the validity of the routing function while the broadcast is taking place, we allow that such messages arriving to the node n be routed through an output link which is on a valid path to reach node n_d. We will do so by introducing a new routing rule:

Rule 1: If a message m arrives to a node n by the input link l_i and has for destination process p, and $\mathcal{R}(l_i, L_n(p)) = $ g, then $\Pi(l_i, p) = \cup_{l=(n',n)\in LI}\mathcal{R}(l, L_n(p))$.

The validity of the Π function between two broadcasts implies that this situation can only occur while the broadcast is taking place. Furthermore, the validity of function $\mathcal{R}$ guarantees that even in this case, $\Pi(l_i, p)$ is not empty.

With the introduction of this new rule, the resulting routing function is valid, but we had introduced a new dependency between the physical resources. Even if this situation hardly happens in practice (a message arrives in a node of V_T just after this node has received the

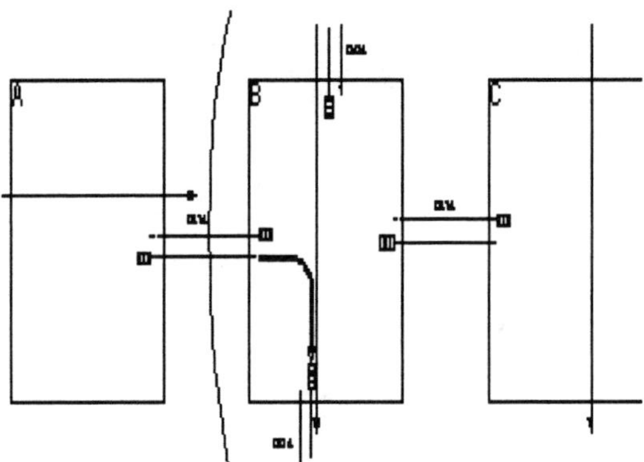

Figure 5.

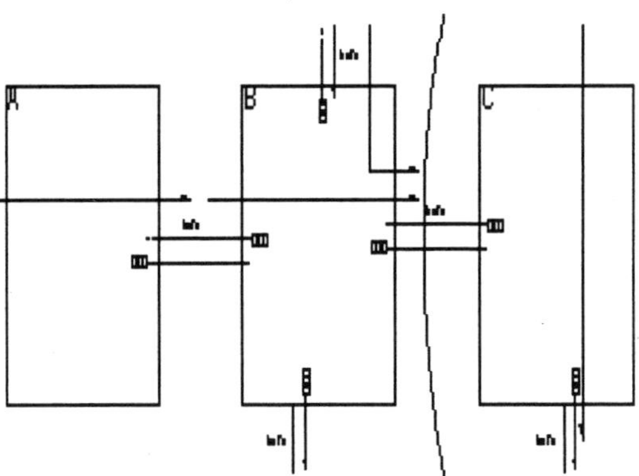

Figure 6.

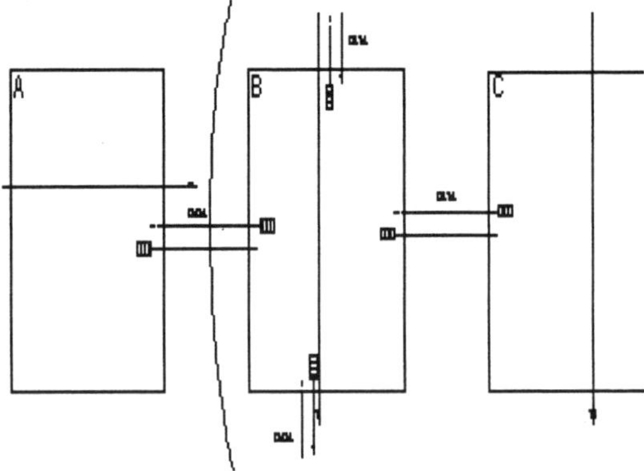

Figure 7.

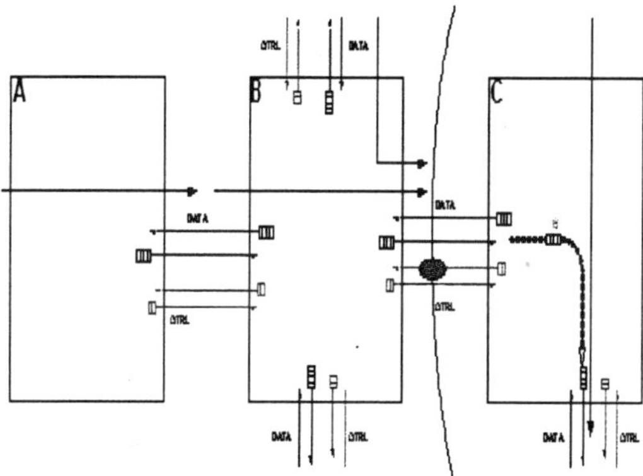

Figure 8.

control message, but before it has broadcasted it to its neighbours), deadlock situations may occur. Classical deadlock avoidance solutions [4] cannot take into account the new dependencies generated by our routing rule. In order to solve this problem, we have introduced additional buffers to store the messages received in a node while the broadcast is taking place locally. We also need to create reserved control channels to send the control messages from a node to its neighbours, so they do not compete with standard messages to use the link buffers, and thus the time needed to send them is bounded.

The detailed resulting handling of control messages is done as follows:

- when a node receives a control message from one of the control links (from one of its neighbours), it stops routing standard messages;

- it sends an acknowledgement of the control message to the issuing neighbour through the same control link;

- the node decides, according to the broadcasting algorithm described above, if it has to discard, fully broadcast, or only partially broadcast the control message and sends it to the selected neighbours;

- it updates its localization function if needed;

- it waits for the acknowledgement messages of all the nodes it has sent the control message to;

- upon reception of the last acknowledgement, it restarts routing standard messages.

During the time that the node n had stopped routing messages, and until the neighbours have received the control messages, they may have routed some standard messages according to their previous localization function, and already stored them on the buffers of the outgoing links (these buffers can independently be placed in the output link of the previous node or in the input link of node n).

When those messages will arrive to n, they will be routed using our additional routing rule, and can be a source of deadlock situations. In order to avoid such possible deadlock situations, we have introduced additional input buffers of the same size than the buffers of the link. Indeed, there are at most as many messages routed using the old localization function as the size of the link buffers, since we have stopped routing messages in this node. Such additional buffers will only be used by messages that are routed using the routing rule stated above.

We can then notice the followings:

- number of misrouted messages requesting these new buffers is bounded and smaller than the capacity of the additional buffers;

- these messages are placed in the buffer during the finite time of the update of the routing information;

- the buffers are emptied after the update, so that there are no more requests from some other messages.

We can then easily conclude that no cyclic request of physical resources is added. Hence, the Π-routing remains deadlock-free.

3.3.2 Memory space management

Another important issue we need to address is the memory space needed to store the routing information at each node, and since the $\mathcal{R}$ function is a classical host-address based routing function, we can use several existing techniques (e.g. interval routing) to reduce the memory needed for storing the required information [14, 18, 28]. We will focus in this section on the implementation of the localization functions L_n, and present a technique to store only the information concerning the processes that are effectively running and for which the node has to be informed of its migration.

In order to reduce the amount of memory needed to store the information of the L_n function, we use the following naming scheme for process identifications: a process name is obtained by the concatenation of the address of the node where it was created, and an identification unique to that node (for example, the number of processes created before in that node). Disregarding of the process migrations, and thus of the node where it is actually running, its identification remains constant until it finishes. The use of such a naming scheme allows us to deduce from a process identification, the host where it was created. In the case where a node routes a message to a process it has not been informed of any migration of, it can easily compute a default localization: the address of the node where it was created. Therefore, we do not need to store any localization information on each node when the system starts or when a process is created. The localization function can be completely isolated from the process placement algorithm.

When a process migrates for the ith time, the control messages sent to the nodes of the V set include the number of the migrations (here i). Upon reception of such a control message by a node, it can discard any previous localization information for that process, and replace it with the new one, but it needs to store the value of i. We can therefore represent the localization function information as a table containing three fields for each row: the process identification, the node where it has migrated to for the last time (actual node's knowledge), and the number of that migration. To route a message, the L_n function starts by making a lookup on that table, and if there is no entry for the destination process of the message, it computes the default localization (where it has been created), by slicing the process identification.

Finally, when a process finishes, we can dispose of the entries of the nodes which have been informed of its migrations. We propose the following algorithm for implementing a garbage collection without needing to store at any single node the list of the nodes which have been informed of the previous migrations of each process that finishes:

- When a process finishes, the system verifies if it has arrived to that node as a result of a migration (a process may finish at the node where it was created, after a succession of several migrations). If this is the case, it sends a control message to all of its neighbours to inform them of the end of its execution.

- Upon reception of such a termination control message, a node verifies if it has an entry for that process on its localization table. If it has one, it suppresses it and broadcasts the termination control message to all of its neighbours. Else, it discards it.

We can easily prove that, even if the process had migrated several times, this algorithm completely delete any routing information from the tables of the L_n functions of all the nodes.

A conflict may arise if there were still control messages from previous migrations being broadcasted on the network, and if on one node the termination control message arrives just before the notification message. Such a race condition can occur particularly if the notification message is already on a buffer from a neighbour when we receive the termination message. This can result on a permanent lost of memory space. In order to solve further this problem, we can delay the deletion of the entry on the table until we are sure that the buffers have been emptied. The following algorithm details the handling of the termination control messages:

- upon reception of a termination control message, and if the node already had an entry for that process in its localization table, it sets its migration number to a maximum value, so that any migration notification control message is discarded;

- it broadcasts the termination control message to its neighbours and checks if there are any messages on the incoming control links until it is sure that a conflict is not possible (either the buffers are empty and the control message has been acknowledged, or it has read enough messages from the control links to be sure that all the messages there have been treated);

- then it deletes the entry from the table.

Using both this naming scheme for processes identifications, and the garbage collection algorithm, we can bound the amount of memory space needed for the L_n functions at each node to be equal to the number of processes actively running and which have notified the node of their migrations.

3.3.3 Examples and evaluations

In this section we present as an example the results obtained on three different network topologies: a non-regular graph, and for performance comparison purposes, two regular networks: a 2-dimensional mesh, and a binary tree.

Non-regular graph

The above general graph consists of several subnets connected by an interconnection backbone. We consider in this example that a process migrates from node A_s to node E_d respectively on the subnets connected to the backbone by the nodes A and E. For increased readability, we have only represented a subset of the routing function (the routes that concern the A and E nodes), but we suppose that:

- the routing function gives identical output links for every node of a given subnet (i.e. the route to node A is also accepted to route messages to node A_s)

- the resulting $\mathcal{R}$ function is valid and deadlock free for a general network (see for instance [18]).

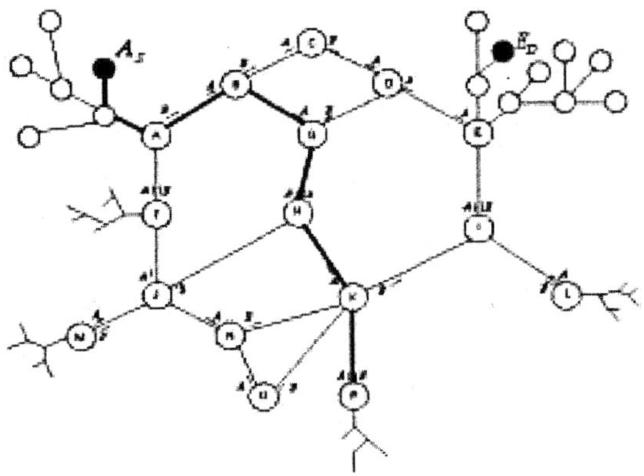

Figure 9. Non-regular graph

If we use the $\mathcal{R}$-equivalence and implement the broadcast algorithm described above, we obtain the set V that bellow. This figure also shows the path that messages outgoing from a process located on node P will follow.

Mesh

In order to compare the Π routing functions to other dedicated techniques for routing on regular networks, we will analyze how the Π routing model behaves when implemented on a 2-dimensional mesh using a classical X-Y routing as being the $\mathcal{R}$ function. The figure 3.2 above illustrates the V set obtained after the migration of a process from node to a node n_d.

The broadcast algorithm ends with the Π function producing a minimal routing scheme. The number of nodes in the V set is:

$$\text{card}(V_T) = N.(\Delta x + 1) \text{ et card}(V_E) = 2.N$$

and the mean path length obtained is:

$$l_{may}(\gamma) = \left|x'' - x'\right| + \left|y'' - y'\right| = \Delta_x + \Delta_y$$

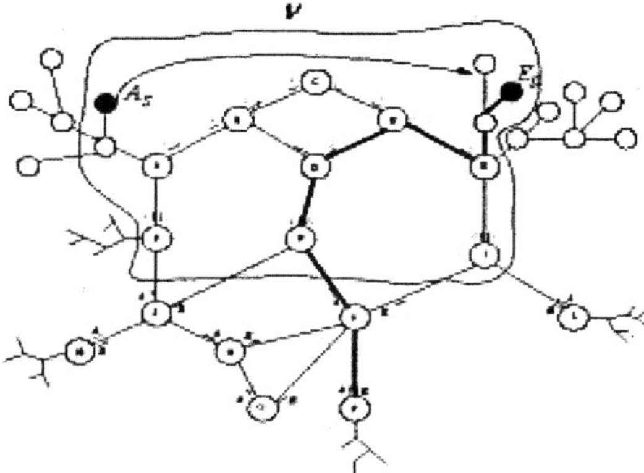

Figure 10. Non-regular graph

Tree

More detailed discussion can be found in [9, 27] for the Π routing model applied to a balanced binary tree network. We use there an usual minimal routing function $\mathcal{R}$, and the $\mathcal{R}$-equivalence broadcast algorithm as for the previous examples. For a process p that migrates from a node n_s to a node n_d on the tree, let δ be the depth of the tree, and respectively δ_s and δ_d the depth of the nodes n_s and n_d in the tree.

We can then easily compute the number of nodes that have been notified of the migration:
card(V) = 2.d(n_s, n_d) -1 + nbc(n_s) + nbc(n_d) + isroot(n_x)
with d(n_s, n_d) the distance between nodes n_s and n_d, "nbc" the function giving the number of children of a node, and "isroot" a function which gives 1 for the root, and 0 for the rest of the nodes; n_x being the root of the minimal subtree containing both n_s and n_d.

The resulting routing function is minimal, as for the example of the mesh. We can compare the mean path length obtained by this function, and compare the result to the value we had obtained if we would had used a forwarding technique instead. The mean path length for the Π routing function is:

$$\mu_\Pi = ((2^{\delta+1}(\delta + \delta_{nd} - 3) + 2^{\delta-\delta nd+2} + 2 + \delta_{nd})/(2^{\delta+1} - 2)$$

4　Future work

The Π routing model has been developed to support, at a network level, the correct routing of messages between mobile processes by using selective pruning of broadcasting communication. It has proved to offer reasonable path lengths size, which can even be minimal, while reducing the overhead of control communications by broadcasting only to a subset of the network nodes.

Further work on this subject should focus on the complexity of the implementation of the Π routing model over existing routing hardware and ad-hoc networks. It should be particularly interesting to study ways of reducing the overhead induced by a two-stage route computation.

Finally, it would also be interesting to study the possibility of mixing the Π routing model and existing routing techniques to handle the mobility of the nodes.

References

[1] J. A Bergstra, A. Ponse, S.A. Smolka (eds). *Handbook of Process Algebra*, Elsevier, 2001

[2] F. Douglis, J. Ousterhout. *Transparent process migration: Design alternatives and the sprite implementation.* Software-Practice and Experience, 21(8): 757–785, August 1991.

[3] W. J. Dally, C. L. Seitz. *Deadlock-free message routing in multiprocessor interconnection networks.* IEEE Transactions on Computers, C-36(5), May 1987.

[4] J. Duato. *A necessary and sufficient condition for deadlock-free routing in cut-through and store-and-forward networks.* IEEE Transactions on Parallel and Distributed Systems, 7(8), August 1996.

[5] C. Ene, T. Muntean. *A broadcast based calculus for communicating systems*, Proc. of Int. Conf. on Formal Methods for Parallel Programming Teory and Applications, IEEE-FMPPTA, San Francisco, 2001

[6] C. Ene, T. Muntean. *On the expressive power of point-to-point and broadcast communications*, Foundations of Theoretical Computing, LNCS 1864 – Iassy, Sept 1999

[7] C. Ene. *Un model formel pour les systèmes mobiles à diffusion*, PhD Univ. de la Méditerranée, Marseille, Dec. 2001

[8] C. Ene, T. Muntean. *Testing theories for broadcasting systems*, ISPDC'2002

[9] J. Garmendia, L. Mugwaneza, T. Muntean, S. Rivas. *Compact and Correct Adaptive Routing for General Networks*, in "Communication Networks, Distributed Systems Modelling and Simulation" Conf. CNDS, San Diego, 2000

[10] M. Hennessy, J. Rathke. *Bisimulations for a calculus of broadcasting systems*, Theoretical Computer Science, 200, 1998

[11] M. Hennessy, *Timed process algebras: a tutorial*, in Marktoberdorf Summer School on process design calculi, 1992

[12] C. A. R. Hoare. *Communicating Sequential Processes*. Internat. Series in Computer Science. Prentice-Hall, 1985.

[13] J.P. Jung, I. Sakho, *A methodology for devising optimal all-to-all broadcast algorithms in two-dimensional tori*, IEEE Proceeding Conference HSLN'03, Bonn (Germany), October 2003

[14] J. van Leeuwen R. B. Tan. *Interval routing*. The computer Journal, 30(4), 1987.

[15] N. Lynch, M. Tuttle. *An introduction to I/O automata*, Centrum voor Wiskunde en Informatica, Amsterdam, also MIT/LCS/TM-373

[16] R. Milner. *Communication and Concurrency*, Prentice Hall 1989

[17] R. Milner. *Communicating and Mobile Systems: Pi-calculus*, Cambridge Univ. Press, 1999

[18] L. Mugwaneza, T. Muntean, I. Sakho. *A deadlock-free routing algorithm with network size independent buffering*, LNCS 457, pages 490-501, 1990.

[19] T. Muntean, J. Garmendia, S. Rivas. *A Routing Model for Mobile Agents*, Proceedings of Parallel and Distributed Computing and Systems –PDCS'00, ACM-IASTED Conf. Las Vegas, Nov. 2000

[20] T. Muntean. *Towards Multi-Models Parallel Programming and Communications*. ACM MIT Workshop on "Future Directions in Computing Research", G. Agha (ed), MIT Press, 1997

[21] K. Ostrovsky. *Higher order broadcasting systems*, PhD thesis, Chalmers University of Technology, Göteborg, 2002

[22] I. Phillips. *CCS with priority guards*, in Concur-2001, LNCS 2154

[23] KVS Prasad. *A Calculus of Broadcasting Systems*, TAPSOFT'91, LNCS 493

[24] KVS Prasad. *A Calculus of Broadcasting Systems*, Science of Computer Programming, 25, 1995

[25] KVS Prasad. *Broadcast Calculus Interpreted in CCS up to Bisimulation*, Electronic Notes in Theoretical Computer Science, 52, Elsevier Science Publishers, 2002

[26] A. W. Roscoe. *The Theory and Practice of Concurrency*. Internat. Series in Computer Science. Prentice-Hall, 1997.

[27] S. Rivas. *Routage adaptatif dans les réseaux généraux*, PhD Université de la Méditerranée, Marseille, 1999

[28] N. Santoro, R. Khatib. *Labelling and implicit routing in networks*. The Computer Journal, 28(1) : February 1985.

[29] B. Thomsen, Plain. *CHOCS: a second generation calculus for higher-order processes*, Acta Informatica, 30, 1993

Concurrent Information Processing and Computing
D. Grigoras and A. Nicolau (Eds.)
IOS Press, 2005

131

A Compositional Semantics for Petri Net Reactive Modules

Ferucio Laurentiu Ţiplea   Aurora Ţiplea

Faculty of Computer Science
"Al.I.Cuza" University of Iaşi, Romania
E-mail: `fltiplea@infoiasi.ro`

Abstract. In this paper we model (discrete) reactive systems that may interact with each other by *Petri net modules* which are classical Petri nets together with a distinguished subset of *interface places*. We consider then an *asynchronous composition operation* of modules and, closely related to it, a *decomposition operation*. We show that any process (concurrent execution) of a composition of two modules can be decomposed into processes of "shifted" components for which a p-composition function exists, and vice versa. Based on this result, a *compositional semantics* of modules is then defined. The concurrent execution of a module inside a system is called a *process sample/fragment* of the system w.r.t. that module. We show that, in some circumstances, all the process samples of a system can be generated by *e-modules* which abstract from some parts of the behaviour by collapsing many consecutive steps into a single one. Finally, some applications of the results mentioned above are pointed out.

1   Introduction and Preliminaries

In spite of the impressive progress in the development of methods for system design and verification, many realistic systems are still too large to be handled. Thus, it is important to find techniques that can be used in conjunction with the symbolic methods to extend the size of the systems that can be verified. Two such techniques, generally recognized as the only methods can ever scale up to handle industrial-size design and verification, are the *abstraction* and *modularization* which break the task of verifying a large system into several smaller tasks of verifying simpler systems. Modularization exploits the modular structure of a complex system composed of multiple processes running in parallel. In such systems it is essential to study and analyse each process as a *reactive system* (which is a collection of variables that, over time, change their values in a sequence of rounds). That is because, from the point of view of each process, the rest of the system can be viewed as an environment that continuously interacts with the process. Then, an obvious strategy is to derive properties (proofs) of the whole system from partial (local) properties involving (abstractions of) its modules (components). Generally speaking, modular design and verification requires:

- an ability to describe and compose modules with different synchrony assumptions, and at different level of abstraction;

- an ability to decompose verification tasks into subtasks of lower complexity.

For details and significant work in this direction the reader is referred, for example, to [1, 2, 5, 7–9, 11, 12, 22–24].

In this paper we model (discrete) reactive systems that may interact with each other by *Petri net modules* which are classical Petri nets together with a distinguished subset of places (modelling the set of *interface/shared variables*). We consider then an *asynchronous composition operation* of modules that allows us to build systems from components and, closely related to it, a *decomposition operation* of systems in smaller parts (components). We show that every process (concurrent execution) of a system which is a composition of two modules can be decomposed into processes of its "shifted" components and, moreover, these processes can be related each other by means of a *p-composition function*. Conversely, composition of processes of shifted components, which are related by some p-composition function, are processes of the system. These two results lead naturally to a compositional semantics of modules, which is then defined. The concurrent execution of a module inside a system is called a *process sample/fragment* of the system w.r.t. that module. We show that, in some circumstancies, all the process samples of a system can be generated by e-modules which *abstracts* from some parts of the behaviour by collapsing many steps into a single one. Finally, some applications of the results mentioned above are pointed out.

In the remainder of this section we recall basic definitions and notations in Petri net theory (for further details the reader is referred to [3, 6, 13, 14]).

The empty set is denoted by $\emptyset$, and $|A|$ denotes the cardinality of the finite set A. $A \subseteq B$ denotes the inclusion of the set A into the set B, and $\mathcal{P}(A)$ is the set of all subsets (the power set) of A. The set of integers is $\mathbf{Z}$, and the set of nonnegative integers is $\mathbf{N}$. For a binary relation R, $Dom(R)$ and $Cod(R)$ denote the domain and the codomain, respectively, of R, $R(x)$ is the image of x under R, and R^+ (R^*) is the transitive (reflexive and transitive) closure of R. If $f_i : A_i \to \mathbf{Z}$ are functions, $i = 1, 2$, $f_1 + f_2$ is the function from $A_1 \cup A_2$ into $\mathbf{Z}$ given by $(f_1 + f_2)(a) = f_1(a)$ for all $a \in A_1 - A_2$, $(f_1 + f_2)(a) = f_2(a)$ for all $a \in A_2 - A_1$, and $(f_1 + f_2)(a) = f_1(a) + f_2(a)$ for all $a \in A_1 \cap A_2$. In a similar way is defined $f_1 - f_2$. The restriction of a function $f : A \to B$ to the set $C \subseteq A$ is denoted by $f|_C$; f^{-1} is the function from B into the powerset of A given by $f^{-1}(b) = \{a \in A | f(a) = b\}$ for all $b \in B$.

A (finite) *Petri net* (or *net*, for short) is a 4-tuple $\Sigma = (S, T, F, W)$, where S and T are two finite sets (of *places* and *transitions*, respectively), $S \cap T = \emptyset$, $F \subseteq (S \times T) \cup (T \times S)$ is the *flow relation*, and $W : (S \times T) \cup (T \times S) \to \mathbf{N}$ is the *weight function* of Σ verifying $W(x, y) = 0$ iff $(x, y) \notin F$. In our paper we shall suppose that all the nets we consider do not have isolated transitions (but they may have isolated places). When $W(x, y) \leq 1$ for all $(x, y) \in F$, we may (and will) simplify the 4-tuples (S, T, F, W) to the 3-tuple (S, T, F).

A *marking* of a net Σ is any function $M : S \to \mathbf{N}$ (when S is empty, M is the empty function); it will sometimes be identified with a vector $M \in \mathbf{N}^{|S|}$. The operations and relations on vectors are componentwise defined. For $x \in S \cup T$ we set

$$^\bullet x = \{y | (y, x) \in F\}, \quad x^\bullet = \{y | (x, y) \in F\}, \quad ^\bullet x^\bullet = {}^\bullet x \cup x^\bullet,$$

and extend usually these notations to subsets $X \subseteq S \cup T$.

A *marked net* is a pair $\gamma = (\Sigma, M_0)$, where Σ is a net and M_0, the *initial marking* of γ, is a marking of Σ. A *labelled marked net* is a 3-tuple $\gamma = (\Sigma, M_0, l)$, where the first two components form a marked net and l, the *labelling function* of γ, assigns to each transition either a letter or the empty word λ. In the sequel we shall often use the term "Petri net" or "net" whenever we refer to a structure γ as defined above. In all the definitions above Σ is called the *underlying net* of γ. A marking (place, transition, arc, weight) of a net γ is any marking (place, transition, arc, weight) of the underlying net of γ.

Pictorially, a net γ is represented by a graph. Then the places are denoted by circles and transitions by boxes; the flow relation is represented by arcs. The arc $f \in F$ is labelled by $W(f)$ whenever $W(f) > 1$. The initial marking M_0 is presented by putting $M_0(s)$ tokens into the circle representing the place s and the labelling function is denoted by placing letters into the boxes representing transitions (when some boxes are empty we will understand that the corresponding transitions are labelled by themselves).

Let γ be a net and M a marking of it. The *transition rule* states that a transition t is *enabled* at M, denoted $M[t\rangle_\gamma$, if $M(s) \geq W(s, t)$ for all $s \in S$. If t is enabled at M then t may *occur* yielding a new marking M' given by $M'(s) = M(s) - W(s, t) + W(t, s)$, for all $s \in S$; we abbreviate this by $M[t\rangle_\gamma M'$. The transition rule is extended to sequences of transition $w \in T^*$ in the usual way. If $M_0[w\rangle_\gamma M$ then M is called *reachable*; $[M_0\rangle_\gamma$, called the *reachability set* of γ, denotes the set of all reachable markings of γ. The notation "$[\cdot\rangle_\gamma$" will be simplified to "$[\cdot\rangle$" whenever γ is clear from context.

The concurrent behaviour of Petri nets is well-expressed by the notion of a *process*. Generally speaking, processes of Petri nets are obtained by running the nets and solving conflicts in an arbitrary fashion as and when they arise. A process of a net is also a net; these nets are called *occurrence nets* and they are classical nets $N = (B, E, R)$ (B is the set of places, E is the set of transitions, and R is the flow relation) satisfying:

(i) $|{}^\bullet b| \leq 1$ and $|b^\bullet| \leq 1$, for all $b \in B$;

(ii) R^+ is acyclic, i.e. for all $x, y \in B \cup E$, if $(x, y) \in R^+$ then $(y, x) \notin R^+$.

Usually the elements of B are called *conditions* whereas the elements of E are called *events*. The *partially ordered set induced* by N is $(B \cup E, \prec_N)$, where $\prec_N = R^+$. A *B-cut* of N is any maximal subset $C \subseteq B$ of incomparable elements according to the relation $\prec_N$. As we will only use B-cuts we call them shortly *cuts* (see [3] for more details). The *initial (final) cut* of N is ${}^\circ N = \{b \in B || {}^\bullet b| = 0\}$ ($N^\circ = \{b \in B || b^\bullet| = 0\}$). A *path in N from x to y* is any finite sequence of elements $x = x_1, \ldots, x_n = y$ such that for all $1 \leq i < n$, $(x_i, x_{i+1}) \in R$. In defining processes we need V-*labelled occurrence nets* which are couples $\pi = (N, p)$, where N is a occurrence net and p is a total function from $B \cup E$ into an alphabet V. The above definitions (partial order, cut, initial and final cut) are transferred to labelled occurrence nets π by means of N; the corresponding notations are obtained by changing "N" into "π" (e.g. $\prec_\pi$, ${}^\circ \pi$, π°). Let $\Sigma = (S, T, F, W)$ be a Petri net, $\pi = (N, p)$ an $(S \cup T)$-labelled occurrence net such that $p(B) \subseteq S$ and $p(E) \subseteq T$, and C a subset of conditions of π. Define the *marking induced by C in Σ* as being $M_C(s) = |p^{-1}(s) \cap C|$, for all $s \in S$. There are two alternative definitions of a process, axiomatic and inductive, and it is well-known that for Petri nets of finite synchronization they yields exactly the same objects [3]. We adopt here the axiomatic definition (the inductive one will be given in Section 3.2 as a particular case of the inductive definition of processes of jumping nets). A *process* of $\gamma = (\Sigma, M_0)$ is any $(S \cup T)$-labelled occurrence net $\pi = (N, p)$ satisfying:

(i) $p(B) \subseteq S, p(E) \subseteq T$;

(ii) $M_0(s) = |p^{-1}(s) \cap {}^\circ N|$ for all $s \in S$;

(iii) $W(s, p(e)) = |p^{-1}(s) \cap {}^\bullet e|$ and $W(p(e), s) = |p^{-1}(s) \cap e^\bullet|$ for all $e \in E$ and $s \in S$.

Processes of labelled nets $\gamma = (\Sigma, M_0, l)$ are obtained from processes $\pi = (N, p')$ of (Σ, M_0) by replacing the function p' by p, where $p(x) = p'(x)$ for any condition x, and $p(x) = l(p'(x))$ for any event x. That is, the events are labelled by $l \circ p'$. From this reason we will use sometimes $l \circ p'$ instead p (with the meaning above). The set of all processes of a net γ is denoted by $\Pi(\gamma)$. A *path* in a process π is any path in its underlying occurrence net.

2   Petri Net Modules and their Asynchronous Composition

As we have said in the first section, we model discrete reactive systems that may interact with each other by Petri net modules which are defined as follows.

Definition 2.1. *A Petri net module (PN-module or module, for short) is a couple* $\mathcal{M} = (\gamma, S^c)$, *where* $\gamma = (\Sigma, M_0, l)$ *is a net, called the* underlying net *of* $\mathcal{M}$, *and* S^c *is a subset of places of* γ, *called the* set of interface *or* shared places *of* $\mathcal{M}$.

For a module $\mathcal{M}$, the set $S^i = S - S^c$ is called the *set of internal places* of $\mathcal{M}$. When $S^c = \emptyset$ we say that $\mathcal{M}$ is *closed*; otherwise, it is called *open*. All the concepts referring to nets (place, transition, marking, process etc.) are transferred to modules by means of their underlying nets.

The interface places are used by a module to interact with an environment. During an execution, their content is updated by the system (module) or by the *environment*. The content of the internal places can be updated only by the module itself. The distinction between internal and interface places is similar to the distinction between controlled and external variables in the Alur and Henziger's formalism of reactive modules [1], or to the distinction between unobservable owned variables and observable variables in the formalism of fair Kripke structures as given in [9] [1].

The environment interacts with a module $\mathcal{M}$ by updating, from time to time, the content of the interface places. Such an interaction can be mathematically modelled by a binary relation $R \subseteq \mathrm{N}^{S^c} \times \mathrm{N}^{S^c}$. A pair $(M^c, \overline{M}^c)$ means that the environment reads the content M^c of the interface places and then update it to $\overline{M}^c$. From the module $\mathcal{M}$ point of view this updating is done in exactly one step.

Definition 2.2. *An* environment *for a module* $\mathcal{M} = (\gamma, S^c)$ *is any binary relation* R *on the set of markings* N^{S^c}.

A couple $\mathcal{J} = (\mathcal{M}, R)$, where $\mathcal{M}$ is a module and R is an environment for $\mathcal{M}$, is called an *environmental module* (*e-module*, for short); $\mathcal{M}$ is called the *underlying module*, and R the *environment*, of $\mathcal{J}$. E-modules will be mainly used to describe in a compact way the behaviour of modules; they will abstract from some parts of the behaviour of modules by collapsing many consecutive steps into a single one.

---

[1]The set of interface places can be partitioned further into two sets, the set S^{in} of *input places* and the set S^{out} of *output places*. In this way we have a full analogy with the formalisms mentioned above. However, for our purposes such a partition is not important and we will not consider it.

Definition 2.3. *Let* $\mathcal{J} = (\mathcal{M}, R)$ *be an e-module. The* transition relation *of the e-module* $\mathcal{J}$ *is the binary relation* $[\cdot\rangle_{\mathcal{J}}$ *on* $\mathbf{N}^S$ *given by*

$$M[x\rangle_{\mathcal{J}}M' \quad \Leftrightarrow \quad x \text{ is a transition and } M[x\rangle_{\gamma}M', \text{ or}$$
$$x = (M^c, \overline{M}^c) \in R \text{ and } M|_{S^c} = M^c \text{ and } M' = M - M^c + \overline{M}^c,$$

for all $M, M' \in \mathbf{N}^S$.

It is important to note that the environment of an e-module may update the content of the interface places whenever it is possible. That is, whenever a marking M is reachable in the e-module, $M|_{S^c} = M^c$, and $(M^c, \overline{M}^c) \in R$, then the environment may change the marking on S^c to $\overline{M}^c$. Then, the module can execute further [2].

We define now the *asynchronous parallel composition* of modules. Generally, a parallel composition operation on models of distributed systems combines two models into a single one whose behavior captures, in some sense, the interaction between that two models. There are two major ways of forming the parallel composition of two models, *synchronous* and *asynchronous*, and for each of them different variants are known [2,9]. In synchronous parallel composition, the models run in parallel and synchronize on actions from a given set of actions. The main use of such an operation is for coupling a system with a *tester* which tests for the satisfaction of a given property. Opposite to the synchronous parallel composition is the asynchronous parallel composition, which does not assume any action synchronization but the systems may communicate via a set of shared variables (locations). The execution of such a system can be viewed as the *interleaved execution* of the components. For examples of parallel compositions of Petri nets the reader is referred to [5, 10, 18, 23–25].

In order to avoid some annoying and totally unessential things for our purpose we assume that two disjoint countable sets $\mathcal{S}$ and $\mathcal{T}$ are given, and all the nets we consider have the sets of places and transitions included in $\mathcal{S}$ and $\mathcal{T}$, respectively. For a finite set $S^c \subset \mathcal{S}$ and a marking M_0^c on S^c (that is, $M_0^c : S^c \rightarrow \mathbf{N}$) consider the set $PN(S^c, M_0^c)$ of all modules whose set of places includes S^c and whose initial marking agrees with M_0^c on S^c. Two modules $\mathcal{M}_0$ and $\mathcal{M}_1$ in this set are called *compatible* if $S_0 \cap S_1 = S^c$ and $T_0 \cap T_1 = \emptyset$.

Definition 2.4. *Let* $\mathcal{M}_0, \mathcal{M}_1 \in PN(S^c, M_0^c)$ *be two compatible modules. The* asynchronous parallel composition *of* $\mathcal{M}_0$ *and* $\mathcal{M}_1$, *denoted by* $\mathcal{M}_0 \circ \mathcal{M}_1$, *is the componentwise union of* $\mathcal{M}_0$ *and* $\mathcal{M}_1$, *that is:*

- $\mathcal{M}_0 \circ \mathcal{M}_1 = (\gamma, S^c)$, $\gamma = (\Sigma, M_0, l)$, *and* $\Sigma = (S, T, F, W)$;

- S, T, F, W, M_0 *and* l *are the union of the sets of places, transitions, flow relations, weight functions, markings and labelling functions of* $\mathcal{M}_0$ *and* $\mathcal{M}_1$, *respectively.*

We note that the unions of functions in Definition 2.4 are well-defined. In the case of M_0 we can write $M_0 = M_0^0|_{S_0^i} + M_0^c + M_0^1|_{S_1^i}$, where M_0^0 and M_0^1 are the initial markings of $\mathcal{M}_0$ and $\mathcal{M}_1$, respectively. The module $\mathcal{M}_0 \circ \mathcal{M}_1$ is an element of $PN(S^c, M_0^c)$.

To have a flexible notation we will identify a module $\mathcal{M} = (\gamma, S^c)$ by its underlying net γ, whenever S^c is clear from context; correspondingly, an e-module $\mathcal{J} = (\mathcal{M}, R)$ will

---

[2]The approach we considered for an environment, and for the corresponding transition rule, does not take into account the internal structure neither of the module nor of the environment. This one could appear unrealistic. But, we want to use e-modules for abstraction purposes, and if we should take into consideration the entire internal structure of the module and of the environment then such a purpose can be never reached. However, an intermediate variant of taking into account partial information about their internal structure (or to use something like semaphor variables) could be an worthy idea.

be written as $\mathcal{J} = (\gamma, R)$. Moreover, for $\gamma_0, \gamma_1 \in PN(S^c, M_0^c)$ we will write $\gamma_0 \circ \gamma_1$ instead of $\mathcal{M}_0 \circ \mathcal{M}_1$ and we call it the *composition of* γ_0 *and* γ_1 *along* S^c or, simply, the *composition of* γ_0 *and* γ_1.

Let $ePN(S^c, M_0^c)$ be the set of all e-modules whose underlying modules are alements of $PN(S^c, M_0^c)$. Two e-modules in this set are called *compatible* when their underlying modules are compatible. The asynchronous parallel composition can be extended to compatible e-modules in $ePN(S^c, M_0^c)$ by

$$\mathcal{J}_0 \circ \mathcal{J}_1 = (\mathcal{M}_0 \circ \mathcal{M}_1, R_0 \cup R_1).$$

The asynchronous parallel composition of (e-)modules in $(e)PN(S^c, M_0^c)$ is a partially defined binary operation. It is commutative and associative whenever it is defined; that is, $x_0 \circ x_1 = x_1 \circ x_0$ and $(x_0 \circ x_1) \circ x_2 = x_0 \circ (x_1 \circ x_2)$, for all pairwise compatible (e-)modules x_0, x_1 and x_2. Moreover, the module $\gamma_\emptyset = ((S^c, \emptyset, \emptyset, \emptyset), M_0^c, \emptyset)$, or $(\gamma_\emptyset, \emptyset)$ in case of e-modules, is the unit of this operation [3].

An important and intensively used method for trying to verify a system is to decompose the system, to verify properties of individual components, and to infer from these some properties of the system. There are many ways to decompose a system into components. The one we consider is closely related to the asynchronous parallel composition; it is a *decomposition along* a set of places. It is obvious that, given a net γ and a subset of places S^c, the decomposition along S^c is not unique and, moreover, if we want to have some properties of components, it is not all the time possible. For example, if we consider the net γ in Figure 1 and $S^c = \{s_1\}$, then there is no decomposition of γ into two modules each of them having one transition and such that their asynchronous composition lead to the original net γ. However,

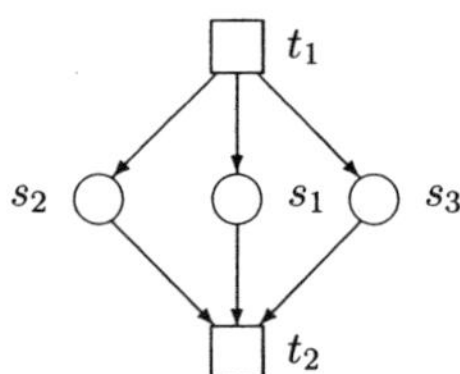

Figure 1. A Petri net with no module decomposition

the decomposition based on subnets generated by subsets of transitions is indeed the inverse operation of the asynchronous composition. If $\Sigma = (S, T, F, W)$ is a net and T_1 is a subset of T, by the *subnet generated by* T_1 we understand the net $\Sigma_1 = (S_1, T_1, F_1, W_1)$, where $S_1 = {}^\bullet T_1^\bullet$, and F_1 and W_1 are the corresponding restrictions of F and W to S_1 and T_1. The subnet generated by $T - T_1$ will be called the *difference* of Σ and Σ_1, and it will be denoted by $\Sigma - \Sigma_1$ (the set ${}^\bullet T_1^\bullet \cap {}^\bullet(T - T_1)^\bullet$ plays the role of interface places between Σ_1 and $\Sigma - \Sigma_1$). These concepts can be naturally extended to (labelled) marked nets. It is clear now that the asynchronous composition of two nets γ_1 and $\gamma - \gamma_1$ as above, along the common set of places, leads to the net γ.

---

[3]One may consider the equivalence relation $\equiv$ on $PN(S^c, M_0^c)$ induced by isomorphisms of labelled nets which preserve S^c (that is, their restrictions to S^c is the identity on S^c) and their initial markings, and define the asynchronous parallel composition on equivalence classes by means of any two compatible representatives of that classes. Then, this operation is totally defined on the quotient set $PN(S^c, M_0^c)/\equiv$ and structures it as a monoid.

We close the section by an example of decomposition which will be used in the next section in order to exemplify process decomposition and process sample generation. The net in Figure 2.2 is a Petri net model of the *Owicki-Lamport's Mutex algorithm*. It consists essentially of two sites: the *writer* and *reader* site, the first one to the left, and the second one to the right, of the dashbox in figure. The net uses three flags: the flag *writer detached* (s_2) signals to the reader that the writer is presently not striving to become *writing*, the flag *reader detached* (s_3) likewise signals to the writer that the reader is presently not striving to become *reading*, and the flag *writer involved* (s_1) is just the complement of writer detached (for a detailed discussion about this net model the reader is referred to [15]). That two sites

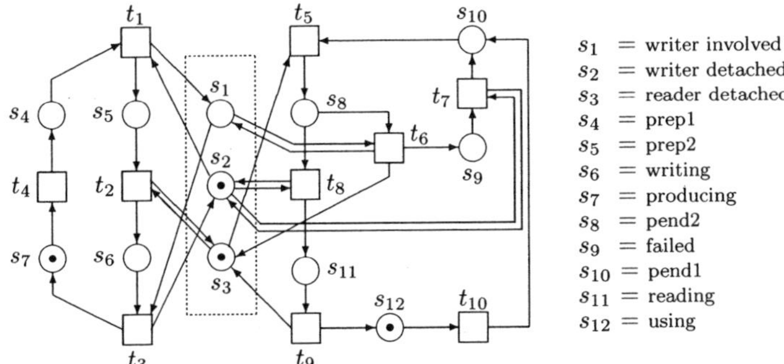

$$
\begin{aligned}
s_1 &= \text{writer involved} \\
s_2 &= \text{writer detached} \\
s_3 &= \text{reader detached} \\
s_4 &= \text{prep1} \\
s_5 &= \text{prep2} \\
s_6 &= \text{writing} \\
s_7 &= \text{producing} \\
s_8 &= \text{pend2} \\
s_9 &= \text{failed} \\
s_{10} &= \text{pend1} \\
s_{11} &= \text{reading} \\
s_{12} &= \text{using}
\end{aligned}
$$

Figure 2. Owicki-Lamport's Mutex algorithm

of the net in Figure 2 are connected each other by means of s_1, s_2 and s_3. We may separate them into two nets γ_0 and γ_1 by multiplying twice these places togheter with their initial markings (Figure 3). Thus, we obtain two nets γ_0 and γ_1 whose asynchronous composition

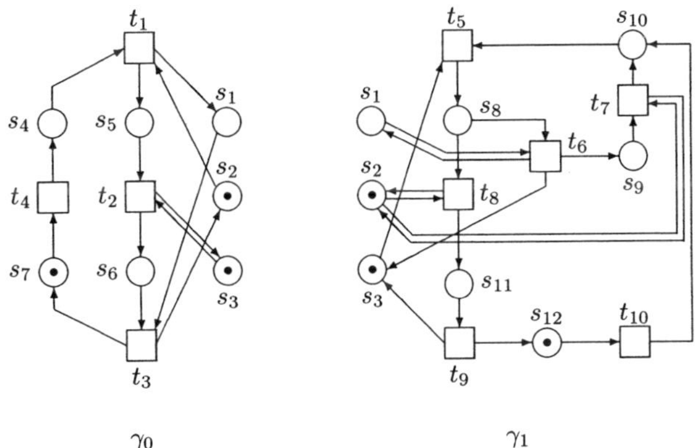

Figure 3. A decomposition of the Petri net in Figure 2

along $\{s_1, s_2, s_3\}$ is γ.

3   Process Decomposition w.r.t. Asynchronous Composition

This section addresses two main problems with respect to the asynchronous parallel composition of two modules $\mathcal{M}_0$ and $\mathcal{M}_1$ with the same set of interface places:

1. What is the structure of processes of $\mathcal{M}_0 \circ \mathcal{M}_1$? Can we decompose them into processes of $\mathcal{M}_0$ and $\mathcal{M}_1$? Can we get them by composing arbitrary processes of $\mathcal{M}_0$ and $\mathcal{M}_1$?

2. Can we generate "fragments" of processes of $\mathcal{M}_0 \circ \mathcal{M}_1$ corresponding to $\mathcal{M}_0$ or $\mathcal{M}_1$?

In what follows, we will give a complete answer to the first question, and a partial answer to the second question.

Let us consider the process π pictorially represented in Figure 4, of the net γ from Figure 2. This process can be split into two parts (occurrence nets) π_0 and π_1 as in Figure 5, according to the decomposition of γ (Figure 3). The initial cut of π_0 generates a marking

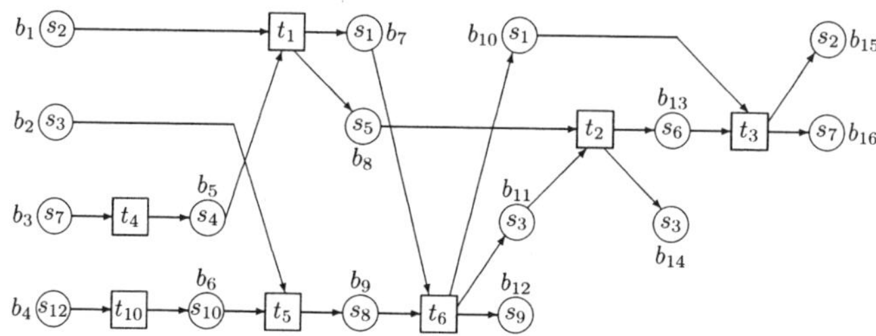

Figure 4. A process of the Petri net in Figure 2

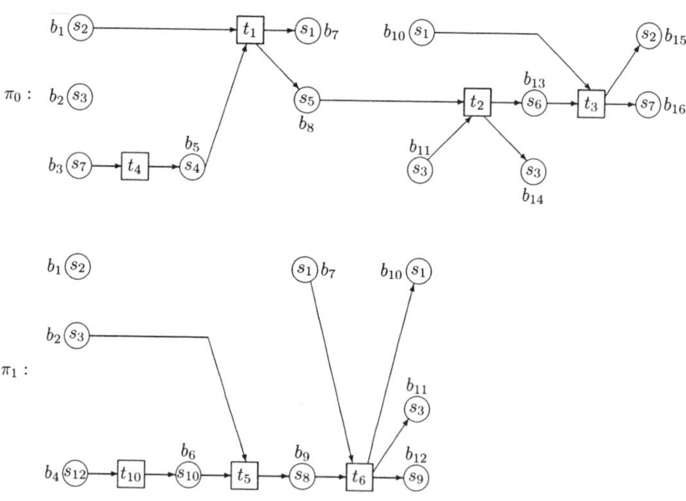

Figure 5. A decomposition of the process in Figure 4

of γ_0 with one token in s_1 and two tokens in s_3, which is neither reachable in γ nor in γ_0; similarly, the initial cut of π_1 generates a marking of γ_1 with one token in each of the places

s_1, s_2 and s_3, which is neither reachable in γ nor in γ_1. However, π_0 (π_1) can become a process of γ_0 (γ_1) if we increase the initial marking of γ_0 (γ_1) by one token in s_1 and one in s_3 (one token in s_1). This fact is not a fortuitous one but it is a particular case of the process decomposition theorem as we will see later.

First, we mention that labelled occurrence nets are particular nets whose places are labelled as well. Therefore, we can extend the definition of composition along a set S^c to the case of these nets by requiring supplementary $p_1(s) = p_2(s)$ for all $s \in S^c$ (p_1 and p_2 are the corresponding labelling functions). Then, we adopt one more notation. For a Petri net $\gamma = (\Sigma, M_0, l) \in PN(S^c, M_0^c)$ and a marking $M \in \mathbf{N}^{S^c}$, we denote by $(\gamma + M)$ the Petri net $(\Sigma, M_0 + M, l) \in PN(S^c, M_0^c + M)$. For every two compatible nets $\gamma_1, \gamma_2 \in PN(S^c, M_0^c)$ and every marking $M \in \mathbf{N}^{S^c}$ we have $((\gamma_1 \circ \gamma_2) + M) = (\gamma_1 + M) \circ (\gamma_2 + M)$.

Theorem 3.1. (Process decomposition theorem)
Let $\gamma_0, \gamma_1 \in PN(S^c, M_0^c)$ be two compatible nets. For each process $\pi \in \Pi(\gamma_0 \circ \gamma_1)$ there are two markings $M', M'' \in \mathbf{N}^{S^c}$ and two processes $\pi_0 \in \Pi(\gamma_0 + M')$ and $\pi_1 \in \Pi(\gamma_1 + M'')$ such that $\pi = \pi_0 \circ \pi_1$ (the composition of processes is along some set of common conditions).

Proof. [20].　　　　　　　　　　　　　　　　　　　　　　　　　　　　$\square$

The occurrence net π_0 (π_1) in the theorem above will be called a *process sample of π w.r.t. γ_0 (γ_1).* The set of all process samples of γ w.r.t. γ_0 will be denoted by $\Pi(\gamma, \gamma_0)$.

π_0 and π_1 in Figure 5 are processes of $(\gamma_0 + (1, 0, 1))$ and $(\gamma_1 + (1, 0, 0))$, respectively (the order on the interface places is s_1, s_2, s_3). Therefore, π_0 is a process sample of π w.r.t. γ_0, and π_1 is a process sample of π w.r.t. γ_1.

We will consider now the converse of Theorem 3.1. Let $\gamma \in PN(S^c, M_0^c)$, π a process of γ, and let $C(\pi)$ be the set of all conditions of π labelled by places in S^c. A *p-partition* of $C(\pi)$ is a couple of sets $(A, C(\pi) - A)$ such that $A \subseteq C(\pi)$, $(\forall b \in C(\pi) - A)(|{}^\bullet b| = 1)$, and $(\forall b \in C(\pi))(|{}^\bullet b \cup b^\bullet| = 2 \Rightarrow b \in C(\pi) - A)$.

Let $\gamma_0, \gamma_1 \in PN(S^c, M_0^c)$, $\pi_0 \in \Pi(\gamma_0)$ and $\pi_1 \in \Pi(\gamma_1)$. A *p-composition function* from π_0 to π_1 is any labelled-preserving bijection $f : A_0 \to A_1$ such that:

(1) $(A_0, C(\pi_0) - A_0)$ is a p-partition of $C(\pi_0)$, and $(A_1, C(\pi_1) - A_1)$ is a p-partition of $C(\pi_1)$;

(2) $(\forall b_0, b_1)(f(b_0) = b_1 \Rightarrow |{}^\bullet b_0 \cup {}^\bullet b_1| \leq 1 \wedge |b_0^\bullet \cup b_1^\bullet| \leq 1)$;

(3) $(\forall b_0, b_1)(f(b_0) = b_1 \wedge |{}^\bullet b_0 \cup {}^\bullet b_1| = 1 \Rightarrow |b_0^\bullet \cup b_1^\bullet| = 1)$;

(4) $(\not\exists b_0, b_1, b_0', b_1')(f(b_0) = b_1 \wedge f(b_0') = b_1' \wedge b_1 \prec_{\pi_1} b_1' \wedge b_0' \prec_{\pi_0} b_0)$.

Moreover, if f satisfies

(5) $M' = M_{\{b \in Cod(f) \mid |{}^\bullet b| = 1\}}$ and $M'' = M_{\{b \in Dom(f) \mid |{}^\bullet b| = 1\}}$,

then it is called *compatible with M' and M''.*

Theorem 3.2. (Process composition theorem)
Let $\gamma_0, \gamma_1 \in PN(S^c, M_0^c)$ be two compatible nets, $M', M'' \in \mathbf{N}^{S^c}$, $\pi_0 \in \Pi(\gamma_0 + M')$ and $\pi_1 \in \Pi(\gamma_1 + M'')$. Then, for every p-composition function $f : A_0 \to A_1$ from π_0 to π_1 compatible with M' and M'', there is a process $\pi_1' \in \Pi(\gamma_1 + M'')$ such that:

(1) π_1' is obtained from π_1 by renaming its elements (but not the labels) [4];

(2) $\pi_0 \circ \pi_1' \in \Pi(\gamma_0 \circ \gamma_1)$ (the composition of processes is along A_0, whereas the composition of nets is along S^c).

Proof. [20]. □

Theorems 3.1 and 3.2 give a complete answer to our first question. Moreover, they lead to a compositional semantics of modules, as follows. For a net $\gamma \in PN(S^c, M_0^c)$ define

$$\Pi_m(\gamma) = \bigcup_{M \in N^{S^c}} \Pi(\gamma + M).$$

Consider then the process composition operator $\circ_{M_0^c}$ as suggested by the composition theorem. Formally, let $\gamma_0, \gamma_1 \in PN(S^c, M_0^c)$ be two compatible nets. Then, for every $M', M'' \in N^{S^c}$, $\pi_0 \in \Pi(\gamma_0 + M')$ and $\pi_1 \in \Pi(\gamma_1 + M'')$, $\pi_0 \circ_{M_0^c} \pi_1$ is the set of all processes $\pi_0 \circ \pi_1$, where the composition, whenever it is possible, is along some set A_0 of conditions such that there is a p-composition function from π_0 to π_1 compatible with M' and M'' and whose domain is A_0. Extend then this operation, by union, to sets of processes.

Corollary 3.1. *Let $\gamma_0, \gamma_1 \in PN(S^c, M_0^c)$ be two compatible nets. Then,*

$$\Pi(\gamma_0 \circ \gamma_1) = \Pi_m(\gamma_0) \circ_{M_0^c} \Pi_m(\gamma_1).$$

Proof. Directly from definitions, composition and decomposition theorems. □

Define now the composition operator $\circ_{\geq M_0^c}$ on processes of compatible nets $\gamma_0, \gamma_1 \in PN(S^c, M_0^c)$, as follows. For every $M', M'' \in N^{S^c}$, $\pi_0 \in \Pi(\gamma_0 + M')$ and $\pi_1 \in \Pi(\gamma_1 + M'')$, $\pi_0 \circ_{\geq M_0^c} \pi_1$ is the set of all processes $\pi_0 \circ \pi_1$, where the composition, whenever it is possible, is along some set A_0 of conditions such that there is a p-composition function from π_0 to π_1 compatible with $M' - M$ and $M'' - M$ and whose domain is A_0, for some marking M smaller than both M' and M''. Extend then this operation, by union, to sets of processes.

Corollary 3.2. *Let $\gamma_0, \gamma_1 \in PN(S^c, M_0^c)$ be two compatible nets. Then,*

$$\Pi_m(\gamma_0 \circ \gamma_1) = \Pi_m(\gamma_0) \circ_{\geq M_0^c} \Pi_m(\gamma_1).$$

Proof. [20]. □

A partial answer to the second question was given in [19], where a technique based on e-modules was proposed. Let us recall first the concept of a *jumping (Petri) net* in a slightly different way than in [17]; this concept is a natural generalization of the concept of an e-module by allowing more sets of interface places.

---

[4]Formally, there is a bijection $\varphi : B_1 \cup E_1 \rightarrow B_1' \cup E_1'$ such that:

(i) $p_1(x) = p_1'(\varphi(x))$, for all $x \in B_1 \cup E_1$;

(ii) $x \prec_{\pi_1} y$ iff $\varphi(x) \prec_{\pi_1'} \varphi(y)$, for all $x \in B_1 \cup E_1$

(p_1 and p_1' are the labelling functions of π_1 and π_1', respectively). In fact, this is the classical concept of *isomorphism* of processes. We did not consider it yet because in Section 4.1 we will introduce a more general concept of isomorphism – see also the concept of a (j, λ)-*isomorphism* in the next section.

Definition 3.1. *A* jumping net (marked jumping net, labelled marked jumping net) *is a couple* $\mathcal{J} = (\gamma, R)$, *where* γ *is a net (marked net, labelled marked net) and* R *is a finite union of sets, each of which being a binary relation on* $\mathrm{N}^{S'}$ *for some* $S' \subseteq S$.

The elements of R are called *jumps* of $\mathcal{J}$. A jump (M, M'), where $M, M' \in \mathrm{N}^{S'}$ and $S' \subseteq S$, is called *local on* S'. For technical reasons we extend jumps to the whole set S of places of γ, as follows:

$$M\,R\,M' \;\Leftrightarrow\; M|_{S'}\,R\,M'|_{S'} \text{ and } M|_{S-S'} = M'|_{S-S'},$$

for all markings $M, M' \in \mathrm{N}^S$, where $S' \subseteq S$ and $(M|_{S'}, M'|_{S'})$ is a local jump on S'.

A computation step in a jumping net $\mathcal{J} = (\gamma, R)$ is performed either by a transition, in the usual way, or by a jump. That is,

$$M[x\rangle M' \;\Leftrightarrow\; \text{either } x \in T \text{ and } M[x\rangle_\gamma M', \text{ or } x \in R \text{ and } M\,R\,M'.$$

In the case $R \subseteq \mathrm{N}^{S'} \times \mathrm{N}^{S'}$ for some $S' \subseteq S$, labelled marked jumping nets correspond exactly to e-modules (with the set S' of interface places).

Local jumps which do not affect all places of a net can occur concurrently with each other or concurrently with transition occurrences. This is formally reflected in the following definition of processes of jumping nets (for convenience we will adopt an inductive definition). Let $\mathcal{J} = (\gamma, R)$ be a marked jumping Petri net, t a transition and $r = (M, M')$ a local jump on a subset $S' \subseteq S$. Then:

- an *elementary occurrence net* associated to t is a labelled occurrence net $\pi = (N, p)$ with the properties: π contains only one event e labelled by t, $W(s, t)$ preconditions and $W(t, s)$ postconditions of e labelled by s, for all $s \in S$, and no other element;

- an *elementary occurrence net* associated to r is a labelled occurrence net $\pi = (N, p)$ with the properties: π contains only one event e labelled by r, $M(s)$ preconditions and $M'(s)$ postconditions of e labelled by s, for all $s \in S'$, and no other element;

- an *initial occurrence net* of γ is an occurrence net (N, p) which does not contain any event and, for each $s \in S$, it contains exactly $M_0(s)$ conditions labelled by s.

Definition 3.2. *Let* $\mathcal{J} = (\gamma, R)$ *be a marked jumping net. The* set of processes *of* $\mathcal{J}$, *denoted by* $\Pi(\mathcal{J})$, *is the smallest set with the properties:*

(1) $\Pi(\mathcal{J})$ *contains all the initial occurrence nets associated to* $\mathcal{J}$;

(2) if $\pi_1 \in \Pi(\mathcal{J})$ *and* π_2 *is an elementary occurrence net associated to a transition* t *such that* $^\circ\pi_2 \subseteq \pi_1^\circ$, *then the composition of* π_1 *and* π_2 *along* $^\circ\pi_2$, *whenever it is possible, is in* $\Pi(\mathcal{J})$;

(3) if $\pi_1 \in \Pi(\mathcal{J})$ *and* π_2 *is an elementary occurrence net associated to a local jump* $r = (M, M')$ *on a subset* S' *of places such that* $|\pi_1^\circ \cap p_1^{-1}(s)| = M(s)$ *for all* $s \in S'$, *then the composition of* π_1 *and* π_2 *along* $^\circ\pi_2$, *whenever it is possible, is in* $\Pi(\mathcal{J})$.

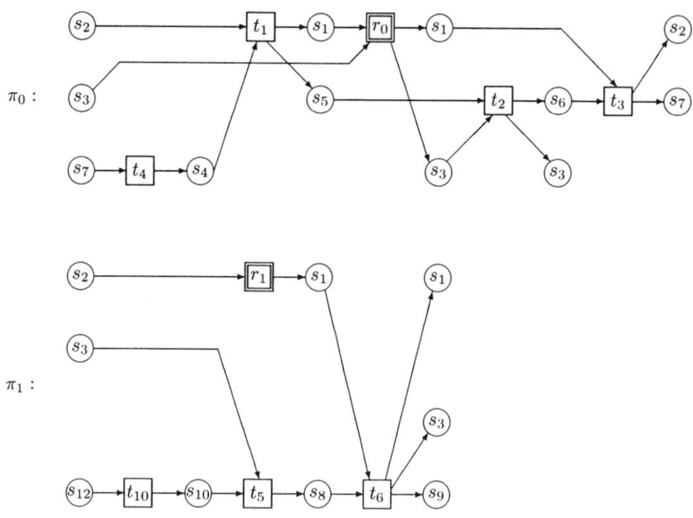

Figure 6. Processes of jumping Petri nets

Let $\mathcal{J}_0 = (\gamma_0, R_0)$ and $\mathcal{J}_1 = (\gamma_1, R_1)$, where γ_0 and γ_1 are the nets in Figure 2, and R_0 and R_1 are relations on $\mathbf{N}^{S^c}$ containing $r_0 = ((1,0,1),(1,0,1))$ and $r_1 = ((0,1,1),(1,0,1))$, respectively. Then, π_0 *(π_1)* in Figure 6 is a process of $\mathcal{J}_0$ *($\mathcal{J}_1$)*.

Let us note that a subnet γ_1 of a net γ may *induce* some jumps for the net $\gamma - \gamma_1$. Moreover, it may induce the same jump at different markings of γ. If the jumps induced by γ_1 do not depend on the internal configuration of γ_1, but just on the marking on the interface places, then γ is called γ_1-*context free*.

Let $\mathcal{J} = (\gamma, R)$ be a jumping net. For each process π of $\mathcal{J}$ we define a new occurrence net by removing all the events labelled by jumps (and the corresponding arcs). Let $\Pi'(\mathcal{J})$ be the set of all these occurrence nets. We note that for every $\mathcal{J} = (\gamma, R)$, $\Pi(\gamma) \subseteq \Pi'(\mathcal{J})$.

Theorem 3.3. (Process sample generation theorem)
Let $\gamma_0, \gamma_1 \in PN(S^c, M_0^c)$ be two compatible nets, and $\gamma = \gamma_0 \circ \gamma_1$. If γ is γ_1-context free then $\Pi(\gamma, \gamma_0) = \Pi'(\mathcal{J})$, where $\mathcal{J} = (\gamma_0, R_0)$ and R_0 is the set of jumps induced by γ_1 in γ.

Proof. [20].   □

4   Applications

In this section we sketch four main applications of the decomposition results in Section 3.

Concurrent Behavior and Replacement   Many transformations of Petri nets may be simply described by "replace the subnet γ_1 of γ by the net γ_2"; that means the subnet γ_1 will be removed from γ and the net γ_2 is inserted in its place (denote the result by $\gamma[\gamma_1 \leftarrow \gamma_2]$). When γ_2 is "more detailed" than γ_1, this operation is usually called a *refinement*; otherwise it is called an *abstraction*. Both of them are particular cases of *replacement*. One of the main problem in connection with replacement is the following: find some equivalence relations on nets, $\approx_1$ and $\approx_2$, such that $\gamma_1 \approx_1 \gamma_2$ implies $\gamma \approx_2 \gamma[\gamma_1 \leftarrow \gamma_2]$.

Based on process decomposition results in Section 3, two such pairs of equivalence relations have been proposed in [18] (see also [20]). They are very powerful because they preserve the process and partial word semantics of Petri nets.

Proving Correcteness of Petri Net Structural Transformations   Many structural transformations on Petri nets can be described in terms of subnet replacement, where the subnets are generated by subsets of places. In such cases, the results in Section 3 can be successfully used in order to prove the correctness of the transformation, as it has been shown in [20].

Validation of Petri Net Models   One aim of simulation is to *validate* the model w.r.t. some desired behavioural properties (that is, to check whether the desired properties are reflected or not in the simulated runs of the model). As we could expect, many problems are encountered when dealing with simulation of a Petri net model: fairness, alternatives (solving conflicts), termination conditions, visualization and property checking for large processes, etc. All these problems could be grouped into two main classes: *generation* and *analysis* of processes. Therefore, it turns out to be an important task to look for an adequate tool to represent and generate processes as well as for an efficient strategy for analyzing them.

The results developed in Section 3 can be used for validation of Petri net models, based on decompositions

$$\gamma = \gamma_0 \circ (\gamma_1 \circ \cdots \circ (\gamma_{n-1} \circ \gamma_n) \cdots)$$

(when they exist). The validation is then performed bottom up, starting with γ_n, then defining a jumping net $\mathcal{J}_{n-1}$ in order to generate process samples and validate γ_{n-1} in the context of γ_n, and so on. For details concerning this technique the reader is referred to [19] or [20].

Model Checking Petri Net Modules   The decomposition results in Section 3 lead naturally to the following question: is it possible to find a modular model checking methodology for Petri net models ? The answer to this question is positive as it has been shown in [21].

5   Conclusions and Related Work

Nets equiped with subsets of interface places (modules, in our paper) appear naturally when a distributed systems is modelled as a set of actors communicating through buffers by message passing. In this context, composition of nets by merging places (asynchronous composition, in our paper) is an important operation. In literature, different variants of modules and asynchronous compositions have been considered. In [4], the modules (called there *open interface nets*) are non-labelled and endowed with a set of markings on the internal places (called stable states). Our modules are exactly those from [24] (called there *host nets*) or [23] (called there *net components*), with the difference that in [23] they are not labelled; the asynchronous composition for modules we considered is like in [24] (called there *place composition*). The set of interface places may be partitioned (as we have already said in Section 2) into subsets of input and output places as in [10]. The concept of an e-module is a new one; however, the idea of considering the interaction between a module and an environment has been touched on in [24] (by adding two transitions t_s^- and t_s^+, for each interface place s), in [23] (by means of *actions*, which are jumps in our paper), and in [10], but in a totally different way and with different purposes than ours. The terminology of *Petri net (reactive) module*, as we considered, seems to be the most adequate one in the context of modelling reactive systems which may interact with each other.

Section 3 considers the (plain) process semantics together with a notion of process isomorphism (different than the classical one), suitable in proving correctness of Petri net transformations. It is shown that processes of composed nets can be decomposed in processes of "shifted" components (that is, components whose initial markings are increased), and vice versa. Clearly, this semantics is not compositional with respect to the operation of composition we considered, but with a little effort we can obtain a compositional one (Corollary 3.2); it is totally diferrent than the semantics considered in the papers cited above. For example, the process semantics in [10] was suitable modified such that the compositional property was achieved, and the CFFD-semantics in [23] is a conjunction of stable failures, divergence traces, and infinite traces (which lead to compositionality). The paper [19] takes into consideration the generation of process samples of a module w.r.t. some submodules. The generation is done via e-modules which are particular cases of jumping nets (as we have mentioned, [23] consideres actions which are jumps in our terminology, and which are used as an abstraction mechanism but in a different way than us; the concept of a jump and its main use as an abstraction mechanism goes back to [16] and [17]).

Finding efficient methods to describe or approximate the set of jumps induced by submodules is of great importance for practical applications. Certainly, there is no general method to that; we have to restrict ourself to subclasses of (safe) nets, and this one could be an interesting subject of study. By taking into consideration partial information about the internal structure of the module and/or environment (as it has been already mentioned in Section 2) we can reduce the size of the set of jumps. On the other side, using semaphor variables (as partial information), the interface places may be regarded both as input and output places, without a specific distinction. When some semaphor variable is on, the module and the environment may work together; when the variable is off, only the environment may work. The environment is setting this variable; the module has just to use read arcs [25] in order to know when it has the right to work.

References

[1] R. Alur, Th.A. Henziger: *Reactive Modules*, in: Proc. of the 11th IEEE Symposium on Logic in Computer Science LICS, 1996, 207–218.

[2] S. Berezin, S. Campos, E.M. Clarke: *Compositional Reasoning in Model Checking*, in: Proc. of the International Symposium "Compositionality: The Significant Difference" COMPOS'97, Bad Malente (Germany), Sept 8–12, 1997, Lecture Notes in Computer Science 1536, Springer-Verlag, 1998, 81–102.

[3] E. Best, C. Fernandez: *Nonsequential Processes. A Petri Net Point of View*, EATCS Monographs on Theoretical Computer Science, Springer-Verlag, 1988.

[4] G. Chehaibar: *Replacement of Open Interface Subnets and Stable State Transformation Equivalence*, in: Advances in Petri Nets 1993, Lecture Notes in Computer Science 674, Springer-Verlag, 1993, 1–25.

[5] W. Damm, G. Döhmen, V. Gerstner: *Modular Verification of Petri Nets. The Temporal Logic Approach*, in: Proc. of the REX Workshop on Stepwise Refinement of Distributed Systems, Models, Formalisms, Correctness (J.W. Bakker, W.-P. de Roever, G. Rozenberg, eds.), Lecture Notes in Computer Science 430, Springer-Verlag, 1989, 180–207.

[6] J. Desel, W. Reisig: *Place/Transition Petri Nets*, in: Lectures on Petri Nets I: Basic Models (W. Reisig, G. Rozenberg, eds.), Lecture Notes in Computer Science 1491, Springer-Verlag, 1998, 122–173.

[7] O. Grumberg, D.E. Long: *Model Checking and Modular Verification*, ACM Transactions on Programming Languages and Systems 16, 1994, 843–871.

[8] B. Josko: *Verifying the Correctness of AADL-Modules Using Model Checking*, in: Proc. of the REX Workshop on Stepwise Refinement of Distributed Systems, Models, Formalisms, Correctness (J.W. Bakker, W.-P. de Roever, G. Rozenberg, eds.), Lecture Notes in Computer Science 430, Springer-Verlag, 1989, 386–400.

[9] Y. Kersten, A. Pnueli: *Modularization and Abstraction: The Keys to Practical Formal Verification*, in: Proc. of the 23rd International Symposium on Mathematical Foundations of Computer Science MFCS'98, Lecture Notes in Computer Science 1450, Springer-Verlag, 1998, 54–71.

[10] E. Kindler: *A Compositional Partial Order Semantics for Petri Net Components*, in Proc. of the 18th International Conference on Application and Theory of Petri Nets, Toulouse (France), Lecture Notes in Computer Science 1248, Springer-Verlag, 1998, 235–252.

[11] O. Kupferman, M.Y. Vardi: *Modular Model Checking*, in: Proc. of the International Symposium "Compositionality: The Significant Difference" COMPOS'97, Bad Malente (Germany), Sept 8–12, 1997, Lecture Notes in Computer Science 1536, Springer-Verlag, 1998, 381–401.

[12] Z. Manna, A. Pnueli: *The Temporal Logic of Reactive and Concurrent Systems. Specification*, Springer-Verlag, 1992.

[13] J.L. Peterson: *Petri Net Theory and the Modelling of Systems*, Prentice-Hall, 1981.

[14] W. Reisig: *Petri Nets. An Introduction*, EATCS Monographs on Theoretical Computer Science, Springer-Verlag, 1985.

[15] W. Reisig: *Elements of Distributed Algorithms. Modeling and Analysis with Petri Nets*, Springer-Verlag, 1998.

[16] F.L. Ţiplea: *Contributions to the Language Theory of Petri Nets*, Ph.D. Thesis, "Al.I.Cuza" University of Iasi (Romania), 1993.

[17] F.L. Ţiplea, T. Jucan: *Jumping Petri Nets*, Foundations of Computing and Decision Sciences 19, 1994, 319–332.

[18] F.L. Ţiplea, M. Katsura, M. Ito: *On Replacement of Petri Nets and Some Applications*, in: Proc. of the Workshop on Semigroups, Formal Languages and Computer Systems, RIMS Kokyuroku 960, Kyoto (Japan), 1996, 178–180.

[19] F.L. Ţiplea, J. Desel: *Petri Net Process Decomposition with Application to Validation*, in: Proc of the 6th Workshop "Algorithmen und Werkzeuge für Petrinetze", Frankfurt am Main (Germany), Oct 11–12, 1999.

[20] F.L. Ţiplea, A. Ţiplea: *Petri Net Reactive Modules*, Technical Report 1999-7, Institut für Informatik, Universität Uagsburg (Germany), 1999, 50 pp.

[21] F.L. Ţiplea, A. Ţiplea: *A Simulation Preorder for Abstraction of Reactive Systems*, in: Proc. of the 3rd International Workshop on Verification, Model Checking, and Abstract Interpretation, Venice (Italy), LNCS 2294, 2002, 272–288.

[22] R. Valette: *Analysis of Petri Nets by Stepwise Refinement*, Journal of Computer and System Science 18, 1979, 35–46.

[23] A. Valmari: *Compositional Analysis with Place-Bordered Subnets*, in Proc. of the 15th International Conference on Application and Theory of Petri Nets, Lecture Notes in Computer Science 815, Springer-Verlag, 1994, 531–547.

[24] W. Vogler: *Modular Construction and Partial Order Semantics of Petri Nets*, Lecture Notes in Computer Science 625, Springer-Verlag, 1992.

[25] W. Vogler: *Efficiency of Asynchronous Systems, Read Arcs, and the MUTEX-Problem*, in: Proc. of ICALP'97 (P. Degano, R. Gorrieri, A. Marchetti-Spaccamela, eds.), Lecture Notes in Computer Science 1256, Springer-Verlag, 1997, 538–548 (full version as Technical Report 352, Institut für Informatik, Universität Augsburg, 1996).

Concurrent Information Processing and Computing
D. Grigoras and A. Nicolau (Eds.)
IOS Press, 2005

Transaction Processing for Clustered Virtual Environments

Christian Schallhart

Institut für Informatik
Technische Universität München
`schallha@cs.tum.edu`

Abstract. This paper introduces Massively Multi-Player Online Role Games (MMORGS) which are currently a main focus of the gaming industry. MMORGS are Networked Virtual Environments (NVES) where a player can navigate his or her character through a large game-world which is populated by thousands of other players and non player characters. Based the problems arising in the context of MMORGS, we will motivate the development of a domain-independent middleware to support MMORG in particular and networked NVES in general. Finally, we will introduce APEIRON, a middleware which is based on a flexible transaction processing framework. APEIRON is designed to serve as basis for the next generation MMORG.

1   Introduction

In this paper we will motivate the development of a middleware which is projected as basis for networked virtual environments (NVES). Today, applications from diverse domains such as cooperative work and military simulations are collectively called NVES. To cope with the differing requirements which are associated with these applications, a couple of frameworks have been proposed and implemented, see [7] for a categorization of these approaches and an overview over of corresponding implementations.
Each of these frameworks was built without any separation between the domain-specific and domain-independent issues. Therefore, these solutions tend to be relatively inflexible.

Currently, the entertainment industry is developing so-called Massively Multi-Player Online Role Games (MMORGS). A MMORG simulates a game-world which is populated by thousands of different characters. Some of these characters are controlled by human players while others are controlled by the MMORG system. The user is connected to the virtual game world through the internet and observes his or her character from the third person perspective. MMORGS are challenging for several reasons such as high scalability and realism.

We propose a transaction based middleware, called APEIRON, to support MMORGS. Because of the real-time character of such simulation, the common transaction semantics must be expanded to guarantee non-blocking access. We choose transactions as the central abstraction in our middleware, since they allow to state the required synchronization guarantees in an abstract and uniform way. Thus, we do not confront the application developer with a number of low-level primitives but with a single method to organize the synchronization of different applications. Also a number of different implementations can be used with the same principal interface such that different platforms can be supported effectively and more importantly, an incremental development is manageable in clean way.

The paper starts with a brief introduction of NVES. In the following section, MMORGS are described and presented as an interesting research object. Section 4 gives an overview on the domain specific services of a MMORG. Finally, Section 5 proposes a domain-independent middleware solution for MMORGS in particular (and NVES in general) followed by some concluding remarks.

2 Networked Virtual Environments

The terms virtual reality and virtual environment have been used with varying meanings. The ambiguity of these terms is rooted in the wide range of applications which are based upon virtual reality. Examples for such applications include military simulations, educational systems, as well as entertainment applications. Thus, many definitions on different flavors of virtual reality systems have been introduced, to distinguish between these varying technologies which are related to virtual environments. For example, in augmented reality, the real environment is seen through a display which shows some overlaid virtual environment. As a common denominator, we will use the following definition [10] which summarizes the most common characteristics of virtual environments.

> A virtual environment (VE) is an interactive, immersive, multi-sensory, 3 dimensional, synthetic environment.

The appearance of the modern PC with its high-resolution graphic displays and the widespread use of the Internet allow the development and broad deployment of networked virtual environments (NVES) supporting multi-user applications such as large-scale simulations or collaboration tools. In the context of virtual environments, networking is employed for two ends.

- First, networking can be used to distribute the load of the computations which are associated with a large-scale virtual environment over a number of computers.

- Second, networking allows a number of geographically dispersed persons to interact with each other within the same virtual environment.

Both types of distribution with respect to virtual environments share a number of problems. NVES are usually soft real-time applications [5], i.e., the average response time of the NVE should be low. Because of the complex interactions which arise between the objects of an NVE, this requires a comprehensive synchronization and communication layer.

In addition, both aspects of networking have specific problems. In the first case, a relatively small number of nodes is usually interconnected within a cluster, i.e., the complete environment is dedicated to the NVE. Ideally, such a cluster should mimic the behavior of a single machine, so for example, the different tasks should be tightly synchronized and the load should be dynamically balanced. SMP become more and more attractive and should be utilized effectively.

In the second case, if the Internet is used to allow a geographically dispersed group of people to interact within a virtual environment, the main problem is that the connection between the server system and client is not under the control of the NVE-system. Consequently, the central problem is to provide a responsive and consistent environment to the user in the presence of long transmission times and frequent packet loss [9].

3 MMORGS

3.1 The World of MMORGS

Massively Multi-Player Online Role Games (MMORGS) enable a large number of players to explore a persistently stored virtual game world using a fictionary character. Although the background stories of these games include different genres such as the middle-ages, fantasy, and science fiction, the principal appearance is always the same: A typically human-like character controlled by the player and observed by the player on the computer screen is acting in a virtual game world which may feature 3-dimensional geographical and architectural entities such as open landscapes, buildings and dungeons. The virtual game world is inhibited by a number of human controlled characters and computer controlled characters (non player characters or NPCS). ¿From the player's perspective, one important goal of his/her interactions with the virtual game world is the development ("improvement") of the fictionary character by gaining experience, e.g., by exploring certain areas, by victories in fights with computer or human controlled characters. The other central motivation to play a MMORG is the interaction with other players within the virtual environment. Chatting, exchanging items of the game world, and exploring the game world collaboratively are essential to the experience of a MMORG player. Usually, MMORG players maintain their evolving characters over relatively long periods of time. It is not uncommon that players use the same the character over more than a year. To this end, a MMORG must maintain the game world itself and the characters persistently.

3.2 Research Interest into MMORGS

MMORGS are generally considered to be the most important recent development in the computer game industry. The first economically successful MMORG was *Ultima-Online*. The success of *Ultima Online* was inspiring – other MMORGS entered the emerging market, most notably *Everquest, Asheron's Call*, and *Anarachy Online*. In comparison to games which did not feature networked gaming (or only LAN-based gaming), these early MMORGS had a relatively weak game quality, especially with respect to graphics. The new generation of MMORGS, such as *Everquest II* and *Asheron's Call II*, presents to the player a world of almost the same quality as a traditional game. The economic interest into this genre is underlined by the fact that major companies in the IT-industry such as Sony, AT&T, and Microsoft show a strong interest in MMORGS and are actively developing products in this domain. The reason for the strong interest of the gaming industry into MMORGS is rooted in the fact that MMORGS are client-server applications which require players to authenticate themselves. Therefore the possibility to use illegal copies is eliminated. Moreover, for the same reason, it is possible to charge each player a monthly subscription fee.

¿From the technical and organizational point of view, MMORGS offer a new challenge to the gaming industry. So for example, the computational resources necessary to host a MMORG are by far larger than for any other kind of game. Also, the components which run server-side must be more reliable than usual game code. In general, the software qualities necessary to build a MMORG successfully, cannot be achieved by traditional game development strategies. For a long time, the game development community had been relatively uninterested into academic developments. However, as an article of the *Game Developer Magazine* titled "In Defense of Academe" (November 2002) shows, the gaming community becomes more and more interested in a more academic and methodologically grounded approach. More specifically, the following goals are shared by today's MMORG projects – and none of them is able to reach all of them.

- Today's MMORGS are supposed to allow 3.000 or more human players to be in the same simulated world. Roughly 30.000 NPCS must be maintained in the same world. This requires significant computational resources.

- MMORGS have to offer the player a logically consistent world, i.e., the world should follow its inherent game logic while the underlying implementation should not cause any unmotivated events. Of particular importance is the *seamlessness* of a MMORG. A MMORG is called seamless, if the distribution of a game world over a number of server-nodes does not lead to synchronization artifacts which can be observed by players.

- The world of any MMORG has to evolve over time. Changes on MMORGS include small changes such as the tuning of certain parameters to keep the game in balance[1], expansions such as adding a new area or a new non playing character, and global changes such as adding a new skill to all characters in the game. Such changes should happen in a fair manner, i.e., they should happen simultaneously for all characters. And ideally – changes should be executed without down-times of the MMORG server system.

- MMORGS are soft real-time services [5], i.e., a MMORG-system is required to respond to requests within a given time-bound on average with a small variance.

- Achieving high reliability is a prominent goal in the MMORG-community. Most of today's MMORGS display weak reliability which is degrading consumer satisfaction.

- Clients of MMORGS must be considered hostile since a certain fraction of players will always try to cheat. Any possibility to obtain some advantage in a MMORG will be exploited by cheating players.[2]

Summarized, MMORGS combine several features which make them an interesting object for research. First, MMORGS are a growing market which is currently conquered by industry. Second, MMORGS are technically very challenging and today's tools are not sufficient to build a MMORG which satisfies all these design goals. Third, the gaming industry has acknowledged the need for a more methodological approach and for academic support. Fourth, MMORGS are still games, i.e., while the goals of any MMORG-project are ambitious, partial failures are tolerable. Finally, we believe that MMORGS subsume many properties of other NVES. Therefore, a middleware which is able to satisfy the needs of a MMORG should be usable in a much broader context.

---

[1] A game is balanced, if there is no dominating strategy. For example, if a certain character type, such as a warrior, is always superior to another character type (e.g., a priest), then the game is unbalanced. To make a game interesting to players, it is important to balance a game as to ensure a diversity of characters and game approaches.

[2] If there is any advantage in crashing the MMORG servers, cheating players will do so. In 2001, *Asheron's Call* has been a victim of such an attack. The attackers' goal was to duplicate a set of given items. To achieve this, they moved these items from one server to another. But with a fine-tuned timing, the attackers were able to crash the first server just after leaving it. Therefore, the item was still stored in the backup of this server and at the same time in the hands of the player's character, thus it has been duplicated. Once the reboot of the crashed machine had finished, they attackers returned to obtain the duplicate.

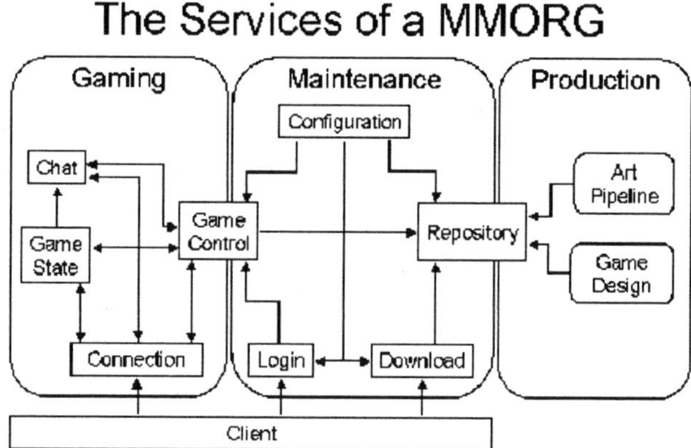

Figure 1. MMORG-Domain

4   MMORG Services

In this section, we will present a model for the domain specific services of a MMORG. To do so, we subdivide the domain of a MMORG-system into three sub-domains, namely the *gaming domain*, the *maintenance domain*, and the *production domain*, see Figure 1. The gaming domain contains all services which are needed by the clients to play the game while the maintenance domain consists of those services which are needed for the management of the produced content, subscription management and other administrative tasks. Finally, the content-production domain embodies all services which are necessary to produce the content itself. Here, we will consider the content-production domain only in so far as we need to describe the gaming and maintenance domain.

In the following, we will briefly introduce these three sub-domains with their respective services.

4.1   Gaming Domain

The services of the gaming domain collaboratively maintain the game state and allow the client to access this state. These services have to operate under soft-realtime constraints, must be highly available, and have to scale well. In total there are the following four services.

Game-State Server: A MMORG's game-state is held and continuously processed by a cluster of game-state servers. A specific game-state server handles a set of zones, i.e., the server executed the control loop of all active objects, such as non playing characters, which are located in this zone. Therefore, a single game-state server must access the set of distributed, persistent, and active objects which constitute each of its zones and process their control loop.

Connection Server: Each connection server for a MMORG is responsible for managing the connections for a number of clients, i.e., to mediate the messages between its clients and the game-state servers which are currently holding the characters of these clients. To do so, the connection server has to select, prioritize and bulk the data which is sent to the client. This data is provided by the game-state and chat servers. On the other hand, the connection server has to validate each (potentially hostile) datum sent from the client to the server at the application level. In the case of a positive validation it has to forward each datum to the responsible server.

Chat Server: Because of the large number of chat messages which typically occur in MMORGS, dedicated chat servers are required. A chat server should mimic features of a commonly accepted chat system, such as the Internet Relay Chat (IRC). In addition to these standard features, there must be a special chat channel which is geographically segmented, i.e., which allows geographically near objects to exchange messages. To achieve this goal, the chat servers need to communicate with the game-state servers. The chat servers also need to communicate with the connection servers which constitute the interface to the client.

Game-Control Server: The game-control server of a MMORG governs all services of the gaming domain of the MMORG. It controls their start-up, shut-down, patching, and balancing. In general, the game-control server acts as facade of the gaming domain with respect to the maintenance domain.

The gaming services are tightly bound to each other, since they all access the game state. The game-state server is maintaining the objects which constitute the game-state, i.e., it keeps them active by executing their control loops. The connection server needs to map changes in the game-state to messages to be sent to the client and has to send the client-requests to these objects. The chat server has to know the geographic position of the characters, and finally, the game-control server has to execute global transactions on the game-state, such as expanding it. All these operations are required to be synchronized and thus all these services should be based on the same common middleware services and distribution middleware.

4.2　Maintenance Domain

The maintenance services do not share the extensive scalability and realtime constraints of the gaming domain. In contrast, they provide standard services and might be based on commercial-off-the-shelf (COTS) products. To achieve the required availability, simple duplication of the corresponding services suffices.

Login Server: The login process into a MMORG can be divided into two steps. First, the subscriber's identity and permissions have to be checked. If this validation is successful, then in the second step the connection has to be established. The first step is entirely handled by the login server while the second step is mainly delegated to the game-control server which activates the subscriber's character and initiates the connection (by issuing the necessary operations on the game-state and connection servers). The login server receives the IP-address of the selected connection server and forwards it to the client.

Download Server: The download servers of a MMORG must provide all software and data which is needed by the clients to enter the game. Because of the continuous development of a MMORG, the download server must also provide incremental patches such that a client can update itself by downloading only a minimal amount of data.

Update Server: The update server is responsible for providing the patches which arise from the changes and expansions of the MMORG's world. In other words, the update server is the interface to the content-production domain. The finally produced content needs to be submitted to the update server in terms of a corresponding client and server patch. The client patches have to be deployed to the download servers and after an appropriate period of time the associated server patch has to be executed by the game-control server. Once the game-control server applies a server patch, the connection servers will be informed to require each connecting client to be patched with the associated client update. Thus the update server provides the patches but it does not control their application.

Configuration Server. The configuration server is responsible for maintaining the complete configuration of all the services which constitute the running MMORG, i.e., it will associate a gaming domain cluster with a set of login, download and update servers. It will also know the current configuration of the MMORG with respect to patching and issue the complete patching procedure, that is, it will upload a client patch onto the download server to make it publicly available, and later, it will command the game-control server to apply the corresponding server patch to the game-state.

By using a configuration server to establish an association between the different services, it is also possible to use the same services for several MMORG-instances. For example, it will be necessary to maintain several test games which use the same update server as the publicly running game.

The services of the maintenance domain are relatively loosely coupled. The login server maintains its subscription database completely isolated from the other services, it only interacts with the game-control server to initiate the connection establishment. The download server is the data-source for the data distribution, the only occurring interaction with the other services is the upload of new patches from the update server. The update server is the interface between the content production domain and the maintenance domain and provides distinct interfaces to both domains. From the perspective of the maintenance domain, the update server provides a simple data-repository which is used by the game-control and download server. This interface might be a standard protocol such as FTP. The configuration server will employ a standard database product to manage its configuration data. Again, the configuration server can be designed as a classical stand-alone database application.

4.3   Content-Production Domain

The content-production domain can be further subdivided into the art-pipeline and the game-design. Both domains are populated by applications which are used to create and maintain the game world. We will not discuss the concrete applications of these two domains since any concrete production domain will be specific to the concrete game and especially to the graphical representation.

The **art-pipeline** is based on standard graphics tools for 3D-modeling. Typically, these tools are expanded by custom scripts and plug-ins, to form a pipeline. Because of the massive amount of work to be done by the art-team, the organization of this work is critical. Therefore, the content-production domain is characterized by the integration and modification of existing tools to form an effective production environment. In addition to the graphics-tools, there need to be extensive version control facilities for binary as well as for textual data. Finally, the raw-models produced by the art-pipeline must be transformed into the client's data-format and for each model a description of the corresponding object which is sufficient for the game-state servers must be generated.

The **game-design** uses these models to build, modify and expand existing areas. The main challenge is again the integration of different tools. In the ideal case, a game-designer can employ an environment which allows her or him to place different objects visually in an area and to program these objects both visually and in terms of a scripting language. Naturally, the game-designer must be able to test new areas. The integration of testing facilities can be done in a number of different forms, ranging from a special client which comes with a completely integrated game-logic to the utilization of the common client connecting to a test gaming environment.

4.4 Domain Independent Services

In this subsection, we will discuss which of the three sub-domains gaming, maintenance, and production can be supported effectively by a domain independent middleware. Furthermore, we will discuss the characteristics which should be met by such a middleware.

The common characteristic of the **gaming domain's services** is that they access a shared database in a highly concurrent manner requiring replication, persistence and synchronization primitives under the pressure of soft-realtime constraints. This database represents the game-world which consists of a set of active objects, i.e., objects which are changing their state pro-actively.

Not building the gaming domain on a shared general middleware will lead to the stovepipe system anti-pattern [2]. This anti-pattern arises when all interfaces between pairs of communicating subsystems are distinct and mutually incompatible. In such a situation usually multiple infrastructure mechanisms are used to integrate these subsystems. This leads to difficulties in modifying or even describing the architecture. The consequences of such a development approach are large semantic gaps between architecture documentation and implemented software. The software might even comply to the paper requirements but it does not meet the user expectations, system maintenance becomes surprisingly costly, the project takes more resources than expected for no obvious reason, the system complexity increases heavily on even slight expansions.

There are two situations which justify to follow this anti-pattern consciously – the exploration of a yet unknown domain and the quick development of a partly functional prototype. But in such a situation, it is usually necessary to restart the project from scratch afterwards.

In contrast, the **maintenance domain's services** are loosely coupled and might be assembled in a heterogenous manner by utilizing standard packages for the corresponding tasks. For example, the login-server might be developed based on the Apache Web-Server and a commercially available billing package, and the download server can be a simple FTP-server. The interface between the maintenance domain and the gaming domain is provided by the game-control server. This server will provide an interface to the maintenance domain which is not based on the middleware, therefore the maintenance domain is completely independent from the middleware.

The **content-production domain** will consist of a set of diverse applications. Many of these applications will not use a live gaming environment. Typically, they will be third-party provided graphical tools which are used to model the graphical appearance of the artifacts in the game-world. Thus, these applications can be kept completely independent from the middleware.

On the other hand, some of the applications in the content-production domain will require access to a (running) game-world. For example, there could be a world-editor, which allows to compose new zones from base elements such as terrain types, houses, items etc. Ideally, such an editor would not utilize some specific implementation of the game but would use the same implementation as the gaming domain itself, i.e., would be based upon the same middleware. However, game-editors display completely different access patterns than the services of the gaming domain. Also, a MMORG will not be built with a single editor but with a (growing) set of editors which provided for different and specific tasks. Thus such a shared middleware must provide the means to integrate new applications which follow different access patterns at ease, i.e., the middleware must allow to compose the complete system out of applications which are built as independently as possible. Consequently, there must be a single shared horizontal interface such that compliance to this interface ensures integrability. This situation is one more strong reason to seek a strong horizontal layer and to avoid the consequences of a stovepipe system.

Summarized, the gaming domain must be the main focus of a middleware for MMORGS, i.e., the middleware has to enable a cluster to maintain a shared and persistent database of active objects which provides a broad set of synchronization primitives and which supports replication for the sake of efficiency and fault-tolerance. Furthermore, the middleware must be designed to meet soft-realtime constraints, since the operations of the gaming domain require response times with small variances. The operations on the database which are executed by the gaming domain cause relatively small changes to the game state but might require to read a comparatively large set of objects. In addition to the services of the gaming-domain, various editing applications of the content-production domain must access the shared database. These applications are operating on the database as a whole, for example, they might need to change a complete zone in the world or might require to change a large set of objects simultaneously.

Thus, a middleware for MMORGS has to support a wide variety of different access patterns. In particular, different synchronization modes must be available, i.e., the applications must be able to choose between serializable access forms and less isolated access forms, such as reading a possibly outdated but consistent snapshot of the database.

Taking this starting point, we will propose a middleware which allows a cluster of SMP machines to maintain a database of active objects. The middleware will be based on an expanded transaction concept which enables its applications to access the database with a broad set of synchronization strategies.

5   Transaction-based Gaming Domain

5.1   Transactions with Weak Isolation Levels

NVES (and even MMORGS) have a very broad set of different requirements such that it appears impractical to build a specific solution directly. Thus, we are developing a middleware, called APEIRON, as a domain-independent middleware which is designed to support the domain-specific services introduced in Section 4 on page 154.

The most natural modeling of an MMORG (and VES in general) is a database of optionally active objects. Each active object is continuously updating its state based on the current state of its environment. Ideally, such an object is implemented without any knowledge on the underlying distribution and concurrency issues. However, this ideal is hardly achievable. While it is possible to handle the distribution of the database internally by the middleware, it is not possible to handle concurrency issues implicitly.

If the implementation of the active objects has to deal with concurrency related issues explicitly, then the primitives for the synchronization should be as uniform as possible. Also, they should be abstract such that different concrete algorithms can be used to implement these primitives. The transaction is a concept which is flexible enough to offer different synchronization strategies but offers quite a uniform interface.

The classical notion of transactions are the ACID semantics. ACID is an acronym for atomicity, consistency, isolation, and durability. Atomicity refers to the fact, that all operations of an ACID transaction are executed completely or none of them. Consistency means that such a transaction transforms one consistent state of the database into another one. A transaction is isolated, if it is not affected by any other transaction, i.e., the transaction is accessing the database virtually exclusively. Finally, durability means that the effects of a transaction once executed are made durable. [3]

Because of their serializability, ACID-transactions alone are insufficient. In addition to executing serializable transactions, the services of the gaming domain must be able to access objects in a non-blocking manner. For example, the decision what a non playing character is going to do next has to be made within soft-realtime, i.e., the time until the decision is found must be within a given bound almost all the time. Usually, the NPC has to know the state of the objects in its neighborhood to determine its next step. However, the decision of the NPC can be based on slightly outdated data.

To fit different synchronization scenarios, the transactions used in APEIRON allow the application to specify *isolation levels* for each accessed object [1]. The isolation-level of an accessed object describes the guarantees which are associated with this object with respect to all other objects which are locked within the same transaction. For example, the states of two different objects which are locked within a single transaction might be required to be mutually consistent.

The isolation levels of APEIRON form a hierarchy, i.e., every isolation-level includes the guarantees of the preceding ones. We list them below, starting at the weakest (committed) and finishing with the strongest (exclusive).

Committed: The object versions which are accessible under this isolation level are only guaranteed to be committed. Therefore, if two object are accessed under this isolation level, it is perfectly possible that the first object is accurately presented while the second one is already outdated.

   If a transaction writes on an object under this isolation level, then lost updates might occur, i.e., the object might have been changed independently in the meantime.

Monotone: All objects which are locked under this isolation level (or a higher one) within the same transaction behave monotone with respect to the database development over time. More precisely, once an object state is made accessible to the application which incorporates modifications of a transaction T, then every object state which is locked afterwards must incorporate the changes of T. The behavior in case of a modifying access is the same as for the committed isolation level.

---

[3]The ACID semantics were introduced in [3]. For a general overview on classical transactions and their implementation, see [6].

Consistent: This isolation level allows to lock a set of objects within a so-called consistency group, i.e., if one these objects reflects the effects of a transaction T, then all objects in this group must reflect the changes of T. If an object which is locked under the consistent isolation level is modified, then APEIRON enforces that no lost update occurs.

Accurate: If an object is locked under this isolation level, then the presented version must be up-to-date and no other transaction is allowed to change the object in the meantime. This scheme corresponds to classic ACID-transactions.

Pessimistic: The isolation level accurate and pessimistic are interchangeable – the correctness of a transaction is independent of this choice. However, such a change will have a strong impact on the performance of a transaction: If an object is locked with isolation-level pessimistic, then it is guaranteed that the corresponding transaction will succeed in validating the accesses this object. In other words, once the transaction has a pessimistic transactional lock on all locked objects, it knows it will be committable.
This isolation-level is useful for accessing high-contention data, i.e., objects which are modified by many transactions concurrently such that conflicts arise often. Naturally, obtaining a pessimistic lock might fail more often than acquiring an accurate lock.

Exclusive: This isolation-level gives exclusive access to an objects, thus it subsumes the guarantees of pessimistic. This isolation-level is mainly used as a synchronization primitive.

More precisely, APEIRON allows the application to specify an isolation-level which is required immediately and another one which is required directly before committing to the database.

We call the first isolation-level the **running isolation-level**. The application uses the running isolation-level to specify the isolation-level which is required such that the transaction itself does not crash. For example, a transaction might crash if the referential integrity of a set of objects is not guaranteed. In such a case, the application locks them under the running isolation-level consistent. Summarized, the running isolation-level is used to ensure that the transaction itself does not crash. However, it does not ensure that the transaction can be committed correctly.

The second one is called the **commitment isolation-level**. This isolation-level is enforced during the commitment of the corresponding transaction. This isolation-level can only be stronger than the running isolation-level (since the isolation-level can only be expanded over time). The commitment isolation-level is used to describe the guarantees which are required for a transaction such that its outcome is correct. For example, a transaction might access only two objects under the running isolation-level committed but might require a commitment isolation-level accurate. In this case, the transaction must be programmed such that inter-object inconsistencies does not cause the transaction to crash, but the outcome of the transaction must only be correct, if the locked states of the two objects were up-to-date and are unmodified at the moment of commitment.

5.2   Services as Active Objects

As pointed out in [4], the migration of a character is comparable to the migration of an process. In both cases an active objects has to be suspended, transfered to another node, and resumed again. In the case of the migration of a character, the additional difficulty is to achieve migration as quickly as possible – the character should be seamlessly observable.

In an NVE-cluster, the objects which are observable from more than one node must be replicated in order to achieve the real time character of the simulation. The replicas will not be perfect but slightly outdated with respect to the master instance. The weaker isolation levels which allow to access slightly outdated versions of an object can use such replicated versions of an object. If a character moves from one node to another, typically it has been replicated at the new node for quite some time. In such a situation, the migration is only required to change a former slave replica into a master replica and vice versa.

Since each NVE-cluster solution must come up with a solution for character migration, it is actually providing a solution for process migration. Therefore, within APEIRON, services are modeled in terms of active objects. In consequence, all features associated with common objects are available for services. Particularly, services can be maintained in fault-tolerant manner and can be migrated for the sake of load-balancing.

5.3 Incremental Implementation

The transaction interface is the main interface for applications. As stated in the preceding subsections, we are using transactions as interface since they allow to state different synchronization strategies uniformly. At the same time, they are sufficiently abstract such that a variety of different implementations can be applied. In particular, it is possible to build the underlying implementation incrementally.

An implementation can be restricted in terms of a conservative implementation, i.e., instead of implementing an isolation level, the implementation can just use the next higher isolation level.

Another option for incremental development is to vary the implementation of the distribution mechanisms. The common application interface of APEIRON does not give allow to manipulate the distribution of objects. This interface only allows to constrain the replication of an object – the way these constraints are enforces is not observable through the interface.[4] Therefore, it is possible to start with a relatively simple implementation for SMP machines without any distribution, or to build an implementation which does not maintain any replicas for the sake of fault-tolerance.

6 Conclusion

We presented MMORGS and motivated the design of APEIRON by the requirements of MMORGS. However, APEIRON itself is domain-independent and provides a general and consistent set of functionality to the application developer. Therefore, we think that APEIRON can be used as basis for other types of NVES – at least to solve the problem of load distribution. APEIRON leaves the problem of geographical distribution to the domain-specific and/or application level since there is no general solution for it.

The key-concept of APEIRON is a transaction interface which is based on weak isolation levels. Such an interface is intuitive to application developers and clearly separates the applications from any low-level operations. Therefore, it becomes possible to develop applications atop of APEIRON using a uniform interface concept, based on varying implementations.

---

[4]There is a separate interface which allows to access and manipulate the underlying meta-data which contains the underlying platform parameters and the configuration of the active databases.

Currently, we are deriving a complete architecture for APEIRON and started to implement basic modules. We hope to have a running prototype for SMP-machines supporting at least two weak isolation levels by the end of 2004.

References

[1] Atul Adya. *Weak Consistency: A Generalized Theory and Optimistic Implementation for Distributed Transactions.* PhD thesis, MIT, 1999.

[2] William J. Brown, Raphael C. Malveau, Hays W. McCormick, and Thomas J. Mowbray. *Anti Patterns.* Wiley & Sons, 1998.

[3] T. Härder and A. Reuter. Principles of transaction-oriented database recovery. *Computing Surveys*, 15(4), 1983.

[4] J. Huang, Y. Du, and C.-M. Wang. Design of the server cluster to support avatar migration. In *Virtual Reality*, pages 7–14, 2003.

[5] Hermann Kopetz. *Real-Time Systems.* Kluwer Academic Publishers, 1997.

[6] Nancy Lynch, Michael Merritt, William Weihl, and Alan Fekete. *Atomic Transactions.* Morgan Kaufmann, 1994.

[7] Michael R. Macedonia and Michael J. Zyda. A taxonomy for networked virtual environments. *IEEE MultiMedia*, 4(1):48–56, – 1997.

[8] Douglas C. Schmidt and Stephen D. Huston. *C++ Network Programming, Volume 1: Mastering Complexity with ACE and Patterns.* C++ In-Depth Series. Addison-Wesley, 2002.

[9] Sandeep Kishan Singhal. *Effective Remote Modelling in Large-Scale Distributed Simulation and Visualization Environments.* PhD thesis, Stanford University, 1996.

[10] R. Stuart. *The Design of Virtual Environments.* Computing McGraw-Hill, 1996.

Concurrent Information Processing and Computing
D. Grigoras and A. Nicolau (Eds.)
IOS Press, 2005

159

The Challenges and the Promise of Quantum Parallelism

Dan C. Marinescu   Gabriela M. Marinescu

School of Computer Science
University of Central Florida
Email: {dcm,magda}cs.ucf.edu

Abstract. In this paper we discuss the relationship between the entanglement and quantum parallelism and then present Shor's algorithm. Like most factorization algorithms, Shor's algorithm reduces the factorization problem to the problem of finding the period of a function, but uses quantum parallelism to find a superposition of all values of the function in one step.

1   Introduction

A *quantitative version of the Church-Turing principle* allows us to relate the behavior of the abstract model of computation provided by the Universal Turing Machines (UTM) with the physical computing devices used to carry out a computation. This thesis can be formulated as "any physical computing device can be simulated by a Turing machine in a number of steps polynomial in the resources used by the computing device". While no one has been able to find counter-examples for this thesis, the search has been limited to systems constructed based upon the laws of classical mechanics.

Yet, the universe is essentially quantum mechanical, therefore there is a possibility that the computing power of quantum mechanical computing devices might be greater than the computing power of classical computing devices [6]. If this is true, then problems such as factoring integers, or finding discrete logarithms, for which no polynomial time algorithms are known, could be solved in linear time by a quantum device. Therefore, the investigation of quantum computing devices and of quantum algorithms is well motivated [4].

Quantum computers, computers based upon quantum circuits which behave according to the laws of quantum mechanics, allow us to transgress the well-defined boundary between polynomial and exponential computations. We suspect that the source of this incredible power of quantum computers is the phenomenon of entanglement, characteristic to quantum systems [2]. Quantum entanglement does not have a classical counterpart.

In a recent paper [8] Peter Shor classifies the quantum algorithms known to offer a significant speed-up over their classical counterparts into three broad categories:

(i) Algorithms that find the periodicity of a function using Fourier transform methods. Simon's algorithm [9], Shor's algorithms for factoring and for computing discrete logarithms [7], and Hallgren's algorithm to solve Bell equation are all members of this class.

(ii) Search algorithms which can perform an exhaustive search of N items in $\sqrt{N}$ time. Grover's algorithms [1] belong to this class.

(iii) Algorithms for simulating quantum systems, as suggested by Feynman. This is a potentially large class of algorithms, but not many algorithms in this class have been developed so far. Once quantum computers become a reality we should expect the development of a considerable number of programs to simulate quantum systems of interest.

Yet, quantum algorithms have not witnessed the same effervescent developments we have seen in quantum information theory, or in quantum complexity. Clearly, the development of quantum algorithms requires a very different thinking than the one we are accustomed to for classical computers. To offer a considerable speed-up a quantum algorithm must rely on superposition states and this is a foreign concept for those unaccustomed with quantum mechanical thinking.

In addition to this obvious reason, Peter Shor speculates [8] that the number of problems the quantum algorithms may offer a substantial speedup over the classical algorithms may be very limited. To see the spectacular speedups we have to concentrate on problems not in the classical computational class P. Many believe that quantum algorithms solving NP-complete problems in polynomial time do not exist, even though no proof of this assertion is available at this time. Shor argues that if we assume that no polynomial time quantum algorithms exist for solving NP-hard problems, then the class of problems we have to search for, is neither NP-hard, nor P, and the population of this class is relatively small.

2   Quantum Parallelism

We show that if we are given a quantum circuit able to compute a function $f(j)$, with j a binary string of length n, in polynomial time, then we are able to compute a superposition of all 2^n possible values of the function f, in polynomial time with a single copy of the quantum circuit. An alternative formulation of this statement is that we require only a polynomial effort to compute f. In contrast, if we wish to calculate the 2^n values of the function f using a classical circuit which computes f in polynomial time, then we need an exponential number of copies of the circuit.

This "magic" effect is called *quantum parallelism*. To achieve this remarkable result we construct a quantum circuit able to compute f in polynomial time and prepare its input in a superposition state, as shown in Figure 1. The input to the quantum gate array is the result of transforming the state obtained as the tensor product on the n qubits in state $\mid 0\rangle$ by a quantum circuit whose transfer matrix is the tensor product of the n transfer matrices of the Hadamard gate

$$H \otimes H \ldots \otimes H(\mid 0\rangle \mid 0\rangle \ldots \mid 0\rangle) = \frac{1}{2^{n/2}}(\mid 0\rangle + \mid 1\rangle)^n = \frac{1}{2^{n/2}} \sum_{j=0}^{2^n-1} \mid j\rangle.$$

with

$$H = \frac{1}{2}\begin{pmatrix} 1 & 1 \\ 1 & 0 \end{pmatrix}$$

The quantum gate array implements a function $f : \{0,1\}^n \longmapsto \{0,1\}$ mapping an n-bit input string $j = (j_0, j_1, \ldots j_{n-1})$ to a binary value, 0 or 1, in polynomial time. The transformation carried out by the quantum gate array is

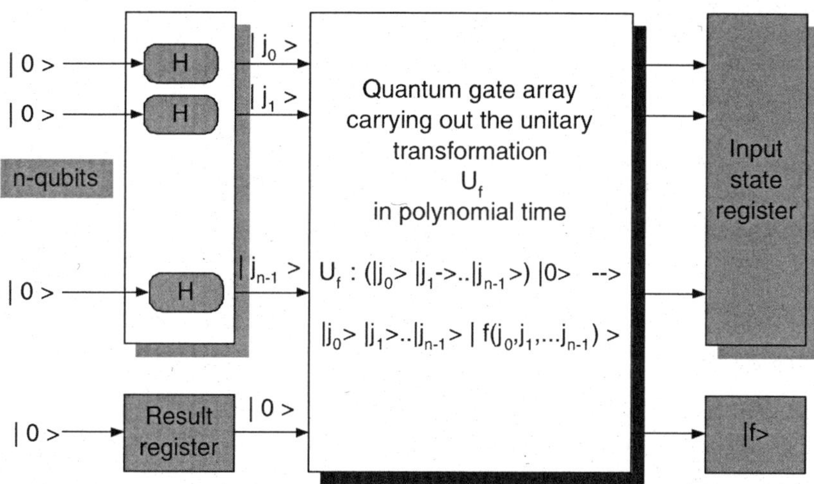

Figure 1. A quantum computer with two input registers, j and the result register and two output registers. j consists of n qubits, $\mid j_0\rangle, \mid j_1\rangle, \ldots \mid j_{n-i}\rangle$. The result register is initially set to zero, $\mid 0\rangle$. The quantum gate array implements a function $f : \{0,1\}^n \mapsto \{0,1\}$ mapping an n-bit input string to a binary value, 0 or 1 in polynomial time. The actual input to the quantum gate array consists of the tensor product of n input qubits in state $\mid 0\rangle$ in a superposition state created by n Hadamard gates. There are 2^n possible values of the input string and the final result is a superposition of the 2^n possible evaluations of the function $f(j)$.

$$U_f : [\mid j_0\rangle \mid j_1\rangle \ldots \mid j_{n-1}\rangle] \mid 0\rangle \mapsto [\mid j_0\rangle \mid j_1\rangle \ldots \mid j_{n-1}\rangle] \mid f(j_0, j_1, \ldots j_{n-1})\rangle$$

If the input is a superposition state created by the n Hadamard gates, then the result is a superposition of all possible values of function f

$$\mid f\rangle = \sum_{j=0}^{2^n - 1} \mid j\rangle \mid f(j)\rangle.$$

This relatively simple quantum circuit setup makes us wonder if the superposition is the source of the enormous power of computers based upon quantum effects. The state of a system consisting of n bits is a vector, but in a 2^n dimensional vector space. If we have n qubits the state of the system is also a vector in the 2^n-dimensional Hilbert space $\mathcal{H}^{2^n}$ which is the tensor product of n, two-dimensional Hilbert spaces

$$\mathcal{H}^{2^n} = \bigotimes_{k=1}^{n} H_2.$$

Thus, there is an isomorphism between the state space of a system of n qubits $(\bigotimes_{k=1}^{n} H_2)$ and the state space of a single particle with 2^n states, $\mathcal{H}^{2^n}$.

The crucial observation is that *in addition to the classical states corresponding to all possible binary vectors of length n, the state space $\mathcal{H}^{2^n}$ includes also entangled states. The entangled states reflect the critical distinction between the Cartesian product in an Euclidian space and the tensor product in a Hilbert space.*

We now ask ourselves if a single classical system with 2^n states could emulate the behavior of a quantum system of n qubits. We can construct a system where each qubit is represented by a classical wave system and select two modes of vibration to represent the basis states $|\,0\rangle$ and $|\,1\rangle$. We can then construct the superposition corresponding to $|\,0\rangle + |\,1\rangle$. Finally, we use n copies of such systems to obtain a product state.

For example, we may use an elastic string with fixed end points; then the two modes used to represent the basis states could be the lowest energy modes. A set of n such elastic strings will represent a product state. Joszsa argues that in such an experiment the joint state of the n strings is always a product state of n separate vibrations [2]. It may be possible for the 2^n modes of a classical vibrating system to emulate the behavior of n qubits and exhibit entangled states, but we would need to expand an exponential amount of energy to emulate the behavior of entangled quantum particles.

Another alternative may be feasible. A physical system with infinitely many discrete energy levels could be used to represent the superposition of exponentially many modes, using a constant energy. In this case the levels will be exponentially crowded together and we would need an exponential amount of energy to distinguish among them.

We conclude this discussion with the observation that the state of n qubits requires an energy that grows linearly with n while the energy required by a classical system which mimics the behavior of the n-qubit system grows exponentially with n. It should also be painfully clear to us that a rigorous assessment of computational complexity must consider all computational resources, including energy, as opposed to the traditional complexity theory focused on time and space complexity.

Quantum parallelism is best illustrated by the solution to the so-called "Deutsch's problem". Consider a black box characterized by a transfer function that maps a single input bit x into an output, $f(x)$. The transformation performed by the black box, $f(x)$, is a general function and might not be invertible. We assume that it takes the same amount of time, T, to carry out each of the four possible mappings performed by the transfer function $f(x)$ of the black box and it takes no time to compare the results

$$f(0) = 0, \quad f(0) = 1, \quad f(1) = 0, \quad f(1) = 1.$$

The problem posed is to distinguish if $f(0) = f(1)$ or $f(0) \neq f(1)$.

Using a classical computer one alternative is to compute sequentially $f(0)$ and $f(1)$ and then compare the results, see Figure 2(a) for a total time $2T$. A classical parallel solution is illustrated in Figure 2(b) where we have two replicas of the circuit and we feed 0 as input to one of the replicas of the black box and 1 to the other, and then compare the partial results. In this case we obtain the answer after time T but we need two copies of the system, rather than one.

Consider now a quantum computer with a transfer function U_f that takes as input two qubits $|\,x\rangle$ (control) and $|\,y\rangle$ (target) and two outputs, $|\,x\rangle$ and $|\,y\rangle \oplus f(x)\rangle$. We have the choice of selecting the states of the two qubits $|\,x\rangle$ and $|\,y\rangle$. We choose the first qubit in the state $|\,x\rangle = \frac{1}{\sqrt{2}}(|\,0\rangle + |\,1\rangle)$ and the second qubit in the state $|\,y\rangle = \frac{1}{\sqrt{2}}(|\,0\rangle - |\,1\rangle)$.

We shall show that the first output qubit of the circuit is $|\,f(0) \oplus f(1)\rangle$. Thus,

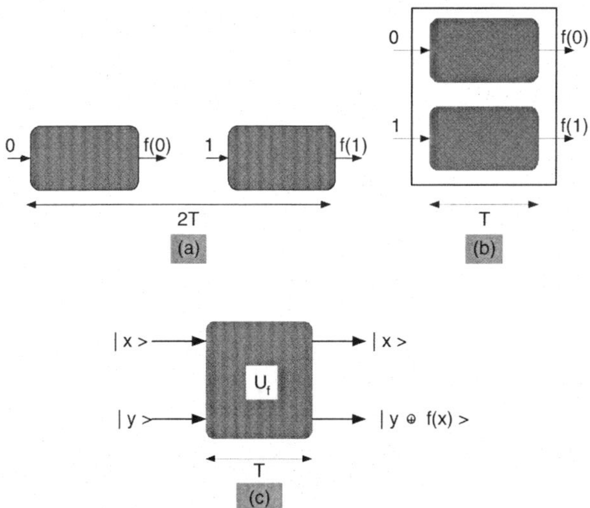

Figure 2. Classical and quantum parallelism. (a) Sequential solution to Deutsch's problem using a classical computer. (b) A parallel solution to Deutsch's problem using a classical computer. (c) The quantum black box with a transfer function U_f. It evaluates $f(0)$ and $f(1)$ simultaneously.

(i) if $f(0) = f(1)$ then this qubit is 0 (indeed $0 \oplus 0 = 0$ and $1 \oplus 1 = 0$) and

(ii) if $f(0) \neq f(1)$ then this qubit is 1 (indeed, $0 \oplus 1 = 1$ and $1 \oplus 0 = 1$).

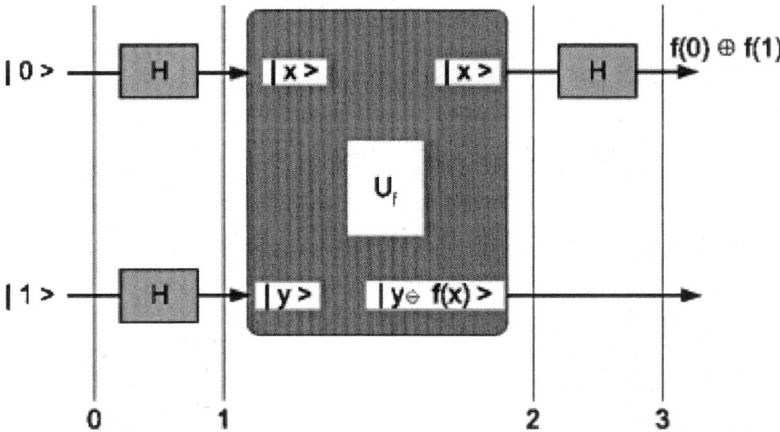

Figure 3. A quantum circuit for solving Deutsch's problem. The first output qubit of the circuit is $|\ f(0) \oplus f(1)\rangle$. Thus if $f(0) = f(1)$ then this qubit is 0 and if $f(0) \neq f(1)$ then this qubit is 1.

Figure 3 illustrates the quantum circuit for solving Deutsch's problem. To compute the output state of this circuit we consider the four stages of this circuit and we examine the four vectors, ξ_0, ξ_1, ξ_2 and ξ_3 describing the state of the system at each stage.

The input vector is

$$| \xi_0 \rangle = | 0\,1 \rangle = \begin{pmatrix} 1 \\ 0 \end{pmatrix} \otimes \begin{pmatrix} 0 \\ 1 \end{pmatrix} = \begin{pmatrix} 0 \\ 1 \\ 0 \\ 0 \end{pmatrix}.$$

the transfer matrix of the first stage is

$$G_1 = H \otimes H = \frac{1}{\sqrt{2}} \begin{pmatrix} 1 & 1 \\ 1 & -1 \end{pmatrix} \otimes \frac{1}{\sqrt{2}} \begin{pmatrix} 1 & 1 \\ 1 & -1 \end{pmatrix} = \frac{1}{2} \begin{pmatrix} 1 & 1 & 1 & 1 \\ 1 & -1 & 1 & -1 \\ 1 & 1 & -1 & -1 \\ 1 & -1 & -1 & 1 \end{pmatrix}$$

Now

$$| \xi_1 \rangle = G_1 \xi_0 = \frac{1}{2} \begin{pmatrix} 1 & 1 & 1 & 1 \\ 1 & -1 & 1 & -1 \\ 1 & 1 & -1 & -1 \\ 1 & -1 & -1 & 1 \end{pmatrix} \begin{pmatrix} 0 \\ 1 \\ 0 \\ 0 \end{pmatrix} = \frac{1}{2} \begin{pmatrix} 1 \\ -1 \\ 1 \\ -1 \end{pmatrix}$$

or

$$| \xi_1 \rangle = \frac{1}{2}(| 00 \rangle - | 01 \rangle + | 10 \rangle - | 11 \rangle) = \left[\frac{| 0 \rangle + | 1 \rangle}{\sqrt{2}} \right] \left[\frac{| 0 \rangle - | 1 \rangle}{\sqrt{2}} \right]$$

The two qubits applied to the input of the black box are

$$| x \rangle = \left[\frac{| 0 \rangle + | 1 \rangle}{\sqrt{2}} \right] \qquad | y \rangle = \left[\frac{| 0 \rangle - | 1 \rangle}{\sqrt{2}} \right]$$

We know that $| 0 \oplus f(x) \rangle = | f(x) \rangle$ thus:

$$| y \rangle \oplus | f(x) \rangle = \frac{(| 0 \rangle - | 1 \rangle)}{\sqrt{2}} \oplus | f(x) \rangle = \frac{(| f(x) \rangle - | 1 \oplus f(x) \rangle)}{\sqrt{2}}.$$

But $| 1 \oplus f(x) \rangle$ is equal to 0 when $f(x) = 1$ and it is equal to 1 when $f(x) = 0$ thus:

$$| y \rangle \oplus | f(x) \rangle = (-1)^{f(x)} \frac{(| 0 \rangle - | 1 \rangle)}{\sqrt{2}}.$$

Then

$$| y \rangle \oplus | f(x) \rangle = \begin{cases} \frac{(| 0 \rangle - | 1 \rangle)}{\sqrt{2}} & if \ f(x) = 0 \\ -\frac{(| 0 \rangle - | 1 \rangle)}{\sqrt{2}} & if \ f(x) = 1 \end{cases}$$

When $f(0) = f(1)$ the second output qubit of the black box, $\mid x \otimes (y \oplus f(x))\rangle$, is

$$
\mid \xi_2\rangle =
\begin{cases}
\left[\frac{\mid 0\rangle + \mid 1\rangle}{\sqrt{2}}\right] \left[\frac{\mid 0\rangle - \mid 1\rangle}{\sqrt{2}}\right] = \frac{1}{2}\begin{pmatrix} 1 \\ -1 \\ 1 \\ -1 \end{pmatrix} & if\ f(0) = f(1) = 0 \\[20pt]
-\left[\frac{\mid 0\rangle + \mid 1\rangle}{\sqrt{2}}\right] \left[\frac{\mid 0\rangle - \mid 1\rangle}{\sqrt{2}}\right] = -\frac{1}{2}\begin{pmatrix} 1 \\ -1 \\ 1 \\ -1 \end{pmatrix} & if\ f(0) = f(1) = 1
\end{cases}
$$

It is easy to show that if $f(0) \neq f(1)$, then the output of the black box is

$$
\mid \xi_2\rangle =
\begin{cases}
\left[\frac{\mid 0\rangle - \mid 1\rangle}{\sqrt{2}}\right] \left[\frac{\mid 0\rangle - \mid 1\rangle}{\sqrt{2}}\right] = \frac{1}{2}\begin{pmatrix} 1 \\ -1 \\ -1 \\ 1 \end{pmatrix} & if\ f(0) = 0\ and\ f(1) = 1 \\[20pt]
-\left[\frac{\mid 0\rangle - \mid 1\rangle}{\sqrt{2}}\right] \left[\frac{\mid 0\rangle - \mid 1\rangle}{\sqrt{2}}\right] = -\frac{1}{2}\begin{pmatrix} 1 \\ -1 \\ -1 \\ 1 \end{pmatrix} & if\ f(0) = 1\ and\ f(1) = 0
\end{cases}
$$

Combining these two results we have

$$
\mid \xi_2\rangle =
\begin{cases}
\pm\left[\frac{\mid 0\rangle + \mid 1\rangle}{\sqrt{2}}\right] \left[\frac{\mid 0\rangle - \mid 1\rangle}{\sqrt{2}}\right] = \frac{1}{2}\begin{pmatrix} 1 \\ -1 \\ 1 \\ -1 \end{pmatrix} & if\ f(0) = f(1) \\[20pt]
\pm\left[\frac{\mid 0\rangle - \mid 1\rangle}{\sqrt{2}}\right] \left[\frac{\mid 0\rangle - \mid 1\rangle}{\sqrt{2}}\right] = \frac{1}{2}\begin{pmatrix} 1 \\ -1 \\ -1 \\ 1 \end{pmatrix} & if\ f(0) \neq f(1)
\end{cases}
$$

The transfer matrix of the third stage of the quantum circuit in Figure 3 is

$$
G_3 = H \otimes I = \frac{1}{\sqrt{2}}\begin{pmatrix} 1 & 1 \\ 1 & -1 \end{pmatrix} \otimes \begin{pmatrix} 1 & 0 \\ 0 & 1 \end{pmatrix} = \frac{1}{\sqrt{2}}\begin{pmatrix} 1 & 0 & 1 & 0 \\ 0 & 1 & 0 & 1 \\ 1 & 0 & -1 & 0 \\ 0 & 1 & 0 & -1 \end{pmatrix}
$$

If $f(0) = f(1)$ then

$$
\mid \xi_3\rangle = \pm\frac{1}{\sqrt{2}}\begin{pmatrix} 1 & 0 & 1 & 0 \\ 0 & 1 & 0 & 1 \\ 1 & 0 & -1 & 0 \\ 0 & 1 & 0 & 1 \end{pmatrix}\frac{1}{2}\begin{pmatrix} 1 \\ -1 \\ 1 \\ -1 \end{pmatrix} = \pm\frac{1}{\sqrt{2}}\begin{pmatrix} 1 \\ -1 \\ 0 \\ 0 \end{pmatrix} = \pm \mid 0\rangle\frac{\mid 0\rangle - \mid 1\rangle}{\sqrt{2}}
$$

If $f(0) \neq f(1)$ then

$$|\xi_3\rangle = \pm \frac{1}{\sqrt{2}} \begin{pmatrix} 1 & 0 & 1 & 0 \\ 0 & 1 & 0 & 1 \\ 1 & 0 & -1 & 0 \\ 0 & 1 & 0 & -1 \end{pmatrix} \frac{1}{2} \begin{pmatrix} 1 \\ -1 \\ -1 \\ 1 \end{pmatrix} = \pm \frac{1}{\sqrt{2}} \begin{pmatrix} 0 \\ 0 \\ 1 \\ -1 \end{pmatrix} = \pm |1\rangle \frac{|0\rangle - |1\rangle}{\sqrt{2}}$$

We observe that

$$f(0) \oplus f(1) = \begin{cases} 0 & if \ f(0) = f(1) \\ 1 & if \ f(0) \neq f(1) \end{cases}$$

Finally, we rewrite $|\xi_3\rangle$

$$|\xi_3\rangle = \pm |f(0) \oplus f(1)\rangle \left[\frac{|0\rangle - |1\rangle}{\sqrt{2}} \right].$$

This expression tells us that by measuring the first output qubit of the circuit in Figure 3 we are able to determine $f(0) \oplus f(1)$ after performing a single evaluation of the function.

3   Shor's Factoring Algorithm and Order Finding

We now address possibly the most important application of quantum computing and we discuss algorithms for integer factorization. In 1994 Peter Shor [5] found a polynomial time algorithm for factorization of n-bit numbers on quantum computers and generated a wave of enthusiasm for quantum computing. Like most factorization algorithms, Shor's algorithm reduces the factorization problem to the problem of finding the period of a function, but uses quantum parallelism to find a superposition of all values of the function in one step. Then the algorithm calculates the quantum Fourier transform of the function, which sets the amplitudes into multiples of the fundamental frequency, the reciprocal of the period. To factor an integer the Shor's algorithm measures the period of the function. A powerful version of the technique used by Shor is the phase-estimation algorithm of Kitaev [3].

The relationship between integer factorization algorithms and the quantum Fourier transform is quite convoluted. We argue that integer factorization reduces to another problem, namely order finding. We can construct an algorithm to determine the prime factors of N based upon the procedure to determine the order of integers $x \ mod \ N$.

But, for our factorization algorithm to be efficient, we have to choose wisely the integers x, we cannot simply try all $x < N$. Now the phase estimation comes into picture. Phase estimation is the name given to the algorithm that allows us to estimate the eigenvalue associated with the eigenvector of a unitary operator. Phase estimation is the cornerstone of several algorithms in quantum computing. The QFT is used by the phase estimation algorithm.

The relationships between these algorithms are summarized in Figure 4.

We reiterate the fact that efficient integer factorization is a very important practical problem because the security of widely used cryptographic protocols is based upon the conjectured difficulty of large integers factorization. To factor an integer N means to write N as a product of prime numbers:

$$N = p \times q_1 \times q_2 \dots \times q_n.$$

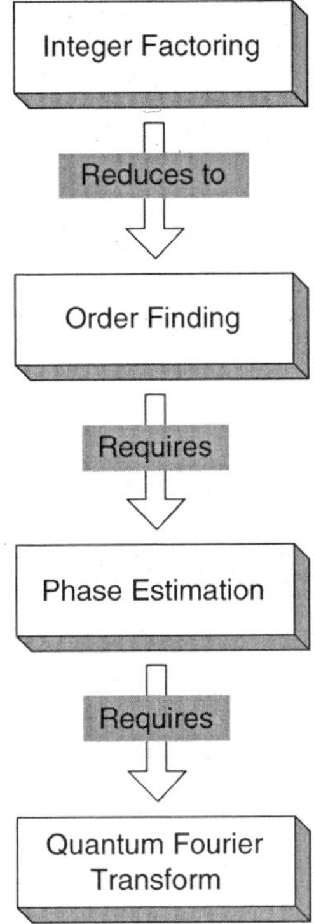

Figure 4. The relationship between integer factorization and Quantum Fourier Transform .

The integer p is said to be a "proper factor" of N if

(i) another integer q exists such that $N = pq$,

(ii) $p \neq 1$, and

(iii) $p \neq N$.

To factor an integer we examine its last digit and if it is even then, the integer is even and has 2 as a factor. It is trivial to factor a small integer. The proper factors of 14 are $p = 2$ and $q = 7$, while the proper factors of 39 are $p = 3$ and $q = 13$. The problem gets harder and harder as the integer to be factored becomes larger and larger. For example, it is practically unfeasible to factor the integer 2841877 without the use of a calculator, or even better, a computer program. By trial and error we could find that $p = 19$ is a proper factor, thus $2841877 = 19 \times 149573$ but then we have to factor the integer 149573.

Given two integers r and N *the order of r modulo N* is the smallest integer k such that $r^k = 1 \mod N$ with two additional conditions

(i) $r^1 \neq 1 \mod N$, and

(ii) $(r^{k-1} + r^{k-2} + \ldots + r^2 + r + 1) \neq 1 \mod N.$

Computing the order k for an integer q such that $q^k = 1 \mod N$ can be represented graphically as a cycle of length $k - 1$.

Several examples of finding the order of an integer modulo N by direct search are given below. First, we wish to find the order of 11 modulo 21, i.e., to find the smallest integer k such that $11^k = 1 \mod 21$. We start with $k = 2$ and continue with $k = 3, 4, 5, 6$.

$$11^2 = 121 = 5 \times 21 + 16 \qquad\qquad \mapsto 11^2 = 16 \mod 21$$

$$11^3 = 11 \times 11^2 = 11 \times 16 \mod 21 = 176 \mod 21 = 8 \mod 21 \mapsto$$
$$11^3 = 8 \mod 21$$

$$11^4 = 11 \times 11^3 = 11 \times 8 \mod 21 = 88 \mod 21 = 4 \mod 21 \mapsto$$
$$11^4 = 4 \mod 21$$

$$11^5 = 11 \times 11^4 = 11 \times 4 \mod 21 = 44 \mod 21 = 2 \mod 21 \mapsto$$
$$11^5 = 2 \mod 21$$

$$11^6 = 11 \times 11^5 = 11 \times 2 \mod 21 = 22 \mod 21 = 1 \mod 21 \mapsto$$
$$11^6 = 1 \mod 21$$

Thus, the order of 11 modulo 21 is $k = 6$. Indeed, the length of the cycle is $k - 1 = 5$, as shown in Figure 5.

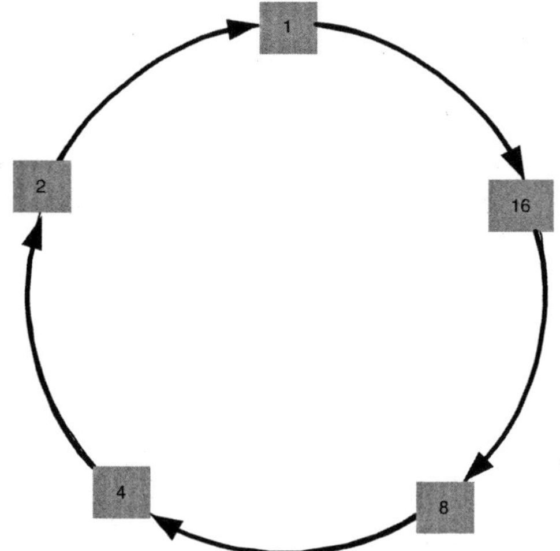

Figure 5. The multiplicative cycle for 11 mod 21. **Each number on the cycle is obtained by multiplying the previous one by** 11 mod 21.

Let us observe that to compute r^k we need only to compute several powers of r. We can express $k = k_{m-1}2^{m-1} + k_{m-2}2^{m-2} + \ldots k_1 2^1 + k_0$ with $k_i = 0$ or $k_i = 1$. Then

$$r^k = r^{k_{m-1}2^{m-1}} \times r^{k_{m-2}2^{m-2}} \times \ldots r^{k_2 2^2} \times r^{k_1 2^1} + r^{k_0}$$

To compute r^k we need at most $m - 1$ exponentiations

$$r^{2^1}, r^{2^2}, r^{2^3}, \ldots r^{2^{m-1}}.$$

For example, when we wish to compute 17^{29} we can write $29 = 16 + 8 + 4 + 1 = 2^4 + 2^3 + 2^2 + 2^0$. Thus

$$17^{29} = 17^{16} \times 17^8 \times 17^4 \times 17^1.$$

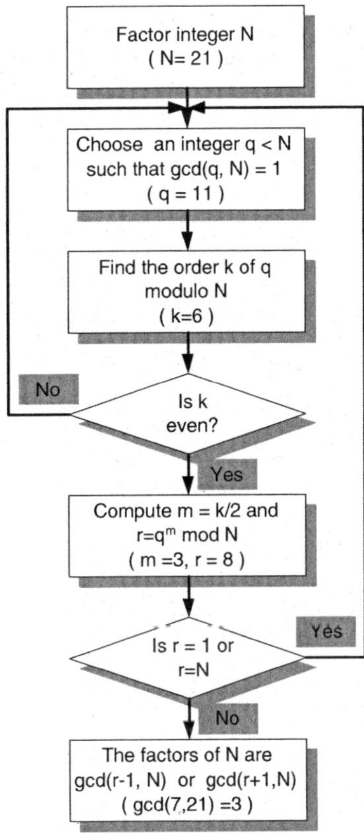

Figure 6. The flowchart of the factorization algorithm based upon order finding.

The pseudo code to carry out this computation is

```
power:= 1
for i=0 to m-1

    if (r^k == 1) then
          power := power × r^(2^i)   mod N

       endif
endfor
```

The condition $r^k = 1 \mod N$ implies that $r^k - 1$ is divisible by N. Equivalently, this means that an integer m exists such that

$$r^k - 1 = (r - 1)(r^{k-1} + r^{k-2} + \ldots + r^2 + r + 1) = mN.$$

This equation shows that either $(r - 1)$ or $(r^{k-1} + r^{k-2} + \ldots + r^2 + r + 1)$ share a common factor with N. Assume that $r - 1$ is such a factor, or shares a common factor with N. We show that the greatest common divisor (gcd) of N and $r - 1$ is indeed a proper factor of N, namely $\gcd(N, r - 1) \neq 1$ and $\gcd(N, r - 1) \neq N$. Consider two cases

(i) if $r - 1 < N$ then the common factor of $r - 1$ and N cannot be N.

(ii) if $r - 1 \geq N$ then $\gcd(N, r - 1)$ could be N if $r - 1$ is a multiple of N. But $r - 1$ is not a multiple of N due to the condition $r^1 \neq 1 \mod N$ that can also be written as $(r - 1) \neq 0 \mod N$.

Thus the $\gcd(N, r - 1)$ is a proper factor of N. Moreover, efficient algorithms to compute the greatest common divisor of two integers exist, e.g., Euclid's algorithm.

We conclude that *the problem of finding the factors of N is reduced to the problem of order finding*. To clarify this idea, let us give several examples. First, we consider the easier case when N is neither even, nor a power of primes. In this case we are looking for an integer r with the property that $r^2 - 1$ is a multiple of N but neither $r - 1$ nor $r + 1$ are multiples of N, i.e., $r \neq 1 \mod N$ and $r \neq -1 \mod N$.

For example, when $N = 21$ a possible choice for r is $r = 8$. Indeed, $r^2 - 1 = 64 - 1 = 63 = 3 \times 21$. As expected, $r - 1 = 8 - 1 = 7$ is a proper factor of $N = 21$.

The pseudocode for finding a proper factor p of an integer N based upon the order finding algorithm is

```
Step 1. If N is even then return  p=2.

Step 2. If N is a power k of a prime integer p then return p.

Step 3. Randomly pick q, 1 < q < N-1.

        If p = gcd(q,N) > 1 then return p. Else go to Step 4.

Step 4. Determine the order k of q modulo N.

        If k is not even then go to Step 3.

Step 5. Let k = 2 m and determine r,
        the m-th power of q modulo N with 1 < r < N.

        If 1 < p = gcd(r-1, N) < N   then return p.

        If 1 < p = gcd(r+1, N) < N   then return p.

        Else (if we fail to find a proper factor of q) go to Ste
```

The flowchart of the algorithm is shown in Figure 6. In our example the order of $11 \mod 21$ is $k = 6$. But $6 = 2 \times 3$. Thus, $m = 3$ and $r = q^m \mod N = 11^3 \mod 21 = 8$. Then, $r - 1 = 8 - 1 = 7$ and $p = \gcd(r - 1, N) = \gcd(7, 21) = 7 < 21$ is a factor of $N = 21$.

As we pointed out earlier, the key to the efficiency of the algorithm is the choice of q.

4 Acknowledgments

The research reported in this paper was partially supported by National Science Foundation grants MCB9527131, DBI0296107, ACI0296035, and EIA0296179.

References

[1] L. K. Grover. *A Fast Quantum Algorithm for Database Search.* Proc. ACM Symp. on Theory of Computing, ACM Press, 212–219, 1996.

[2] R. Josza. *Entanglement and Quantum Computation.* Geometric Issues in the Foundations of Science, Eds. S. Hugget, L. Mason, K.P. Tod, S.T. Tsou, and N. M. J. Woodhouse, Oxford University Press 1997. Also Preprint, http://arxiv.org/archive/quant-ph/9707034 v1, 1997.

[3] A. Yu. Kitaev. *Quantum Measurements and the Abelian Stabilizer Problem.* Preprint, http://arxiv.org/archive/quant-ph/9511026 v1, 1995.

[4] D. C.Marinescu and G. M. Marinescu. Lectures on Quantum Computing. Prentice Hall Publishing, Upper Saddle River, New Jersey, 2004.

[5] P. W. Shor. *Algorithms for Quantum Computation: Discrete Log and Factoring.* Proc. 35 Annual Symp. on Foundations of Computer Science, 124–134, IEEE Press, Piscataway, New Jersey, 1994.

[6] P. W. Shor. *Polynomial - Time Algorithms for Prime Factorization and Discrete Logarithms on a Quantum Computer.* Preprint, http://arxiv.org/archive/quant-ph/9508027 v2, 1996.

[7] P. W. Shor. *Polynomial-Time Algorithms for Prime Factorization and Discrete Logarithms on a Quantum Computer.* SIAM J. Computing 26:1484–1509, 1997.

[8] P. W. Shor. *Why Haven't More Quantum Algorithms Been Found.* Journal of the ACM, 50(1): 87–90, 2003.

[9] D. R. Simon. *On the Power of Quantum Computation.* SIAM J. Computing 26:1474–1483, 1997.

Papers

Common Mechanisms for Supporting Fault Tolerance in DSM and Message Passing Systems

Ramamurthy Badrinath   Christine Morin

IRISA/INRIA
Campus universitaire de Beaulieu,
35042 Rennes Cedex, France
badri@cse.iitkgp.ernet.in, Christine.Morin@irisa.fr

Abstract. Backward error recovery involving checkpointing and restart of tasks is an important component of any system providing fault tolerance to applications distributed over a network. A central problem to checkpointing and recovery is the ability to track dependencies and arrive at a consistent global checkpoint. Traditionally literature treats one of either distributed shared memory (DSM) or message passing as the interprocess communication mechanism when considering the issue of fault tolerance. This paper describes preliminary investigation into common mechanisms that can be implemented to support a wide variety of protocols in both shared memory and message passing systems. In effect it can be used in a system that combines both these IPC mechanisms.[1]

1   Introduction

In distributed systems, the concept of a consistent global state is an important component in algorithms that recover the system from a faulty state. A consistent global state [3] is a set of local states which maintain causal consistency. Causal interrelation between states of different tasks arises from inter-process communication (IPC).

One encounters two kinds of distributed systems depending on the type of IPC used - one which uses message passing (called **MP** systems in this paper), and one where there is a distributed shared virtual memory for all tasks in the system (called **DSM** systems in this paper). For this study we consider shared memory reads and writes, and explicit message passing using send-receive pairs as the only form of IPC. We refer to these collectively as *interactions*.

A *local state* consists of the processor state and the private memory state of a task. In pure MP systems, all memory of a task is private. In case of DSM systems private memory for a task is usually only its stack.

A *local checkpoint* is a saved local state. For MP systems the set of local checkpoints which are consistent forms a global state to which the system may recover. In the case of DSM systems we must additionally restore the shared virtual memory to a state that is consistent with the states of all the tasks. In fact one can view the units of shared memory as entities themselves like tasks and make sure these are consistent with the tasks' local states on recovery. This is the view we take in this paper.

---

[1]The work presented in this paper was carried out while the first author was at IRISA/INRIA, on leave from the CSE Department, Indian Institute of Technology, Kharagpur – 721302, INDIA

The objective of checkpointing and recovery algorithms is to compute the *latest* global state to which the system can recover on failure. This is called the *recovery line*. It is not our purpose in this paper to describe or compare different checkpointing or recovery protocols. These are available in excellent surveys for both MP [4] and DSM [10] systems. Instead we focus on describing mechanisms that can be used in building support for these protocols, assuming the fail-stop model. Still for completeness sake let us describe the major classification of algorithms in this area. Broadly speaking there three classes of checkpointing (and corresponding recovery) protocols for tasks:

- *Coordinated checkpointing:* Here tasks coordinate with each other so that at any time the set of latest checkpoints for all tasks forms a recovery line. The advantage of this mechanism is that recovery is simple and it keeps only the latest checkpoint of each task. The disadvantage is the fact that coordination is needed to establish such a checkpoint.

- *Uncoordinated checkpointing:* Here tasks take checkpoints independently. The advantage is that checkpointing involves no coordination and hence is simpler. The disadvantage is that recovery is complex. Usually recovery requires us to maintain a number of checkpoints for each task as well as a history of the interactions.

- *Communication Induced Checkpointing:* Here tasks take independent checkpoints, but in addition to these they also take additional checkpoints referred to as *forced* check-points. Thus one may view this as introducing some amount of coordination into an uncoordinated checkpointing protocol. The forced checkpoints help make the recovery line progress. Hence we may not need to maintain as much history information as in the case of uncoordinated checkpointing.

In all the above cases dependency tracking plays an important role in the checkpointing and recovery protocols and in optimizations of them for implementation.

In our discussion we will be considering two kinds of entities that need checkpointing - tasks (with private states), and shared memory pages. Though choosing pages as the unit of memory can lead to false sharing, we prefer to use this model because it is easily supportable in practice. Each entity (page and task) will maintain enough information to know what other entities it *directly* depends on. This information will be used then to compute globally consistent states required for recovery.

In this paper we propose mechanisms that can be used to support a wide variety of checkpointing and recovery protocols on both DSM and MP systems. The rest of the paper is organized as follows. In Section 2 we present our communication and state model and introduce the formalism to represent dependency. Section 3 discusses the proposed mechanism and Section 4 shows its application to the major classes of protocols. We then discuss implementation issues in Section 5. Finally, in Section 6 we compare the work in this paper to other related work.

2   Communication and State Model

We now describe a model to clarify our notion of entity state and of IPC. We can then relate our mechanisms to this model and describe how it works in practice.

We consider direct communication between tasks as consisting of a *message* send-receive pair. The communication channel is considered unreliable, implying that messages may be

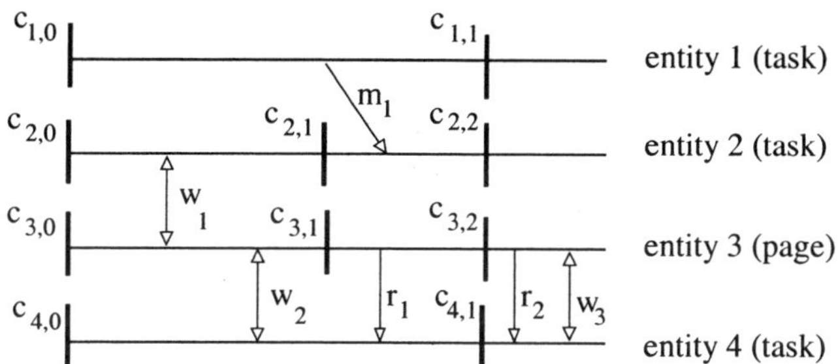

Figure 1. An illustration of interactions causing interdependencies.

lost. Each received message generates a dependency. We say that there is a dependency from the sender to the receiver, or that the receiver is dependent on the sender. If the sender is rolled back to a state before the send, then the receiver needs to be rolled back to a state before the receive. This maintains meaningful causal relationship.

Direct communication also happens between a shared memory page and a task, caused by read and write operations. On a *read* from a page a task state becomes dependent on the corresponding page state. If the page is rolled back to a state prior to the read then the corresponding task may also need to be rolled back to a state prior to its read. This is very similar to the send-receive pair described above, with the additional note that there is no equivalent of a "lost" message. Note that not every interaction results in a new dependency. This is an implementation issue that is discussed in Sections 3 and 5.

A *write* to a page presents an interesting difference from message passing. A write always succeeds and when a write happens, it causes a *two way dependence* as noted by Gunaseelan and LeBlanc [5]. This means that after the write, if the task is rolled back to a state before the write, then so must the page. Similarly if a page is rolled back to a state before the write, then so must the task.

These three varieties of dependencies are depicted in Figure 1. $c_{i,j}$ is the jth checkpoint of entity i. w_1, w_2, w_3 are shared memory writes, r_1, r_2 are shared memory reads and m_1 is a message passed from a sender to a receiver. The figure also shows the other event of interest to us which is the checkpoint event. The checkpoints of a tasks are serially ordered with $c_{i,j}$ representing the jth checkpoint of entity i. We discuss the example in more detail after introducing some formalism.

We can now formalize the above dependencies in the context of checkpointing and roll-back recovery. We do so by extending the now well established "happened before" relation [1, 12]. We note that when the system recovers from a failure each entity is either left untouched in its current state or is rolled back to a checkpoint. We may assume for convenience of argument that the current state of an unfailed entity is a temporary checkpoint too, and hence we will focus on a formalism that establishes dependencies between checkpoints.

We say that $c_{l,m}$ *depends on* $c_{i,j}$, denoted $c_{i,j} \rightarrow c_{l,m}$ if and only if one of the following conditions holds:

1. $i = l$ and $j < m$

2. $i \neq l$ and entity l and i are tasks and task i sends a message after $c_{i,j}$ that task l receives before $c_{l,m}$.

3. $i \neq l$ and entity i is a page and entity l is a task and the task reads the page after the page's checkpoint $c_{i,j}$ but before the task's checkpoint $c_{l,m}$.

4. $i \neq l$ and one of the entities is a page and the other is a task, and the task writes to the page after $c_{i,j}$ and before $c_{l,m}$.

Conditions 1 and 2 are typically used to define dependencies in message passing systems. Conditions 3 and 4 follow from our description of dependence between tasks and shared memory. Condition 4 brings out the property that a write creates a two way dependency. Referring to Figure 1, $c_{1,0} \rightarrow c_{1,1}$ by condition 1, $c_{1,0} \rightarrow c_{2,2}$ by condition 2 (caused by m_1), $c_{3,1} \rightarrow c_{4,1}$ by condition 3 (caused by r_1), and $c_{2,0} \rightarrow c_{3,1}$ by condition 4 (caused by w_1). Also note that the other effect of w_1 is that $c_{3,0} \rightarrow c_{2,1}$.

An interesting result of viewing the page as a separate entity is that certain "Write after Write" dependencies that arise between tasks [2] are naturally handled by this model. In the example of Figure 1, if entity 4 fails immediately after w_2, and rolls back to $c_{4,0}$ then [2] tells us that entity 2 must recover to the state prior to w_1, i.e., to $c_{2,0}$. This is explicit in our model. On entity 4 failing, we must rollback entity 3 to $c_{3,0}$ which in turn implies that we must rollback entity 2 to $c_{2,0}$. In fact our model also tells us that if after w_1 and w_2 if entity 2 fails before $c_{2,1}$ then we must roll back entities 3 and 4 to $c_{3,0}$ and $c_{4,0}$ respectively.

For this paper we assume a *fail stop* failure model. Our mechanisms do not assume any specific limit on the number of failures itself. That is an issue that will depend on the details of the checkpoint and recovery protocols.

3 Mechanism for Dependency Tracking for Recovery Line Computation

In this section we describe the dependency tracking mechanism and describe how it can be used to compute the recovery line for both MP and DSM systems. Our mechanisms are based on ideas from the work of Baldoni *et. al.* [1], and that of Gunaseelan and LeBlanc [5].

3.1 Basic Mechanism

We associate with each entity (i.e., each page and each task) an integer called a *sequence number*. This is initialized to 1 when the entity begins its existence. This is incremented only when the entity takes a checkpoint. The sequence number of the source of a dependency is delivered to the destination of the dependency whenever a dependency is created. For instance in Figure 1, r_1 causes the current sequence number of entity 3 to be delivered to entity 4. A write will cause sequence numbers of the task to be made available to the page and *vice-versa*. Over time an entity receives a number of such sequence numbers from other entities. These are stored in a vector called the *direct dependence vector* (**DDV**) of the entity. If there is a dependence from entity i to j (for instance a message is sent from task i to task j), and the sequence number (of i) sent in the interaction is sn, and $ddv[j]$ is the local dependence vector with entity j, then on the event at j, we execute the following code:

$$ddv[j][i] = \max\{ddv[j][i], sn\}$$

Initially for an entity j, $ddv[j]$ contains all zeros. One may consider the initial image of an entity to be its zero-th checkpoint just for ease of argument. The local value of sn will always be the *checkpoint number* of the next checkpoint to be taken for the entity. Whenever we checkpoint an entity j we store along with the local checkpoint, the corresponding

DDV, i.e., $ddv[j]$. This saved DDV is called the *time-stamp* of the corresponding checkpoint. Whenever a checkpoint is taken at a node j we execute the following code:

$$ddv[j][j] = sn; sn + +; \text{save the time-stamp } ddv[j].$$

We will refer to the time-stamp associated with the kth checkpoint of entity j as $ddv_k[j]$. Note that $ddv_k[j][j] == k$. For completeness sake, the time-stamp for the zero-th checkpoint for all entities has all zeros.

This mechanism essentially records direct dependencies between checkpoints of various entities. So for instance if entity i decides to rollback to checkpoint number n, then for entity j if $ddv[j][i] > n$, then clearly entity j needs to rollback to a checkpointed state for which $ddv[j][i] \leq n$. Of course this covers only direct dependencies. The recovery line computation is the responsibility of the recovery protocol.

With this mechanism in place it is possible to detect all direct dependencies. Yet, in the case of shared memory, some optimization is possible. Consider a page that has not been changed between the two checkpoints $c_{i,j}$ and $c_{i,k}(k > j)$ for the page, then clearly any read after $c_{i,k}$ still refers to the version checkpointed at $c_{i,j}$ provided the page has not yet been modified before the read after $c_{i,k}$. Recording the newer sequence number by the reader results in an artificial dependence. Hence in a read of a page we may prefer to use an older value than the actual sequence number of the page. For this we introduce for each page another counter called the *last write number* (**lwn**). On a read the *lwn* of the page is 'received' by the reading task rather than the *sn* of the page. Also this means that on write to a page, the page must update *lwn* to its current value of *sn*. Typically, algorithms such as that of Janakiraman and Tamir [6] use a bit called the *dirty since checkpoint* (or **dsc**) bit to optimize the overhead of checkpointing. This bit is set to zero when a checkpoint is taken and set to one when a write is done. One may note that the value of the *dsc* bit is simply the value of the boolean expression $lwn == sn$. Note that not every interaction incurs the overhead mentioned in this section. This is an implementation issue that we discuss further in Section 5.

3.2 Usage in Checkpointing and Dependency Tracking

A local checkpoint for a task is its current private state and the corresponding DDV. A local checkpoint for a page is the current page content, the DDV and the *lwn*. Notice that the value of *sn* is in the DDV itself.

With this we are now in a position to track dependencies in the system which could be caused by message passing or shared memory or a combination of both. Thanks to the result by Wang *et. al.* [12], the direct dependency information is sufficient to detect the recovery line. In the next section we will show how this may be used in a few typical scenarios.

4 Usages in Different Protocol Families

It is possible to use these mechanisms to implement several well established protocols and their optimizations for recovery. We take the three families of protocols - coordinated checkpointing, communication induced checkpointing and uncoordinated checkpointing and corresponding recovery strategies.

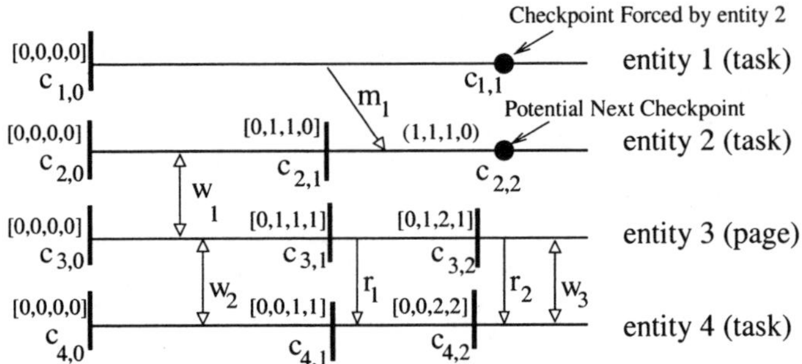

Figure 2. An example of a coordinated checkpointing scenario.

4.1 Coordinated Checkpointing

In the case of coordinated checkpointing whenever the system makes a decision to checkpoint one or more entities, it will make sure that the resulting set of checkpoints (one from each entity) forms a recovery line. This requires coordination among potentially all tasks during the checkpointing phase. The two common optimizations that are necessary for this to be efficient in practice are (1) ability to detect which entities need to be checkpointed, and (2) ability to save the checkpoints asynchronously to the storage. The current work is relevant to the former of these two points. If an entity i takes a checkpoint with the corresponding time-stamp $ddv_k[i]$, then for each other entity j if $ddv_{k-1}[i][j] \neq ddv_k[i][j]$, then entity j must be checkpointed as well, and this protocol has to be applied recursively at entity j. The entities corresponding to the tree of dependencies thus generated can be coordinated and we can generate a coordinated checkpoint. If the entity is a page for which $lwn == sn$, then it means that no updating of the page content information is needed [6].

Consider our example in Figure 2. Corresponding to each checkpoint the time-stamp is shown above the checkpoint label, in square brackets. The DDV for entity 2 immediately after the receipt of m_1 is shown in round brackets. If the latest checkpoints are $\{c_{1,0}, c_{2,1}, c_{3,2}, c_{4,2}\}$, then if entity 2 decides to take the checkpoint $c_{2,2}$ as indicated, then it forces entity 1 to take the checkpoint $c_{1,1}$ because $ddv[2][1] = 1$ but $ddv_1[2][1] = 0$.

For recovery the solution is quite straight forward. The fault detector or some other recovery management mechanism will detect identities of the faulted entities and broadcast them to all unfailed entities. If a non faulty entity i receives notification that entity j is rolling back, then if $ddv[i][j] \neq ddv_{sn-1}[i][j]$, where sn is the current sequence number at i, then clearly entity i has received a dependency from entity j since its last checkpoint, and hence entity i has to rollback as well. This needs to be done recursively just as in the checkpointing phase.

Consider our example in figure 3. The vector in the round brackets is the DDV at entity 4 after w_3. If the set of latest checkpoints is $\{c_{1,1}, c_{2,2}, c_{3,2}, c_{4,2}\}$, then if entity 3 failed after the write w_3 then the recovery would require entity 3 to restart at checkpointed state $c_{3,2}$. When this information reaches entity 4, it compares locally the value of $ddv[4][3]$ and $ddv_2[4][3]$ and find them to be 3 and 2 respectively, requiring it to rollback to its previous checkpoint $c_{4,2}$. On the contrary, note that if the failure was after r_2 but before w_3, then entity 4 would have only received the lwn value with the page read which means $ddv[4][3]$ would only be 2, hence not requiring any action on the part of entity 4.

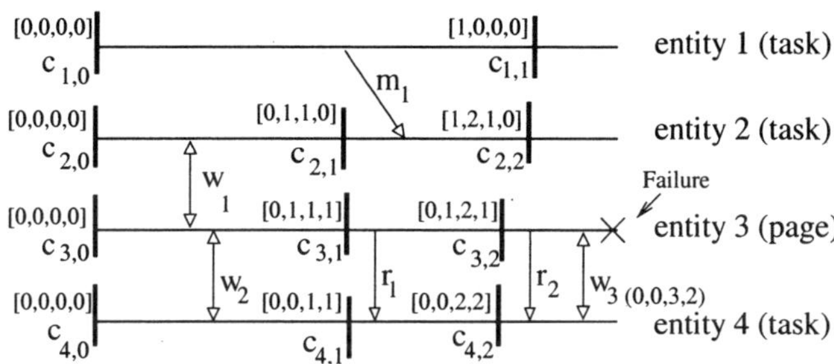

Figure 3. A recovery scenario for coordinated checkpointing.

4.2　Communication Induced Checkpointing

The checkpoints in the case of communication induced checkpointing are of two kinds - independent and forced. When an entity independently decides to checkpoint, it takes an independent checkpoint and does not communicate with other entities. This kind of checkpoint is what creates potential inconsistencies between latest checkpoints of tasks, requiring rollback to older checkpoints. When there is an interaction, then the destination entity of the dependency takes a checkpoint before actually allowing the interaction to affect the computation, if indeed the dependence is new. This is a heuristic to make the recovery line progress. Formally, if the interaction creates a dependency from entity i to entity j, carrying the sequence number x (from i), then entity j must take a checkpoint before completing the interaction causing the dependence provided that $ddv[j][i] \neq x$. This check detects that the independence is new, it makes sure that not every dependency causing interaction leads to a forced checkpoint.

The recovery protocol is identical to that for uncoordinated checkpointing, described next.

4.3　Uncoordinated Checkpointing

In the case of uncoordinated checkpointing the checkpointing phase is straightforward and similar to the independent checkpointing phase of the communication induced checkpointing scheme.

In the recovery phase we need to recover to a globally consistent state. This means we need to compute a recovery line from the set of checkpoints stored. Indeed in this case a *domino effect* [11] may occur leading to a lot of lost computation. This is the potential overhead paid for no coordination at all in the checkpointing and communication phases. The recovery line can be computed in the traditional fashion by presenting the full set of time-stamps to a central "decider process" and letting it compute the recovery line. The recovery line can be computed by constructing the checkpoint graph [4] from the time-stamps. Then one can use reachability analysis to compute the set of checkpoints to recover from. Indeed if the entire set of time-stamps is broadcast, then each entity can run this algorithm and decide for itself the point to which it should rollback. A typical uncoordinated checkpointing algorithm is optimized by implementing a garbage collection algorithm [4] that collects the time-stamps and computes the recovery line. In the process it removes unnecessary history information. This too uses the same set of time-stamps.

5 Implementation Notes

For efficiency reasons it is important to keep the overheads low in the checkpointing and recovery protocols, and during all interactions. In this section we evaluate the overheads introduced by the mechanisms explained in this paper. All interactions must carry a sequence number which is an integer. The code to be executed with the sequence number itself is also small as shown earlier. It is important to note that not all reads or writes need to incur this overhead. In a typical DSM implementation [9] based on sequential consistency with a write-invalidate coherency protocol, the first write is associated with a page fault, leading to a *page grab*, invalidating other copies of the page. It is only at this time that we need to carry the sequence number. Successive writes can proceed without any overhead. Similarly a read request usually requires one to get a *read only* copy of the page. It is only during this *page get* that the overhead of sequence number management is required, not during successive reads.

Secondly, during checkpointing and recovery we need to store or share information in the form of the DDV. The size of the DDV therefore is a concern. Since tasks may interact with other tasks or pages, their DDV size will be as large as the number of tasks and the number of pages. For the pages, we need only maintain a DDV as large as the number of tasks, as pages only interact directly with tasks. This may represent a considerable savings for applications where the number of pages is large and the number of tasks is not very large. Recovery for coordinated checkpointing does not require exchanging of the DDV between entities. But uncoordinated checkpointing may require several DDV's from each entity to be sent to a central recovery manager for computing the recovery line. The alternate of distributed recovery will require several DDV's to be broadcasted from each entity. Hence keeping more smaller DDVs is beneficial. In fact one can keep DDV's in a compressed form (rather than explicit array representation) if the communication delays and latencies are high for the system.

6 Related Work

In this section we compare the description in the current paper with other work in the area. Apart from the work of Gunaseelan and LeBlanc [5], this paper seems to be the only one that talks about time-stamps for shared memory. Their paper deals explicitly with IPC based on RPC retaining shared information. They also talk about specific language support for their study. Also, they do not concern themselves with issues related to fault tolerance as such.

Janssens and Fuchs [7] talk about analyzing all the communication that takes place in a DSM system and abstracting it to the actual resulting inter task dependencies. Our approach is different in that we consider the pages themselves as entities, like tasks, thereby making the basic building blocks from which the dependencies are constructed, different. We also note that they use time-stamps with the aim of rebuilding the ownership information state of DSM pages. Both [7] and [6] talk only about coordinated checkpointing and recovery.

Our work borrows the ideas of time-stamps and direct dependence vectors from the work of Baldoni *et. al.* [1]. Their aim was to compute the *"first global checkpoint that contains"* or *"follows"* a given set of local checkpoints. They also do not talk about application to DSM systems. Their work in turn borrows theoretical ideas from the work of Wang *et. al.* [12], in particular the fact that direct dependency information suffices for constructing consistent global checkpoints.

7   Conclusion

This paper describes common mechanisms for implementing a variety of checkpointing and rollback recovery protocols for both message passing and distributed shared memory systems. The idea is to treat pages as separate entities like tasks and provide a mechanism for tracking direct dependencies among tasks and memory pages. Apart from the fact that it is a mechanism common to both DSM and MP systems over a variety of protocols, it is efficient for implementation since the overhead for each interaction is very low - both in terms of the computation required and the amount of control information exchanged. We also note that the mechanism is sufficient to support several of the optimizations discussed in literature.

The mechanisms proposed in this paper are currently under implementation in the Kerrighed cluster OS [9] which supports both DSM and message passing for IPC. Concerning Kerrighed DSM, mechanisms and optimizations similar to those studied in our previous work on Icare recoverable DSM [8] for efficiently saving checkpoints in memory will be implemented.

References

[1] R. Baldoni, G. Cioffi, J. Helary, and M. Raynal. Direct dependency-based determination of consistent global checkpoints. *International Journal of Computer Systems Sciences and Engineering*, 16(1):43–49, 2001.

[2] M. Banatre, A. Gefflaut, P. Joubert, C. Morin, and P.A. Lee. An architecture for tolerating processor failures in shared-memory multiprocessors. *IEEE Transaction on Computers*, 45(10):1101–1115, 1996.

[3] K.M. Chandy and L. Lamport. Distributed snapshots: Determining global states of distributed systems. *ACM Trans. Computer Systems*, 3(1):63–75, February 1985.

[4] M. Elnozahy, L. Alvisi, Y-M. Wang, and D.B. Johnson. A survey of rollback-recovery protocols in message-passing systems. Technical Report CMU-CS-99-148, Carnegie Mellon University, June 1999.

[5] L. Gunaseelan and R.J. LeBlanc Jr. Event ordering in a shared memory distributed system. In *International Conference on Distributed Computing Systems*, pages 256–263, 1993.

[6] G. Janakiraman and Y. Tamir. Coordinated checkpointing-rollback error recovery for distributed shared memory multicomputers. In *Symposium on Reliable Distributed Systems*, pages 42–51, 1994.

[7] B. Janssens and W.K. Fuchs. Reducing interprocessor dependence in recoverable distributed shared memory. In *Symposium on Reliable Distributed Systems*, pages 34–41, 1994.

[8] Anne-Marie Kermarrec, Christine Morin, and Michel Banâtre. Design, implementation and evaluation of ICARE: an efficicent recoverable DSM. *Software Practice and Experience*, 28(9):981–1010, July 1998.

[9] Renaud Lottiaux, Christine Morin, and Geoffroy Vallée. Containers: an architecture for an efficient cluster operating system. Publication interne 1442, IRISA, February 2002.

[10] C. Morin and I. Puaut. A survey of recoverable distributed shared virtual memory systems. *IEEE Transaction on Parallel and Distributed Systems*, 8(9):959–969, 1997.

[11] B. Randell. System structure for software fault tolerance. *IEEE Trans. on Software Engineering*, 1(2):220–232, 1975.

[12] Y.M. Wang, A. Lowry, and W.K. Fuchs. Consistent global checkpoints based on direct dependency tracking. *Information Processing Letters*, 50:223–230, 1994.

Concurrent Information Processing and Computing
D. Grigoras and A. Nicolau (Eds.)
IOS Press, 2005

Synchronization Based on Global States as a General Control Method in Parallel Programs

J. Borkowski[1], M. Tudruj[1,2], D. Kopanski[1]

[1] *Polish-Japanese Institute of Information Technology,*
86 Koszykowa Str., 02-008 Warsaw, Poland
[2] *Institute of Computer Science, Polish Academy of Sciences*
21 Ordona Str. 01-237 Warsaw, Poland
{janb, tudruj, damian}@pjwstk.edu.pl

Abstract. New parallel program synchronization mechanisms are presented. A specialized synchronizer process, or a hierarchy of such processes, gather information about process states and construct Strongly Consistent Global States, using time interval timestamps. Global predicates evaluated by synchronizers can cause synchronization signals to be send to processes, the signals trigger asynchronous computation activation or cancellation. The proposed framework is integrated with a message passing system - it is added to the GRADE graphical parallel programming environment to enhance its message-passing based features. Architecture and implementation of the enhancement are discussed.

1 Introduction

Message passing has become one of the most popular and most successful parallel programming paradigms, especially due to standardization enabled by PVM and MPI libraries. Nevertheless writing programs based on message passing libraries is still difficult since many technical details have to be known by a programmer. To ease parallel programming, program design tools are becoming popular. Message passing is lacking a systematic way for process synchronization. The code responsible for synchronization is mixed with the computational code and the synchronization conditions are expressed in terms of low-level operations (send/receive, barrier). In a program organized in a better way, data transfer operations should be separated from synchronization. Accidentally used synchronization primitives should be transformed into a generalized system where synchronization is used as a top-level factor that constitutes a framework for general program execution control. Some proposals in this direction have been already published [19], however, they have not been implemented yet in practice. De-coupled implementation of synchronization in program execution control is consistent with the current tendencies of the systematic design of parallel systems. Much work has been done on efficiency of various forms of synchronization operations [9, 24, 29]. However, these tendencies are very scarcely supported by the design of adequate parallel program design tools. This project is an attempt to partially fill this gap.

An advanced synchronization environment for parallel applications has been proposed in [2, 3]. To a big extent, the control in a parallel application program is dependent on synchronization, which is based on asynchronous evaluation of high-level conditions defined on application global states. The conditions are specified explicitly in special fragments of the program code. Processes react to a fulfilled synchronization condition in a way that is another novel feature. They can be temporally or permanently suspended if higher priority or more relevant actions are to be activated by a synchronization condition. In such situation, a process receives a synchronization message that immediately activates a procedure, which is an integral part of the application. In an alternative case, computations can be cancelled. Due to this some scarce computer resources can be liberated and made available for other tasks. In the proposed synchronization environment, synchronization-driven program execution control can be specified.

In this paper we describe how the ideas mentioned above are combined with standard message passing in the graphical parallel program design environment GRADE [17, 18, 25]. GRADE is meant for programmers who want to write parallel message passing programs without learning details of message passing library procedures. The programmer has only to draw a graph representation of a program divided into parallel processes, to fill the nodes with sequential C code and to assign which variables should be sent/received in which points of the program. GRADE presents a high level approach to parallel program design. However, it lacks more sophisticated and structured synchronization features that can be provided accordingly to above-mentioned principles. We discuss problems, which arise here and propose relevant solutions.

The paper is composed of 3 parts following this introduction. In the part 2, the idea of execution control in parallel programs based on process synchronization is explained. It includes verification of predicates defined on elements of global states in asynchronous systems and reactions on predicates as asynchronous activation and cancellation of computations in application programs. The next part contains a description of new synchronization features added to GRADE. In part 4, physical implementation issues of communication and synchronization for the proposed solution are discussed.

2 Process synchronization based on global predicates

Global application states are used in parallel/distributed application monitoring and debugging to see if the application execution fulfils necessary conditions (global predicates) that warranties correct execution [8, 14, 15, 21, 33]. We suggest using global predicates to control directly program behaviour. In this way, the control/synchronization scheme in a program can be made correctly by construction and also immediately verifiable. Also, synchronization conditions expressed separately as global predicates will be easy to understand and modify. The proposed system works as follows. Application program processes send messages on their states to special globally accessible processes called synchronizers. Each state message is labeled with a timestamp. A synchronizer collects state messages and determines if a consistent global state [8, 15, 28] has been reached. On each global state reached, one (or more) synchronization condition(s) (control predicate(s)) is (are) computed. If a predicate value is true, then a number of synchronization signals are sent by the synchronizer to selected application processes. On reception of these signals, application processes break their standard computation and the control in these processes is transferred to signal handling procedures. The procedures perform actions that constitute reactions to synchronization of application process states that has been reached.

In a parallel system without common clock and without shared memory it is difficult to observe global states of applications. To solve the problem, logical vector clocks [6, 20] or partial synchronization of processor local clocks [28] can be used. Messages about process local states with attached timestamps should be sent to a synchronizer, and the synchronizer task is to combine the received information to identify consistent application global states. The actual sequence of global states cannot be observed with certainty; a synchronizer can only enumerate all the possible alternative execution scenarios. It is not possible to answer whether the actual application execution has passed through a state satisfying a given predicate, because we do not know which scenario happened in real, so what are the exact states the application has passed through. This difficulty has led to a definition of global predicate modalities [8, 12, 14, 15, 28]. Modalities give answers to questions concerning global predicate satisfaction. We need to know on-line, as early as possible, what is the actual application state. So we need a modality, which deals with real application states and with the actual application execution history, which can be evaluated on-line and which imposes low overhead. These conditions are met best by modality *Instantly* [28]. To be able to apply it, we need to synchronize process local clocks with an assumed tolerance ε . For a predicate φ if *Instantly(φ)* is satisfied then there was a period in real time (and this period is known), when the application was in such a state, that φ was satisfied. Such states are called Strongly Consistent Global States (SCGS). It is possible for an application to pass a state satisfying φ while *Instantly(φ)* is not detected, only when such a state lasts less then 2ε. Because this condition is clearly defined, a programmer can deal with it reasonably. The cost of SCGS detection is acceptable - $O(EN \log N)$ [28], where E is the number of events at one process and N is the number of application processes. Other modalities have higher costs (even exponential) for unrestricted predicate forms. *Instantly* requires timestamps to be attached only to messages sent to a synchronizer, timestamps contain just two clock readouts.

Synchronizers observe application program states and evaluate pre-defined predicates. Whenever a predicate is satisfied, the synchronizer activates a reaction in some parts of executed application program. In a message passing system, it is done by sending to them control messages - signals. We want the processes to be able to react on signals possibly immediately by clearly defined actions. These goals are met by asynchronous activation and cancellation [3,5]. In the code of a process, designated regions are made sensitive to incoming signals. If the process control is inside a region sensitive to a signal of a given type a reaction is triggered when such a signal arrives. The reaction can be either activation or cancellation. Synchronization driven activation makes the current computation to be suspended and a reaction code associated with the region to be executed. After completion of the reaction code the suspended computing resumes. Synchronization driven cancellation makes the current computation to be stopped and a cancellation handling procedure associated with the region to be performed. The program execution resumes just after the abandoned region. Fig. 1 illustrates this concept.

An example of efficient program execution control of this type can be a branch-and-bound (B&B) algorithm [2, 4]. The synchronizer knows the best solution found so far in a parallel B&B search. It can react immediately to prevent search processes from solving subtasks if their bounds are lower then the current best solution. A load balancing scheme can be included to the program implemented as an action activated by the synchronizer, triggered in global states with unbalanced load.

3   Implementation of proposed synchronization features in GRADE

GRADE is a parallel programming environment based strictly on message passing. It can be extended by adding control and synchronization methods based on application global state

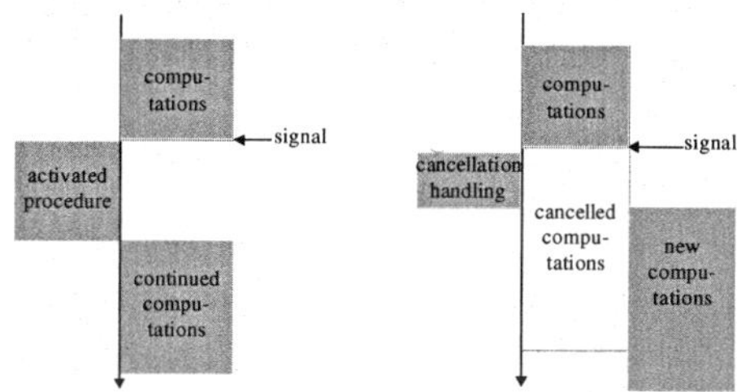

Figure 1. Principle of asynchronous activation (left part) and cancellation (right part)

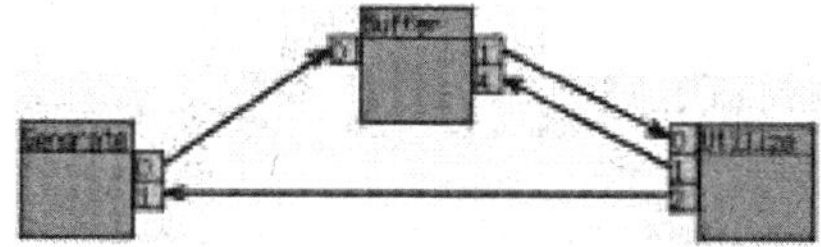

Figure 2. Processes and their interconnections in GRADE

analysis. GRADE allows a user to specify parallel processes, their interconnection and the internal structure of each process. The programmer specifies a program by the use of a graph-ical user interface and does not need to know any technical details of any communication li-brary. Fig. 2. shows application processes and communication channels with three processes connected by links through communication ports.

A separate window can be opened for each process, to specify the process behavior, drawn as a flow diagram, see Fig. 3. To create and modify such diagrams a programmer is supported with GRED graphical editor [18]. There are three main types of nodes used in the algorithm design: control statements (representing if, for, while,...), text blocks (sequential C language code can be put there) and communication nodes. Each communication node has commu-nication ports assigned. In such a way the communication specified on a process level is translated onto the application level. The text blocks are filled with C code with the help of a text editor. The completed graphical program specification is translated into C language to be compiled and linked with GRADE libraries [10].

A synchronizer, as described above, is represented as a special kind of a process. Using dedicated channels, application processes send to it messages about their local states, these messages are properly time stamped. The synchronizer constructs SCGSs using obtained information, evaluates defined predicates on them and sends back synchronization signals. We need here to specify how process state is expressed. The synchronizer has a number of input ports to receive state information from processes. The values sent to the ports are stored in arrays (after proper processing, see further explanations), one array per port, messages from process i are stored at array index i. So, the synchronizer sees the process states abstracted as values of array elements. Each array represents one aspect of process states, e.g. one can hold information about current workload, another about a problem currently being solved. Whenever a process wants to inform the synchronizer about a change in its local state, it sends a message with a proper value to a relevant synchronizer port. Synchronizer operates as shown in Fig. 3.

A synchronizer is shown at application level as a block similar to a standard computa-

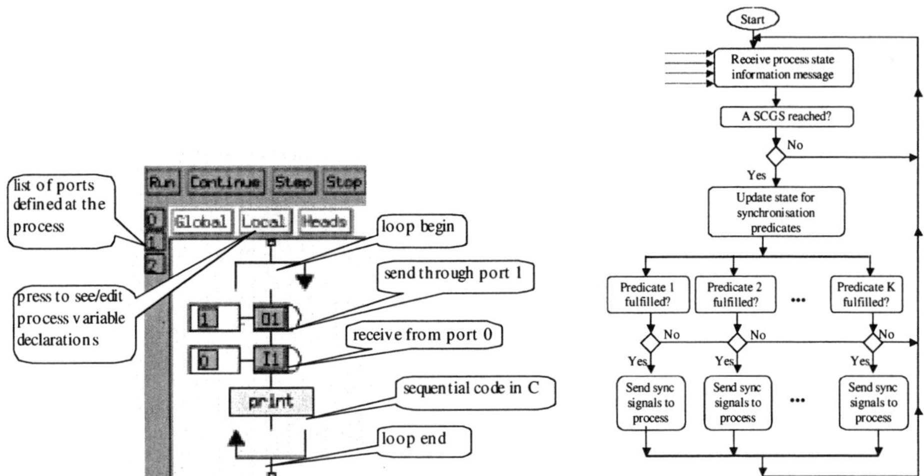

Figure 3. left: Flow diagram fragment of a process , right: Control flow diagram of a synchronizer

tional process, Fig. 4. It has ports and channels that connect it with other processes. Its input ports accept process local state information messages, while output ports send synchronization signals. If we click on a synchronizer block, we open a separate window that shows its internal details. This window shows predicates defined in the synchronizer. Attached input ports determine the state information used by a predicate. A predicate evaluation can cause signals to be sent by attached output ports.

When we click on a predicate symbol, we get another window, in which we can specify the predicate details. The specification takes form of a control flow diagram. Execution of a predicate starts when the synchronizer reaches a SCGS. In the predicate control flow diagram, there are input statements which read in relevant values of a SCGS array bound to specified input ports. Predicates are calculated according to included definition. Output statements contained in the block dispatch synchronization signals. The signals are messages handled by processes in a special way.

Synchronization signals arriving at application processes can provoke a procedure activation or computation cancellation. GRADE process control flow diagram had been extended to express the new functionality. A simplified example of a control flow diagram made sensitive to synchronization signals is presented in Fig. 5. The normal execution flow goes along the path marked by a dotted line. If a signal arrives on ports 1 or 3 when the process execution is within a dashed rectangle, then the control is transferred to the right-hand side block.

For a large number of processes, and for complex predicates, the amount of computations and communication a synchronizer have to perform can be problematic. There is a simple way to decentralize the synchronization control and to improve efficiency. It is by introduction of many synchronizers, each one responsible for a separate synchronization task. Moreover, synchronizers can be organized into hierarchies. Application processes can be split into groups. Each group can cooperate with its own synchronizer that can be connected to a higher-level synchronizer, Fig. 6. There can be many levels in the hierarchy. Higher-level synchronizers act in the same way as low-level synchronizers. Lower level synchronizers

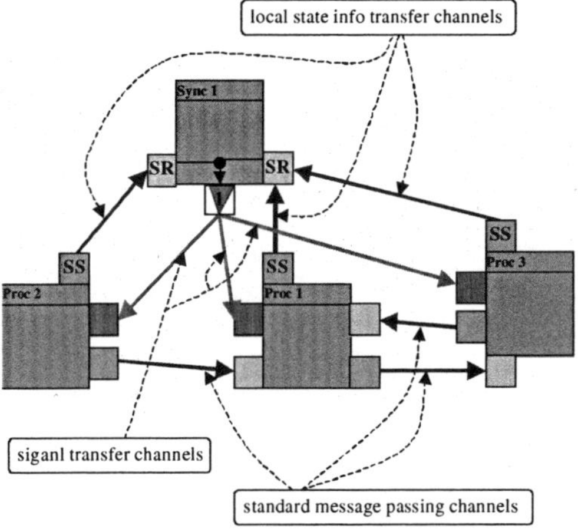

Figure 4. Application level window - three processes with a synchronizer

send state messages to their higher lever synchronizers. A state message is send up in the hierarchy as a result of a predicate evaluation by a lower level synchronizer. A higher-level synchronizer computes SCGSs of subordinate synchronizers. It can know which predicates at the subordinate synchronizers are satisfied. Higher-level predicates can be constructed based on that knowledge and their evaluation can produce synchronization signals. The signals can be propagated to lower levels until they reach application processes. In such a way predicate evaluation and synchronization signal communication is performed in a parallel and distributed way.

GRADE produces C programs based on standard PVM/MPI libraries. In general, such programs cannot be asynchronously interrupted to run a procedure and then to resume previous actions [5]. MPI, PVM, and numerous standard C library procedures are not re-entrant. An application process cannot always react instantaneously on incoming signals. We propose to mark sections of the GRADE process control flow diagram as freely interruptible, uninterruptible or interruptible at defined points only. If an interruption cannot take place right away,

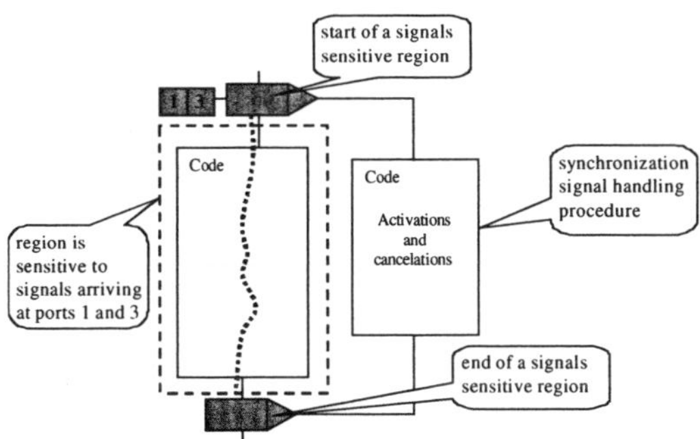

Figure 5. Flow diagram sensitive to synchronization signals

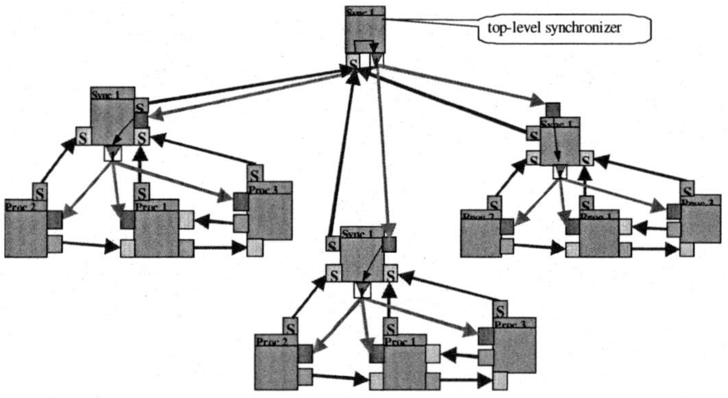

Figure 6. A hierarchic structure of synchronizers

a flag is set, and the signal is to be handled at the first opportunity in the future.

4 Practical implementation solutions

Practical implementation of the proposed system implies the following additions to existing GRADE.

    a) synchronization of clocks in processors which execute application programs

    b) state message exchange with timestamps

    c) detection of consistent global states in processors

    d) programming asynchronous process reaction to synchronization signals

    e) extension of the graphical interface in existing GRADE.

For clock synchronization the Network Time Protocol [26] will be used, as immediately available. Fast Ethernet is used in our platform and we expect to synchronize the clocks with tolerance about 50 μs, so to be able to detect SCGS lasting at least twice that long. Given current CPU speeds, much can happen within that time period. Another solution is planned to be used in the future. It is the RBS protocol [11] or hardware counters based on PCI counter cards controlled in a global way. Then clock tolerance of few microseconds can be achieved. The timestamps can be easily introduced within GRADE communication library. A SCGS detection algorithm planned to be used is described in [28]. The algorithm waits for current process state termination before taking it into account. We want to eliminate waiting for state termination. A watch-dog mechanism in a synchronizer can solve the problem. When a process state starts (after a change), the synchronizer sets a timer. If no message with the state termination arrives soon, the timer triggers a dummy state termination. When the real termination comes, a dummy one is simply replaced by the real. Timer delay is set to $2\varepsilon + Dmax - Dmin$, where ε is the accuracy of clock synchronization, $Dmax$ and $Dmin$ are the maximal and minimal message transfer times, respectively. This way dummy termination will be issued only for states lasting at least 2ε, i.e. long enough to be considered. $Dmin$ and $Dmax$ are determined experimentally. Synchronizer monitors current transfer times and it can adjust the $Dmax$ value.

Signals arriving at a process should trigger the handling procedure immediately. Standard message passing does not offer relevant mechanisms. The functionality of Active Messages [22] is useful, but they provide a low-level implementation and need advanced network hardware (e.g. Myrinet). PVM message handlers [13] are at a higher level, however, they are not triggered immediately upon a message arrival and they are not helpful for cancellation implementation, either. UNIX Real-Time signals can provide necessary features [3, 5]. Within one system they can be delivered and handled within a few microseconds, while message passing and dispatcher processes can be used to transfer them between computers. The time between a process reports its new state to a synchronizer and receives a synchronization signal can be then estimated as twice the message transfer time + watch-dog timer delay + SCGS detection algorithm runtime. This value determines parallel task synchronisation granularity, which can be managed effectively by a synchronizer in our environment. In a FastEthernet cluster based on LAM MPI VIA [7] the transfer time for a message up to 32 byte long is below 70 μs. In this environment, we expect the average synchronisation response time to be around 450 μs. The granularity becomes much finer with an introduction of a faster network. The use of GigaBitEthernet network based on zero-copy MPI EMP [1] provides latency of 23 μs for transfers of messages of 1.5 KB. In this case the obtained reaction time will be shorter than 180 μs. The use of Myrinet 2000 network with MPI provides short-message latency (up to 100 bytes long) of 8.5 μs [My03]. In this case, we expect the synchronisation response time with MPI communication to be below 100 μs i.e. much better than that of GigaBitEthernet. The use of very fast DIMNET network [32] can provide the net short message transfer time of less than 1.2 μs. One can expect to be able to decrease the MPI synchronisation response time to around 10 μs. An ideal solution here would be to use a separate network dedicated for synchronization and control purposes, as in CRAY T3E system [29]. In this case, one can expect the synchronisation response time decreased below 2 μs. A more up-to-date dedicated controller for synchronisation/communication in cluster systems has been proposed in [16]. It enables hardware implementation of fuzzy synchronization [27] inside code regions in parallel application programs with a latency of 1.2 μs for 16 processes. An example of implementation of the distributed synchronization as a dedicated hardware has been described in [30]. With 100 MHz processors, it provides 200 ns latency for 256 processes in a barrier. It shows the potential of hardware distributed implementation of synchronization primitives.

5   Conclusions

A parallel programming environment which combines the standard message-passing paradigm with an advance synchronization and control model based on application global state predicates has been presented in this paper. Global predicates are used to control application program execution together with asynchronous activation and cancellation mechanism. Data transmissions are de-coupled from synchronization and relevant control infrastructure in programs. The synchronization and control code is well separated from the proper application computational code and is easy to understand and verify. Global predicates can implement application control and synchronization, which is correct by construction. The paper contains a discussion of the implementation problems and gives viable solutions.

The proposed programs execution control method will be implemented as a user-friendly parallel program graphical design system. Such a system is currently under work by enhancing an existing GRADE graphical parallel programming environment. This project is implemented within a co-operation with the SZTAKI Institute in Budapest who has been a designer of the GRADE system. Some of proposed elements do not exist in current software environments, e.g. asynchronous activation/cancellation, and will constitute an original extension of current programming methodology. Structural design of the control interface in our proposal is close to GRADE user interface philosophy, which will facilitate their integration. We hope the integrated system will be easily understandable to a programmer and will enable to him a new more useful style of parallel program design. An operational system that we hope to have in few months will let us practical evaluation of all proposed solutions.

References

[1] M. Apte, S. Chakravarthi, J. Padmanabhan and A. Skjellum, A Synchronized Real-Time Linux Based Myrinet Cluster for Deterministic High Performance Computing and MPI/RT, Ninth International Workshop on Parallel and Distributed Real-Time Systems (WPDRTS 2001), April 2001, San Francisco, CA.

[2] J. Borkowski, Towards More Powerful and Flexible Synchronization Primitives, in Proc. of Inter. Conf. on Parallel Computing in Electrical Engineering PARELEC 2000, August 2000, Trois-Rivieres, Canada. IEEE PR00759, pp.18-22

[3] J. Borkowski, Interrupt and Cancellation as Synchronization Methods, in Proc of 4th Int. Conf. Parallel Processing and Applied Mathematics PPAM 2001, Naleczow, Poland, Springer 2001, LNCS 2328

[4] J. Borkowski, D. Kopaski, M. Tudruj, "Adding Advanced Synchronization to Processes in GRADE", in Proceedings of the Int. Conf. on Parallel Processing and Electrical Engineering PARELEC 2002, Warsaw, Poland, IEEE 2002

[5] J. Borkowski, D. Kopaski, M. Tudruj, Implementing Control in Parallel Programs by Synchronization-Driven Activation and Cancelation, Proc. of the Eleventh Euromicro, Genova, Italy, IEEE 2003

[6] O. Babaoglu and K. Marzullo, "Consistent global states of distributed systems: fundamental concepts and mechanisms", in: Distributed Systems, Addison-Wesley, 1995

[7] M. Bertozzi, M. Panella, M. Reggiani, Design of a VIA Based Communication Protocol for LAM/MPI Suite, Ninth Euromicro Workshop on Parallel and Distributed Processing (PDP '01) ,February 07 - 09, 2001, pp. 27-33.

[8] R. Cooper and K. Marzullo, "Consistent detection of global predicates, "Proceedings ACM/ONR Workshop on Parallel Distributed Debugging, pages 163-173, 1991.

[9] Cohen W.E., Dietz H.G., Sponaugle, Dynamic Barrier Architecture for Multi-Mode Fine-Grain Parallelism Using Conventional Processors, 1994 Int. Conf. on Parallel Processing, pp. I 93-96.

[10] D. Drts, P. Kacsuk, GRAPNEL To C Translation in the GRADE Environment Computers and Artificial Intelligence, Vol. 18, No. 4. pp. 415-424, 1999.

[11] J. Elson, L. Girod and D. Estrin. "Fine-grained network time synchronization using reference broadcasts." In Proceedings of the Fifth Symposium on Operating System Design and Implementation (OSDI 2002), Boston, Massachussetts, USA, December 2002.

[12] Eddy Fromentin and Michel Raynal, "Characterizing and detecting the set of global states seen by all observers of a distributed computation," Proceedings of the Fifteenth International Conference on Distributed Computing Systems, pages 431-438, 1995.

[13] Al Geist Advanced Tutorial on PVM 3.4 New Features and Capabilities, http://www.csm.ornl.gov/pvm/EuroPVM97/

[14] Detection of weak unstable predicates in Distributed programs, V.K Garg, B. Waldecker, In IEEE Transactions on Parallel and Distributed Systems, 5(3), pp. 299–307, March 1994.

[15] V. K. Garg, B. Waldecker, Detection of Strong Unstable Predicates in Distributed Programs, IEEE Trans. on Parallel and Distrib. Systems, Vol. 7, No. 12, December 1996 (pp. 1323-1333)

[16] K. Hyakawa, S. Sekiguchi, Design and Implementation of a Synchronization and Communication Controller for Cluster Computing Systems, 4-th Int. Conference on High Performance Computing in Asia-Pacific Region, Vol. 1, May 2000, pp. 76- 81.

[17] Kacsuk, P., Dzsa, G. and Fadgyas, T., GRADE: A Graphical Programming Environment for PVM Applications Proc. of the 5th Euromicro Workshop on Parallel and Distributed Processing, London, 1997, pp. 358-365

[18] The GRED Graphical Editor for the GRADE Parallel Program Development Environment P .Kacsuk, G. Dzsa, T. Fadgyas and R. Lovas Future Generation Computer Systems, No. 15 (1999), pp. 443-452.

[19] M. Tudruj, P. Kacsuk, Extending Grade Towards Explicit Process Synchronization in Parallel Programs, Computers and Artificial Intelligence, vol 17, 1998, No. 5 pp 507-516

[20] F. Mattern. Virtual Time and Global States in Distributed Systems. Proc. Workshop on Parallel and Distributed, Algorithms, Chateau de Bonas, Oct. 1988, M. Cosnard et al. (eds.), Elsevier / North Holland, pp. 215-226, 1989.

[21] M. Minas, Detecting Quantified Global Predicates in Parallel Programs, Europar 95 , Stockholm, Sweden. Proceedings. Lecture Notes in Computer Science, Vol. 966, Springer, pp 403-414

[22] P. J. Mucci, "An Efficient Transport Independent Active Messaging Implementation for PVM", Technical Report UT-CS-98-399, 1998, http://citeseer.nj.nec.com/93955.html

[23] Myricom Corp. GM 1.6.4 API Performance with PCI64B and PCI64C Myrinet/PCI Interfaces, April 2003, http://www.myri.com/myrinet/performance/index.html

[24] Olnovitch, H.T., ALLNODE Barrier Synchronization Network, 9-th Int. Parallel Processing Symposium, April, 1995, pp. 265-269.

[25] The P-GRADE Visual Parallel Programming Environment, http://www.lpds.sztaki.hu/teaching materials/P-GRADE/index.htm

[26] Request for Comment RFC1305 Network Time Protocol (Version 3) Specification, Implementation and Analysis

[27] R. Gupta, The Fuzzy Barrier: A Mechanizm for High Speed Synchronization of Processors, Proc. of the 3rd ASPLOS Conference, April 1989, pp. 54-63.

[28] Scott D. Stoller: "Detecting Global Predicates in Distributed Systems with Clocks". Distributed Computing, Volume 13 Issue 2 (2000) pp 85-98

[29] Scott S. L., Synchronization and Communication in the T3E Multiprocessor, Proceedings of the 7-th ASPLOS Conference, 1996, pp. 26-36.

[30] S. Shang, K. Hwang, Distributed Hardwired Barrier Synchronization for Scalable Multiprocessor Clusters, IEEE Trans. On Parallel and Distributed Systems, vol. 6, June 1995, pp. 591 - 605.

[31] P. Shivam, P. Wyckoff, D. Panda, EMP: Zero-copy OS-bypass NIC-driven Gigabit Ethernet Message Passing, Proceedings of Conference on High Performance Networking and Computing, Denver, Colorado, Nov. '01,pp. 57 - 57

[32] N. Tanabe et al., Low Latency Communication on DIMMnet-1 Network Interface Plugged into a DIMM Slot, Proceedings of the Int. Conf. on Parallel Computing in Electrical Eng., Warsaw, Sept. 2002, pp. 9 - 14.

[33] A. Tarafdar and V.K. Garg. Predicate Control for Active Debugging of Distributed Programs. Symposium on Distributed and Parallel Debugging, 1998.

Concurrent Information Processing and Computing
D. Grigoras and A. Nicolau (Eds.)
IOS Press, 2005

Middleware-based Load Balancing for Communicating Java Objects

Violeta Felea, Bernard Toursel

Laboratoire d'Informatique Fondamentale de Lille (LIFL) UMR CNRS 8022
University of Sciences and Technologies of Lille
59655 Villeneuve d'Ascq CEDEX - FRANCE
Ecole Polytechnique Universitaire de Lille (Polytech'Lille)
{felea, toursel}@lifl.fr

Abstract. In the context of heterogeneous networks, like clusters of workstations, the design of programming and execution environments aims to adapt automatically execution to fluctuations that may appear in the execution of Java distributed and parallel applications. ADAJ, our proposal of a development and execution environment for Java applications, addresses this aim through conceptual tools expressing parallelism, at the development level, and through a dynamic load balancing mechanism, at the execution level. The last one is based on dynamic observation of the application, in order to consider both object activity and communication links. Communications define attraction relations between objects and this article presents a type of asynchronous applications for which the communication aspect is important.

1 Introduction

Heterogeneous systems rise two kinds of problems for distributed applications. The first aspect concerns transparency: applications should be designed as transparently as possible of the heterogeneity and distribution of available resources (CPU, memory, operating system). The second aspect concerns execution, which is supposed to support irregularities in the evolution of the application and in availabilities of resources (share of CPU and/or memory with other processes, new provided resources). Java deals with some heterogeneity problems and its distributed model, JavaRMI [11], allows communication between remote objects; however, Java tools do not adapt automatically execution to fluctuations which may appear during execution of applications.

In the context of distributed execution platforms formed by several Java virtual machines (JVMs), hosted by a cluster of workstations, efficiency of execution should be achieved not only through conceptual tools (oriented towards distribution or parallelism), but also through a load balancing mechanism.

The dynamic load balancing scheme in ADAJ (Adaptive Distributed Applications in Java) is a transparent tool at the middleware level which makes the execution reactive to irregularities in the evolution of the application and to changes in the resource availabilities. This adaptability requires the use of a profiling tool, concurrent with the execution of an application, and not prior to it. Profiling is done using an observation mechanism [3] of the application which predicts its evolution in future, depending on the recent past. The ADAJ load balancing strategy uses these information in order to correct, dynamically, detected load imbalances by good initial object distribution or by object redistribution. The JavaParty distributed object model [9] offers the needed features to achieve our objectives: remote creation and migration of *remote objects*.

Dynamic object migrations are determined by exploiting observation mechanisms of the evolution of the application. Similar work is presented in [4], where allocation decisions are taken at runtime, depending on dynamic load measures. Unlike ADAJ, the language defines directives that specify allocation needs for application components.

The focus of this article is on the load balancing strategy which considers only the evolution of the application for good object redistribution, in the context of communicating objects. We present the approach of a dynamic and transparent intra-application load balancing strategy in ADAJ and its evaluation on a concrete application. The article is organised as follows. The next section describes the load balancing mechanism and the interactions between its different components. Section 3 makes a short overview of the observation mechanism, while section 4 describes how information issued from the observation of the application is exploited. Section 5 discusses implementation issues concerning the load balancing architecture. Experimental results on a communicating application and conclusions are given next.

2　Load Balancing Scheme

In ADAJ, efficiency of applications execution is achieved through the use of a profiling tool. This is aimed towards the application behaviour: objects are observed in order to describe their activity during execution. A distributed graph of objects is drawn, dynamically, which reflects both communication links and object activity. The idea of disposing of a graph of communicating objects is not original: dynamic graph partitioning has been proposed for the load distribution [10], but in the context of a one-unit graph. Load redistribution based on a distributed graph is a more complex operation, which needs either centralising information, or diffusing it. Both of these solutions are expensive, and consequently, in ADAJ, no optimal solution is searched, but an improvement of object distribution, in respect of load balance and communicating objects locality (remote objects communicating intensively should be brought close together).

The observation information are exploited by the three components of the load balancing mechanism:

- the observation component,

- the decision component,

- the correction component.

The observation component contains a load extractor and the object relation observer. The first defines the load of a virtual machine, depending on the observation information (offered by the second) and the number of threads. Every machine load is communicated periodically to the decision component which analyses it and decides the machines which are participating in the load redistribution. The machines concerned are notified and they apply, in a distributed manner, the correction algorithm, which achieves the redistribution process.

3　Observation Mechanism of Relations

Remote objects are particularly interesting in load balancing mechanisms because they are able to migrate. In ADAJ, the load balancing mechanism is based on an observation tool [3] of the evolution of the application. The observation concerns only the remote objects, as they can balance load by migration. The remote objects which are to be observed are called *global objects*. The Java local objects are not remote accessible, cannot migrate and are not observed.

The ADAJ relation observation mechanism maintains a history of the relations of every global object with the environment. We distinguish three types of relations :

- of a global object with another global object (on the same, or different virtual machine),

- of a global object with all other local objects,

- of all other global or local objects with a particular global object.

In object-oriented environments, these relations are generated by method invocations. This remark allowed us to quantify relation intensity by the number of method invocations and not by the method execution time or parameter size as in other projects (Dome [1] or Isatis [2]). Method invocations generate work on global or local objects, and work can only be created through method invocations.

For each of these relations, counters are associated. Counter values are submitted to a smoothing mechanism in order to take into account both past evolution and present value. Smoothing is meant to weight the current behaviour with the previous ones, because sudden, not persistent fluctuations should be neglected.

This ingenious idea of relation quantification is less costly and less complex than other techniques and gives a rating of object activity.

4   Exploiting Observation Information

Load Extractor   Load in a Java virtual machine is generated by the activity of the objects it contains. The methods invoked on objects, generating the activity, are executing in the main thread of the virtual machine, or in the user threads. Thus, the load of a virtual machine is generally measured by the number of threads. In fact, in the JVM there is only one thread running (on a mono-processor machine), the other threads being runnable or not runnable. The portable information which can be extracted, from the virtual machine, is the number of active threads, which can be either runnable or not runnable. The difference between the two kinds of threads is done in ADAJ using the workload of JVMs, the two criteria defining the load of a JVM. The *workload of a JVM*, noted *WP*, sums the workloads of every global object the JVM contains. As mentioned before, an object's workload is generated by method invocations. All input invocations and also invocations towards local objects characterise the *workload of a global object*.

Decision Component   The decision component classifies JVMs as overloaded, normally loaded and underloaded. The algorithm is the following:

- if there are a lot of threads,

    - if WP is close to zero (not runnable threads), then JVM is underloaded,

    - if WP is important (running threads), then JVM is overloaded,

- if there are few threads (no work in the JVM), then JVM is underloaded,

- if there is a normal number of threads,

  - if WP is close to zero (not runnable threads), then JVM is underloaded.

Close to zero and important values are defined using a customise K-Means algorithm: in a preliminary phase, detection of their existence is done (using statistical metrics, as variation coefficient), and then, if it is the case, the values having these properties are identified, using the K-Means classification method [8]. This identification forms three classes of values: the class of values close to the smallest value (associated to the close to zero values), the class of values close to the biggest value (associated to the important values), and the class of values around the mean (associated to the normal values). These associations are possible because "close to zero"/"few" and "important"/"a lot" characterisations (for the JVM workload and respectively, for the number of threads) are relative, and not absolute.

Correction Component   The correction component concerns only the overloaded machines, which decide on the objects to remove and on their destination.

Between all global objects a virtual machine has, some are particularly interesting to remove: objects which do not have strong communication links towards the other global objects remaining on the machine, and those which have an average workload. The first feature avoids the generation of new remote communications, while the second assures some workload will be really removed.

The two constraints are simultaneously considered using an aggregation function, the weighted sum [7]. This technique imposes that values were on a same scale, that's why relative values are considered.

The best classified object, in the respect of the previous function, is to be moved to another virtual machine. This decision depends on its external attraction (communication with global objects in another address space), and on the workload of the destination machine. The previous technique of aggregation is used in order to take into account both criteria.

5   Technical Issues

The three components of the load balancing mechanism (see figure 1) are instances of the: `LocalLoad` remote class (for the load extractor), `LoadDecision` local class (for the decision component) and `LoadBal` remote class (for the correction component).

The `LocalLoad` object is responsible of extracting load measures, from both the observation mechanism (implemented by a local `AsynchObserver` object, which is updated by a remote `LocalJVMObserver` object), and the execution environment of the Java Virtual Machine (number of threads). The two measures are packed into a local `InfoLoad` object, and transmitted to the decision component.

The `LoadDecision` object is unique and has the functionality of applying the decision algorithm for the load measures gathered from all the machines. It activates, if necessary, the `LoadBal` object on every overloaded machine, which applies the location policy, implemented by a local `Decision` object. Remote observation information is recovered from the remote `LocalJVMObserver` objects of the underloaded machines.

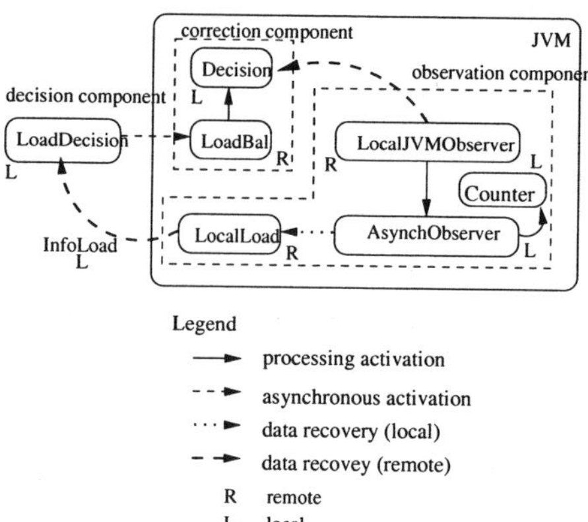

Figure 1. Load balancing scheme components.

6   Experimental Results

The load balancing mechanism in ADAJ was experimentally tested for a distributed and parallel genetic algorithm solving the TSP (Travelling Salesman Problem) problem. This algorithm uses the island model, where the initial population is divided into sub-populations, on which a classical genetic algorithm is applied, in parallel, for a number of evolutions. Afterwards, the best individuals are exchanged between sub-populations. A possible implementation in ADAJ makes the sub-populations remote objects that can migrate.

Experiments consider the execution of the algorithm on a cluster of workstations, with no external load. Initial distribution of objects is voluntarily unequal. Previous tests [6] show good behaviour: gains up to 30% in execution times are achieved, compared to a version which does not use the load balancing mechanism. The tendency is to approach to an equal distribution of objects or equal quantities of processing on every node, which minimises considerably the waiting time in synchronisations.

The TSP application shows situations where the quantity of processing to be executed is not necessarily well distributed, because of unequal sub-population distributions or because of different sub-population sizes. But communications are not taken into consideration. The focus of this article is on another kind of application, which makes use of communication. It is the simulation of an algorithm which solves numerical problems, using an iterative waveform method (see the Medico Akzo Nobel problem [5]). The direct method finds the exact solution after a finite number of operations, while the iterative method gives an approximative solution, after a number of iterations, but has a lower complexity.

The skeleton of this kind of algorithm consists of local computing phases, in parallel over different data, and of information exchange with the neighbour, in a ring fashion.

In ADAJ, the simulation of such an algorithm considers a number of global objects, every global object executing a sequence of communication towards the next global object, followed by a local computation. The communication consists of requesting the same kind of computation, as the local one.

Internal towards External Communication In an object-oriented application, communication links are generated by method invocations. Communication between global objects placed on different virtual machines includes serialisation and network passing cost. When global objects are placed on the same virtual machine, the network cost is eliminated. The difference between the two types of communication induces the definitions of *internal communication*, corresponding to method invocations between global objects in the same address space, and of *external communication*, which is generated by method invocations between global objects in different address spaces.

The objective of the load balancing mechanism is to take into account the communication links in the correction algorithm in order to avoid creating new external communications, and to replace external communications with internal ones. Even if an internal communication is always remote (using the serialisation mechanism), the execution time can be improved eliminating the network traffic overhead.

This results from a test which makes n invocations between two remote objects. The execution platform was made of two homogeneous PIII machines, 733 MHz, having 128M RAM, linked by 100 Mb/s throughput. Table 1 shows an average slowdown of 22% for an external communication, compared to an internal one[1].

Table 1. Execution times and overheads of external communications compared to internal ones

	internal communication (ms)	external communication (ms)	overhead (%)
n=500	117	140	19.65
n=1000	224.66	275.33	22.55
n=5000	1094	1366	24.86
n=10000	2217.66	2728.66	23.04

The network throughput has an important role in these measurements: a slow traffic makes external communication even slower.

The penalty induced by the external communication is even more important if communication optimisation can be introduced: remote objects which are on the same virtual machine can communicate locally (see the JavaParty 0.98 version). In this case, a remote communication can become an internal local one, using object migration.

Communicating Application The communication pattern presented in figure 2 shows that every object executes, concurrently, a computation requested by the previous object, through a communication, and a local computation (except for the last one which does not perform any communication, and for the first one which is not requested the computation). The local processing is blocked during the communication, because of the synchronous call.

Communications are considered by the correction component. The load balancing mechanism in ADAJ balances the load, with the aim of optimising communications, and does not react to communication imbalances. Thus, the initial distribution of objects is voluntarily unbalanced, and makes communications random. For example, if objects are indexed from 0 to 12, their initial distribution on four machines is shown in figure 3.

---

[1] values are averages of 5 execution times, from which the best and the worst time were removed

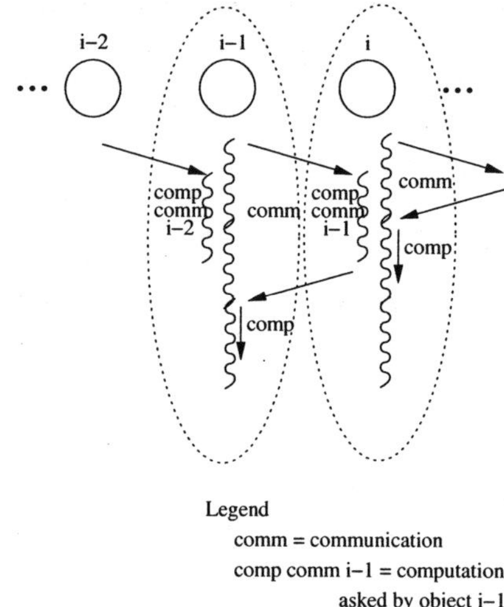

Figure 2. Skeleton of a communicating application.

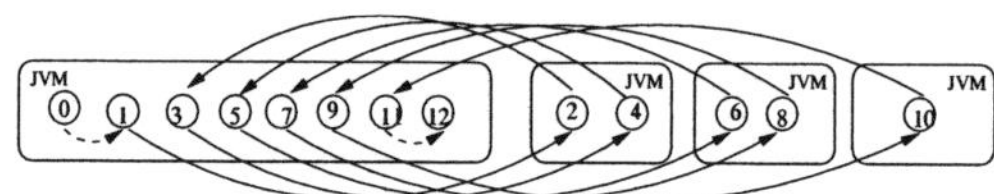

Figure 3. Initial deployment of the communicating application.

This distribution generates 10 external communications, and 2 internal ones. The load balancing mechanism should react to the load imbalance, correct object distribution, by a good placement, which consequently increases the number of internal communications.

Application Behaviour　The objective of the experiments on the communicating application was to analyse the decisions of the load balancing mechanism in respect of communications. Three cases were tested, concerning the choice of the destination machine:

- both communication links and machine workload are important,

- only communication links are important,

- only workload of destination machines is important.

In the first situation, two of the final distributions in figure 4, show a good load balance, and external communications were diminished from 10 to 6 (in average).

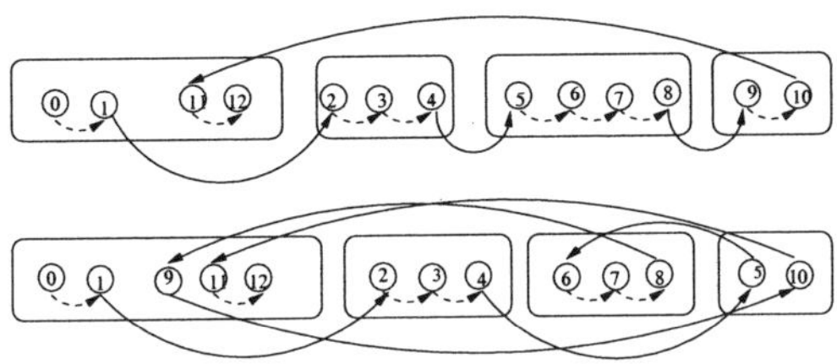

Figure 4. Final deployments of the communicating application.

If communications, only, are considered, experiments show a similar behaviour, because the destination machines are however chosen between the least loaded. On the contrary, when communications are not at all considered, in the third case, loads are balanced, but there is no improvement for external communications (figure 5), or worse, they may be increased.

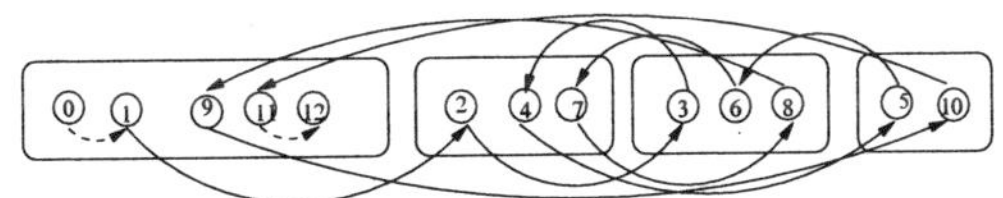

Figure 5. Final deployment of the communicating application.

These experiments testify that load balancing in ADAJ is able not only to balance loads, but also to reestablish a good communication pattern, lost because of inadequate object deployment.

7　Conclusions

Efficiency of execution for distributed and parallel object-oriented applications is an important issue in designing execution environments. In this article we have presented an approach to deploy transparently and dynamically applications over a cluster of workstations. Our solution is a load balancing mechanism at the middleware level which uses profiling information on the application behaviour, in terms of object activity and communication links. The main hypothesis is that application behaviour in the near future resembles to its behaviour in the recent past.

Our previous results [6] showed good performances, compared to executions using no load balancing mechanism strategy. Gains up to 30% in execution times were measured. This article is focused on the behaviour of a communicating application, when load balancing is activated. Random redistribution of objects may balance load, but they cannot always improve communication links, by bringing closer (on the same virtual machine) remote communicating objects. The load balancing mechanism in ADAJ considers communication links during the correction policy and thus is able to recover a good communication pattern, by improving the number of internal communications.

References

[1] J. Arabe, A. Beguelin, B Lowekamp, E. Seligman, M. Starkey, and P. Stephan. Dome : Parallel programming in a heterogenous multi-user environment. Technical report, Carnegie Mellon University, Avril 1995.

[2] Michel Banâtre, Yasmina Belhamissi, Valérie Issarny, Isabelle Puaut, and Jean-Paul Routeau. Adaptive Placement of Method Executions within a Customizable Distributed Object-Based Runtime System - Design, Implementation, and Performance. ISSN 1350-2042 TR 64, IRISA and CRIN-Nancy, 1994.

[3] A. Bouchi, R. Olejnik, and B. Toursel. A New Estimation Method for Distributed Java Object Activity. In *IPDPS 2002 - Workshop on Java for Parallel and Distributed Computing*, Fort Lauderdale, USA, 2002.

[4] A. Corradi, L. Leonardi, and F. Zambonelli. High-Level Directives to Drive the Allocation of Parallel Object-Oriented Applications. In *Proceedings of HIPS'97*, Amsterdam, Pays Bas, 1997.

[5] CWI - The National Research Institute for Mathematics and Computer Science in the Netherlands. *Test Set for IVP Solvers*. http://www.cwi.nl/ftp/IVPtestset/descrip.htm.

[6] V. Felea. Exploiting Runtime Information in Load Balancing Strategies. In P. Kacsuk and D. Kranzlmller and Z. Nmeth and J. Volkert, editor, *Distributed and Parallel Systems - Cluster and Grid Computing*, pages 21–29, Linz, Austria, 2002. Kluwer Academic Publishers.

[7] P.C Fishburn. A survey of multiattribute/multicriteria evaluation theories. In S. Zionts, editor, *Multicriteria problem solving*, pages 181–224. Springer Verlag, Berlin, 1978.

[8] J. A. Hartigan and M. A. Wong. A K-Means Clustering Algorithm. *Applied Statistics*, 28:100–108, 1979.

[9] M. Phillippsen and M. Zenger. JavaParty - Transparent Remote Objects in Java. In *ACM 1997 Workshop on Java for Science and Engineering Computation*, Las Vegas, USA, June 1997.

[10] K. Schloegel, G. Karypis, and V. Kumar. Graph Partititioning for High Performance Scientific Simulations. Technical Report: TR 00-018, Dept. of Computer Science and Engineering, University of Minnesota, 2000. To be included in CRPC Parallel Computing Handbook.

[11] *Sun Products - Remote Method Invocation JDK1.2.* http://java.sun.com/products/jdk/1.2/docs/guide/rmi/index.html, 1998.

Concurrent Information Processing and Computing
D. Grigoras and A. Nicolau (Eds.)
IOS Press, 2005

An XML/RDF-based Proposal to Exchange Information within a Multi-Agent System

Sabin Buraga[1], Sînică Alboaie[2], Lenuţa Alboaie[1,2]

[1] *Faculty of Computer Science, "A.I. Cuza" University of Iaşi, Romania*
`{busaco,adria}@infoiasi.ro`
[2] *Institute of Theoretical Computer Science, Romanian Academy, Iaşi branch*
`abss@iit.iit.tuiasi.ro`

Abstract. The paper presents different platform-independent methods of exchanging information between the members of a multi-agent system. We describe first a multi-agent infrastructure – called *Omega* – that can be considered as a hierarchical space of a set of distributed objects that models the Web resources. We propose an XML/RDF-based model that can be used as an universal manner for serialization and metadata description of the objects processed by the agents. Various relationships that can be established between the entities of a multi-agent system will also be described by RDF constructs.

1 Introduction

The primary goal of Tim Berners-Lee's vision of the Semantic Web [4, 12] is to enable intelligent queries for knowledge on the Web instead of the conventional mechanisms to access the resources. To do this, computer scientists need to achieve the following: to understand the semantic mechanism of all kinds of queries, and what kind of components the process of questioning the Web formally consists of; and to rigorously capture, represent or symbolise the knowledge available on Web.

To accomplish this goal, we are designing and implementing an infrastructure for agent software development, called *Omega* [2], viewed as a tree-like space of a set of distributed objects that models the Web resources by using XML/RDF assertions. The *Omega* system offers a flexible framework for building agent-oriented distributed applications on the Web – consult section 2 for details. To assure the Web scalability, independently designed programs – especially Web agents – must be able to exchange and process the meaning of data and metadata in an independent manner. Semantic interoperability can be completed only if different users (agents, Web services, other Web clients, etc.) interpret RDF statements in the same way.

The *Omega* framework offers an addressing space for the Web objects and a mechanism for remotely accessing the Web distributed resources (that can be viewed as objects). To enable the flexible querying and accessing mechanisms about the distributed Web resources, we must offer a facility for serialization – in an independent manner – the data and metadata (objects) processed by the *Omega* multi-agent system. The paper investigates various possibilities of serialization given by the XML family [6, 23]. Some of the drawbacks due of the lack of a description language regarding the objects' properties can be elegantly resolved by XML.

The serialization of the Web objects presented in section 3 can be considered as a flexible way to exchange information between software agents. Additionally, for each object, different metadata constructs can be attached to specify several semantic properties. These descriptions are written in RDF and presented in section 4.

Several relationships can be established between the entities of the multi-agent system. Following [8, 9], these relations can be easily expressed by RDF assertions. This machine-understandable approach can ease the development of Web-oriented software applications – e.g., Web intelligent agents, Web mediators or Web services – for different activities such as resource discovery and queries that involve time.

2　*Omega* Multi-Agent Infrastructure

2.1　Motivation

We can consider as the fundamental resources that computers expose to the software components (i.e. operating system, applications) or users the following items: the computing capabilities, (volatile or non-volatile) memory, local and remote data (documents), metadata (different descriptions about several properties of the resources: content, structure, layout/interface, dynamics, security issues, etc.).

Of course, there are other modalities to describe these properties without using XML-based assertions, but with the penalty of the platform and software independence. Obviously, these documents (including XML resources) are made to be read and processed in a (mobile) distributed system (the Web itself). To easily access and obtain the knowledge contained by a specific document, there must exists an universal mechanism/model – based on the XML family – to accomplish that. This is the seminal idea of the Semantic Web [4].

2.1.1　WWW Space as a Distributed Hypermedia System

The Web can be viewed as a distributed hypermedia system that uses Internet technologies, a global system of heterogeneous networked computers. Advances in networking and Web/Internet technology are leading to a network-centric computing model, and the Web and Internet itself are evolving into the infrastructure for global network computing. By populating this infrastructure with object-based components and combining them in various ways, the development and deployment of interoperable distributed object systems is fast migrating on Web [22].

The object model provides the ability to mimic real world processes in a fluid, dynamic and natural way. The WWW space allows for objects to be distributed to servers thereby centralizing access, processing, and maintenance, provides a multiplexing interface to distributed objects, and function as a catalyst for the rapidly-growing world of thin-clients – i.e. mobile phones, handheld devices, intelligent appliances. We can safely now state that **Web + Object** integration is a viable reality. This is emphasized by different software organizations and companies – especially in the e-business domain – that are using Web-enabled distributed object technology, in the form of intranets and extranets, to solve their computing problems, and the emergence of an industry that provides Web and object interfaces to distributed object tools.

After the CGI standard, with the advent of Java, and the distributed object infrastructures CORBA/IIOP and OLE/DCOM, the stage was set to evolve the Web from a document management system to a platform for distributed object computing and electronic commerce.

Existing legacy applications can even co-exist with distributed objects through the use of object wrappers [22]. The interface could either be the client browser or browser-like with superpositioned distributed object infrastructures.

2.1.2　Mobile Agents

An important step towards *Internet/Web Computing* is represented by the mobile computations. A mobile object, usually called an *agent* when operating on behalf of a user, is a downloadable, executable object that can independently move (code and state) at its will – the mobile agent is not bound to the system in which it began the code execution and can travel from one node on a network to another.

Mobile agents present the following important attributes: *reactive* (the ability to respond to changes within agent environment), *autonomous* (the mobile agent is able to exercise control over its own actions), *goal-oriented* (the agents have a planned itinerary, they do not simply act in response to the environment), *communicative* (the ability to communicate with other agents, by exchanging information/knowledge), and *mobile* (the mobile agents can transport themselves from one host to another).

Mobile agents provide a way to think about solving software problems in a networked environment that fits more naturally with the real world. Mobile agents can be used to access and manage information that is distributed over large areas [5, 15, 16].

The main benefit is that the software components can be integrated into a coherent and consistent software system – e.g. a multi-agent system – in which they work together to better meet the needs of the entire application (utilising autonomy, responsiveness, pro-activeness and social ability).

Current mobile agent systems – available as commercial or open-source applications – are implemented in C++, Java, Tcl, Scheme, and Python programming languages (to name only few).

2.2　General Architecture of *Omega*

2.2.1　Overview

The *Omega* is an agent-based system that offers an addressing space (viewed as a tree) for the Web objects and different techniques to remotely access the Web distributed resources (viewed as objects) [2].

Each object processed by *Omega* can be considered as a collection of objects included in that one. The links (edges) between the vertices of the tree are given by the aggregation relationship exposed by the object-oriented methodologies.

To emphasize the aggregation relationship, we attach to each object a name or an index, and in this way we can uniquely refer each object of the tree by its name/index (viewed as an identifier). Each object will have an unique list of the identifiers that represent its "address" in the addressing space used by the *Omega* agents. An identifier can be considered as an IName object (at the implementation level, an IName object can be viewed as an object-tree path or a list of object identifiers). By using a tree of objects, we can structure more easily the distributed resources for a given local web (such as a cluster or an intranet).

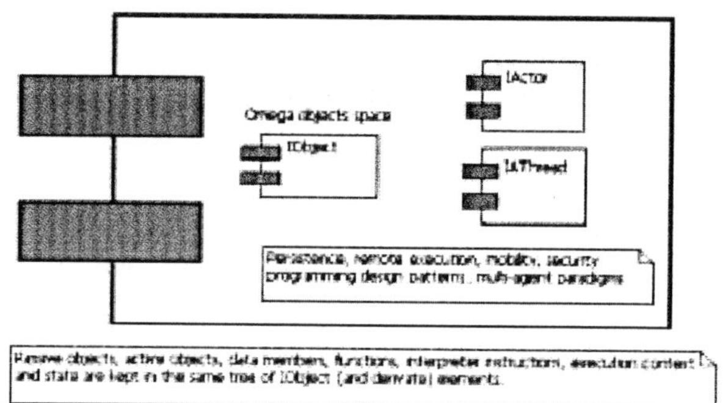

Figure 1. *Omega* objects

2.2.2 Functionality

We choose to use an interpreted environment for our multi-agent model and distributed object structure. Using such an environment, it was easier to implement serialization and various execution control mechanisms [10] which contributed to the implementation of the *Omega* distributed objects system.

Omega offers a distributed object structure, and its initial goal was to determine some good representations of data, types, instructions, functions and objects of an object-oriented language that can be used as a programming language for mobile agents. The result of this effort is a system written in C++ that is able to unify the notions behind the object-actor duality, namely the duality between passive and active objects.

Currently, *Omega* offers to active programs what the World-Wide Web space provides by default for presentation of some static entities (documents), namely an infrastructure able to support Web-based distributed applications (e.g., agents used in clusters or Grid [20]).

2.2.3 *Omega* Classes

The `IObject` class is the base-class for every other class that has memory regions stored within a local system. Every object and function that needs a store space in *Omega* will use `IObject`. In this way, *Omega* assures a space model provided by a common distributed memory. This model is based on the existence of a given node of an `IObject`'s tree, which is easily addressable from the network.

The *Omega* system offers a number of object types which provide functionality to the following classes: *String*, *Number*, *List*, and *Control* agent-execution (i.e. support for virtual threads, scripting languages etc.). Data is represented by different classes such as `IString`, `INumber`, `IOmegaStack`, `IOmegaList` that are derived from the `IObject` generic class (see also figure 1).

Omega offers two categories of data types [2]: *simple data types* – have no components (i.e. `INumber`, `IString`, etc.) – and *compound data types* – represent a mix-up of two or more simple types (e.g., `IName`, `IOmegaList`, `IAThread`).

2.3 *Omega* Language

Omega provides an active part, namely an execution part, which is the implementation of a script-like programming language. In this active part, we are trying to integrate the object space with notions such as execution thread, function, instruction, data types to be modeled with the help of `IObject` abstraction.

Therefore the *Omega* object environment and the *OmegaKernel* mini-interpreter provide – this makes *Omega* able to execute small scripting programs –: a data model (base type-system, the construction of new objects), an address space (every object has its own Internet-consistent address), and techniques to implement the high-level programming level statements.

The language provided by the *Omega* framework may be easily extended with other instructions to build a more complex computational model of the developed agents. An important step was to create a mechanism for representing data structures, statements and objects under the same abstraction (`IObject`) that is a network shared entity.

3 Serialization Mechanism

Several interactions between the Web agents developed within *Omega* system can be accomplished by using serialization mechanisms.

All classes derived from `IObject` must implement the *serialization* (*marshalling*) and *deserialization* (*unmarshalling*) methods. The process of building of the new data types is based on the fact that an `IObject` has a member of the `IOmegaList` type. That member stores associated links which are instances of the derived classes. In this manner, the serialization of the new types of objects can be automatically accomplished by *Omega* via members' serialization and the call of the overloaded own methods. Of course, for several types of objects (e.g. `IOmegaSockets` used for socket operations) the serialization and deserialization activities can not be viewed as a proper solution.

The object serialization do not imply the serialization of the whole subtree that has as root the object in cause. For an object, only the serialization of the object itself and of the `IName` list of its children [1].

3.1 XML-based Serialization

As an optimal manner to serialize the *Omega* objects, we choose an XML-based representation. To describe these objects, we could adopt an RDF-based model. The RDF assertions could give the possibility to express semantics of an *Omega* object.

We are using the XML namespaces defined by the XML Schema specification [13] to retain the primary types of the data exchanged by agents in the serialization and deserialization processes. The *Omega* encoding style is based on the usual XML Schema's data types. All data types used within the *Omega* system of agents must either be taken directly from the XML Schema or derived from *Omega* data types.

An example follows [1]:

```
<element name="local_address_type" type="...">
  <simpleType name="local_address_type" base="xsd:string">
    <enumeration value="tree_id" />
    <enumeration value="unique_name" />
  </simpleType>
```

```
</element>
<element name="local_address" type="..." />
  <complexType name="local_address">
    <element name="la_type" type="local_address_type" />
    <element name="la_value" type="xsd:string" />
  </complexType>
</element>
<IName>
  <IOmegaDomain> ... </IOmegaDomain>
  <local_address>
     <la_type> tree_id </la_type>
     <la_value> 1 </la_value>
  </local_address>
  <local_address>
     <la_type> unique_name </la_type>
     <la_value> member_name </la_value>
  </local_address>
</IName>
```

3.2   SOAP Object Serialization

SOAP – or other protocols that use the RPC over XML approach (e.g., XML-RPC) – will
be used to transport the serialized data. *SOAP* (*Simple Object Access Protocol*) [14, 23] is a
simple lightweight protocol used for structured and strong-type information exchange in a
decentralized, distributed environment. The protocol is based on XML and consists of three
parts: an envelope that describes the contents of the message and how to use it, a set of rules
for serializing data exchanged between applications, and a procedure to represent remote
procedure calls, that is, the way in which queries and the resulting responses to the procedure
are represented.

Similar to object distribution models (e.g., IIOP and DCOM), SOAP can call methods,
services, components, and objects on remote servers. However, unlike these protocols, which
use binary formats for the calls, SOAP uses text format (Unicode), with the help of XML, to
structure the nature of the exchanges.

SOAP can generally operate with several protocols, such as FTP (File Transfer Protocol)
or SMTP (Simple Mail Transfer Protocol), but it is particularly well-suited for the HTTP
(HyperText Transfer Protocol) [23]. It defines a reduced set of parameters that are specified
in the HTTP header, making it easier topass through proxies and firewalls. Using SOAP over
HTTP also enables resources already present on the Web to be unified by using the natural
request/response model of HTTP protocol.

We use an existing tool named *gSoap* [21], which is able to generate the code for serialization from a user-defined specification. The *gSOAP* compiler tools provide an unique
SOAP/XML-to-C/C++ language binding to ease the development of SOAP/XML Web services and clients in C and/or C++ languages.

4   Describing *Omega* Objects in RDF

4.1   Resource Description Framework

4.1.1   Short General Presentation

Resource Description Framework (*RDF*) allows the description of the metadata associated
of the Web documents (resources). RDF consists of a model for the representation of the
named properties and property values. This is suitable to model objects behaviours. RDF

properties may be thought of as attributes of resources and in this sense correspond to traditional attribute-value pairs. RDF properties can also signify relationships between resources. In object-oriented design terminology, resources correspond to objects and properties correspond to instance variables [7, 18].

To facilitate the definition of metadata, RDF is based on *classes*. A collection of classes, typically designed for a specific purpose or domain, is called a *schema* [7]. Through the sharability of schemas, RDF supports the reusability of metadata definitions. The RDF schemas may themselves be expressed in RDF. The RDF syntax is XML-based.

4.1.2 RDF Model

The basic model of RDF consists of three object types [18]:

resources All objects being described by RDF expressions are called *resources* and they are always named by *Uniform Resource Identifiers* (*URI*) plus optional anchor identifiers. Using URI schemas, every type of resource can be identified in the same manner.

properties A *property* is a specific aspect, characteristic, attribute, or relation to describe a resource. Each property has a specific meaning, defines its permitted values, the type of resources it can express, and its relationship with other properties (via RDF Schema).

statements A specific resource together with a named property, plus the value of that property for that resource is an RDF *statement*. These three individual parts of a statement are called, respectively, the *subject*, the *predicate*, and the *object*. The object of a statement (e.g., the property value) can be another resource or a literal.

RDF also specifies three types of container objects: *Bag* (an unordered list of resources or literals), *Sequence* (an ordered list of resources or literals), and *Alternative* (a list of resources or literals that represent alternatives for the single value of a property). The containers may be defined by a URI pattern. RDF can also be used to make statements about other RDF statements (higher-order statements).

The RDF data model provides an abstract, conceptual framework for defining and using metadata. Currently, there are several proposals of model-theoretical semantics for RDF and RDF Schema [11, 17, 23].

4.2 Using RDF to Capture the State of the *Omega* Objects

For each object of the *Omega* multi-agent system, we can attach different metadata. These meta-descriptions will assure the control versioning (the version and the last verification timestamp for each object) and the owner/parent of the created objects. For security purposes, the object metadata will retain the list of the associated object's permissions. This approach is inspired from our RDF-based model used for accessing resources of the distributed file systems [8].

The system keeps these descriptions as RDF assertions that can be transported to other objects during the information updating activities (object replication).

In the stub object of any shared objects, certain metadata is available to inform other objects about the object's author and about the permission list to access this object. The system verifies this information to grant or to deny the access to considered object. The meta-descriptions regarding the permissions and the identity of the user who want to access *Omega* objects must provide a certain cryptographic support.

4.3 Expressing Relations between *Omega* Entities

To catch the dynamics of the involved agents built within *Omega* and the links between them, a high-level RDF-based description of temporal relations can be adopted. The temporal relationships between objects could be stored by RDF constructs, too. This approach is very similar to our model used to retain temporal relations established between (fragments of) Web sites [9].

The proposed model is mainly focused on the description of interval temporal relations. The temporal structure introduced by Interval Temporal Logic (ITL) is a simple linear model of time and is detailed in [3].

For this, an XML-based language is proposed – *Temporal Relation Specification Language* (*TRSL*) [9]. For each time relation, TRSL offers an element that corresponds to a specific relation (e.g. <Meets> element for *Meets* relation from ITL model). The beginning and ending of time periods are denoted by begin and end attributes, respectively. Also, TRSL defines the dur attribute for specifying a known or predictive time period (this will allow Web agents to reason about different actions that may need to be performed).

The syntax and the semantics of TRSL language is detailed in [9].

4.3.1 Example

We consider the following scenario. An object-maintainer Web agent can discover different temporal relations between the *Omega* objects distributed in an intranet and can automatically generate the following TRSL document:

```
<rdf:RDF>
  <rdf:Bag id="RecentlyChanged">
    <rdf:li resource="object1" />
    <rdf:li resource="object2" />
  </rdf:Bag>
  <rdf:Description rdf:aboutEach="#RecentlyChanged">
    <f:Location f:dns="www.site.org">
       193.231.30.1 <!-- spatial information -->
    </f:Location>
    <f:Owner> <!-- metadata information -->
       <rdf:Description rdf:about="http://www.omega.site/">
          <f:Login f:uid="714">busaco</f:Login>
       </rdf:Description>
    </f:Owner>
    ...
    <!-- temporal information -->
    <t:link t:type="temporal" t:action="Serialize"
            t:end="Mon Mar 17 19:35:14 EET 2003">
       <t:Finishes t:dur="2sec" />
    </t:link>
  </rdf:Description>
</rdf:RDF>
```

A collection of objects to be serialized is denoted by RecentlyChanged identifier. This objects are stored on www.site.org machine and the serialization action is planned to be performed on March 17 2003. The metadata information describes the *Omega*'s host and the login name of the system maintainer.

This approach can be used for the resource discovery activities performed in a distributed (mobile) environment, in a machine-understandable manner.

Also, TRSL can store information about simple queries for temporal databases and can be used as an universal XML-based language for expressing different assertions in temporal query languages.

5　Related Work

Althrough there is not a formal framework for multi-agent systems development, due to dependence on application domains, it has been that the construction of these systems requires a different approach from that of conventional software systems development [5, 15].

We are aware of multiple platforms developed both in academia and software industry companies [19]. This confirms that many computer scientists are considering the agent-oriented software as a possible paradigm, designed and implemented especially in very dynamic environments (such as Web). However, the existing implementations have not convinced the whole community or do not cover/provide some facilities desired by programmers or final users. Some proprietary solutions, though well developed, are not built as open systems and can not be easily extended or modified. On the other hand, we were not impressed by the available open-source platforms.

The existing multi-agent platforms use different approaches for communication between agents, by using low-level communication protocols (TCP/IP or HTTP) or standard high-level languages – such as KQML (Knowledge Query Manipulation Language) [5].

The *Omega* system presents an advantage, by adopting an XML-based platform-independent approach in serialization and exchanging information between agents. The SOAP model is more flexible and easy to use than CORBA or DCOM solutions. Some of the *Omega*'s facilities could be also integrated in the *MAIS (Mobile Agents Information System)* – a platform for creating dynamic clusters [16].

6　Conclusion

Omega represents an infrastructure able to support the agent-oriented programming. By this approach, we tried to emphasize a trend which is shaping the evolution of the software development techniques for open distributed applications.

The paper focused on different platform-independent methods of exchanging information between the entities of a multi-agent infrastructure. We proposed an XML/RDF-based model that can be used as an universal manner for serialization and metadata description of the objects processed by the agents. Various properties and relations established between the components (agents, objects, processes) of a multi-agent system can be expressed in a standardized and machine-understandable manner. This approach provides semantic descriptions of the Web resources and could be an interesting solution for exchanging knowledge between intelligent or/and mobile agents.

Also, we intend to experiment an XML-based version of the *Omega* language that can be used to exchange mobile code of the software agents coded within the *Omega* framework.

References

[1] S. Alboaie, S. Buraga, L. Alboaie, *An XML-based Serialization of Information Exchanged by Software Agents*, Proceedings of the 7th World Multiconference on Systemics, Cybernetics and Informatics – SCI 2003, Orlando, Florida, 2003

[2] S. Alboaie, G. Ciobanu, *Designing and Developing Multi-Agent Systems*, in International Symposium on Parallel and Distributed Computing (ISPDC) Proceedings, Scientific Annals of the "A.I. Cuza" University, Computer Science section, Tome XI, "A.I. Cuza" University Press, Iaşi, 2002

[3] J. Allen, P. Hayes, "Moments and Points in an Interval-based Temporal Logic", *Computational Intelligence*, 5 (4), 1989

[4] T. Berners-Lee, *Weaving the Web*, Orion Business Books, London, 1999

[5] J. Bradshow, *Software Agents*, AAAI Press, 1997

[6] T. Bray *et al.* (eds.), *Extensible Markup Language (XML) 1.0 (Second Edition)*, W3C Recommendation, Boston, 2000: `http://www.w3.org/TR/REC-xml`

[7] D. Brickley, R. V. Guha, *Resource Description Framework (RDF) Schema Specification 1.0*, W3C Candidate Recommendation, Boston, 2000: `http://www.w3.org/TR/2000/REC-xml-20001006`

[8] S. Buraga, *A Model for Accessing Resources of the Distributed File Systems*, in Advanced Environments, Tools and Applications for Cluster Computing, D. Grigoraş *et al.* (eds.), Lecture Notes in Computer Science – LNCS 2326, Springer-Verlag, 2002

[9] S. Buraga, G. Ciobanu, *A RDF-based Model for Expressing Spatio-Temporal Relations Between Web Sites*, in Proceedings of the 3rd International Conference on Web Information Systems Engineering (WISE 2002), 12-14 December 2002, Singapore, IEEE Computer Society Press, 2002

[10] C. Callsen, *Open Distributed Heterogeneous Computing*, PhD Thesis, University of Illinois at Urbana-Champaign, 1997

[11] W. Conen, R. Klapsing, *A Logical Interpretation of RDF*, in Linköping Electronic Articles in Computer and Information Science, 5, 2000.

[12] S. Decker *et al.*, *Knowledge Representation on the Web*, in F. Baader (ed.), International Workshop on Description Logic (DL'00): `http://www.cs.vu.nl/~frankn/abstracts/DL00.html`

[13] D. Fallside (ed.), *XML Schema*, W3C Recommendation, Boston, 2001: `http://www.w3.org/TR/xmlschema-0/`

[14] C. Gorman, *Programming Web Services with SOAP*, O'Reilly and Associates, 2001

[15] S. Green, F. Somers, *Software Agents: A Review*: `http://www.cs.tcd.ie/research_groups/aig/iag/iag.html`

[16] D. Grigoraş *et al.*, *MAIS – The Mobile Agents Information System Support for Creating Dynamic Clusters*, in Proceedings of ICA3PP, Beijing, 2002

[17] P. Hayes (ed.), *RDF Model Theory*, W3C Working Draft, Boston, 2002: `http://www.w3.org/TR/rdf-mt/`

[18] O. Lassila, R. Swick (eds.), *RDF Model and Syntax Specification*, W3C Recommendation, Boston, 1999: `http://www.w3.org/TR/REC-rdf-syntax/`

[19] E. Mangina, *Review of Software Products for Multi-Agent Systems*, AgentLink.org, 2003: `http://www.agentlink.org/`

[20] L. Moreau, *Agents for the Grid: A Comparison with Web Services (Part I: the transport layer)*, in IEEE International Symposium on Cluster Computing and the Grid Proceedings, Berlin, Germany, May 2002

[21] * * *, *SOAPware*: `http://www.soapware.org/`

[22] * * *, *Web Object Integration*: `http://www.objs.com/survey/web-object-integration.htm`

[23] * * *, *World Wide Consortium's Technical Reports*, Boston, 2003: `http://www.w3.org/TR/`

Concurrent Information Processing and Computing
D. Grigoras and A. Nicolau (Eds.)
IOS Press, 2005

A Pattern-based Software Engineering Tool for Grid Environments

Maria Cecília Gomes[1]   José C. Cunha[1]   Omer F. Rana[2]

[1]*Faculdade de Ciências e Tecnologia, Universidade Nova de Lisboa,*
Campus FCT, 2829-516 Caparica, Portugal, [2] *Department of Computer Science, Cardiff University,*
5 The Parade, PO BOX 916, Cardiff cf24 3xf, UK

Abstract. A pattern-based software engineering tool for constructing workflow based applications is described. The tool provides a novel way of composing applications executing over Grid resources. The tool provides a structured design approach, centered on the manipulation of patterns through pre-defined pattern operators. Patterns and operators are divided into two categories: structural and behavioural. Structural operators act upon structural patterns to build reusable architectures. Behavioural patterns define the data and control flow dependencies between components in the architecture. Components within a pattern are subsequently instantiated with particular executables, and behavioural operators allow subsequent execution control and reconfiguration of the application.

1 Introduction and Related Work

The Grid [1] provides an important paradigm for large scale distributed computing. A primary objective within such a paradigm is to provide co-ordinated sharing of geographically distributed services (which may include hardware, software and information resources) across multiple administrative domains. Hence, Grid environments may be heterogeneous and dynamic – thereby necessitating software design approaches and tools which can more effectively exploit such environments. Such tools must support application configuration, execution control and reconfiguration of software services. Our contribution comprises a software engineering tool where the composition of Grid resources results from manipulating patterns through pre-defined pattern operators. The tool provides a library of pre-defined and user defined pattern templates, and a library of pre-defined operators. The operators also allow the subsequent execution control and reconfiguration of the application.

Patterns abstract common interactions between components in Grid environments, enabling reuse. Hence, a user may build an application in a structured fashion by selecting the most appropriate set of patterns, and by combining them according to operator semantics. Furthermore, we divide patterns into 'structural' and 'behavioural' categories, allowing users to choose the most appropriate combinations. Structural patterns encode component connectivity (e.g. a set of components connected in a ring fashion), whereas behavioural patterns capture temporal or flow dependencies (data and control flow dependencies) between components (e.g. a Client/Server model or a Producer/Consumer model). Operators define actions that can be applied over patterns and they are also divided into structural and behavioural categories. Structural operators manipulate structural patterns (e.g. adding an element to a ring pattern) and behavioural operators manage temporal or flow dependencies (e.g. to stop and resume the execution of a behavioural pattern). Behavioural operators allow the user to control application execution and reconfiguration. Pattern operators may be applied in an ordered combination and the sequence may be shared among users. To implement pattern templates and pattern operators we have extended the Triana [9] workflow tool to support patterns. At present, only structural patterns and operators are implemented. They are the major focus of this paper.

There has been considerable research since GoF [2], on identifying relevant patterns for different application areas. The Grid community has also recognised the importance of patterns [4] as a way to re-use expert knowledge. Patterns are not just a modeling abstraction, but have also been included into development tools, as first class entities. Furthermore, application re-usability and maintenance is improved if (design) patterns are still identifiable in the final code. Component paradigms also provide patterns as first class entities, where patterns may be defined, stored and reused independently of the components. Tools like the ones mentioned in [16, 17] provide a pattern-based approach for component composition – the *ObjectAssembler* visual development environment provides a catalogue of patterns for connecting JavaBean components. Similarly, the *Pacosuite* tool supports component composition through *composition patterns* which define component interactions.

Our approach also treats patterns as first class entities, but differs in that the user may explicitly define structural constraints between components, separately from the behavioural constraints. Such structural constraints may be useful, for example, to represent common software architectures in high-performance computing applications. The major benefit of our approach is an easy manipulation of pattern instances through operators, which simplifies the design process. Additionally, pattern refinement can be undertaken as a sequence of operators. Our approach aims at providing a novel way to access and compose Grid services. Major focus of other related efforts in the context of Grid computing is application centered, such as the DataGrid [19] and the MyGrid [18] projects. As a consequence, the resulting solutions are in some way restricted by the application area. The DataGrid project, for example, aims to provide scientific "collaboratories" through a middleware supporting cross-application resources in the areas of High-Energy Physics (mainly), Biology and Earth observation. Our approach is more generic in scope, and more widely applicable. Our approach is primarily aimed at two kinds of users: (1) software developers interested in abstracting common interaction patterns within a workflow tool (independent of any application), and (2) computational scientists familiar with particular application-domain specific software libraries, and interactions between these. Pattern based programming may not be a useful approach for highly tuned applications on particular architectures (such as for 'production' codes), or when the user is unfamiliar with the types of interactions between different software components.

2 Pattern Templates and Pattern Operators

This section presents a set of structural patterns, followed by structural operators.

2.1 Structural Patterns

Structural patterns may be divided into two groups: topological and non-topological. Topological patterns represent structures that frequently occur in Grid systems. For illustration purposes, we introduce three basic structures represented by the *pipeline*, the *ring*, and the *star* patterns. The non-topological patterns correspond to a sub-set of state-of-the-art design patterns ([2]), selected because of their utility in Grid systems. We select the *Adapter*, the *Facade*, and the *Proxy* patterns.

The *pipeline* pattern represents a sequence of ordered stages, where one stage produces data to the next. For example, in a signal processing application the first stage may consist of a signal generator service producing data to a set of intermediate stages for filtering. Frequently, the last stage consists of a visualisation service for observing results. Formally, the pattern's structure can be defined by three components, as represented in the left-hand side of figure 1. The structure is represented in UML notation [5] and was adapted from the *Pipes and Filters pattern* [3]. The first component (*DataSource*) produces data to a *Connector* component from which data is then consumed by a third component (*DataSink*). The *ring* pattern can be seen as an extension to the pipeline, as it also consists of a set of stages, but with the "last" stage connected to the "first". The *ring* pattern can be represented similarly to the *pipeline* pattern: instead of the *DataSource* and *DataSink* components, they are replaced with a single *Component* with two links to the *Connector*. In Grid environments, the ring topological structure can be found in a number of applications, both in the context of application execution (such as for modelling interactions within a local area network) to logical topologies such as supporting an authentication chain when approving participants with multiple Certificate servers. Each server delegates an authentication request to the next domain, and the final server replies to the original client. This chain based mechanism can also be found in resolving the address/location of an executable file using a directory lookup service – such as Globus MDS [7].

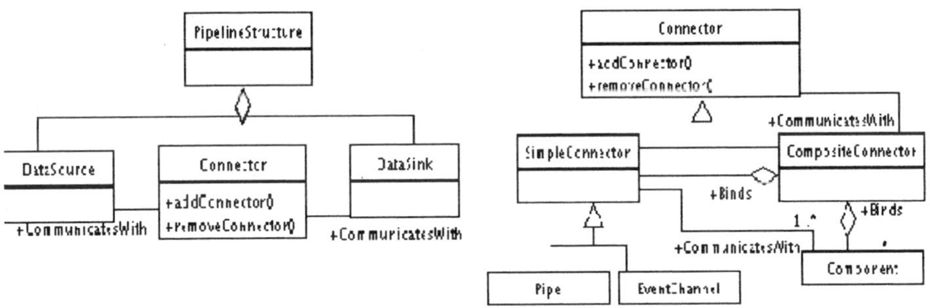

Figure 1. The Pipeline and Connector patterns.

A *star* pattern consists of a *nucleus* which communicates through *simple connector*s to *satellite* components (a single *connector* links a single *satellite* to the *nucleus*). All services based on a centralised resource sharing model in Grid environments may be seen as matching the star structure.

The *Adapter* pattern allows communication between two elements when they do not have the same interface (see [2] for a formal definition). In Grids, the *Adapter* pattern may be used to model wrappers for legacy codes (such as Fortran binaries). If the client is expecting a different interface from the one provided by the server, the adapter can act as a translator. This pattern is also particularly useful for providing a mapping between the interface of an existing code and a pre-defined component data model for Grids, such as CCA [8]. The *Facade* pattern (see [2]) may be used to restrict access to a set of sub-systems (such as an IP domain), through a common interface (the facade). The *Proxy* pattern (see [2]) allows the local presence of an entity's surrogate which transparently supports access to the remote entity. Grid services, for example, are usually accessed through a proxy (or gatekeeper).

2.2 Structural Operators

Structural operators are used to modify and manipulate structural patterns.

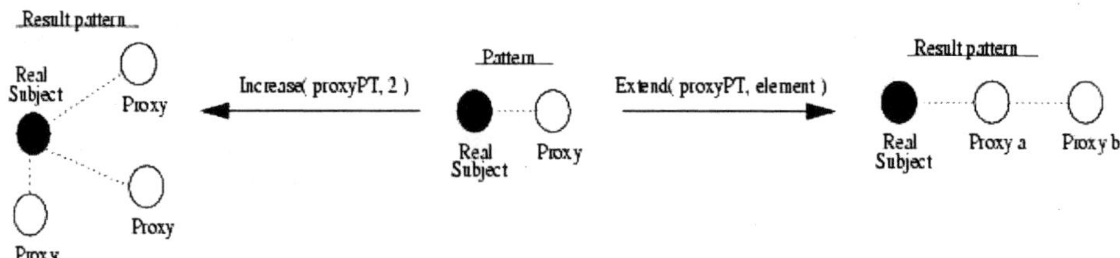

Figure 2. The Increase (left-side) and Extend (right-side) operators over a proxy pattern.

Increase(P, n): the number of elements in a pattern P is increased by n. Like any structural operator, the increase operator keeps the structure of the pattern invariant. The left-hand side of figure 2 shows the application of the increase operator to a proxy pattern for the creation of two proxy elements. Similarly, when using **Decrease(P, n)**, 'n' elements are removed from the pattern.

Extend(P, element): an element is added to a pattern, and its structure is augmented. Figure 2 shows the Extend operator being applied to a proxy pattern. The proxy pattern is extended by adding a component to an existing *proxy*. This situation occurs in mobile agent/object systems, where the sequence of proxies is used for locating the agent/object (via a chain of message forwarders, for instance). Using the **Reduce(P, element)** operator, an element is removed from a pattern.

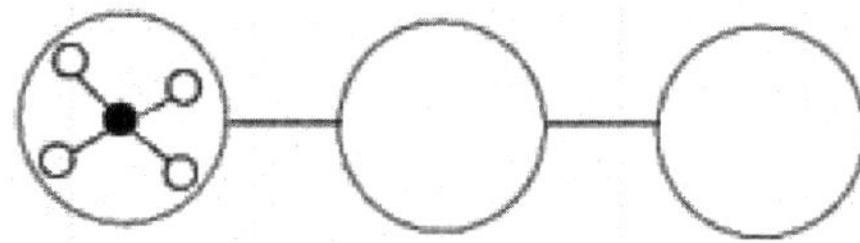

Figure 3. Result of the application of the Embed operator to a pipeline pattern to include a star pattern into the first element of the pipeline.

Embed(P1, P2): pattern P1 is added into a higher-level pattern P2. The concept of hierarchy is supported here by enabling component place holders to contain other patterns. Figure 3 shows the embedding of a star pattern into the first element of a pipeline pattern. Similarly, **Extract(P1, P2)** causes a pattern P1 to be removed from a higher-level pattern P2. **Rename(P1, P2)** causes a structural pattern P1 to be transformed to pattern P2. Using the **Replace(P1, P2)** operator, pattern P1, as a single entity, is replaced within pattern P2. With **Replicate(P, n)**, pattern "P" is replicated "n" times, and the resulting replicas are independent of each other. **Group/Aggregate(P1,...,Pn)** enables a group of "n" patterns to be seen as a single pattern, and behave as a single entity. We define an operator catalogue which may be used to modify structural patterns. The sequence of usage of operators is also significant.

3 Pattern Supported Workflow

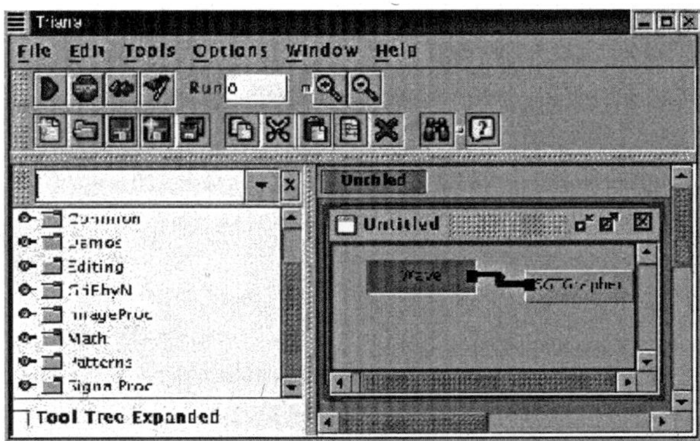

Figure 4. The Triana Graphical User Interface.

Triana [9] is a workflow based tool (see figure 4) for integrating different components to build scientific applications. By default, Triana comes with a toolbox of pre-defined services/tools (called *units*) for signal processing, mathematical calculations, audio and image processing, etc. Triana also provides a wizard for the creation of new services, which are then added to the toolbox. Users compose applications: 1) by selecting *units* from toolboxes, and dragging and dropping them onto a scratchpad, and 2) by connecting (linking) components using the Triana interface. An application in Triana consists of a network of components connected into a *TaskGraph* – with connectivity between components checked based on data types associated with the input and output ports of components. Figure 4 shows a simple example with two components from the signal processing toolbox: a wave generator's output node is connected to the input node of a grapher unit. Execution starts as soon as data arrives in a component's input port(s), and a component is allowed to send results concurrently to several other components. Triana also has a grouping facility to enable a collection of components to be treated as a single group. This "group component" will have nodes (input and output ports) that allow connecting the internal components to outside ones. Finally, users may save the configurations they have defined and reuse them later on.

Once an application has been constructed using the Triana GUI, it must subsequently be executed on distributed computational resources. Figure 5 shows, in a simplified way, how execution is achieved using a collection of JXTA [13] based Triana peers [10, 11]. The peer supporting the Triana GUI acts as a co-ordinator for launching different parts of the *Task-Graph* on other peers; using input from the user, it decides which parts of the TaskGraph to run locally, and which on remote peers. Conceptually, Triana is a two-layered application where the Triana GUI is de-coupled from the Triana Service (see figure 5) responsible for the (distributed) execution. Each peer must support a Triana Service, to enable execution requests to be received from the co-ordinator – essentially the Triana Service acts as a hosting environment to launch and manage task execution on remote resources. A peer may subsequently also sub-contract execution to other peers. A Triana-Service to Globus/OGSA bridge is also being implemented as part of the European GridLab project.

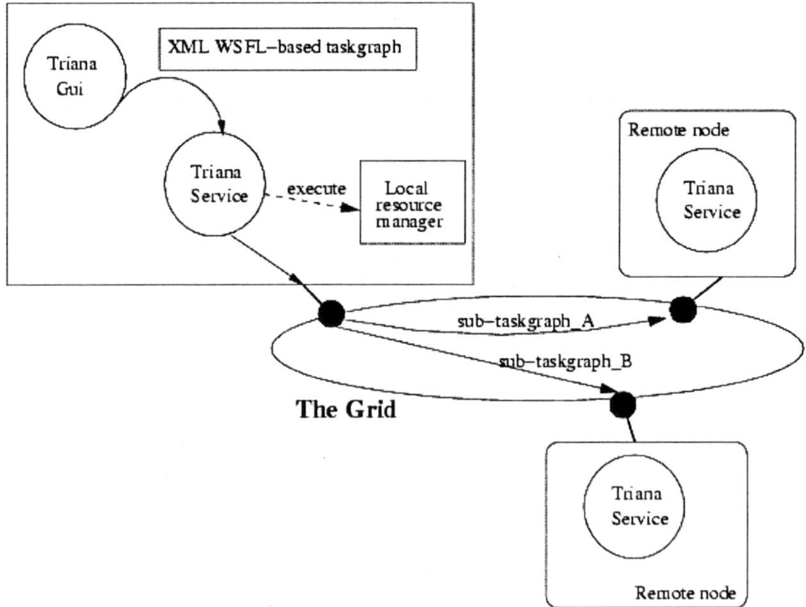

Figure 5. A simplified vision of Triana's distribution model.

3.1   Patterns and Operators in Triana

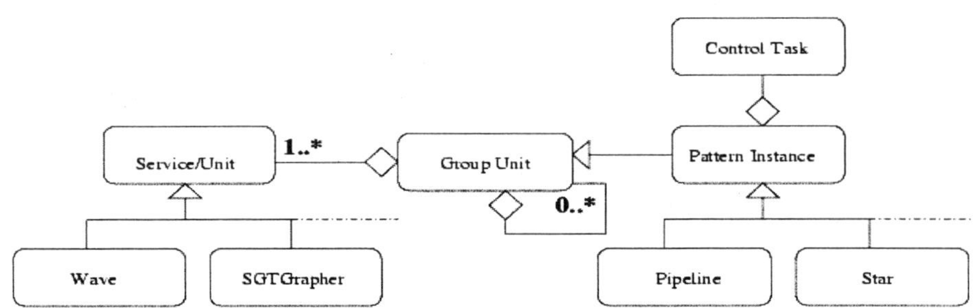

Figure 6. Definition of a pattern instance.

Triana has been extended to support structural patterns and structural operators – which are made available in the Triana toolbox. Intrinsically, a pattern in Triana is a group component, as it contains a set of entities (connected in a pre-defined way), with a particular set of parameters. Group components in Triana can also be recursive, i.e. they can contain other groups of units. Such a component has a set of input/output ports to support the connection to the input/output ports of the encapsulated units. For example, in figure 7 the *Gaussian* unit is connected to the *Wave* unit through an input node owned by the *Pipeline*. A *Pattern Instance* on the other hand, is a pattern with units instantiated to particular executables. Figure 6 shows the definition of a pattern instance in Triana, and figure 7 shows an example of a pattern instance. Initially a pattern consists of place holders for executables, identified as *Dummy Units*. A pattern is therefore not executable, but only becomes executable by instantiating dummy units to particular executable components (the result being a pattern instance). Hence, each pattern instance aggregates units according to a specific structure, and is managed by a *Control Task*.

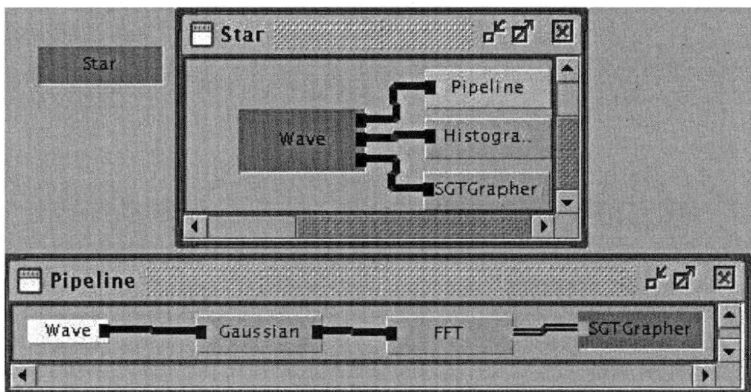

Figure 7. Final configuration.

3.2 A Few Triana Classes

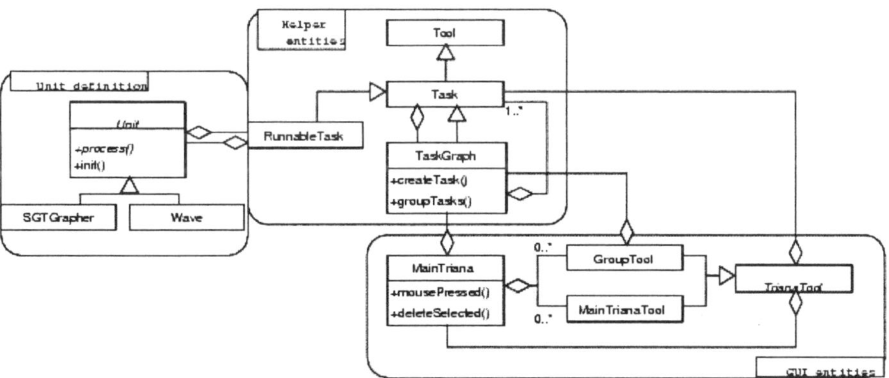

Figure 8. UML simplified description of some Triana classes.

Figure 8 shows the set of classes for implementing patterns in Triana, and is divided into three major areas: *Unit definition* presents the basic class for defining a Triana service/unit; *Helper entities* shows classes for realising the execution of a unit; and *GUI entities* gives an example of classes that support interaction with the users.

A new service is defined by extending the *Unit* abstract class, containing optional and mandatory methods to be implemented. The *process()* method is mandatory and specifies the specific actions to be performed by the unit. For an optional method, like *init()*, a user may define actions that must be executed prior to service execution (i.e. before *process()* is executed). Triana also provides an event mechanism, that allows event listeners to be associated with particular unit parameters. Helper classes like *Tool*, *Task*, and *RunnableTask* provide the necessary code to execute a unit, and to send and receive data. *Tool* defines code common for all units in the toolbox (e.g. parameter management code, like code to get the name of all the service's parameters). *Task* extends *Tool* and represents a task in a *TaskGraph*, i.e. an entity that can be connected to other entities forming a workflow. *RunnableTask* makes the connection between a *Unit* and a *Task*. It initialises an associated unit (e.g. an object of class *Wave*) by calling its *init()* method. Furthermore, it implements the data handling capability of a *Task* (e.g. keeps track of which nodes have data that has not yet been processed, and wakes up a task when there is data ready to be read on all input ports).

A TaskGraph is itself a group *Task* – an idea used to represent hierarchy. A TaskGraph contains a collection of tasks linked by cables. Whenever a task is created, it is always created in the context of a TaskGraph (and contains a reference to this taskgraph as shown in figure 8). A *TaskGraph* provides methods for creating a new task within it (*createTask()*); connecting/disconnecting tasks which belong to the taskgraph; creating a new sub-taskgraph out of a group of tasks that belong to the taskgraph (*groupTasks()*); etc. A TaskGraph may also act as a listener to the tasks that it represents (e.g. it gets notified when a task is disconnected from another task). Besides tasks, it is possible to listen to events from the tasks' ports, and associated configuration parameters for these ports.

3.3   Implementation of Structural Patterns and Operators

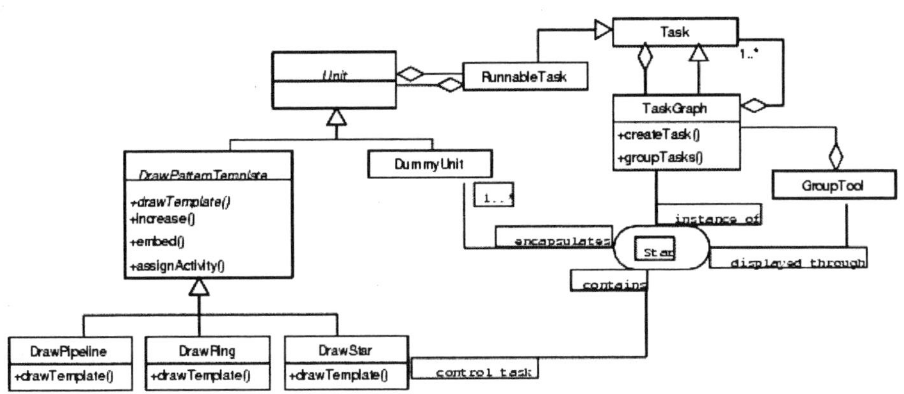

Figure 9. UML definition of the classes for creating structural pattern templates. Particular example of the star pattern template.

Patterns and operators are implemented as extensions to the *Unit* class. For example, *DrawPatternTemplate* (figure 9) is an abstract class that extends *Unit* and implements structural patterns' common behaviour. Particular structural patterns are then support by specific subtypes like *DrawPipeline, DrawRing,* etc. To create a pattern template like *Star* in figure 9, an instance of *DrawStar* creates a new TaskGraph that includes the instance itself. This instance also acts as a "control task" for the pattern. On execution, first it draws a default set of component place holders, i.e. *DummyUnit* tasks, inside the TaskGraph. A DummyUnit must subsequently be instantiated with a specific unit from the Triana toolbox. It is also the responsibility of the control task (i.e. the *DrawStar* instance) to support event handling for these DummyUnits. It also implements structural operators like *increase, embed,* etc. The operators' major code is defined in *DrawPatternTemplate,* and specific actions are left to the subtypes. For example, the *increase* operator needs two actions: a) to create and draw a new *DummyUnit* element, and b) to identify the connection element, i.e. to which of the already existing *DummyUnits* should the new element be attached to. Action a) is common to all subtypes, so it is implemented in the *DrawPatternTemplate* class. Action b), in turn, is specific of each structural pattern. For example, for a *Star* pattern template a new *DummyUnit* has to be attached to the *nucleus* of the star, whereas for the pipeline a new *DummyUnit* is added to one of the ends of the pipeline. As such, each subtype redefines the abstract method *getConnectionElement( )* which identifies the *DummyUnit* that represents the adequate connection point.

To sum up, the *Star* pattern template shown in figure 9 can be described as a group defined by a taskgraph and graphically accessible through a *GroupTool* instance. Moreover, the group is a set of connected *DummyUnits* instances which structural properties are controlled by an instance of *DrawStar*.

4   Conclusion

Ongoing work on implementing a pattern-based software engineering tool for Grid environments is outlined. The tool provides a library of useful pattern templates and pattern operators, primarily aimed at supporting workflow based applications. A variety of scientific applications in Astrophysics, Bio-Informatics, Chemistry fall into this category. Structural pattern templates are manipulated through structural operators that preserve the patterns' structural constraints. A user is able to subsequently select and apply different behavioural patterns, defining and managing in this way various data and control flows between the components. After the instantiation of pattern elements with specific Grid services, a user will be able to control the application's execution and reconfiguration through behavioural operators. The current implementation efforts towards achieving this is described, based on the Triana workflow tool.

Acknowledgements

We would like to thank the Triana group ([9]), in particular Matthew Shields and Ian Wang for their suggestions and invaluable support on explaining the complexities of the Triana code.

This work was possible due a grant from the Agentcities.NET project, to which we would also like to thank.

References

[1] Ian Foster, Carl Kesselman (Editors), "The Grid: Blueprint for a New Computing Infrastructure", Morgan Kaufmann, 1998

[2] E. Gamma, R. Helm, R. Johnson, J. Vlissides, "Design Patterns: Elements of Reusable Object-Oriented Software", Addison-Wesley, 1994.

[3] F. Buschmann, R. Meunier, H. Rohnert, P. Sommerlad, M. Stal, "Pattern-Oriented Software Architecture: A System of Patterns", John Wiley & Sons, 1998.

[4] "Patterns and Skeletons for Parallel and Distributed Computing", F. Rabhi and S. Gorlatch(Eds), Springer, 2002.

[5] M. Fowler, K. Scott, "UML Distilled. Applying The Standard Object Modeling Language", Addison-Wesley, 1997.

[6] Gentleware, The Poseidon UML Tool, Web site at: `http://www.gentleware.com/`. Last visited: December 2002.

[7] ANL, "The Globus System". See Web site at: `http://www.globus.org/`. Last visited: February 2003.

[8] The Common Component Architecture Forum. See Web site at: `http://www.cca-forum.org/`. Last visited: August 2002.

[9] I. Taylor et al., "TRIANA". See Web site at: `http://www.triana.co.uk/`. Last visited: February 2003.

[10] I. Taylor, O. F. Rana, R. Philp, I. Wang, M. Shields, "Supporting Peer-2-Peer Interactions in the Consumer Grid", 8th International Workshop on High-Level Parallel Programming Models and Supportive Environments (HIPS) at IPDPS, Nice, France, April 2003. IEEE Computer Society Press.

[11] I. Taylor, M. Shields, I. Wang, R. Philp, S. Majithia, "Grid-Aware Triana Prototype", GridLab - A Grid Application Toolkit and Testbed, Work Package 3: Work-Flow Application Toolkit (TGAT). See Web site at: `http://www.gridlab.org/`. Last visited: January 2003.

[12] I. Taylor S. Majithia, M. Shields, I. Wang, "Triana WorkFlow Specification", GridLab - A Grid Application Toolkit and Testbed, Work Package 3: Work-Flow Application Toolkit (TGAT). See Web site at: `http://www.gridlab.org/`. Last visited: January 2003.

[13] Project JXTA. See Web site at: `http://www.w3.org/XML`. Last visited: December 2003.

[14] M. C. Gomes, J. C. Cunha, O. F. Rana, "Pattern Operators for Grid Environments", submitted to the "Scientific Programming Journal", March 2003.

[15] J. Bosch, "Design Patterns as Language Constructs", Journal of Object-Oriented Programming, Vol. 11(2), pages 18-32, 1998.

[16] B. Wydaeghe, W. Vanderperren, "Visual Composition Using Composition Patterns", Proc. Tools 2001, Santa Barbara, USA, July 2001.

[17] ObjectVenture, The ObjectAssembler Visual Development Environment. See Web site at: `http://www.objectventure.com/objectassembler.html`. Last visited: March 2003.

[18] The MyGrid Project. See Web site at: `http://www.mygrid.org.uk`. Last visited: January 2003.

[19] The DataGrid Project. See Web site at: `http://eu-datagrid.web.cern.ch/eu-datagrid`. Last visited: January 2003.

Concurrent Information Processing and Computing
D. Grigoras and A. Nicolau (Eds.)
IOS Press, 2005

Parallel Implementation of Multi-population Differential Evolution

Daniela Zaharie and Dana Petcu

West University of Timişoara, B-dul V.Pârvan 4, 300223 Timişoara, Romania,
e-mail: {dzaharie,petcu}@info.uvt.ro

Abstract. A coarse-grained parallelization of an adaptive differential evolution algorithm is described. The parallelization is based on the multi-population model, a random connection topology being used. The results obtained by the implementation of the proposed algorithm on a PC cluster show not only a speedup in execution time, but also an improvement of the convergence behavior by reducing the premature convergence situations.

1 Introduction

Evolutionary algorithms are stochastic optimization methods which are particularly well suited for hard problems where little is known about the search space. They maintain a population of candidate solutions which are iteratively transformed by some nature-inspired operators: *mutation, recombination* and *selection*. The evolutionary process tends to find globally satisfactory, even if not optimal, solutions to the optimization problem. When they are applied to large real problems they may become too slow [14]. To overcome this difficulty either new evolutionary operators or parallelization methods have been proposed.

A result of the efforts in the first direction is the "differential evolution" algorithm (DE), developed by Storn and Price [13], which is an efficient optimization technique on continuous domains. On the other hand there are two main reasons for parallelizing an evolutionary algorithm: one is to achieve time savings by distributing the computational effort and the second is to benefit from the algorithmic point of view [14].

Efficient parallelization of evolutionary algorithms is not a trivial task despite the fact that these algorithms are inherently parallel. This is mainly due to the fact that the population elements interact during the evolution and the effect of operators is sensitive to their control parameters choice. This means that all the empirical knowledge concerning parameters choice gathered from serial implementations is not necessarily useful for parallel implementations (mainly if parallelization implies modification in the population structure). On the other hand there exists different classes of evolutionary algorithms: genetic algorithms, genetic programming, evolutionary strategies and evolutionary programming. Even if they are based on the same natural evolution principle they are different, and so are their parallel implementations.

During the last years, several parallel models have been proposed [1], [3], [14]. The parallelization of an evolutionary algorithm can be made at one of the following levels [14]: objective function evaluation level (*master-slave model*), population level (*multi-population model*, called also *island model* or *migration model*), element level (*cellular model*). The cellular model leads to fine-grained parallelization while the other two lead to coarse-grained parallelization.

The aim of this work is to analyze a parallel implementation of the differential evolution [13] based on the multi-population model. The reasons of choosing the multi-population model were: *(i)* it is inspired from the spatial structure of natural populations; *(ii)* its ability of preserving the population diversity through the migration process.

Due to the absence of a real mutation, differential evolution is highly predisposed to a fast decrease of the population diversity which leads to the undesirable premature convergence (the algorithm is trapped into a sub-optimal state). The multi-population approach could help avoiding such a situation.

Unlike other evolutionary algorithms for which different parallel implementations have been proposed there exists few parallel implementation of differential evolution [9], [12]. These are based on parallelization of the objective function evaluation and on the cellular model, respectively. As is motivated in [9], the multi-population model has been avoided because of the difficulties related with the control parameters choice. Since the algorithm which we propose is adaptive, the parameter choice is no more a difficulty and, as we shall see, the multi-population approach can improve the DE behavior.

The paper is organized as follows. Section 2 presents a short overview of the parallel models for evolutionary algorithms. The adaptive differential evolution and the multi-population approach are detailed in Section 3. Section 4 describes the parallel implementation and the numerical tests performed on a PC cluster. Concluding remarks are presented in Section 5.

2   Overview of parallel evolutionary algorithms

The parallelization at the objective function level has as main motivation the fact that the most costly computation is the objective function evaluation. In this model, all computations excepting the evaluation operation is performed by a master processor. The evaluation step consists in computing the objective function values for all elements of the population and this step is done in parallel in the following way. The master processor transfers elements of the population to slave processors which have only the role of evaluating the objective function for the received element. After the master receives the data from the slaves, it continues with the next step of the algorithm (e.g. selection). This synchronous updating of the population is not very efficient due to the need of waiting until the last slave return the function value. In order to prevent these idle times, in [2] is used an asynchronous update of the population: each new element obtained by mutation and recombination is sent to a slave processor for evaluation without waiting until all new candidates are generated; moreover when a slave returns a result, if the corresponding element is better than the worst element in the population then will replace it. This algorithm was tested in [2] on a concrete problem on a LAN of Sun Sparc workstations using PVM. Parallelization at objective function level is efficient mainly if the objective function is complex [5].

In the multi-population model, the population is divided into sub-populations called *islands* or *demes*. In each island a standard sequential evolutionary algorithm is executed. The communication between sub-populations is assured by a *migration* process: after some generations several elements leave their island and migrate to another. This process has an important role in preserving the population diversity, thus in avoiding premature convergence cases. Its effectiveness depends on the communication topology (a graph structure in which the sub-populations are nodes and the connections indicate the communicating sub-populations). The frequency of migration (number of generations between two migrations), the migration topology, and the selection of migrants have to be established for each evolutionary algorithm because a general rigorous way to choose them is not known at present. From an implementation point of view, the coarse-grained models are suited to distributed memory multicomputers and clusters only if the ratio of computation to communication is high [14].

There exist several implementations of parallel genetic algorithms based on the multi-population model. For example, VEGA [18] implements a distributed genetic algorithm based on the island model with exchange of individuals over a defined connection topology (ring, grid, x-net, hypercube, fully connected); it works on the MIMD computer Intel Paragon and workstation clusters.

In the cellular model (also called *neighborhood* or *diffusion* models) the elements are placed on the nodes of a toroidal one- or two-dimensional grid. The evolutionary transformations take place within a small neighborhood. This model is suited for massive parallel machines.

Different hybrid strategies were also considered. The idea proposed in [10] is to consider an architecture based on the island model at a top level where each island acts based on a cellular model. A process is dedicated to control the islander's evolution, to manage the migration, to collect the local statistics, and finally to generate the global ones.

Choosing the adequate model depends on the problem particularities, on the specific of the evolutionary algorithm, and on the available hardware support.

3   The multi-population adaptive differential evolution

The differential evolution algorithm has been successfully applied in solving continuous optimization problems encountered in engineering design [8]. To describe the algorithm structure we consider the problem of finding the minimum, $x^* \in D$, of an objective function $f : D \subset \mathbb{R}^n \rightarrow \mathbb{R}$ on which we do not impose any restriction.

The classical DE algorithm evolves a fixed size population, $P = \{x_1, \ldots, x_m\}$, which is randomly initialized with elements from D. After population initialization, an iterative process is started, and, at each iteration (generation), a new population is produced until a stopping condition is satisfied. At each generation, each population element (x_l) could be replaced (with probability p) with a new generated element. The new element is a linear combination between a randomly selected element (x_{α^l}) and a difference between other two randomly selected elements (x_{β^l} and x_{γ^l}). For each l, the indices α^l, β^l and γ^l are selected without replacement from $\{1, \ldots, m\}$. Besides the population size (m), the parameters of the algorithm are: $p \in [0, 1]$ (the probability of replacing an element with the new generated one) and $F > 0$ (the factor which amplify the "differential" term). Experimental studies show that DE convergence properties are highly dependent on the algorithm parameters [6], [13], [15]. Thus, as for other evolutionary algorithms, adaptation methods are highly desirable. In [16] is proposed a parameter adaptation based on the idea of controlling the population diversity.

The classical DE is modified as follows. The parameters F and p are replaced with two sets of parameters: $\{F_i\}_{i=\overline{1,n}}$ and $\{p_i\}_{i=\overline{1,n}}$ (a pair of parameters, (F_i, p_i) for each component, x^i). At each generation the variances for all n components are computed as follows:

$$\mathrm{Var}(x^i(g)) = \frac{1}{m} \sum_{l=1}^{m} \left(x_l^i(g) - \frac{1}{m} \sum_{k=1}^{m} x_k^i(g) \right)^2, \quad i = \overline{1, n}.$$

These values are used to compute the new parameters. The parameter modification is based on

---

Random initialization of $P(0) = \{x_1(0), \ldots, x_m(0)\}$, $\{F_i\}_{i=\overline{1,n}}$, $\{p_i\}_{i=\overline{1,n}}$
$g = 0$
Compute $\text{Var}(x^i(0))$, $i = \overline{1,n}$
Repeat
   Perturbation step:

$$z_l^i = \begin{cases} x_{\alpha^l}^i(g) + F_i \cdot (x_{\beta^l}^i(g) - x_{\gamma^l}^i(g)) & \text{with probability } p_i \\ x_l^i(g) & \text{with probability } 1 - p_i \end{cases} \quad l = \overline{1,m}, i = \overline{1,n}$$

   Evaluation step:
     Compute $f(x_1(g)), \ldots, f(x_m(g))$ and $f(z_1), \ldots, f(z_m)$
   Selection step:
     If $f(z_l) < f(x_l(g))$ then $x_l(g+1) = z_l$ else $x_l(g+1) = x_l(g), l = \overline{1,m}$
   Variance computation:
     Compute $\text{Var}(x^i(g+1))$, $c_i(g+1)$, $i = \overline{1,n}$
   Parameters adaptation:
     If g is even then adapt F_i, $i = \overline{1,n}$ according with (1)
     else adapt p_i, $i = \overline{1,n}$ according with (2)
   $g = g + 1$
Until *a stopping criterion is satisfied.*

Figure 1. The general structure of the adaptive DE algorithm

the value $c_i(g+1) = \gamma \text{Var}(x^i(g))/\text{Var}(x^i(g+1))$, with $\gamma > 0$ a *new* control parameter. The values $c_i(g+1)$, $i = \overline{1,n}$ are used to adjust the parameters involved in the computation of the new population, $x(g+2)$. At each generation only one set of parameters is modified. For instance, at even generations the values F_i are modified as follows:

$$F_i = \begin{cases} \sqrt{\dfrac{m(c_i - 1) + p_i(2 - p_i)}{2mp_i}} & \text{if } m(c_i - 1) + p_i(2 - p_i) \geq 0 \\ F_{\text{inf}} & \text{if } m(c_i - 1) + p_i(2 - p_i) < 0 \end{cases} \quad (1)$$

with F_{inf} the minimal value for F. A sufficient condition for increasing the population variance by recombination is that $F \geq 1/\sqrt{m}$, thus we shall use $F_{\text{inf}} = 1/\sqrt{m}$. An upper bound for F_i can also be imposed (empirical results suggest $F_{\text{sup}} = 2$).

At odd generations, the parameters p_i are adapted as follows:

$$p_i = \begin{cases} -(mF_i^2 - 1) + \sqrt{(mF_i^2 - 1)^2 - m(1 - c_i)} & \text{if } c_i \geq 1 \\ p_{\text{inf}} & \text{if } c_i < 1 \end{cases} \quad (2)$$

with p_{inf} the minimal value for p_i. Since $p_i \in [0, 1]$ a minimal value for p_i should be near 0, e.g. $p_{\text{inf}} = 0.01$ while the maximal value should be $p_{\text{sup}} = 1$. When the computed values of the parameters are outside their domain, they are corrected as follows: a value less than the lower bound is replaced with the lower bound, while a value greater than the upper bound is replaced with the upper bound. The general structure of the adaptive DE algorithm is illustrated in Fig. 1.

Unlike other adaptation rules [4] (e.g. self-adaptation) where each population element has specific values of the parameters, the proposed method uses different values for each component. In this way the particularities of the fitness landscape could be "captured" by the parameters adaptation process. Moreover, this will simplify the communication between sub-populations in the multi-population approach, each sub-population having its own set of control parameters.

We consider now a multi-population approach for the adaptive DE. Our model consists in dividing the population in s sub-populations of the same size, μ. On each sub-population an adaptive DE is executed for a fixed number, τ, of generations. Each DE corresponding to a sub-population works with its own set of randomly initialized adaptive parameters.

After every τ generations, a migration process, based on a random connection topology, is started. More specifically, the migration strategy consists in: each element from each sub-population can be swapped (with a given *migration probability, p_m*) with a randomly selected element from a randomly selected sub-population (including the sub-population which contains the initial element).

Due to the migration process, a sub-population with a low diversity can be "revived" after the migration takes place. Hence the multi-population approach allows avoiding premature convergence situations in DE. We shall illustrate this by numerical results obtained for some benchmark test functions (see Table 1). The minimal value for all test functions is 0. Functions f_1 and f_5 have a unique minimum, while f_2, f_3 and f_4 have many local minima beside the global minimum.

Table 1. Test functions

Name	Expression	Domain
Sphere	$f_1(x) = \sum_{i=1}^{n} x_i^2$	$[-100, 100]^n$
Rastrigin	$f_2(x) = \sum_{i=1}^{n} [x_i^2 - 10\cos(2\pi x_i) + 10]$	$[-5.12, 5.12]^n$
Griewank	$f_3(x) = \dfrac{1}{4000} \sum_{i=1}^{n} x_i^2 - \prod_{i=1}^{n} \cos(x_i/\sqrt{i}) + 1$	$[-600, 600]^n$
Ackley	$f_4(x) = -20\exp\left(-0.2\sqrt{\dfrac{1}{n}\sum_{i=1}^{n} x_i^2}\right) - \exp\left(\dfrac{1}{n}\sum_{i=1}^{n}\cos(2\pi x_i)\right) + 20 + e$	$[-32, 32]^n$
Rosenbrock	$f_5(x) = \sum_{i=1}^{n-1} [100(x_{i+1} - x_i^2)^2 + (x_i - 1)^2]$	$[-30, 30]^n$

During the experiments, the following parameters were fixed: $m = 60$ (the population size), $n = 100$ (the problem dimension), $\tau = 100$ (the number of generations between migrations), $p_m = 0.5$ (the migration probability), $r = 10$ (the number of independent runs of the algorithm, used to compute the averaged values). The stopping condition which we used is: "$f_* \leq \epsilon$ or $\langle Var(x) \rangle < 10^{-12}$" ($f_*$ is the best value of the objective function found into the population and $\langle Var(x) \rangle$ denotes the averaged value of the variance computed over all population elements and all their components). The algorithm is considered successful (*Success*) if the first part of the condition is satisfied, and it prematurely converges (*PC*) if only the second part is true. In Tables 2 and 3, for each situation (success or premature convergence) the number of cases (from 10 independent trials) and the averaged number of generations are presented.

Having the aim of verifying if the migration process can avoid premature convergence we used a low value for the control parameter, $\gamma = 0.5$. This value encourages the decrease of population variance thus it can induce a premature convergence on the adaptive DE, but as numerical results in Tables 2 and 3 shows, the multi-population approach assures in most cases a repairing effect. Similar results have been obtained for a deterministic selection of migrants: a copy of the best element of a source sub-population will replace the worst element of a destination sub-population.

Table 2. Influence of migration on the adaptive DE. Test functions: f_1 and f_2, $\epsilon = 10^{-6}, \gamma = 0.5$.

s	μ	p_m	Sphere (f_1)			Rastrigin (f_2)		
			Success cases/gen.	PC cases/gen.	$\langle f_* \rangle$	Success cases/gen.	PC cases/gen.	$\langle f_* \rangle$
1	60	0	-	10/2002	9.2829	-	10/2011	8.1777
2	30	0.5	7/1223	3/1700	0.0001	-	10/2398	3.0844
3	20	0.5	10/1282	-	10^{-6}	2/2852	8/2988	0.9950
4	15	0.5	10/1337	-	10^{-6}	4/3447	6/3552	0.7959
5	12	0.5	10/1410	-	10^{-6}	7/3967	3/4385	0.2984
6	10	0.5	10/1478	-	10^{-6}	7/4631	3/4874	0.3979

Table 3. Influence of migration on the adaptive DE. Test functions: f_3 and f_4, $\epsilon = 10^{-6}, \gamma = 0.5$.

s	μ	p_m	Griewank (f_3)			Ackley (f_4)		
			Success cases/gen.	PC cases/gen.	$\langle f_* \rangle$	Success cases/gen.	PC cases/gen.	$\langle f_* \rangle$
1	60	0	-	10/2251	0.3926	-	10/1613	0.2730
2	30	0.5	6/1205	4/1946	0.0031	3/1616	7/1562	0.0411
3	20	0.5	10/1285	-	10^{-6}	8/1684	2/1922	$2 \cdot 10^{-6}$
4	15	0.5	10/1314	-	10^{-6}	10/1761	-	10^{-6}
5	12	0.5	10/1391	-	10^{-6}	10/1849	-	10^{-6}
6	10	0.5	10/1456	-	10^{-6}	10/1939	-	10^{-6}

4   Numerical tests on the parallel implementation

In this section we present the results obtained running a multi-population adaptive DE implementation on a PC cluster: 8 PC IV 1500 MHz with 256 Mb RAM interconnected via a Myrinet switch and optical fiber cables ensuring a transmission of 2 Gb/s. Such a system is suited for a random communication topology between the processes of a parallel code. The code is written in C and PVM (Parallel Virtual Machine, http://netlib.org/pvm). We used the test functions from Table 1.

Similar numerical tests were performed in [7] on a 16 PC cluster system (Intel PII 400 MHz, 128 Mb, FastEthernet, MPICH) for Rastrigin's function (f_2). A genetic algorithm based on gray-coding, one point crossover and standard mutation is used. The migration is based on a ring topology with connections established in a random manner each time a migration takes place. The tests used the following parameters: migration rate equal to 0.5, population size between 20 and 270, sub-populations number between 1 and 16, and 30 independent trials. The simulation of the island model is stopped when all islands satisfy the termination condition (synchronous operations are needed). The number of generations that ensure a reasonable speedup (12 for 16 processors) is around 40.

The model adopted in [11] distributes all the population elements on a toroidal landscape and the sub-populations are obtained by introducing logical boundaries. The migration strategy is defined by letting a random walk path to cross the boundaries between sub-populations on the bases of a given probability function (flip rate, the same for all boundaries). The master-slave model is used in the implementation on a SGI Power Challenge system with 10 R-1000 processors. The algorithm was applied to the Rastrigin's function with $n = 16$. The

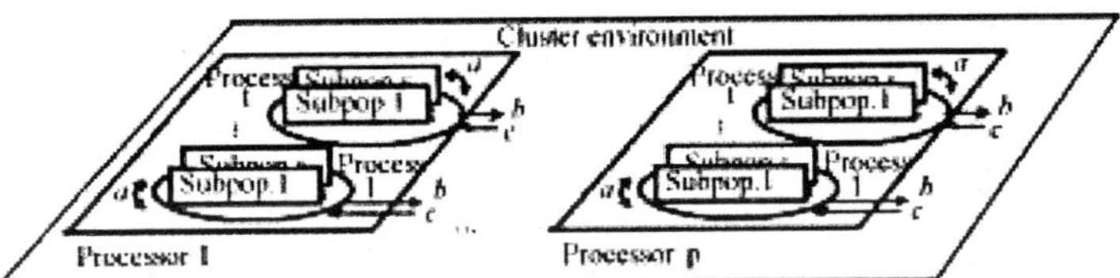

Figure 2. Implementation strategy – the migration process has three stages: (a) internal exchanges of elements from the same process; (b) send the migrants from the current process; (c) receive the elements which replace the migrants

minimum value for the objective function is set to 10^{-6}, three step length for the random walk, populations sizes 64-900, 10 trials, toroidal landscape split in 4 equal regions, flip rate between 0 and 1. Tests show that a clear correlation between the optimal flip rate and the population size cannot be settled and extreme flip rates (0 and 1) are not recommended. For 10 generations the speedup obtained using 4 processors and 900 individuals is 3.8.

We have adopted the following strategy. The user can decide if the sub-populations will be treated by one or more processes. One processor of the cluster system can treat one or more processes. A random communication topology is used in the migration process. An element is moved with respect to a user-defined probability (p_m) in a random position of a randomly selected sub-population. The selected position being occupied by another element, the later one will migrate to the former position of the incoming individual. If the destination sub-population is treated by the same process, it suffices a simple exchange; otherwise the element will be gathered in a message buffer together with the others willing to migrate from the current process. This message buffer is sent to all other processes which will extract data corresponding to the incoming elements and send back the data corresponding to the elements being replaced (Figure 2). The algorithm stops when one sub-population satisfies the termination condition (distance to the minimal value less than $\epsilon = 10^{-6}$).

We have tested the parallel algorithm for the test functions in Table 1, with the problem dimension $n =30, 100, 250, 500$, the population size $m =50, 100, 300$, the sub-populations number $s =1, 2, 3, 4, 6, 8$, the number of processes $t =1, 2, 3, 4, 6, 8$, the number of processors $p =1, 2, 3, 4, 6, 8$, and the probability of migration from one island to another set to 0.5. The number of generations between two consecutive migrations is $\tau = 100$.

In order to measure the speedup due to the parallel implementation we computed the averaged time spent in 100 iterations of the adaptive DE algorithm and the corresponding migration stage. Let $T(p, t, s)$ denote this time spent by p processors treating t processes dealing with s sub-populations. Figures 3 (a) and (b) show that the mean time spent by the implementation of the algorithm with several sub-populations and migrations is approximately the same as that of the algorithm which does not use sub-populations, independent with respect to problem dimension n and to population size m: $T(1, 1, s) \approx T(1, 1, 1)$. Figures 3 (c) and (d) show that a time decrease can be obtained by treating the sub-populations on different processes, due to the fact that each process deals with smaller sub-populations: $T(1, t, s) \leq T(1, 1, s)$ where $1 \leq t \leq s$. This is true at least for $m \geq 100$ or $n \geq 100$.

The computation of the speedup at one stage of the algorithm can be done in three ways:
- algorithmic speedup: $S_p^{(1)} = T(1, 1, 1)/T(p, p, p)$;
- concurrent implementation speedup: $S_p^{(2)} = T(1, 1, p)/T(p, p, p)$;

- parallel implementation speedup: $S_p^{(3)} = T(1, p, p)/T(p, p, p)$.

According to the above remarks we expect that $S_p^{(3)} \leq \min\{S_p^{(1)}, S_p^{(2)}\}$. This is also suggested by Figure 3 (e), in the case of $m = 300$ and $p = 4$ processors. The speedup values are comparable with those from [11] (in our tests we use a smaller population and a higher problem dimension). Figure 3 (f) illustrates the dependence of the $S_p^{(2)}$ values on the problem dimension and population size in the case of $p = 2$ processors. The main remark is that when different values of m and n are used no major differences appear.

The code efficiency is measured using the above defined speedup measures and the number of processors: $E_p = S_p/p$. Figure 3 (g) refers to $E_p^{(2)}$ in the case of the population size $m = 300$ and $s = p$ sub-populations. Note that high efficiency values ($E_p^{(2)} \geq 85\%$) are obtained also in the case of $p = 8$ processors. Figure 3 (h) shows that only small differences appear by changing the problem: $E_p^{(3)}$ is computed in the case of $m = 300$ and $n = 250$. This is due to the fact that the test functions are of similar complexity.

5 Conclusions

We implemented a coarse-grained model of an adaptive differential evolution algorithm on a PC cluster. The parallelization is based on the multi-population model with a random connection topology and a random selection of the migrants. In summary, we obtained the following results: parallel execution on the cluster is able to speedup the DE significantly and improvement of the convergence have been obtained even by sequential implementation due to the ability of the migration process to preserve the population diversity, thus to avoid premature convergence. We applied the same migration strategy in [17] for multi-objective optimization using a similar multi-population model for the adaptive Pareto DE.

Acknowledgements. This work has been supported by the project RO-InfoSoc-3 no. 61/2002.

References

[1] P. Adamidis, Parallel Evolutionary Algorithms: A Review, 4th Hellenic-European Conference on Computer Mathematics and its Applications, Athens, Greece, (1998).

[2] Thomas Bäck, Thomas Baielstein, Boris Naujoks and Jochen Heistermann, Evolutionary algorithms for the optimization of simulation models using PVM, in J. Dongarra, M. Gengler, B. Tourancheau, X. Vigouroux (eds.), Proc. of EuroPVM'95, (1995) 277–282.

[3] E. Cantu-Paz, A survey of parallel genetic algorithms, IlliGal Report No. 97003, (1997).

[4] A.E. Eiben and R. Hinterding, Parameter Control in Evolutionary Algorithms, IEEE Trans. on Evolutionary Computation, 3(2), (1999) 124–141.

[5] C. T. Fogarty and R. Huang, Implementing the genetic algorithm on transputer based parallel processing systems, in Proc. of Parallel Problem Solving from Nature, LNCS **496**, (1991) 145–149.

[6] R. Gämperle, S.D. Müller and P. Koumoutsakos, A Parameter Study for Differential Evolution, in A. Grmela, N.E. Mastorakis (eds.) Advances in Intelligent Systems, Fuzzy Systems, Evolutionary Computation, WSEAS Press, (2002) 293–298.

[7] Tomoyuki Hiroyasu, Mitsunori Miki and Yusuke Tanimura, The difference of parallel efficiency between the two models of parallel genetic algorithms on PC cluster systems, in Proc. 4th Intern. Conf. High Performance Computing in Asia-Pacific region (1999), 945–948.

[8] J. Lampinen, A Bibliography of Differential Evolution Algorithm, Technical Report, Lappeenranta University of Technology, IT Department, Laboratory of Information Processing, (1999).

[9] J. Lampinen, Differential Evolution-New Naturally Parallel Approach for Engineering Design Optimization, in Barry H.V. Topping(ed.), Developments in Computational Mechanics with High Performance Computing, Civil-Comp Press, Edinburgh, (1999) 217–228.

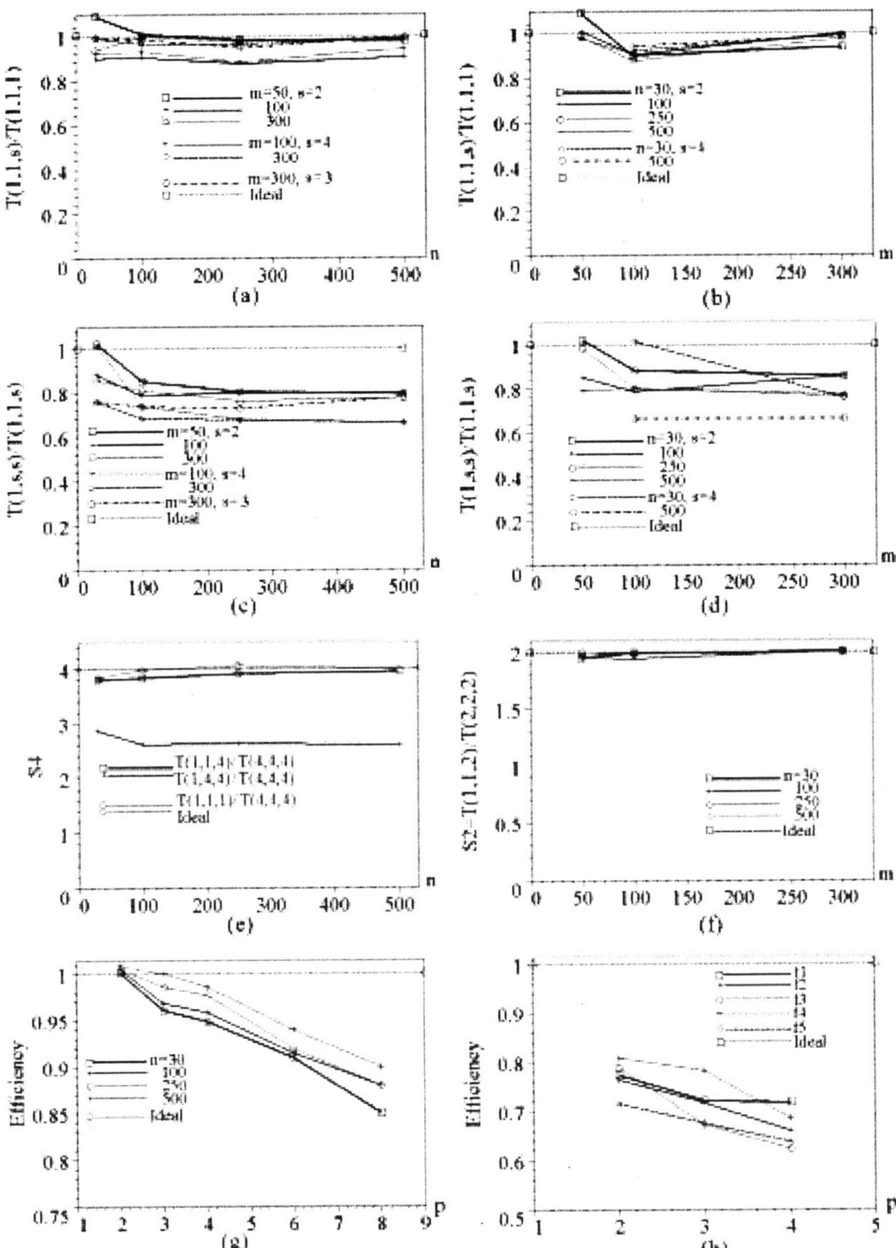

Figure 3. Time, speedup and efficiency of the parallel algorithm applied to Rastrigin's function f_2: (a) comparison between one population and s sub-population cases – n is variable; (b) a similar study – m is variable; (c) influence of the number of processes – n is variable; (d) a similar study – m is variable; (e) different measures of the speedup for $p = 4$; (f) dependence of the speedup on m and n when $p = 2$; (g) parallel code efficiency when $m = 300$; (h) efficiency variation when the code is applied to different test functions

[10] Michael Rocha, Filipe Pereira, Sónia Afonso and Jóse Neves, A genetic and evolutionary programming environment with spatially structured populations and built-in paralallelism, in L. Monosori, J. Váncza and M. Ali (eds.), Proc. IEA/AEI 2001, LNAI, **2070**, (2001) 383–392.

[11] D. Quagliarella and A. Vicini, Sub-population policies for a parallel multiojjective genetic algorithm with applications to wing design, in Proc. of Intern. Conf. on Systems, Man & Cybern., (1998) 3142–3147.

[12] M. Salomon, Parallélisation de l'évolution différentielle pour le recalage rigide d'images médicales volumiques, Technique et science informatiques, **20**(5), (2001) 605-627.

[13] R. Storn, K. Price, Differential Evolution - A Simple and Efficient Heuristic for Global Optimization over Continuous Spaces, Technical Report TR-95-012, ICSI, (1995).

[14] M. Tomassini, Parallel and Distributed Evolutionary Algorithms: A Review, in K. Miettinen, M. Mkel, P. Neittaanmki and J. Periaux (eds.) Evolutionary Algorithms in Engineering and Computer Science, J. Wiley and Sons, Chichester, (1999) 113–133.

[15] D. Zaharie, Critical Values for the Control Parameters of Differential Evolution Algorithms, in R. Matoušek, P. Ošmera (eds.), Proc. of Mendel 2002, 8th International Conference on Soft Computing, (2002) 62–67.

[16] D. Zaharie, Parameter Adaptation in Differential Evolution by Controlling the Population Diversity, in D.Petcu et al. (eds), Proc. of 4th International Workshop on Symbolic and Numeric Algorithms for Scientific Computing, Timisoara, Romania, (2002) 385–397.

[17] D. Zaharie and D. Petcu, Adaptive Pareto Differential Evolution and its Parallelization, Proc. of 5th International Conference on Parallel Processing and Applied Mathematics, Czestochowa, Poland,(2003).

[18] A. Zell and R. Baumann, Distributed Genetic Algorithms on the Intel Paragon, a large MIMD Computer, in T. B. L. J. Fogel, P. J. Angeline (eds), Proc. of the 5th Ann. Conf. on Evolutionary Programming, (1996) 385-394.

Concurrent Information Processing and Computing
D. Grigoras and A. Nicolau (Eds.)
IOS Press, 2005

233

Infection Simulation

Cătălin Bulancea[1]   Mitică Craus[2]

[1] *Institute for Computer Science, Romanian Academy, Iaşi Branch*
[2] *Technical University "Gh. Asachi", Department of Computer Engineering, Iaşi*
[1]`catalinb@academie.is.edu.ro`   [2]`craus@cs.tuiasi.ro`

Abstract. In order to study the infection process, a graph-based model is considered. A number of mutational and decisional schemes for the pathogen agents and a reaction mechanism for the host are defined and tested. In order to make tests, a simulator was built and used. The results have shown that the artificial system evolution is closed to the evolution of the infection in living bodies.

1   Introduction

Artificial life applications have nature as an inspiration source. Many of the multi-agent systems have the functioning mechanisms and principles inspired by the natural collectivity behavior [1]. Simple life forms as the seaweeds or the bacteria, which have almost no individual importance, can organize themselves in complex social systems named colonies. These simple structures were the starting point for evolving into more complex multi-cellular life forms. This is the place were we can find the basic principles of coexistence strictly connected to the adaptation, interaction and selection [2], which are natural processes by excellence.

In nature, the infection is a very complex phenomenon, strictly applicable to evolved multi-cellular life forms. We can identify the host, which is invaded by foreign, usually elementary (not necessarily unicellular) life forms. The host has some protection mechanisms, composed by white cells, antibodies, T-cells, etc. but, in some cases, these can become relatively quickly obsolete by the mutation capacity of the pathogen agents.

In this paper we describe a multi-agent system with two separate populations that interact inside an environment which has its infrastructure modelled as a graph. The graph's nodes can be seen as points with maximum resource concentration (we name resource the substances indispensable for life processes to take place; these resources are consumed by the pathogen agents, with toxins resulting in the end). The nodes are interconnected by communications channels that represent the capillary blood vessels in living bodies. The entities (antigens and antibodies) are modelled as messages, which can travel between the nodes.

Initially, the infection is located in a few nodes. The graph could evolve to supra-infected stage, if the reaction is not efficient, or to clear stage, in the contrary situation. If no "living nodes" remain, the graph becomes dead.

2 The Problem Statement

In nature, the pathogen agents are primitive life-forms (usual viruses and bacteria). In a favorable environment they have considerable reproduction capabilities. They are also exposed to mutations. In few cases, the infection is focused on a single point. Usually, the pathogen agents are grouped around the points with a maximum concentration of the resource (the substances needed for their metabolism). If the resource is consumed, they will migrate to another place were it is possible to find resources. Meanwhile, the immune system is trying to reduce, and if it is possible to destroy them.

3 The Mathematical Model

In this section we will describe the environment, the mutation mechanism of the pathogen agents and the reaction.

In order to model the environment's infrastructure, we consider a graph. As we have already mentioned, the nodes can be considered the maximum concentration resource points. In these points, this substance concentration gradient is zero or doesn't exist at all. Communication channels, represented by the edges of the graph, link such points.

Some functions are assigned to the system and they will measure stability and will correlate this with reaction efficiency.

We can define a graph-based model for the infection problem, as it follows:

A graph $G = (V, E)$ represents the environment's infrastructure. V is the set of nodes ($|V| = n$) and E is the set of edges. ($|E| = m$). Initially, a small number of pathogen agents are placed in a single (or few) node(s). Each node can host a certain number of entities, different from one node to another. We call this the node capacity.

The infection entities have a set of characteristics associated, which can be transferred to the next generation using chromosomes (ch), composed by genes. They can take numerical values. These characteristics are: *acidity, life, sensibility, reproduction_value*.

The genes are exposed to mutations, which can change them and randomly modify their characteristics.

The mutations process is modelled by a mutation operator

$$m : I_{chromosome} \longrightarrow D_{genes} \tag{1}$$

$I_{chromosome}$ is the domain of chromosome indices and D_{genes} is the domain of gene values. This operator can be applied either in the reproduction process or in some special situations given by the local environment toxicity or hostility. Let us denote by ch_i the i-th chromosome belonging to the entity e. For the chromosome ch_i, the operator m can be applied to one or more genes. m is not a common multi-variable function. It will randomly select (one or more) genes that will undergo mutation [3]. There is a restriction: *reproduction_value < sensibility* (*reproduction_value << sensibility* is better). This can be explained by the fact that biological entities (pathogen or non-pathogen agents) rarely reproduce themselves in a hostile environment (where the food is scarce).

Reproduction is modelled using a unary *multiply* operator that acts over a single entity (parent entity) and produces a number of children. In some situations multiplication is accompanied by mutation. This means that the child entity is not an accurate copy of its parents and it could have different characteristics which can make it stronger (or weaker) than its parent.

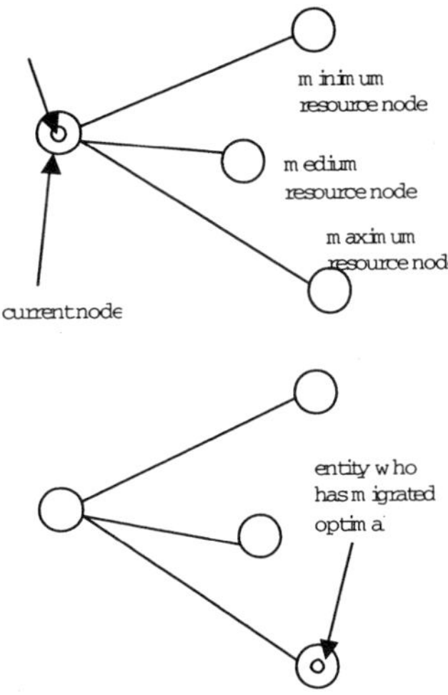

Figure 1. The deterministic migration process

The migrations mechanism can be defined in two ways as it can be seen in Figure 1 and Figure 2.

In the first case (Figure 1), the entity (pathogen agent) migrates following an optimal path. It chooses the node with maximum concentration of resource. This capability is specific to the more evolved unicellular organisms with self movement capacities (scourges).

The second way of migration is specific to rudimentary life forms like viruses and primitive bacteria (Figure 2). They do not feel any concentration gradient and move themselves in a random way. For this kind of migration we developed a strategy to minimize the probability of the entity to turn back to the origin node.

The decision function of the pathogen agents uses a Monte-Carlo strategy. This function generates a partial random number d (partial because there are some dependencies on the local environment, for example current resource quantity). We can consider three stages:

1. If the value d is lower than the first threshold, considered to be the reproduction value, then the entity reproduces itself (the multiply operator is applied)

2. If the value d is greater than the first threshold and lower than the second threshold (sensibility value) the entity stays in the current node and waits for new events;

3. If d is greater than the second threshold, it means this place is not friendly, or has no food (resource) and the entity will migrate to another node.

In our model, the reaction of the host simulates the generation and behavior mechanism of the white cells.

The white cells have external receptors, which are activated by the pathogen agents. When these receptors touch a certain cell, they identify a pattern in the disposition of the constituent substances of the external cell membrane. If this cell is recognized as foreign it is destroyed,

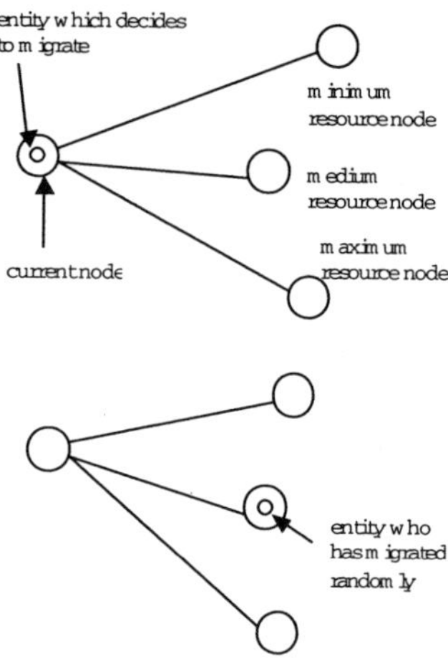

Figure 2. The random migration process

otherwise nothing happens. The white cell are generated in such a manner to not match with body cells, named self. If this happens then the white cell (which is still in a preliminary stage) is destroyed. This generation mechanism is shown in Figure 3.

In our model, the anti-infection agents are generated in special nodes, named active nodes. They are not provided with a migration capacity and their life-time is limited.

4   The Infection Simulator

We have built an infection simulator based on our mathematical model and the message passing paradigm. Graph nodes are processing units. The entities (antibodies and antigens) are numerical messages exchanged between nodes. They are stored in dynamic collections. These collections are parsed sequentially in the processing nodes and every entity is "computed" once. When an entity decides to migrate, it gets a special mark and, at the end of current parsing process, it is removed from the collection in the origin node. It will be stored in a receiving buffer in the the destination node until the parsing process in that node ends. Afterwards it will be added to the dynamic collection of this node and than it will be computed.

In Figure 4 is described the node computational structure.

The migration process has three phases:

1. The migrating entities are moved into the destination node's buffer;

2. The migrating entities are transferred to the dynamic collection, after the current parsing process ends;

3. The effective migration: the entities travel from the source node to the destination node and interact with the other entities in the destination node's area.

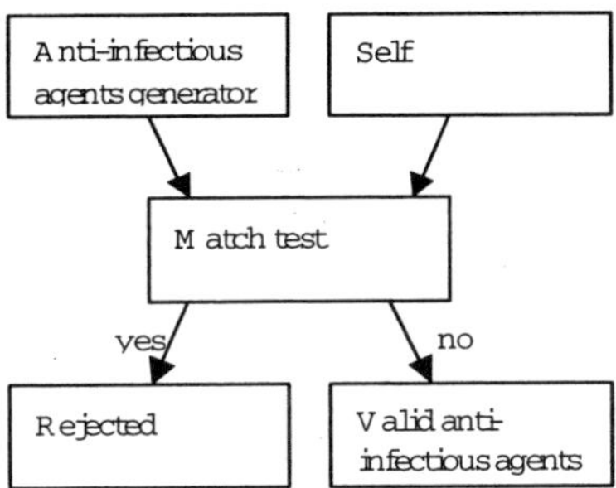

Figure 3. The white cell generation process

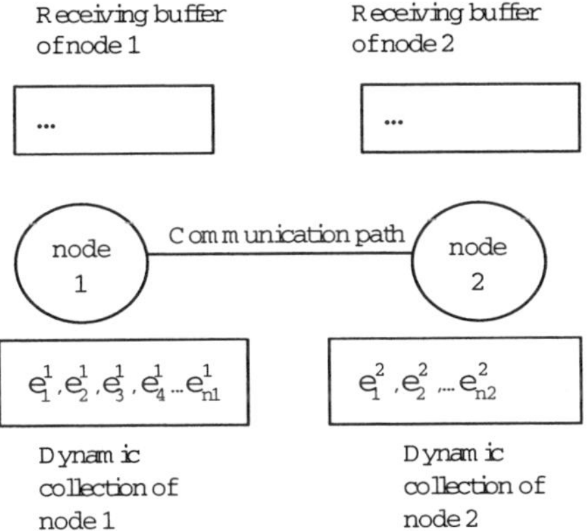

Figure 4. The node computational structure

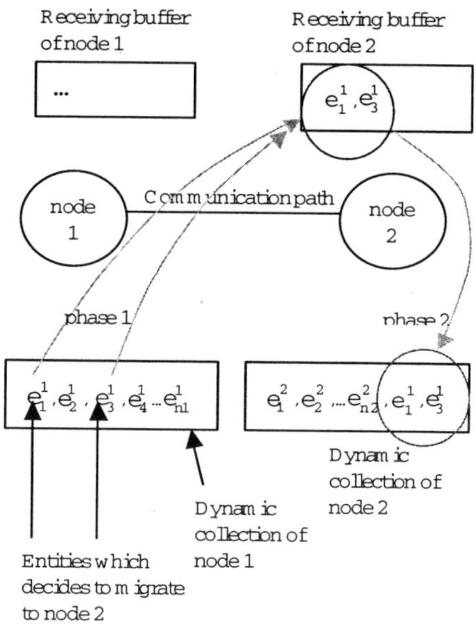

Figure 5. The first two phases of the migration process

The first two phases are illustrated in Figure 5. The blue color represents the first phase and the red color represents the second phase. The transitions are figured with green arrows.

After the second phase ends the effective migration takes place (Figure 6). When the entity reaches the destination node perimeter it can interact with other entities (especially antibodies).

The dynamic collection and the receiving buffer of a node are implemented as object arrays, where objects are entities.

Every node has an associated area where entities can interact. In successive computational steps entities change their position in this zone.

When infection is detected, the nodes begin to generate antibodies. This also takes place in two different phases:

1. At first antibodies with the previous successful receptor sets (that did match any antigens) are generated

2. If the infection persists, white cell's receptors are generated randomly; if these prove to be successful, the receptors combination is stored in an array.

An antibody interacts with the closest entity in the node area (Figure 7). The interaction presumes a matching test between the white cell's receptors and the entity's genes. If the matching test succeeds the entity is destroyed. The matching rule is modelled as it follows:

$$|r_i - g_i| < v \tag{2}$$

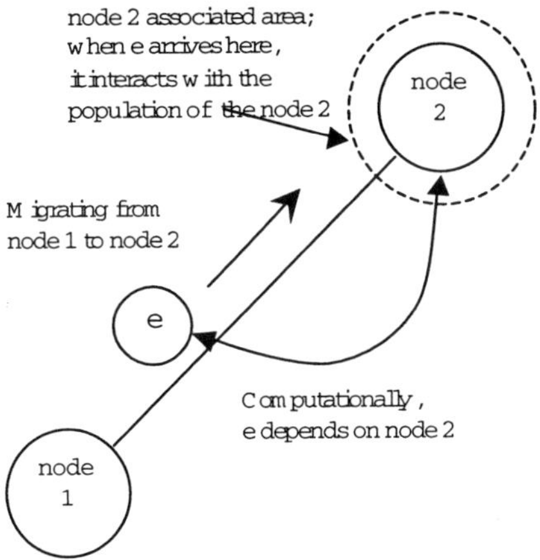

Figure 6. The effective migration

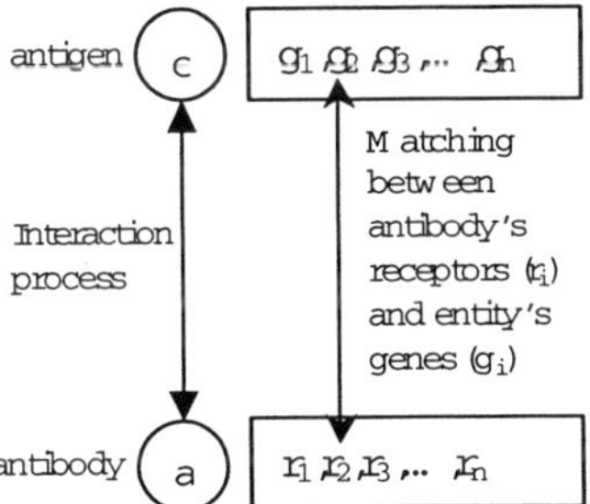

Figure 7. The interaction between the white cell (a) and the antigen (e)

where r_i is the receptor value, g_i is the gene value and v is the value of the threshold below which the matching is considered to be done.

All processes draw their currently computed entities on a common window, in order to allow the observation of the entire phenomenon evolution.

Antigen's color is given partially by their genes. It means that different genotypes antigens have different colors. This allows for the population diversity to be observed easier.

Our simulator is an OOP application. There are four major classes:

1. *mainwindow* (defined in *mainwindow.cs*) - this is where the graphic environment and the application's controls are implemented;

2. *graph* (defined in graph.cs) - implements the generating and initializing functions for the graph environment;

3. *node* (defined in node.cs) - contains the functions for processes and for managing the local entity population;

4. *entity* (defined in *node.cs*) - implements the functions that describe the behavior of the entities and their interaction.

The following four parameters must be initialized before the simulation starts: the initial infected node, the mutation rate, the delay of the thread and the initial number of the infecting entities.

At the end, the simulation time and the evolution of the node population can be seen using the "statistic" module. This module allows us to make comparisons between the antigen population and the reaction intensity. The energy variations can also be visualized.

The generic algorithm for each node, implemented as a separated process is described as it follows:

Algorithm 1 Generic Algorithm

```
for each node parallel do
    if (entity.arrived() then
        population.increase();
    if (node.state=infected) then
        node.activatereaction();
    //lifecycle
    for (each entity in node) do
        if (entity.life=0) then
            entity.dies(); population.decrease();
        entity.decreaselife();
        if (entity.type=white cell) then
            entity.interract();
    else
        entity.decide();
        if (decision=multiply) then
            entity.multiply(); population.increase();
        else
            if (decision=stay) then
                entity.stay();
            else
                entity.migrate(neighbors); population.decrease();
```

Table 1. Initial population = 50 infecting entities ; Mutation rate = 0.2

Experiment number	Experiment time	Antibody efficiency(%)
1	755	9.7
2	691	12.9
3	662	13.2
4	442	16.1

Table 2. Initial population = 50 infecting entities ; Mutation rate = 0.8

Experiment number	Experiment time	Antibody efficiency(%)
1	1023	4.89
2	985	5.32
3	813	6.14
4	715	6.34

Table 3. Initial population = 100 infecting entities ; Mutation rate = 0.2

Experiment number	Experiment time	Antibody efficiency(%)
1	673	18.75
2	531	19.61
3	518	20.9
4	443	23.48

Table 4. Initial population = 100 infecting entities ; Mutation rate = 0.8

Experiment number	Experiment time	Antibody efficiency(%)
1	1980	9.6
2	1408	10.94
3	1195	13.6
4	982	16.5

5   Experiments

The experiments were made with different mutation rates and different initial populations on a graph with 20 nodes. The machine used in tests was a Pentium III processor machine with 512Mb RAM.

We have measured the time for eliminating the infection (experiment time) in life cycles. The experiment results are shown in Table 1-4. It can be observed that a greater value of the mutation rate makes the pathogen agents stronger against the reaction (the infection elimination time increases). Also, the antibody efficiency ($\frac{\text{the number of the successful antibodies}}{\text{the number of the generated antibodies}}$) increases as the initial population of the pathogen agents become more numerous. This can be explained by the fact that the probability to generate an antibody which will meet and eliminate an antigen increases as the population of the infecting entities also increases.

6   Conclusions

The experiments have proved that in our artificial environment the infection evolves the same way it does in a living body. We can conclude that our model is a realistic one.

7   Future work

Improvement of the reaction model is an objective in our future work. There are many unexplored aspects concerning the host reaction. Another goal is to make our graph-based model to more closely resemble a real type of infection and to test it on real data sets.

References

[1] Y. Shi. and R. C. Eberhart, Parameter selection in particle swarm optimization, Evoluionary Programming VII: Proc. EP 98, Springer-Verlag, New York (1998) 591–600

[2] J. Holland, Adaptation in Natural and Artificial Systems, University of Michigan Press (1975)

[3] D. Dumitrescu, Genetic Algorithms and Evolutive strategies, Microinformatica, Cluj-Napoca (2002)

Efficient Fine-grain Computations based on Remote DMA Communication with Rotating Buffers

Adam Smyk[1]   Marek Tudruj[1,2]

[1] *Polish-Japanese Institute of Information Technology,*
86 Koszykowa Str.,02-008 Warsaw, Poland
[2] *Institute of Computer Science, Polish Academy of Sciences*
21 Ordona Str., 01-237 Warsaw, Poland
{*asmyk,tudruj*}*@pjwstk.edu.pl*

Abstract. Efficient implementation of fine-grain computations for MIMD architecture based on Remote Direct Memory Access (RDMA) communication will be presented. RDMA assumes that computation results are written directly to the memory of the destination processor with passing over the operating system and all overheads connected with it. The proposed method assumes that RDMA communication control infrastructure is prepared in advance in a program, to be next used during program execution. The main idea consists in R-DMA rotating buffers that strongly eliminate control time overheads. The method ensures that data are not overwritten if they are still in use during computations. Advantages of the proposed solution are shown on the example of a very fine grain algorithm of the Discrete Fast Fourier Transform (DFFT). Comparison of the efficiency of the RDMA rotating buffers method against MPI communication is presented.

1 Introduction

Efficient computations for many numerical problems might be obtained merely by applying parallel very fine grained algorithms. The main feature of such algorithms is that large degree of a parallelism is exploited at instruction level with a very frequent and irregular communication of small amount of data.

In the most popular contemporary systems which are based on distributed memory architecture (message passing), high communication intensity and the resulting significant time overheads cause that execution of fine grain parallel programs is usually unprofitable. One of solutions, which to some degree improves execution of fine-grained applications, especially on clusters of workstations, is replacing standard communication networks (FastEthernet) with much more efficient communication based on the GigabitEthernet [1], Mirinet [2], Quadrics [3] or InfiniBand [4] networks. There appeared some more innovative and efficient solutions [5], where all communication has been implemented with the use of RAM memory DIMM slot interfaces - DIMMnet network, which improved efficiency 7 times in comparison to the Mirinet2000 network. In the case of popular MIMD multiprocessor systems such modifications are rather difficult to be done. The only viable solution to enhance fine-grain parallel computations in such systems is designing programs at the lowest available programming level, what can guarantee the smallest communication overhead.

In this paper we focused our attention on the last mentioned approach. A relevant solution and its application for fine-grained communication in the multiprocessor supercomputer systems will be presented. The proposed solution is based on the R-DMA communication [6], which was implemented in supercomputers as Hitachi SR2201 [7], Hitachi SR8000 [8], IBM RS/6000 SP [9] and also in clusters of workstations [10] [11]. It is exploiting the fact that each computational node can have direct physical access to the memory of any other computational node. This feature allows us to over-pass services of the operating system. It gives a clear improvement of message passing communication efficiency with relation to MPI (even up to 40% for messages size from 1KB to 100KB) but it entails also the use of additional synchronization instructions to assure that access to the remote memory is fully controlled. Such synchronization instructions prevent the remote nodes form illegal overwriting still unused data until receiving a special permission from the owner of the memory. For such synchronization on fine-grain computation the idea of rotating buffers was introduced. Rotating buffers constitute a special kind of write-only, shared memory between two (or more) computational nodes with periodical access confirmation.

This paper is composed of four parts. In the first part Remote-DMA mechanism is described. In the second part, the rotating buffers applied to RDMA control is presented. In the third part, fine-grain algorithm implementation of the discrete fast Fourier transform based on RDMA with rotating buffers is briefly described [12] and in the last part results of the experiments are shown.

2   Remote DMA Mechanism

Remote DMA (Direct Memory Access) communication, which has been introduced on modern supercomputers like Hitachi SR2201, is a good alternative for commonly known and widely used parallel libraries such as MPI, PVM or Express. Although introducing more complicated way of its programming implementation, it gives us significantly higher speedup, which ranges from $\sim$3.0 to $\sim$5.0 for medium length of messages (from 1KB to 1MB).

This type of communication is based on direct access to memory of a remote computation node from the application program level. It is implemented through creation of appropriate sending-receiving infrastructure [Fig.1] which consists of three main parts:

- RDMA Object - physically allocated memory on both sending and receiving sides which will be used for fast RDMA communication (sending and receiving side);

- RDMA Area - virtual address space on which RDMA object will mapped (sending and receiving side);

- RDMA Field - part of the RDMA area where the received data will be stored (only receiving side).

All components mentioned above might be created using appropriate RDMA functions [6]. A simplified RDMA communication scheme is presented in Fig.2. After creation of such infrastructure, each sending node has to receive permission to write a data to memory (more precisely to given RDMA Fields) of receiving node. Each RDMA Field is specified by unique value (key), which is defined while the fields are created.

To obtain access to remote memory described by the receiving fields, sending application sends to the remote node a special request for "write rights". The write permission is given on condition that the key in sending request is equal to the key on one of receive fields already created on the receiving side. Writing data to remote memory is possible only after reception of all needed authorizations [Fig.3].

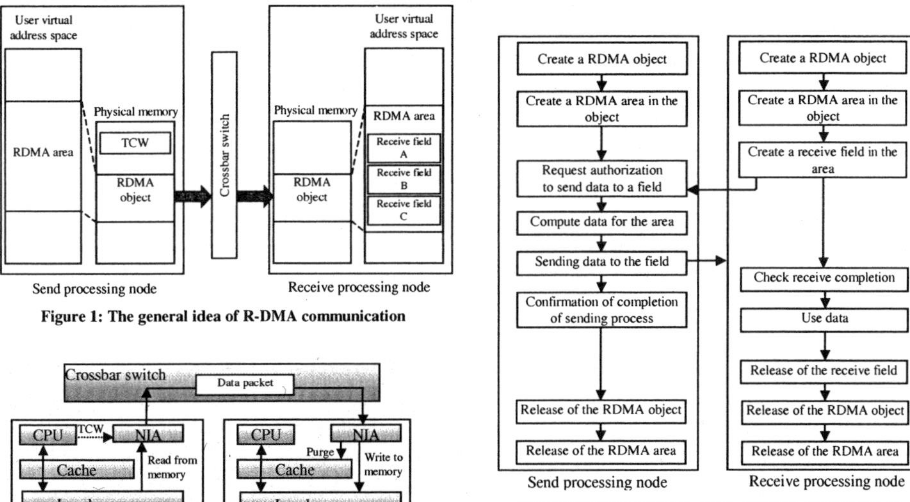

Figure 1: The general idea of R-DMA communication

Figure 2: Remote DMA communication scheme

Figure 3: Control for a single RDMA transmission

Applications on the send and the receive sides create the structure of objects, areas and fields described above. The send node fills its RDMA area with the data to be sent. In the next step, special control structure called TCW (Transfer Control Word) is created. It contains all needed parameters to perform the communication between two nodes such as: number of receive node, RDMA Field key value, RDMA Object identifier, address and size of sending data. The transmission will be started when the correctly created TCW will be written by send processor to NIA (Network Interface Adapter) of send node. From that moment, data transmission process is independent on the processor and it is carried out under the NIA control which divides all send data into packets and sent them through the communication network (crossbar switch) to destination node. To keep data coherency between cache and the local memory, before the TCW will be written to NIA, the processor updates all data from a local memory on suitable data from the cache (NIA does not read data directly from the cache). A full description of all RDMA infrastructure is stored on all nodes in a special table called LCT (Local Combuf Table). The NIA in the received node decodes all arriving packets and on the basis of the key values from the data and the key values from the LCT, determines address in a local memory where received data should be stored. Additionally, to avoid any data incoherency, the NIA purges cache memory if it is necessary (NIA does not write data directly to the cache).

Depending on the type of data communication, we can distinguish several kinds of send methods. The most important and the most often used are: standard blocked send (combuf_send),standard unblocked send (combuf_send_with_flag) and two send methods with TCW reuse (combuf_kick_tcw i combuf_kick_tcw_fast). The basic difference between all methods mentioned above lies is that in the case of standard sends, the new TCW is created for each send independently, what enlarges total communication latency. In the case of sends with TCW reuse, the control word is created only once and it might be used for iterative communication. It can be modified before each data transfer to be used for different data.

Data reception does not consume processor time, because the transmission is executed independently by NIA and a local memory. The receiving application has a chance to check in its local memory if given data have been received or not yet.

In RDMA communication, a send application has no possibility to check if data which have been already sent, have arrived to the local memory on the receive node or have not. The RDMA functions allow us to test only if the send data have already been sent and if the memory area occupied by them may be modified. To obtain confirmation of data reception, a remote node is forced to send an extra message to a source node with information that all data were received and it is ready for next data package. Of course, it increases the total communication time and causes that communication efficiency decreases of 10%-30% depending on the frequency.

3   RDMA Rotating Buffers Method of Communication

A RDMA rotating buffer contains data prepared for moving from one processing node to another. Each processing node has an own local memory which is logically divided [Fig. 4] into two parts: locally accessed area (LAM - Locally Accessed Memory) and remotely accessed area (GAM - Globally Accessed Memory). All data which are needed for local computations are stored in the LAM area while data needed for computations on different nodes are stores in the GAM area. In the GAM area, two sub-parts are distinguished: DRAM (Data Remote Access Memory) i RCA (Remote Confirmation Area). DRAM part is in fact

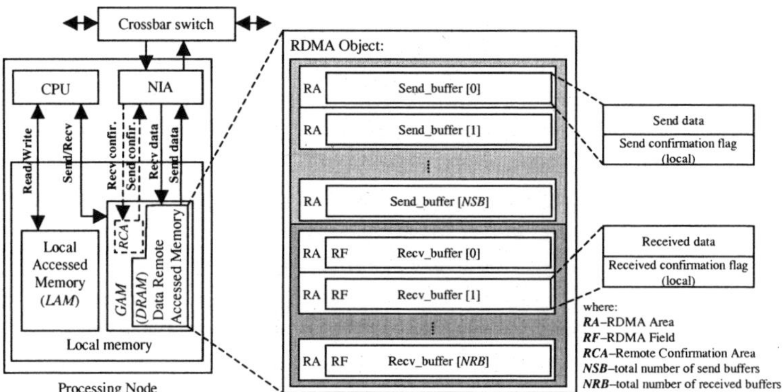

Figure 4: Memory structure in rotating-buffers method (for one processing node)

one RDMA object with specified identifier (ID). The ID allows to distinguish this object among others existing at the same time in one application (max. number of objects is 128). Thus, DRAM is a continuous chunk of allocated memory with separate fields for sending and receiving data. These two fields consist of many adjacent RDMA areas which are linearly assigned to two arrays of pointers (Send_buffer and Recv_buffer), each of length respectively: NSB and NRB (min. 4KB per each). In each RDMA area from receive part of DRAM, one RDMA field is created (in total NRB fields). Each created field is described be a unique number (key), which has to be used to write data to the specified buffer of GAM from the remote node (RN). Each RN that has a combination of RDMA object ID and unique key for all created locally (receive) buffers, sends each of them in a local node (LN) an access

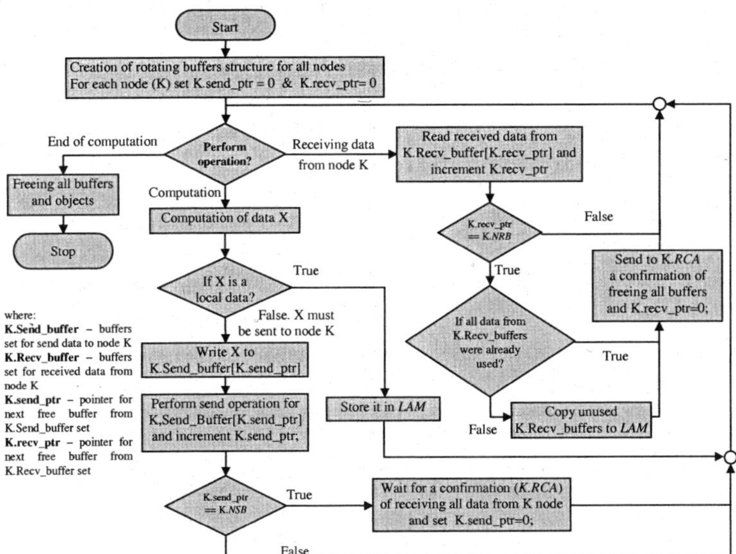

Figure 5: Control flow of the rotating-buffers method (for one processing node)

request. If, on LN, there exists a RDMA object with specified ID and it contains the buffer described by the unique key, LN will send to RN an access right for writing to this buffer. From that time, RN can write (send) data to the remote accessed buffer. Additionally, in each created buffer, the last 32 bytes are reserved for local (send or receive) confirmation flags. It is needed for fast RDMA communication (combuf_spin_wait or combuf_make_tcw functions) which will be used during our experiments.

Another part of GAM is a RCA (Remote Confirmation Area). The internal structure of RCA is quite similar to DRAM, with a slight difference that RCA always contains one send and one receive buffer. These buffers do not store any computational data but they are used to synchronize sender and receiver nodes. Through RCA, the RN confirms that all data sent to it were correctly received and were already used, so, all receive buffers are ready for new data.

Communication between two nodes will be established, if on both of them such a buffer structure is built. If one node sends or receives data from several other nodes, such a structure has to be created independently of each other. The control flow chart for one processing node is presented in Fig. 5. After the structure described above is created for each remote node K, two pointers K.send_ptr i K.recv_ptr are created. These pointers are in fact indexes to arrays of buffers and always indicate a next free buffer for sending data to node K or receiving data from node K, respectively. The pointers K.recv_ptr i K.send_ptr specify rotating, periodical access to the particular and not busy (without any important data) buffer which can be used for current transmission.

4   Discrete Fast Fourier Transform and its Parallel Implementation

The Fourier transform finds a wide application in solving many scientific and engineering problems such as digital signal processing or image filtering [13]. The Fourier transform enables to convert a periodical, N- point sampled signal to its representation in the frequency domain. The Fast Fourier Transform (FFT) is based on the following equation:

$$X'[i] = \sum_{j=0}^{N/2-1} X[2j]\omega^{2ji} + \omega^j \sum_{j=0}^{N/2-1} X[2j+1]\omega^{2ji}$$

Where: $\omega = e^{2\Pi\sqrt{-1}/N}$ twiddle factor, e is a base of natural logarithms. For each input coefficient, the Fourier transform can be computed recursively as two $N/2$-point FFT-s, one for all even points ($X[0], X[2], .$) and one for all odd points ($X[1], X[3], .$). If we assume that i is changing from 0 to $N/2 - 1$, all coefficients can be computed as follows:

$$X'[i] = X[even] + \omega^j X[odd]$$
$$X'[i + N/2] = X[even] + \omega^{j+N/2} X[odd] = X[even] - \omega^j X[odd]$$

In the case of parallel implementation of FFT, (based on ***The Binary − Exchange Algorithm***) the computational complexity can be reduced up to $O(logN)$, on condition that each point of FFT is computed on a separate processing node. Communication scheme for 16-point FFT for each step of computation is shown in [Fig.6]. Depending on the number of available processing nodes, each point of FFT is mapped onto a pre-determined processor. For 8 processors and 16-point FFT for example, on each processor, 2 adjoining (according to their three the most significant bits) points have been mapped. The remaining bits determine placement of each sample on a processor. The communication scheme is independent of the number of processors and it does not change. In case when the number of processors is less then the number of input coefficients, at the final stages (Step 4), all computations will be done locally without any data exchange.

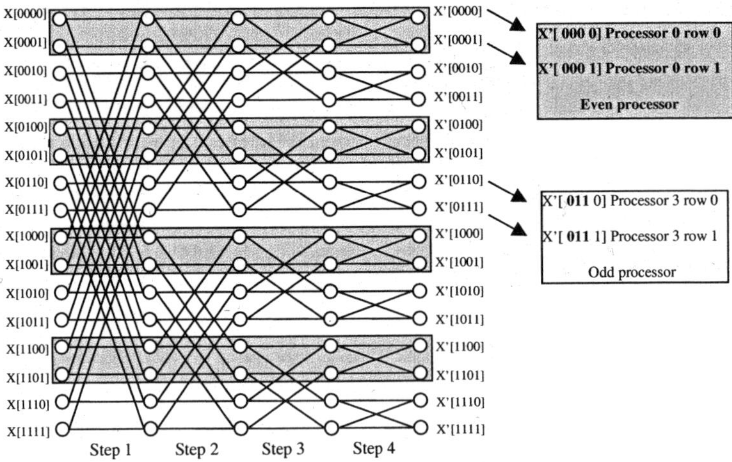

Figure 6: Communication scheme for 16-point *FFT* and 8 processors

5   Experiment Results

The rotating buffers method which is presented in a chapter 3 has been implemented by designing a C++ class called RDMA_RB. The RDMA_RB class makes available several C++ methods to create a memory structure described in Fig.4 and it allows a rotating access to the send and the receive buffers according to the scheme from Fig.5. A single object of this class might be used for bidirectional communication between two established nodes. In RDMA_RB class, three types of send methods are used: standard send RDMA, send with TCW and send with TCW Fast. To receive data, two methods are introduced standard receive RDMA and spin receive RDMA. A full specification of all these methods is available in [6].

To estimate efficiency of the RB method, several tests were carried out and the results obtained were compared to communication efficiency of the MPI library (2 communication functions were used MPI_Send i MPI_Recv). All experiments were run on Hitachi SR2201 supercomputer with 16 nodes (but only 8 nodes were used during the tests). In each test, the number of send buffers was equal to the number of receive buffers. In first experiment,

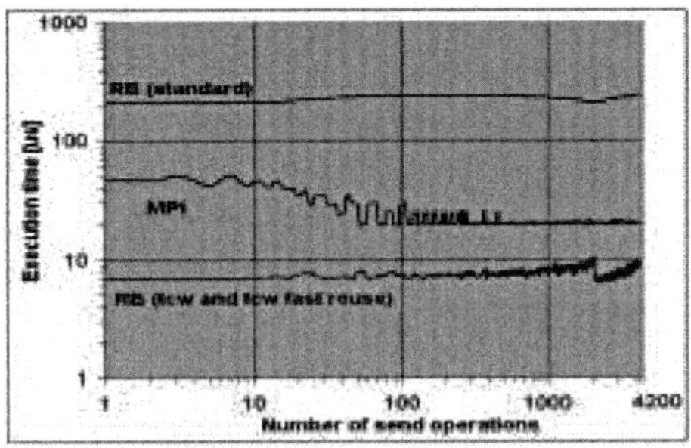

Figure 7: Average execution time for MPI and RB communication (2100 buffers) between 2 processors

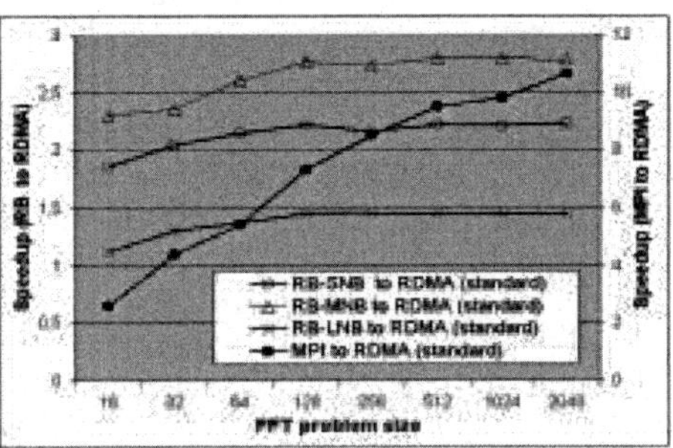

Figure 8: Speedup for MPI and RB method versus RDMA with standard send RDMA for different numbers of buffers (FFT)

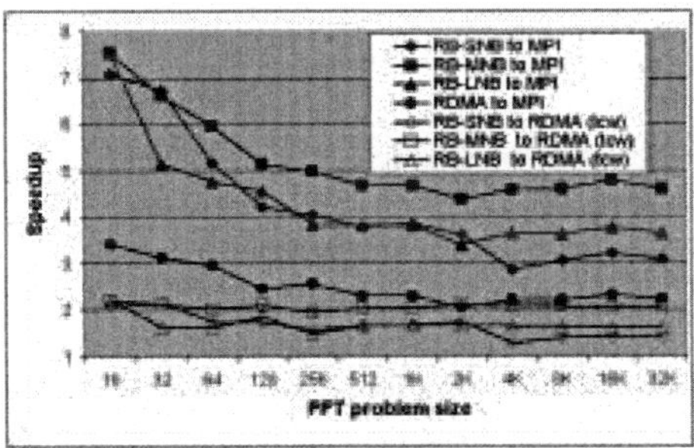

Figure 9: Speedup for MPI and RB method versus RDMA with TCW RDMA communication for different numbers of buffers (FFT)

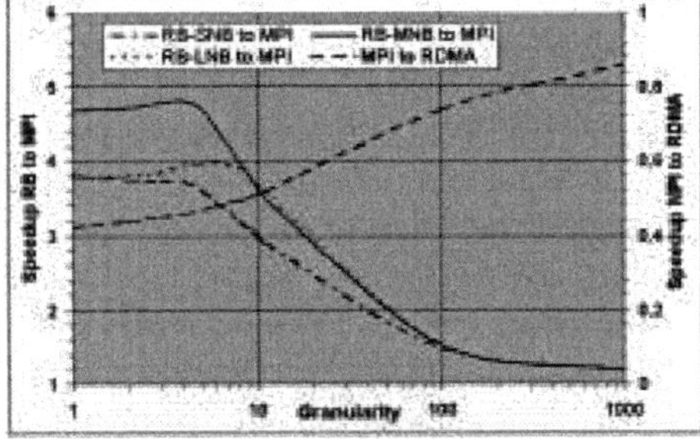

Figure 10: Comparison of speedups for RB RDMA and MPI transmission in terms of granularity (for 2048-point FFT)

a comparison of the execution time of sending functions for three types of configurations (mentioned above) were done. In the case of the RB RDMA method with standard send function, the execution time was the biggest ($\sim 200\mu s$). For each transmission an internal control infrastructure (transfer control word) has to prepared separately (and also canceled after transmission) what significantly decreases performance of communication. In the case of MPI communication which was on average 8 times faster than for RB with standard RDMA communication, the execution time for almost all transmissions was constant and equal to $\sim 20\mu s$. Next two communication methods (RB with TCW and TCW fast reuse) are from 3 to 5 times faster (from $\sim 7\mu s$ to $\sim 18\mu s$) than MPI communication. But as the number of messages which are sent to NIA (injected into inter-processor network) grows, its transmission capabilities can be exceeded. It is due to the NIA overload. In comparison to the MPI communication, NIA has to service much more transmissions at the same time. Additionally, each of them concerns a different part of the operating memory (for each transmission a different buffer is used). It causes that the transmission latency for next send operations can grow even up to 2 times, Fig. 7. To restore full efficiency of the RB method, next sending actions are postponed until all previous ones executed will be completed. Return confirmation transmission allows unloading NIA when all buffers have been used (2100 in our case) and also indicates that rotation of buffers has to be performed. When the total number of buffers decreases, the number of confirmations grows. It allows to keep stability of all consecutive transmissions but it can cause also that the total execution time increases. It means that to obtain the minimum execution time the number of buffers in the RB RDMA method should be well matched to solved problem.

The FFT Binary-Exchange algorithm was executed to check suitability of the RB RDMA method for fine grain applications. Tests were done for FFT algorithm for three types of RDMA_RB class objects: with a small number of buffers SNB (from 1 to 10 buffers), a medium number on buffers MNB (from 10 to 50 buffers) and with a large number of buffers LNB (from 100 to 300 buffers) in one RDMA_RB object. Average values of speedup for mentioned above numbers of buffers RB-SNB, RB-MNB and RB-LNB were measured.

In Fig.8, the speedup for the RB method with standard send RDMA function compared to MPI is presented. In standard send RDMA function, the control word TCW is created and deleted every time when communication was performed what significantly decreases the expected gain from the RB method, while the MPI is implemented with TCW reuse. It causes that as the problem size increases, the efficiency of the MPI communication also increases (up to large problems). It directly results from character of transmissions which are described above, Fig. 7. In the case of RB method with standard send RDMA function, the efficiency is almost 3 times bigger (for RB-MNB) but is visibly smaller than in the MPI case and from that reason all communication functions were implemented with the use of more efficient TCW and TCW Fast methods. Results of performed experiments are presented in Fig.9. It can be observed that the speedup of the RB method in comparison with the MPI communication definitely grows even up to ~ 8 times for small problem sizes. It is because the RB method with TCW reuse offers more stable transmissions than MPI for total small number of transmissions (no more than 100 when the RB method is going to be unstable, Fig. 7). When the problem size grows, the speedup falls to ~ 5 for RB-MNB and to ~ 3 for RB-SNB and it stays almost constant for all configurations of the RB method. Significantly higher performance in the case of the RB-MNB what can result from the total number of confirmations matching the NIA potential. It causes that NIA is not overloaded which assures almost constantly and simultaneously the smallest execution time for each transmission. The difference between the RB-LNB and RB-SNB configurations for big problem sizes comes from too high frequency of confirmations in the case of RB-SNB what increases the total execution time. In comparison to the RDMA communication with TCW reuse, the speedup of the RB method is ~ 2.3 times bigger and it was achieved for the RB-MNB configuration what unambiguously indicates that the RB method with this configuration gives the minimal execution time of the FFT problem, independently on its size.

In next experiment, efficiency comparison of two sending functions (with TCW and TCW fast reuse) which were used in the RB method was done, Table 1. It can be seen that the most significant improvement was obtained for the RB-MNB configuration and it was equal to ∼16,843%. It shows again that the efficiency improvement achieved for this configuration comparing with the RB-MNB and RB-MNB is the biggest what indicates its significant usefulness with implementation of different fine-grain parallel problems.

Table 1.
Comparison of efficiency of *TCW* communication versus
***TCW fast* communication in *RB* method (2048-point FFT)**

Communication method	Communication time [μs]		
	RB-SNB	**RB -MNB**	**RB –LNB**
TCW	10252,40	8536,00	11155,00
TCW Fast	9092,96	7305,53	10116,30
	Improvement [%]		
	RB -SNB	**RB -MNB**	**RB –LNB**
TCW/TCW FAST	12,751 %	16,843 %	10,268 %

In the last experiments, efficiency of communication based on the RB RDMA method, for algorithms with various granularities, was examined. In these experiments, the communication scheme as in the FFT graph was applied (Fig. 7), however, a ratio between computational load in each FFT node, and communication intensity between each two nodes, was changed for each test. In the FFT method described in Chapter 4, the volume A of data to be used in a computation and the volume B of results to be sent to another node are equal (a very fine grain computation). In Fig.10, the speedup of computation with the RB method for the constant value B=1 and the value A changing in from 1 to 1000, is presented. The value A/B=1000 means that for each 1000 data items to be processed during computations on a local node, only 1 data item is send to another computational node. In Fig.10, a comparison of speedups for the RB method (with TCW communication) executed for 2048-point FFT graph with varied granularities, is presented. It can be observed that the efficiency of the RB method depends on the granularity of parallel algorithm which has an significant influence on the communication intensity. The biggest speedup, was obtained for granularity ranges from ∼1 to ∼8 (the finest computations) and it was equal to about ∼5.0 for the RB-MNB configuration. When granularity increases, the speedup falls to ∼1.0 and for very coarse grain problems, the efficiency of the RB method is almost the same as for the MPI communication. It confirms that the RB method based on the RDMA communication performed on SR2201 system behaves well for small grain of computation when granularity is smaller than 10. On the contrary to the RB method, in the case of MPI compared to the RDMA TCW communication the smallest speedup is obtained for small grain problems and it grows to one with increasing granularity. It can be concluded that for efficient implementation of fine grain parallel algorithms the RB RDMA method assures much better performance of computations than the MPI library. For coarse grain problems similar execution times are obtained for both of these methods.

6 Conclusions

In the paper, RDMA communication control based on rotating buffers has been presented. It turned out that such a simple idea speeds up execution of fine-grain applications (the FFT algorithm) in comparison to execution based on the MPI library. The executed application was run in a distributed memory MIMD system and it was characterized by very frequent communication. The speedup of communication was changing in a rather wide range from ~3.0 to ~8.0 depending on several factors such as: number of rotating buffers, total number of communications (size of the problem), granularity and types of send and receive functions. The highest efficiency (speedup ~8.0) was usually obtained when solving small size problems (~16), for a granularity form 1 to 10 and the medium number of buffers. With granularity growing from 10 to 100, the efficiency of the RB method linearly fell and for very large communications it converges to 1.0 for both the RB RDMA (independently of the number of buffers) and MPI methods.

In a future work concerned with this subject, the idea of minimizing the total number of the rotating buffers will be examined. We want to introduce thereby, a more economical management of operating memory, which now is done in a rather greedy way. This work was sponsored by the KBN Grant N. 4T11C 007 22 and by the internal grants of the PJIIT.

References

[1] Rich Seifert, *Gigabit Ethernet: Technology and Applications for High Speed LANs*, Addison-Wesley, May 1998.

[2] A.Smyk, M.Tudruj, *OpenMP/MPI programming in a multi-cluster system based on shared memory/message passing communication.*, LNCS 2326, Springer Verlag, Advanced Environments, Tools and Applications for Cluster Computing, Mangalia, 1-6 Sept. 2001, pp. 241 - 248.

[3] *http://www.quadrics.com/*

[4] J. Liu et al., *Micro-Benchmark Level Performance Comparison for High-Speed Cluster Interconnects*, Hot Interconnects 10, Stanford University. August 20 - 22, 2003.

[5] N.Tanabe, Y.Hamada, H.Nakajo, H.Imashiro, J.Yamamoto, T.Kudoh, H.Amano, *Low Latency Communication on DIMMnet-1 Network Interface Plugged into a DIMM Slot*, International Conference in Parallel Computing in Electrical Engineering PARELEC 2002, 22-25 September , Warsaw, pp. 9 - 14.

[6] Hitachi Ltd, *HI-UX/MPP - Remote DMA -C- User's Guide Manual Number: 6A20-3-021-10(E)*, Second Edition: January 1997

[7] H. Fujii et al. *Architecture and Performance of the Hitachi SR2201 Massively Parallel Processor System*, 11-th Int. Parallel Processing Symposium, Geneva, Switzerland, April 1997, pp. 233-241

[8] T. Lanfear, *SR8000 Concept*, Hitachi Europe GmbH, *http://research.ac.upc.es/HPCseminar/SEM9900/SR8000_concept.ppt*

[9] M. Banikazemi et al., *MPI-LAPI: An Efficient Implementation of MPI for IBM RS/6000 SP Systems*, IEEE Transactions on Parallel and Distributed Systems, Vol. 12, No. 10, October 2001, pp. 1081-1093.

[10] Ariel Cohen, *RDMA offers low overhead, high speed*, Network World, 03/24/03

[11] J. Liu, *High Performance RDMA-Based MPI Implementation over InfiniBand*, Proceedings of 17th Annual ACM International Conference on Supercomputing. San Francisco Bay Area. June, 2003.

[12] B.Willkinson, M.Allen, *Parallel Programming - Techniques and Applications Using Networked Workstations and Parallel Computers*, 1999 Prentice Hall. 6WA

[13] A.Grama, A.Gupta, G.Karypis, V.Kumar, *Introduction to Parallel Computing*, Second Edition, 2003 Addison Vesley.

Concurrent Information Processing and Computing
D. Grigoras and A. Nicolau (Eds.)
IOS Press, 2005

Parallelizing the Training Phase of Back-propagation in a LAN of Workstations

Sorin Babii   Vladimir Creţu

"Politehnica" University of Timişoara, V. Pârvan 2, Timişoara, Romania

Abstract. This article presents the results of some experiments in parallelizing the training phase of a feed-forward, artificial neural network. More specifically, we develop and analyze a parallelization strategy of the widely used neural net learning algorithm called back-propagation.

We describe a strategy for parallelizing the back-propagation algorithm. We implemented this algorithm on several LANs, permitting us to evaluate and analyze their performances based on the results of actual runs. We were interested on the qualitative aspect of the analysis, in order to achieve a fair understanding of the factors determining the behavior of this parallel algorithms. We were interested in discovering and dealing with some of the specific circumstances that have to be considered when a parallelized neural net learning algorithm is to be implemented on a set of workstations in a LAN. Part of our purpose is to investigate whether it is possible to exploit the computational resources of such a set of workstations.

1 Introduction

Training artificial neural networks is a computationally very intensive task, requiring millions of floating point multiplications even for small networks and small problems. Moreover, neural nets require large amounts of memory. These two facts make work on neural nets a very time consuming business, putting an effective limit on the size of the applications.

There are several ways to try to compensate for this disadvantage of the neural networks.

The first approach is by reducing the size of the problem by pre-processing the input data, thereby decreasing either the number of iterations necessary to train the net or the size of the net itself. Such reductions are almost always problem specific, so that this approach cannot be generalized to cover all kinds of problems.

Another possibility is by improving the performance of the back-propagation learning rule, either using ad hoc modifications or by applying results from numerical optimization theory. Work on the so-called conjugate gradient methods belongs to the latter category.

A third approach is to make existing algorithms run faster either by implementing them directly in hardware (using VLSI techniques or optics) or by modifying them to run on some parallel architecture of existing processors. It is this latter part of the third approach, that we are going to deal with in this paper: How to parallelize the back-propagation learning algorithm.

2　Back-Propagation using Data Partitioning

An obvious and easy way of parallelizing an artificial neural network using back-propagation is the *data partitioning* strategy in which the training data are distributed evenly among the workstations. All workstations simulate the entire network but on different sub-sets of the training data. During each learning cycle each processor presents the patterns in its own share of the current batch. We call the gradients calculated this way in the individual processors as *component gradients*, since each of them is the result of presenting only some part of the batch to the network. Once all patterns in the batch have been presented, the resulting component gradients are combined (summed) into one *global gradient*, which is then used to calculate the change on each weight. Following that, the weights are updated and sent to all workstations as the new set of weights to be used in the subsequent presentation of patterns during the next learning cycle.

This is the simplest form of the data partitioning approach to parallelizing artificial neural networks. Implementations and experimental results of this form will be discussed in the following section.

2.1　A Simple Implementation of the Data Partitioning Strategy

The actual process of implementing the data partitioning strategy is quite straight-forward, starting from the sequential back-propagation algorithm. All we have to do is put together a set of workstations interconnected in a LAN, each of which should run the sequential algorithm on its own, independently from the others. With P processors we therefore have P identical copies of the entire network. During each learning cycle, each processor q presents to the network the patterns in its part B_q of the current batch B of training patterns. As a result the following component gradient $\overline{g}^{<q>}$ is calculated in processor q:

$$\overline{g}^{<q>} = \sum_{p \in B_q} \frac{\partial E_p}{\partial \overline{w}} \tag{1}$$

where $\overline{w}$ denotes the set of all weights.

The weight change $\Delta_B \overline{w}$ with respect to the patterns in batch B can be expressed as a sum of component gradients $\overline{g}^{<q>}$:

$$\Delta_B \overline{w}(n+1) = -\eta \sum_{p \in B} \frac{\partial E_p}{\partial \overline{w}} + \alpha \Delta_B \overline{w}(n) = -\eta \sum_{q=0}^{P-1} \overline{g}^{<q>} + \alpha \Delta_B \overline{w}(n) \tag{2}$$

Therefore, only one modification is necessary as compared to the sequential algorithm: A scheme for performing the collection and summation of all component gradients $\overline{g}^{<q>}$ and the distribution of updated weights (a broadcast).

2.2　Communication Schema

We implemented the summation of component gradients using a ring configuration of P processors in such a way that each processor after $P - 1$ steps will hold the total gradient. Initially each processor simply communicates its own component gradient to its predecessor

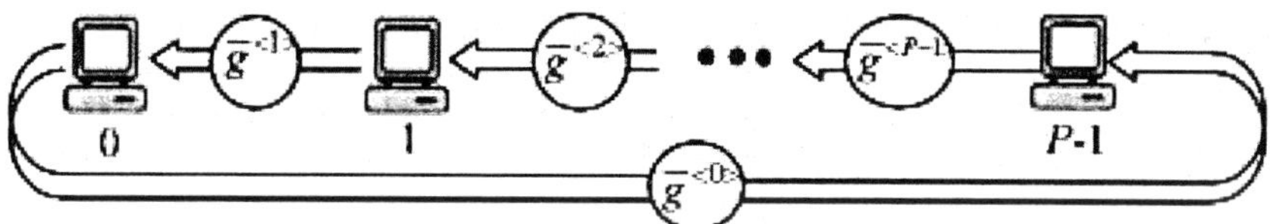

Figure 1. Summation of component gradients.

in the ring (figure 1). Then all processors add the component gradient just received to a temporary sum of component gradients. Each processor sends the received component gradient to the predecessor and receives a new component gradient.

After $P - 1$ steps each processor will have received component gradients from *all* other processors. Thus it will now hold the sum of all component gradients, and it will be able to update the weights as required.

3　Performance of the Algorithm

In this section we are going to present the results of the algorithm when run on two kinds of workstations:

1. up to 12 IBM RS6000 workstations, at 10MB/s,
2. up to 16 SunBlade 150 workstations, at 100MB/s.

The training sets were randomly generated.

We have to define here some terms used below.

We define the speed-up as the ratio of the execution time T_{seq} of the sequential algorithm to the execution time T_{par} of the parallel algorithm, executed on P processors, when both algorithms are applied to that problem:

$$S(P) = \frac{T_{seq}}{T_{par}(P)} \tag{3}$$

We express the efficiency as the ratio of observed to optimal speed-up. Assuming that speed-up is only determined by the effects of concurrent computations, i.e. that $S(P)$ is bounded by P, we can express the efficiency as:

$$E(P) = \frac{S(P)}{P} = \frac{T_{seq}}{T_{par}(P) \cdot P} \tag{4}$$

We have to emphasize at this point that *between* weight updates efficiency *must* be 100% since in those periods all processors work independently of each other, each processor running in exactly the same way as in the sequential neural net simulator. The collection of component gradients and the distribution of the weight updates constitute extra work compared to the sequential algorithm, therefore we need an extra time. Furthermore, the computation of new weight values after all component gradients have been collected is not parallelized at all, since the root processor (0) is performing this task alone. The inefficiency generated by this sequential computation of the weights increases with the number of processors: The more processors used in executing the algorithm, the more processors are inactive during the updating. Of course, this is a very unfortunate property for a parallel algorithm, although the actual computation of the new weight values does not constitute a very large fraction of the total amount of computational work, especially when a large batch size is used.

To summarize: Since between weight updates the algorithm executed in each processor is exactly the same as the sequential algorithm we expect any reduced efficiency that may be observed in the parallel algorithm to be caused primarily by circumstances relating to the updating of the weights.

3.1 Variable Batch Size

The above considerations suggest that efficiency will be low when a small batch is used, and that efficiency will increase if the size of the batch is increased.

Figure 2 shows the results of running a 50-50-50 network with varying batch size, on the maximum number of workstations in each case (12, and 16, respectively). The neural net simulator was run for 10 learning cycles, i.e. the weights were updated the same number of times in all runs. Note, that since the number of processors and the size of the net are fixed, the time necessary for performing one weight update is expected to remain the same in all runs, independently of the batch size used.

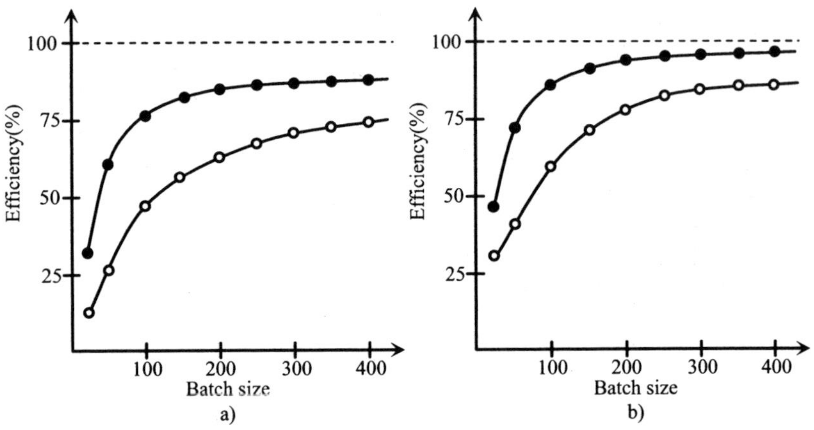

Figure 2. Efficiency shown as a function of batch size: a) RS6000 , b) SunBlade150.

The unfilled circles mark the results of ordinary executions of the algorithm, that is, when the processors actually communicate with each other, as they should. The filled circles give the results of the same runs, only this time no communication is performed. Each time the processors would normally want to communicate they execute a NOP command instead. By looking at the difference between those two graphs we can estimate how the communication affects the global efficiency.

As expected, the efficiency of the algorithm is very low for the smallest a batch size, since each processor in this case presents only one single pattern to the net between each weight update. In other words, the weights are updated relatively often. As the size of the batch is increased, execution time becomes more and more dominated by the time used for presenting patterns and calculating component gradients, since the number of weight updates is not increased. This way the time used for updating the weights becomes a smaller and smaller part of the total execution time, hence efficiency increases.

The second graph consisting of the filled circles confirms, that time spent in actual communication during each weight update is partly responsible for the less than optimal efficiency observed. Furthermore, absolute running times show that time spent in communication is independent of the batch size used, as expected.

However, the graphs also show that there are other equally important sources for inefficiency. Some of this inefficiency may be generated by the supplementary sentences checking the number of successors, extra summations of component gradients, as well as handling communications.

3.2 Variable Number of Processors

We will now present the results on the same workstations, when the problem is fixed and the number of processors is increased. Since increasing the batch size increases efficiency, we can expect that more processors can be used on problems with large batch sizes. The experiments were made using three different fixed batch sizes.

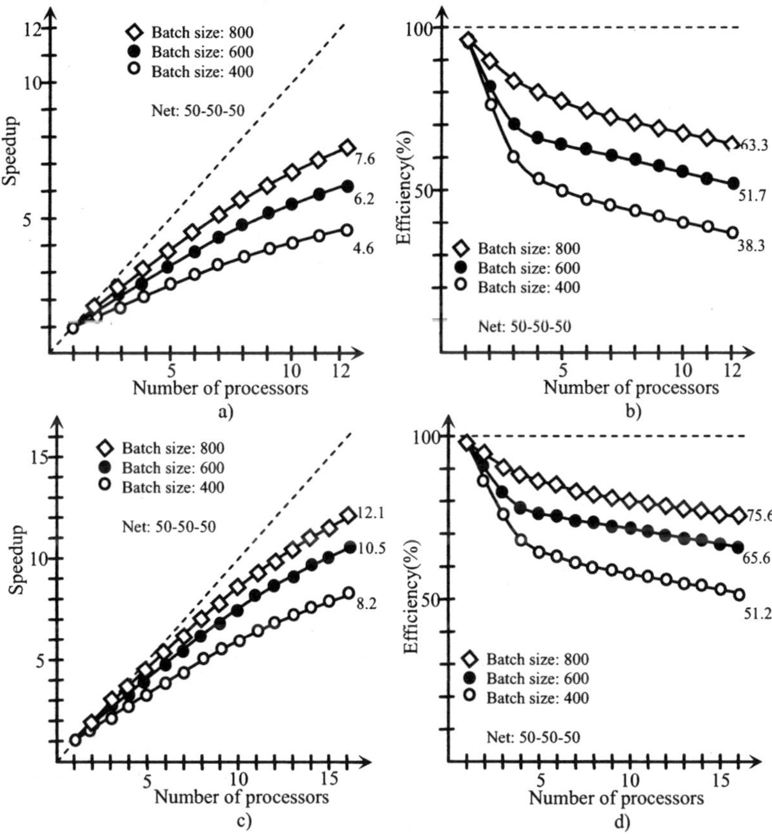

Figure 3. Speed-up for three different batch sizes: a), b) - RS6000, c),d) - SunBlade150

Figure 3 shows the dependency between the speed-up and the number of processors executing the parallel algorithm. It can be seen that for all three batch sizes (except, perhaps, the smallest batch size) speed-up has not yet reached its maximum value even when using the maximum number of processors (12, and 16, respectively). This means that, probably, we can achieve an even greater speed-up if using more workstations.

It can also be seen, though, that as more and more processors are used, efficiency decreases (figure 3b, 3d). Using the results just obtained in the above section we can conclude that there can be one reason for this: As the number of processors is increased each processor handles a smaller and smaller part of the batch. In other words, the batch size per processor is lowered, making the processors run less efficiently as demonstrated in the above section. This effect can also be seen by simply comparing the three graphs in figure 3b, 3d.

However, efficiency depends not only on the batch size per processor, but on the number of processors as well, so there must be other reasons for the falling efficiency as well, since efficiency depends not only on the batch size per processor, but on the number of processors as well. Analyzing figure 3b, 3d, we can see that for the same batch size per processor, the efficiency is decreasing when the number of processor is larger. This is probably because of the time needed for collecting component gradients and distributing the weight updates.

3.3   Scaling Batch Size with the Number of Processors

The third class of experiments was done to examine the effects of scaling the size of the batch with the number of processors used in executing the algorithm. We investigated whether an increase in the number of sub-problems (patterns in the batch) will allow us to increase the number of processors correspondingly without reducing efficiency.

In figure 4 the batch size *per processor* is fixed (in each of the four series of experiments). That is, each processor presents a fixed number of patterns between each weight update, independently of the number of processors.

Figure 4b, 4d show that for large numbers of processors, if increasing the batch size is possible, the number of processors applied to the problem can be increased correspondingly without any significant loss of efficiency.

When compared to figure 3, it can be seen that the efficiency graphs in figure 4 are very similar. In fact, they are nearly identical in shape. This confirms what we have already stated, that this parallel algorithm looses efficiency mainly during weight updates.

We can also use these figures to determine whether it will be useful to add processors to some fixed problem. In other words, for how long an increase in speed-up can be obtained by adding more processors. Raising the number of processors by some factor will only increase speed-up if efficiency is reduced by less than that same factor, as a result of the extra processors.

It would be nice if we could formulate a rule as to how many processors could be applied to some specific problem. Like, say, one should at most use a number of processors corresponding to one fifth of the batch size. That is, as long as each processor handles more than 5 patterns in the batch, adding more processors will increase speed-up. In general, this is possible if the efficiency of the parallel algorithm depends only on the batch size per processor, and not on the number of processors itself (i.e. if the efficiency graphs in figure 4b, 4d, were straight, horizontal lines). As can be seen, this is not the case for this parallel algorithm, and indeed, it seems that no such general rule can be formulated.

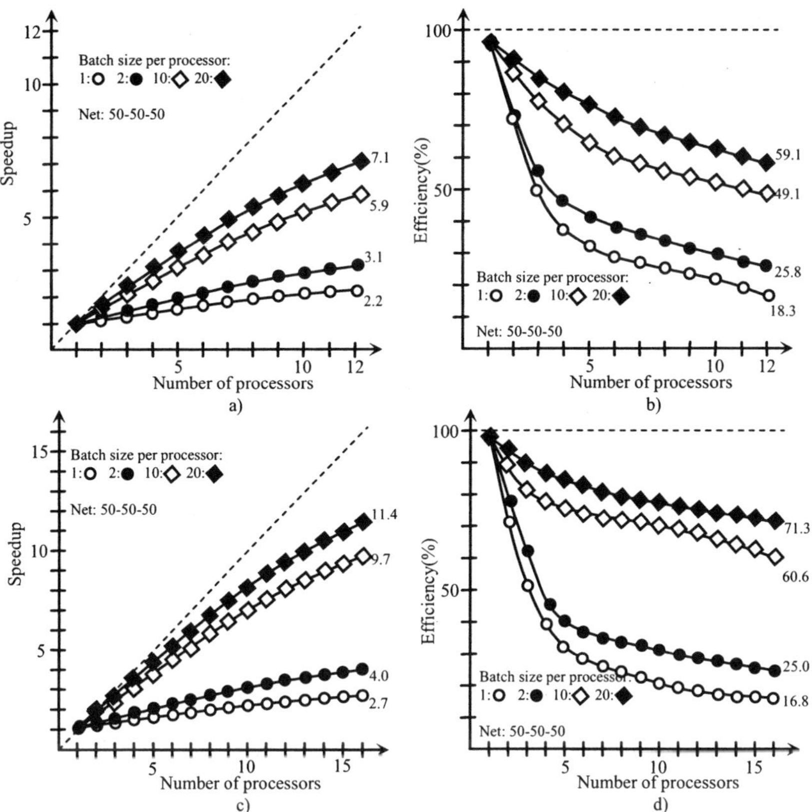

Figure 4. Efficiency as a function of batch size per processor a),b) - RS6000, c),d) - SunBlade150

4   Conclusions

We have seen that it is possible to parallelize the back-propagation algorithm in a very simple way using the data partitioning strategy. Furthermore, the experiments demonstrated that efficiency increases with the size of the batch of training patterns presented to the net between each update of the weights. This means that if very large batch sizes can be used it is possible to gain a substantial speed-up using this kind of parallelization.

An important disadvantage of this algorithm is the somewhat excessive memory requirements resulting from the fact that each processor has to store a copy of the entire network. Such redundancy is not desirable in a parallel algorithm, since this means that the parallelization does not allow an increase in the size of the problems (with respect to memory requirements) that can be undertaken.

References

[1] Rumelhart, D. E., Hinton, G. E. and Williams, R. J., Learning Internal Representations by Error Propagation, in D. E. Rumelhart and J. L. McClelland (Eds.), Parallel Distributed Processing – Explorations in the Microstructure of Cognition, Volume 1 - Foundations. A Bradford Book, MIT Press, (1986) 318–362.

[2] A. Pétrowski, L. Personnaz, G. Dreyfus, C. Girault, Parallel Implementations of Neural Network Simulations, Hypercube and Distributed Computers, F. André & J.P. Verjus Eds., Amsterdam: North Holland (1989) 205–218.

[3] A. Singer, Implementations of Artificial neural networks on the Connection Machine, Parallel Computing, vol. 14, pp. (1990) 305–315.

[4] M. Cosnard, J.C. Mignot, H. Paugam-Moisy, Implementations of Multilayer Neural Networks on Parallel Architectures, 2nd International Specialist Seminar on Parallel Digital Processors, Lisbonne, April 1991.

[5] Alain Petrowski and Gérard Dreyfus and Claude Girault, Performance analysis of a pipelined backpropagation algorithm, IEEE Trans. on Neural Networks, vol. 4, November 1993, 970–981.

[6] Jim Tørresen. Parallelization of Backpropagation Training for Feed-Forward Neural Networks. Ph.D. thesis, (1996).

[7] Jim Tørresen and Shinji Tomita, A Review of Parallel Implementations of Backpropagation Neural Networks, Chapter 2 in the book by N. Sundararajan and P. Saratchandran (editors): Parallel Architectures for Artificial Neural Networks, IEEE CS Press (1998) ISBN 0-8186-8399-6.

Concurrent Information Processing and Computing
D. Grigoras and A. Nicolau (Eds.)
IOS Press, 2005

Task Graph Structuring for Dynamic SMP Clusters with Communication on-the-fly

Lukasz Masko

Institute of Computer Science, Polish Academy of Sciences,
01–237 Warsaw, ul. Ordona 21,Poland
`masko@ipipan.waw.pl`

Abstract. This paper concerns program task graph scheduling for a new parallel system architecture based on dynamically reconfigurable shared memory clusters. Programs are represented by a special type of macro dataflow graphs. The proposed scheduling algorithms are based on simple, atomic transformations applied to program graphs. These transformations reduce the execution time of the whole graph by local actions performed on its local subgraphs. The transformations convert subgraphs of an initial graph in such a way that data transfer operations take advantage of special architectural features such as communication on–the–fly and processor switching between SMP clusters. The paper includes a simple exemplary scheduling algorithm based on such transformations.

1   Introduction

SMP systems provide increased computational power in a simple and convenient way. However, their efficiency depends on the solution of the interconnection network existing between processors and shared memory modules. The simplest network for connecting processing nodes with shared memory modules is a memory bus. In programs, where data exchange between parallel distributed processes and shared memory is intensive, the scalability of bus–based system is poor. System performance can be much improved by organizing many processor clusters as sets of processors using separate memory busses. Such systems, based on fixed size clusters, already exist [1–3]. However, three problems in such systems still need improvement: fixed composition of processors in a cluster, intra–cluster data exchange and inter–cluster data exchange. Fixed number of processors in a cluster can be not adequate to the needs imposed by communication–intensive program areas. Intra–cluster communication needs improvement, especially in bus–based clusters. Inter–cluster communication rarely can be totally avoided. In existing systems it is frequently implemented by message passing, which has much higher latency than intra–cluster communication.

A new architecture, based on dynamic shared memory processor clusters has been proposed [4], which addresses the three problems mentioned above. In this architecture (Fig.1), a dynamic cluster is constituted by a program run–time variable number of processors connected to a shared memory module, modified at program run-time. Memory modules are dual–ported. One port of a memory module is connected to a local cluster bus, which is used for data exchange inside clusters – more precisely between memory modules and processor data caches. The other port is connected to a global bus, which connects all memory modules with all processor data caches. Each bus is supervised by an arbiter, to which processors depose access requests. The global bus can be used only for data reads. Local cluster busses are

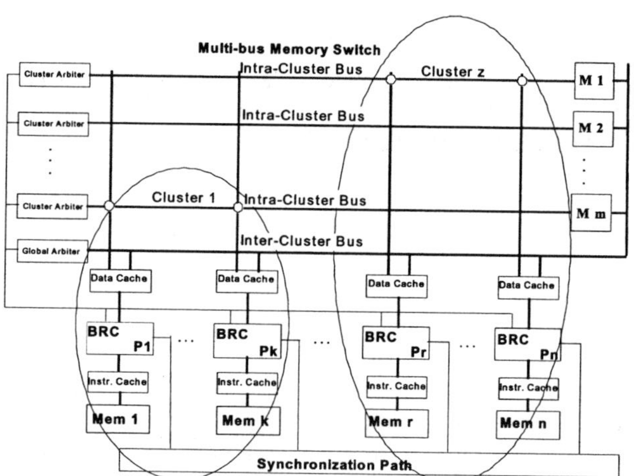

Figure 1. General overview of the system

used both for reads and writes. A processor can be connected to only one local memory bus at a time, but it can be dynamically switched between busses of different memory modules.

Processor operations related to memory busses (i.e. data transfers and processor switching between clusters) are supervised by Bus Request Controller (BRC). This block of a processor is connected to all bus arbiters. It collects in queues transmission requests issued by application programs, performs request selection and communicates with bus arbiters.

Processor switching between clusters solves the problem of fixed cluster size at run–time. System structure can be dynamically adjusted to program needs by displacement of processors between clusters. Intra–cluster data exchange efficiency problem is effectively solved by data transfers on–the–fly included in his architecture. This method, similar to cache injection [5], is based on reading of data in parallel by many processors. It includes automatic cluster bus snooping by BRCs of processors while a write operation takes place on a memory bus. The crossbar switches used for intra–cluster communication cannot easily provide such feature. Inter–cluster communication is improved with the use of a new communication method that takes advantage of both processor switching between clusters and data transfers on–the–fly. It is called communication on–the–fly and consists in switching processors between memory modules with results of computations stored in their data caches. While the switched processor writes data to the cluster memory module, the snooping processors can read in parallel the data to their data caches

We have assumed a new program execution principle called cache–controlled macro data–flow model. A program is decomposed into macro–blocks. Each macro–block of a program can be executed without data transfers to or from shared memory, using only the information stored in processor's cache. Therefore, before a block can be executed, all data required for it must be read from shared memory. After the block is finished, all the results required for other processors must be transferred back to the shared memory module. A program is represented as an extended macro-dataflow graph [6], in which computation nodes correspond to program macro–blocks. The graph also contains structures allowing modeling of special architectural features, such as processor switching, data transfers on–the–fly and synchronization. This representation is described in Section 2. Program graph scheduling consists in special transformations of its subgraphs so as to obtain an equivalent graph, but with smaller execution time. Section 3 presents a set of such transformations, which can be identified as basic. In Section 4 an exemplary scheduling algorithm using these transformations is presented.

2 Program graph representation

Program representation which is used in this paper, is based on a standard macro dataflow graph extended with some new kinds of nodes and edges. Basic nodes are computation and communication nodes. Computation node represents a sequence of computation instructions executed without any data transfers from or to the shared memory module. All data required for a node are read before its execution and held in processor's data cache. Computation results are written back to the shared memory module after the node is executed. A node is denoted in the graph by a rectangle labeled with a task name (i.e. T1, see Fig.2) and the name of the processor, which executes this task (i.e. P1). Basic communication nodes are write and read nodes. They represent data transfers from a processor's data cache to a shared memory module or from a shared memory module to the processor's data cache, respectively. Such operation consists in placing a proper request in the processor's BRC and waiting for data transfer completion. In the graph, read/write operations are denoted by circles. They can be labeled by the names of processors, which execute them.

In order to model other operations such as synchronization or processor switching, some new types of nodes have been added. Processor switching is denoted as a crossed rectangle. It is labeled with the name of the memory module, to which a processor executing this operation is switched to. A switching operation itself consists in communication between a given processor and bus arbiters. The processor must be disconnected from one bus and then connected to another. Both operations can be performed if there is no traffic on an appropriate bus. Synchronization (a barrier operation) is denoted as a horizontal line crossing some (at least two) of the paths in the graph. It is also marked with barrier's label (i.e. B1). Rounded polygons marked with memory module labels mean groups of tasks executed using the same shared memory module.

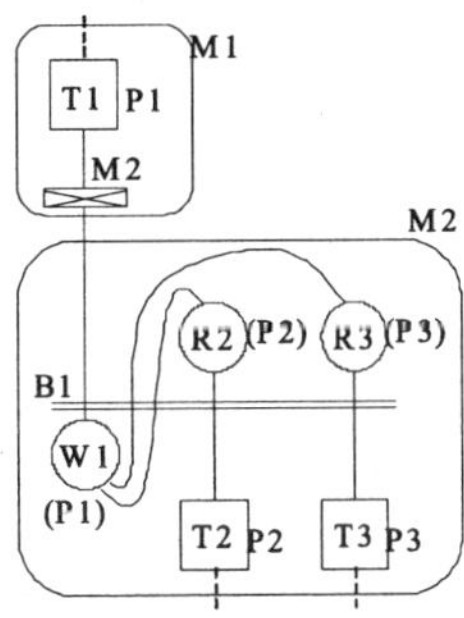

Figure 2. Nodes of the program graph

In a read on-the-fly operation synchronized by a barrier, read nodes have special meaning. In this operation, as shown in Fig.2, they are composed of placing requests in processors' BRCs before a barrier and execution of the data transmission after the barrier is fulfilled. The processor executes its barrier instruction between these actions. Curved edges mean data transmissions. While data are written from the writing processor's (P1) data cache with instruction W1, processors P2 and P3 read this data to their data caches using read on–the–fly technique based on bus snooping.

3 Basic graph manipulations

The main goal of this paper is to identify a set of transformations, which next can be used as a basis for a task scheduling algorithm. What first we require from these transformations is their locality, by which we mean that applying a transformation to a small, local subgraph doesn't change the structure of the rest of the graph. It allows to preserve all the advantages

---

Algorithm 2 Outline of scheduling algorithms

1: Start with initial structuring of the program graph. This step can be very simple, but may also contain some graph transformations.
2: **repeat**
3:     Choose a subgraph of the program graph according to a criterion on which the algorithm is based. Choose one transformation and apply it to the chosen subgraph.
4:     **if** this transformation fulfills an acceptance criterion **then**
5:       validate this transformation in the subgraph.
6:     **else**
7:       reject this transformation.
8: **until** all the pairs: subgraph and transformation have been inspected (no transformation, which can be applied to any subgraph, fulfills the criterion).
9: **end** – now the graph is scheduled

---

of transformations applied to the program graph before the current one. Obtaining locality depends on the performed transformation and can involve introducing processor switchings between clusters. Adding such operations is not expensive. Some of the proposed transformations later remove unnecessary processor switching from the graph.

Algorithm 2 constitutes a framework for different algorithms, which can be created with the use of local transformations of program graphs. Different criteria for all the required choices shown in the algorithm can be assumed, such as the execution time of the whole graph, or just of a local subgraph. Also the choice of a subgraph as well as a transformation to be applied, can be performed in various ways giving different scheduling algorithms.

3.1   Mapping simple pairs of sequential nodes onto the same processor

A simple pair of sequential nodes is a subgraph, which is built of two consecutive computation nodes, with only one write and one read node between them (Fig.3a). Execution of task T2 depends only on results produced by task T1, written to the shared memory by operation W1, and later read only by processor P2 for task T2 with operation R2. The read operation R2 can be performed either by using the global bus (when processors P1 and P2 are connected to different local busses and are therefore in different clusters) or by using the local bus (when both processors are connected to the same memory module). If read R2 uses the global bus, we place both processors in the same cluster and add one processor switching operation in order to maintain locality of transformation in the graph – transformation $a) \rightarrow b)$ in

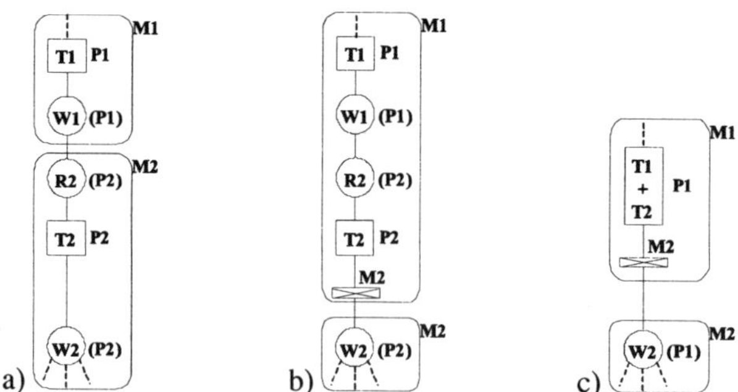

Figure 3. Simple sequence of nodes

Fig.3. If read R2 is performed with a local bus this step is not required. Now we map tasks T1, T2 and all other tasks executed by processor P2 to processor P1. Then we can safely remove the pair of write/read nodes W1 and R2 – transformation *b)* → *c)*, for their are no longer required. As a result, the number of used processors is reduced by one. Furthermore, one memory write and one read operation are eliminated. This reduces execution time of a program code represented by this subgraph. It doesn't reduce the number of memory busses required.

Locality of this transformation is preserved by introduction of processor switching operation. Without itall the nodes subsequent to W2, which are executed by processor P1, would have to use the M1 memory module instead of M2. If there were any data transfer nodes among them using local bus of memory module M2, this would force them to use the global bus instead of local one and introduce changes in the rest of the program graph.

3.2 One–to–many communication scheme (multicast structure)

This communication scheme consists in sending the same or almost the same information to a number of processors (Fig.4a). Processor P2 executes task T2 and writes its results to shared memory module M2. After that, processors P3, P4 and P5 read these data and execute their tasks (T3, T4 and T5 respectively). Reading processors can be in the same (P4) or in different clusters (P3, P5). Proper transmissions use then global or local bus. In such a situation we try to introduce a read-on-the-fly operation. This leads to elimination of almost all read operations and therefore reduces execution time of this subgraph.

Operation proceeds as follows: first, we must determine all read nodes that will be converted to communication on–the–fly. In some cases, conversion of some nodes leads to a deadlock in the graph. The other criterion can be the ready–time of the node. Let's assume, that in the situation given in Fig.4a only nodes R4 and R5 will be transformed. The next step consists in placing all the considered read nodes in the cluster of the corresponding write node. We add processor switching everywhere it is required to preserve locality of the transformation. After this, we introduce a barrier and convert standard read nodes into reads on–the–fly. The result is shown in Fig.4b. In this way, almost all (or all) reads are performed on–the–fly while the write operation takes place. This reduces execution time of such a subgraph. This doesn't reduce a number of used processors or busses.

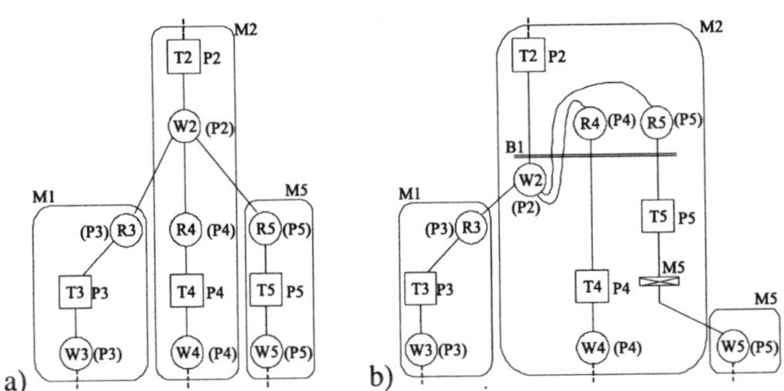

Figure 4. Multicast

3.3   Many–to–one communication scheme (reduction structure)

This communication scheme appears, when one processor reads information from many processors and then uses it for computations (Fig.5a). Writing processors can be connected either to the same memory module, as reading processor (P1) or to different modules (P2, P3, P4).

The first step of this operation is to determine the write nodes that will be included in this graph transformation. In some cases, an improper transformation may lead to deadlock. Also execution time of the read nodes should be close to execution time of write nodes to avoid processor stalls. Let's assume, that in a given example W4 node will not be used during transformation. Second step consists in placing all the considered write and read nodes together in the same cluster. We introduce processor switching operations everywhere it is required for locality. In the next step we transform all possible communication (here: pairs W1–R1, W2–R2, W3–R3) into the on–the–fly pattern (introducing barriers, like in the multicast situation). This eliminates some read operations, which reduces execution time.

As a result, a subgraph is obtained (Fig.5b), in which all (or almost all) the communications are performed via a local bus and they use reads on–the–fly, which reduces the amount of data transferred through the bus and - as a result - the execution time of this subgraph.

3.4   Many–to–many communication scheme ("butterfly" structure)

This communication scheme corresponds to a mixture of several one–to–many (or many–to–one) communication patterns in one subgraph. It can be transformed using a series of transformations given above. The only difference is caused by the fact, that a processor can be connected to only one local bus. Therefore, it is required to select one memory bus which will be used for all transfers. We can assign a new memory module for this operation and switch all writing processors to it, together with their data. If this module is really not required, it will be removed later. Like in previous subsections, there is some space left for modifications. We can choose some of the nodes not to be affected by all the transformations or to be included in only some of them. By default we include all the communication nodes.

An example of such a situation is shown in Fig.6a. Generally, a transformation itself consists in putting all the write and read nodes in the same cluster (connecting processors to the same memory module) and introducing reads on–the–fly. Also computation nodes T4, T5 and T6 are arranged to be executed while processors are connected to the same memory module. This is because a processor can be switched to a different memory module in order

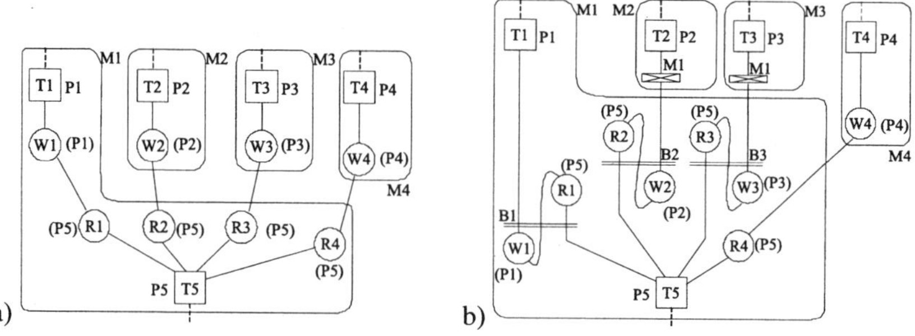

Figure 5. Reduction

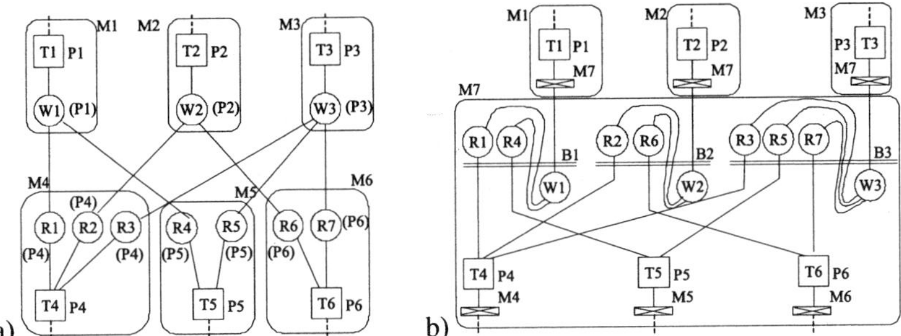

Figure 6. Butterfly subgraph

to move computation results in its cache. Processor switchings after execution of T4, T5 and T6 is required to obtain locality of graph transformations, like in Section 3.1. The result of the transformation is shown in Fig.6b. This operation decreases the number of performed transmissions, which reduces subgraph execution time.

3.5 Mapping computational node sequences onto the same processor

Mapping of sequential code onto the same processor is important not only to decrease the number of used processors, also to decreases the execution time by elimination of communication. Simple situation, when there is one–to–one communication, was described in subsection 3.1. More complicated structures are results of operations described in subsections 3.2–3.4. The idea of this mapping operation is the same as in 3.1, but due to higher complexity, more variants must be considered. The decision is usually taken based on the evaluation of the execution time of the program graph. The variant, which reduces time at most is mainly the one that is introduced in the graph.

A transformation consists in mapping two consecutive computation nodes onto the same processor and removing a read node from between them. In a reduction–like case, we also remove one write node. In the transformed graph, the lack of read operation on the path between two computational nodes labeled with the same processor name indicates, that all the data produced by the first node and required for execution of the second one are carried in the processor's cache.

In the multicast–like situation we must decide, which successor of the writing processor should be unified with it. Usually placing the writing node together with the node performing a standard read operation (like the R3 in Fig.4b) reduces the execution time of the graph at most by eliminating one read operation, but in a general case other choice can be more profitable. In

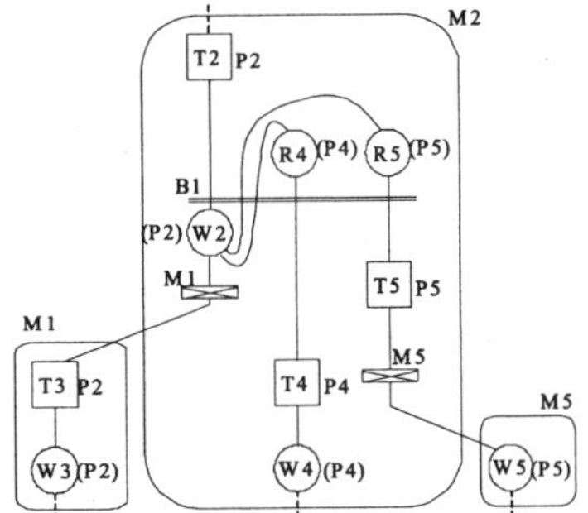

Figure 7. Example of multicast subgraph after processor unification

the situation in Fig.4b, if we want to map tasks from processor P3 to processor P2, we get the subgraph shown in Fig.7. Notice, that a processor switching operation is introduced. This is due to the fact, that further operations are performed using the M1 memory module. In this operation, unlike in subsection 3.1, we cannot remove the write node but in some situations it is possible to reduce its weight, when part of this data is required only for execution of certain task (T3 in this case).

The reduction–like situation should be treated in the opposite way to the multicast. One of writing processors must be chosen and unified with a reading one. The choice of a writing processor seems to be easy — we unify the processor, whose write instruction has the largest amount of data to be transferred. In most cases, such a unification would remove the heaviest message from the bus. But it can be possible that choosing different processor can give better results. Therefore, we must try different possibilities and choose the one which gives the best performance improvement.

In the butterfly situation, as the most complicated one, it is required to check the biggest number of different possibilities for unifying processors. The idea itself is still the same – we can map tasks performed by one of the reading processors to one of its writing predecessors. As a result of this operation, some read operations are removed from the graph. This can lead to no improvement at all, if these reads were to be performed on–the–fly. But, like in the multicast situation, we can get speed improvement by reducing the amount of written data (if some of it can be carried in processors cache, just like in the multicast situation). An important achievement of this transformation is reduction of the number of used processors – in some situations this subgraph can be executed with half as many of processors required at the beginning.

3.6 Merging of processor clusters

This operation is used for two reasons. The first one is to reduce the number of used memory modules. After applying the operations described in previous chapters, the number of busses (shared memory modules) is usually not reduced (situation described in chapter 3.1 is possible, but hardly ever appears in its pure form). Although this produces an optimized code, its execution usually requires more busses then it is available. Therefore, reduction of modules in use is vital. Another thing is, that due to this operation, we can remove some of processor switching operations from the graph. Although such operation itself doesn't take much of processor time, its execution can be delayed because of the traffic on the bus (an arbiter has to wait for its bus to be silent before it can disconnect the processor from it).

A merging operation consists in mapping all memory transfer operations of the two consecutive clusters to the same local memory bus. We are using the bus of the first cluster. If there is any processor switching operation between these two clusters, this operation is then removed form the graph since it is no longer needed.

4 An exemplary scheduling algorithm

As mentioned before, the algorithm consists in application of steps described in Section 3 in various order. Notice, that application of the operation described in Section 3.1 is always profitable because it always reduces the number of used resources and the graph execution time. Application of the operation from Section 3.5 is useful mainly after execution of operations from Sections 3.1–3.4. Also cluster merging should be performed after application of transformation from Section 3.5.

Program scheduling starts with program graph structured in such a way, that all the processing nodes together with its predecessors (read nodes) and successor (write node) are

---

Algorithm 3 Simple scheduling algorithm

1: Initial program graph is structured in such a way that each computation node with its read nodes and write node is assigned to a separate processor. Each processor is assigned to a separate memory module.
2: Apply operation described in Section 3.1 in all places in the graph, where it is possible.
3: Traverse the graph using the BFS (Breadth First Search) rule.
4: **for** every visited node v **do**
5:    Check, which transformations from those described in Sections 3.2–3.4 can be applied to the node v and its neighborhood (check if this node can be a part of subgraph, that has a form of "butterfly", "multicast" or "reduction", in this order). Apply the chosen transformation for the whole subgraph containing the node v.
6:    For the same subgraph, apply one of transformations described in Section 3.5, appropriate for this structure.
7: Traverse the graph in the same order.
8: **for** every visited cluster **do**
9:    Try to unify it with one of its subsequent clusters (apply operation from Section 3.6).

---

executed on separate processors and mapped to separate memory modules. All write operations are performed using separate local busses and all read operations are performed using the global bus. There is no processor switching, because every processor is used only in one cluster. Execution of such structured graph requires potentially unbounded number of resources (processors and memory modules). Furthermore, saturation of the global bus makes execution of such program highly inefficient. The aim of a scheduling algorithm is to reduce execution time of the whole program graph. To achieve it, we must reduce global bus traffic by distribution of data transfers to local busses, and reduce the number of required resources, also leading to reduction of the number of memory operations.

Algorithm 3 presents the simple scheduling algorithm. It consists in scanning the whole graph from its beginning to its end. During this scanning we locate structures matching operations described in Section 3 and apply proper transformations to them. This algorithm doesn't use graph evaluation but all possible operations are applied for all the nodes in the subgraph.

The result of application of consecutive steps of this scheduling algorithm to a simple program graph is shown in Fig.8. Fig.8a contains the initial program graph structured for the maximal number of resources. Fig.8b shows the same graph after application of transformations described in Sections 3.1-3.5. Fig.8c shows the final form of the structured graph. As a result, we obtain a graph, which uses only 2 processors and 1 memory module (opposite to 6 processors and 6 memory modules as in the initial graph). All remaining data transmissions are performed "on–the–fly". If we assume that all the computation nodes T1–T6 have weights 5 and all transmissions have weights 10, the simulated execution time of the initial graph from Fig.8a is 125 time units, while execution of the structured program graph from Fig.8c takes 65 time units.

5 Conclusions

In this paper, basic transformations have been presented, that can be applied for scheduling program graphs to decrease their execution time in parallel architecture based on dynamic SMP clusters. They transform subgraphs of an initial program graph in such a way, that data transmissions, which are present in this subgraph, can be performed using communication and read on–the–fly operations. The transformations show the strong locality property be-

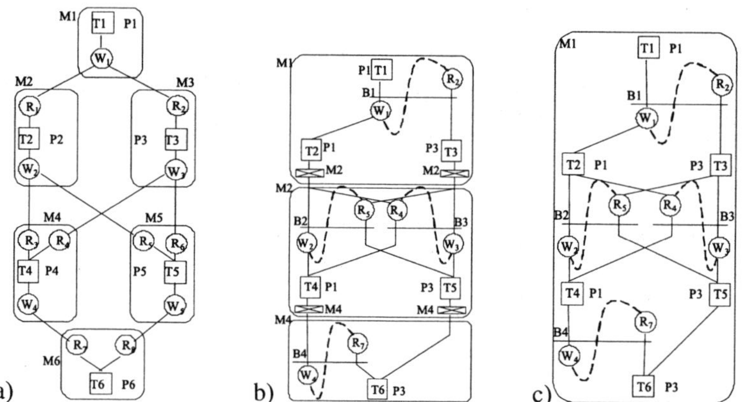

Figure 8. Application of greedy scheduling algorithm to simple program graph

cause they act only on relatively small subgraphs of the whole program graph. The first type of transformation coverts a simple sequence of nodes with communication between them into one computation node with no communication. The second, third and fourth types of transformation convert a multicast–, reduction– and butterfly–like subgraphs in such a way that data transmissions can be done by communication on–the–fly. The fifth type of transformation is similar to the first one, but is used for more complicated subgraphs. Like the first one, it eliminates data transmission nodes from the program graph. The last type of transformation reduces the number of used memory modules and eliminates some processor switching operations. The transformations reduce the execution time of programs, because the number of data transmissions on the busses can be strongly decreased. They distribute data traffic from the global bus to local busses of SMP clusters. They convert programs to equivalent ones, but executed faster than in the initial form. The transformations can constitute a basis for various scheduling algorithms. They reduce the amount of resources required for program execution as well. A presented simple scheduling algorithm confirms usefulness of the proposed transformations.

This work was partially sponsored by the KBN grant No. 4T11C 007 22.

References

[1] *Convex Exemplar Architecture*, Convex Press, 1994, p. 239.

[2] D. Lenoski et al. *The Stanford Dash multi–processor*, IEEE Computer, Vol. 25, N. 3, 1992, pp. 63–79.

[3] *Multimax Technical Summary*, Encore Computer Summary, March 1987.

[4] M. Tudruj, L. Masko, *A Parallel System Architecture based on Dynamically Configurable Shared Memory Clusters*, PPAM 2001 – Parallel Processing and Applied Mathematics 2001, LNCS 2328, 2002.

[5] A. Milenkovic, V. Milutinovic, *Cache Injection: A Novel Technique for Tolerating Memory Latency in Bus–Based SMPs*, Proceedings of the Euro–Par 2000, LNCS 1900, Springer Verlag, 2000, pp. 558–566.

[6] M. Tudruj, L. Masko, *Program Execution Control for Communication On–The–Fly in Dynamic Shared Memory Processor Clusters*, Proceedings of the 3rd International Conference on Parallel Computing in Electrical Engineering, PARELEC 2002, September 2002, Warsaw, IEEE Computer Society Press.

Application of the Runge-Kutta-Fehlberg Method in the Speculative Method of Transient States Analysis

Jaroslaw Forenc[1]   Wojciech Walendziuk[1]   Andrzej Jordan[2]

[1]*Bialystok Technical University, Faculty of Electrical Engineering*
Wiejska 45D Street, 15-351 Bialystok, POLAND
tel. +48-85 742-16-51, fax +48-85 742-16-57
{jarekf, walenw}@pb.bialystok.pl
[2]*Polish-Japanese Institute of Information Technology*
Koszykowa 86 Street, 02-008 Warsaw, POLAND
tel. +48-22 621-03-73
jordana@pb.bialystok.pl

Abstract. In this paper the application of the Runge-Kutta-Fehlberg method in the speculative method of the analysis of transient states will be presented. The speculative method is intended to conduct transient states analysis in electrical circuits in which the transient state is described by a large system of ordinary differential equations, linear or nonlinear. A general idea of this method is based on the decomposition of the time domain. Computations in the particular subintervals of time are conducted in parallel with the use of one of well-known numerical methods of solving ordinary differential equations systems. In the article the application of the Runge-Kutta-Fehleberg method for this purpose will be presented. As the practical example of the application of the speculative method, the analysis of the dynamics of an asynchronous slip-ring motor will be shown.

1 Introduction

The transient states analysis in large electrical circuits is usually time consuming and thereby costly. In such a case, the achievement of high accuracy of computations in a short time requires the application of high performance computer systems [1]. The transient states appearing in electrical circuits are often described by a system of ordinary differential equations, linear or nonlinear (systems of lumped constants). Most of numerical methods of solving ordinary differential equations systems are typical sequential methods. In these methods the knowledge of the values of the state variables from the previous step is necessary in order to determine the values of the state variables in the next step. For some time now various parallel methods of solving ordinary differential equations system have been developed [2].

The speculative method is an original approach to the analysis of transient states appearing in electrical circuits in which the transient state is described by a large system of linear or nonlinear ordinary differential equations. The main aim of the application of this method is to reduce the time of transient states analysis. A general idea of the speculative method is based on the decomposition of the time domain. The computations in the particular subintervals of time are conducted in parallel with the use of one of well-known numerical methods of solving ordinary differential equations systems. In previous papers the application of the fourth-order Runge-Kutta method with a fixed integration step [3, 4] and the application of the same method but with automatic selection of the integration step [5, 6] were presented. In this paper the application of the Runge-Kutta-Fehlberg method [7,8] as the numerical method of solving ordinary differential equations system, the algorithm of automatic selection of the integration step in this method, then general description of the speculative method algorithm will be described. As an example of the application of the speculative method, the analysis of the dynamics of an asynchronous slip-ring motor will be presented. The computations were carried out with the use of a PC and WMPI library [9] - an implementation of MPI standard [10].

2   The algorithm of the Runge-Kutta-Fehlberg method

The execution of computations in the speculative method is based on the application of the Runge-Kutta-Fehlberg method. The Runge-Kutta-Fehlberg method uses the Runge-Kutta method of the fifth order to estimate the local error in the Runge-Kutta method of the fourth order. In this method the solution x_n at the point t_n is known, and the solution x_{n+1} at the next point $t_{n+1} = t_n + h$ with the assumed accuracy ε must be determined. For this purpose k_i $(i = 1, 2, \ldots, 6)$ coefficients are calculated:

$$k_1 = hf(t_n, x_n)$$

$$k_2 = hf(t_n + \tfrac{1}{4}h, x_n + \tfrac{1}{4}k_1)$$

$$k_3 = hf(t_n + \tfrac{3}{8}h, x_n + \tfrac{3}{32}k_1 + \tfrac{9}{32}k_2)$$

$$k_4 = hf(t_n + \tfrac{12}{13}h, x_n + \tfrac{1932}{2197}k_1 - \tfrac{7200}{2197}k_2 + \tfrac{7296}{2197}k_3) \tag{1}$$

$$k_5 = hf(t_n + h, x_n + \tfrac{439}{216}k_1 - 8k_2 + \tfrac{3680}{513}k_3 - \tfrac{845}{4104}k_4)$$

$$k_6 = hf(t_n + \tfrac{1}{2}h, x_n - \tfrac{8}{27}k_1 + 2k_2 - \tfrac{3544}{2565}k_3 + \tfrac{1859}{4104}k_4 - \tfrac{11}{40}k_5)$$

Then, the estimate of the fourth order (2) and the fifth order (3) of the solution are calculated:

$$\hat{x}_{n+1} = x_n + \left(\tfrac{25}{216}k_1 + \tfrac{1408}{2565}k_3 + \tfrac{2197}{4104}k_4 - \tfrac{1}{5}k_5\right) \tag{2}$$

$$x_{n+1} = x_n + \left(\tfrac{16}{135}k_1 + \tfrac{6656}{12825}k_3 + \tfrac{28561}{56430}k_4 - \tfrac{9}{50}k_5 + \tfrac{2}{55}k_6\right) \tag{3}$$

Finally, the error estimate is obtained:

$$\delta_{max} = \|x_{n+1} - \hat{x}_{n+1}\| \tag{4}$$

If the value of the error estimate is less or equal to the assumed accuracy ε, the solution x_{n+1} is accepted as accurate enough. Moreover, if inequality (5) [11] is true (which indicates that h is much smaller then necessary):

$$\delta_{max} < \frac{\varepsilon}{50} \tag{5}$$

then, the integration step h is multiplied by two, otherwise computations are conducted at the next point. When the value of the error estimate is greater than the assumed accuracy (which indicates that h is too large), the solution x_{n+1} is rejected, then the integration step is divided by two and computations for point t_{n+1} are executed again. In the speculative method as the initial value of the integration step $h = (t_N - t_0)/100$ is assumed.

3   The speculative method

In the speculative method the total time of the transient analysis (t_0, t_N) is divided into a given number of N subintervals (Figure 1).

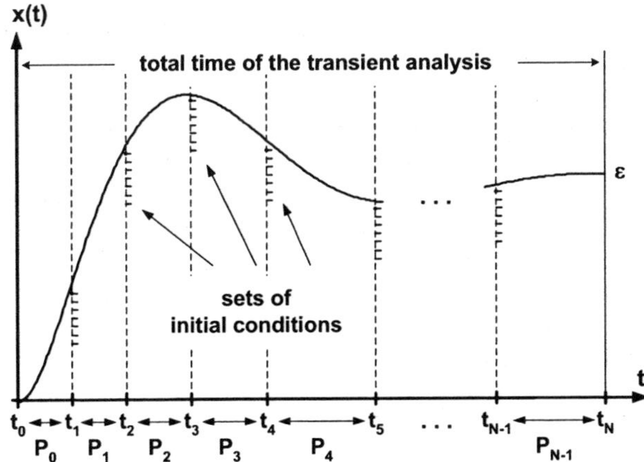

Figure 1. Division of the total time of the transient analysis into subintervals and the definition of the sets of initial conditions.

The set of parallel processes $(P_0, \ldots, P_{N-1})$ is assigned for subintervals (t_{n-1}, t_n), $(n = 1, 2, \ldots, N)$. As computations in particular subintervals are conducted in parallel, the same number of steps should be executed in each subinterval. In the Runge-Kutta Fehlberg method an automatic selection of the integration step is applied. The length of the integration step h, thus the number of steps in particular subintervals, is considerably dependent on the nature of the plot. In this case, applying the simplest, equal, division of the total time of the transient analysis is not optimal. In order to get an optimal division, computations are executed in the whole interval (t_0, t_N) with the assumed low accuracy ε (e.g. $\varepsilon = 10^{-1} \div 10^{-3}$) and approximate solution $x_0^p, x_1^p, \ldots, x_m^p$ at points $t_0^p, t_1^p, \ldots, t_m^p$ $(t_0 = t_0^p$ and $t_N = t_m^p)$ is obtained. Then, the obtained number of points m of approximate solution is divided by the number of subintervals N, obtaining, according to equation (6), points $t_1, t_2, \ldots, t_{N-1}$ which are the division of the total time of the transient analysis.

$$t_i = t_{i(\frac{m}{N})}^p \qquad i = 1, 2, \ldots, N - 1 \tag{6}$$

In this way, the total time of the transient analysis (t_0, t_N) has been divided into nonequal subintervals. The subintervals, in which state variables oscillate, have a shorter length in relation to subintervals in which the function is even (see Figure 3 and Figure 4). Along with the increase of computations accuracy, the number of integration steps usually rises more in those subintervals in which state variables oscillate. For that reason the length of shorter subintervals is decreased, while the length of longer subintervals is increased in relation to the division determined according to equation (6). The value of the low accuracy ε should ensure stability of the solution. In the case of linear equations, the analysis of eigenvalues of the matrix, being the right side of differential equations, could be helpful for determination of the value of the low accuracy ε.

In order to execute parallel computations in particular subintervals, it is necessary to determine the initial conditions for the sets of parallel processes $P_1, P_2, \ldots, P_{N-1}$ at points $t_1, t_2, \ldots, t_{N-1}$ (for each state variable). For the set P_0, these conditions are known from the assumption. In the speculative method, instead of one condition, a set of initial conditions is determined for each state variable (Figure 1). For this purpose, previous computations with a low accuracy ε are used. For each point $t_1, t_2, \ldots, t_{N-1}$ we go back to a previous point of approximate solution and we execute two computations with step $h/2$ (where h is distance between two points of approximate solution). In this way, two solutions at each point are obtained. These solutions are used for determination of the initial conditions. The absolute value of the difference of the computations from both steps, h and $2 \cdot h/2$, at points $t_1, t_2, \ldots, t_{N-1}$, multiplied by a safety coefficient k (assumed "a priori"), determines the length of the section in which the initial conditions for the separate set of parallel processes will be presented. As the beginning of each section, the value computed for the step $2 \cdot h/2$ is assumed. The end of the section is determined by the formula presented below:

$$x_{i,2\cdot h/2} \pm |x_{i,2\cdot h/2} - x_{i,h}| \cdot k \qquad i = 1, 2, \ldots, N - 1 \tag{7}$$

where: $x_{i,h}$ - values computed with step h, $x_{i,2\cdot h/2}$ - values obtained during double computations with step $h/2$, k - a safety coefficient.

The values of the state variables computed for both steps determine the convergence direction to the exact solution. If $x_{i,h} > x_{i,2\cdot h/2}$, then in equation (7) the sign "-" occurs, and if $x_{i,h} < x_{i,2\cdot h/2}$, then the sign "+" occurs. The obtained section, divided for each state variable at points $t_1, t_2, \ldots, t_{N-1}$ into a particular number of subintervals, determines points which are the searched initial conditions. When the initial conditions are determined, the main computations are started. For each set of parallel processes, a particular number of computing processors is assigned. For the first set P_0, only one computing processor (master) is assigned because there exists only one initial condition for each state variable in this set. For the rest of sets of parallel processes, such a number of computing processors (slaves) is assigned as the number of initial conditions they have. All processors (master and slaves) execute parallel computations in their subintervals with a high accuracy ε (e.g. $\varepsilon = 10^{-6} \div 10^{-8}$). When the computations are finished, only one solution in the subinterval (t_0, t_1) is obtained, however, for the rest of subintervals a sequence of the solutions having different initial conditions is obtained.

In the last stage of the algorithm, the master processor determines an optimal final speculative solution which consists of selected solutions from particular subintervals (Figure 2). In the first subinterval (t_0, t_1) we have only one solution which is the exact solution. In the next subinterval (t_1, t_2) we choose such a solution whose initial condition is the closest to the value at the point t_1, obtained during computations in the previous subinterval (the master processor computations). For the rest of subintervals, $(t_2, t_3), \ldots, (t_{N-1}, t_N)$, we proceed similarly as in subinterval (t_1, t_2).

4 Analysis of the dynamics of an asynchronous slip-ring motor

As an example of the application of the speculative method, the analysis of the dynamics of an asynchronous slip-ring motor will be described. The nonlinear equations which describe the transient state of the motor will be presented in the standard form. This form was obtained by a transformation of the stator and rotor current equations with the use of an orthogonal

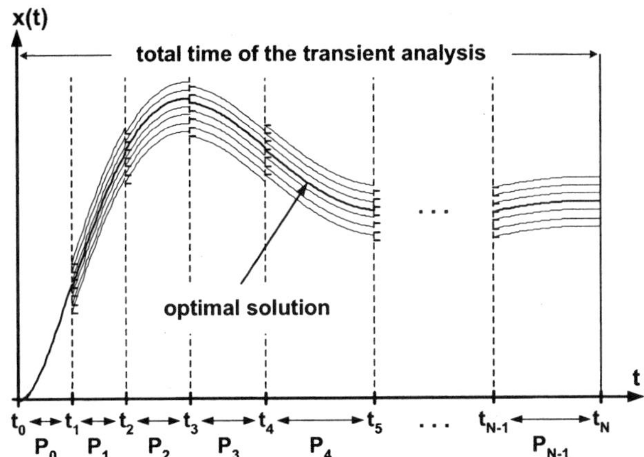

Figure 2. Determination of the optimal solution.

matrix [7]. To simplify the description, only basic motor parameters are presented:

$$P = 10\,kW, \quad a = 1445\,r.p.m., \quad I = 21\,A$$
$$U = 220\,V, \quad \eta = 88.5\,\%, \quad \cos\varphi = 0.8 \tag{8}$$

The standard form of the equations is shown below:

$$\frac{dx_1(t)}{dt} = -a_1 x_1 - a_5 x_2 + a_4 x_3 - b_4 x_2 x_5 - b_3 x_4 x_5 + e_1$$

$$\frac{dx_2(t)}{dt} = a_5 x_1 - a_1 x_2 + a_4 x_4 + b_4 x_1 x_5 + b_3 x_3 x_5 + e_2$$

$$\frac{dx_3(t)}{dt} = a_2 x_1 - a_3 x_3 - a_5 x_4 + b_2 x_2 x_5 + b_1 x_4 x_5 - e_3 \tag{9}$$

$$\frac{dx_4(t)}{dt} = a_2 x_2 + a_5 x_3 - a_3 x_4 - b_2 x_1 x_5 - b_1 x_3 x_5 - e_4$$

$$\frac{dx_5(t)}{dt} = -c_2 x_5 + c_1 x_1 x_4 - c_1 x_2 x_3 - M$$

where: $x_1(t)$, $x_2(t)$ - standard form of the stator current, $x_3(t)$, $x_4(t)$ - standard form of the rotor current, $x_5(t)$ - angular velocity.

The coefficient values on the right side of equations (9) result from the rating data of the motor and its electrical parameters.

For the speculative algorithm, the following parameters of computations were set up: on the basis of computations with a low accuracy $\varepsilon = 10^{-1}$, the total time of transient analysis (t_0, t_N) - $0.0 \div 1.0$ s was divided into 6 non-equal subintervals (sets of parallel processes: $P_0, P_1, \ldots, P_5$) with the length: (t_0, t_1) - 0.0737 s, (t_1, t_2) - 0.0825 s, (t_2, t_3) - 0.0825 s, (t_3, t_4) - 0.095 s, (t_4, t_5) - 0.28 s, (t_5, t_6) - 0.3913 s. For each set of parallel processes, 10 initial conditions and 10 computing processors were assigned. The main computations were carried out with the assumed high accuracy $\varepsilon = 10^{-7}$. The same initial condition $x_i(t) = 0.0$, $i = 1, 2, \ldots, 5$ was assumed for all states variables.

Figure 3 and Figure 4 present the obtained results for state variables $x_1(t)$ and $x_3(t)$, respectively. In order to compare the results obtained by the speculative method, the same computations were carried out with the application of a sequential algorithm of the Runge-Kutta-Fehlberg method with a fixed integration step $h = 10^{-8}s$. The solution of the speculative method is convergent with the solution obtained by the sequential algorithm.

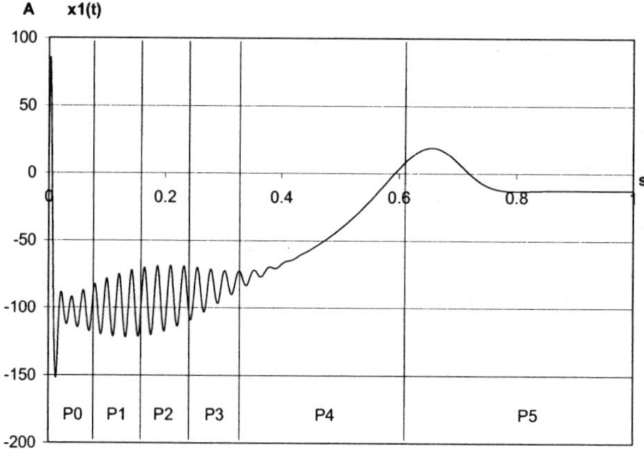

Figure 3. The solution of the state variable $x_1(t)$ - the standard form of the stator current.

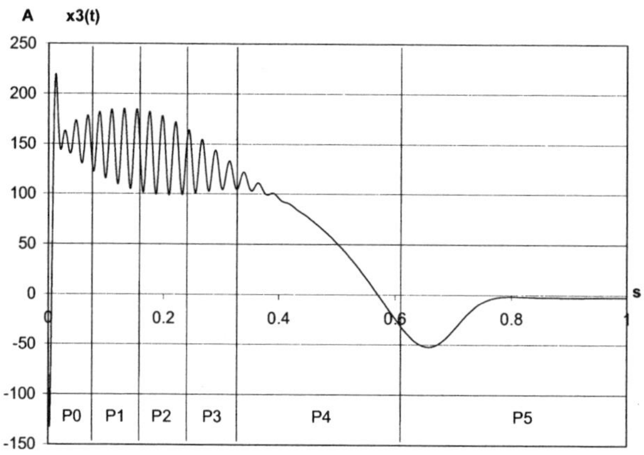

Figure 4. The solution of the state variable $x_3(t)$ - the standard form of the rotor current.

To estimate the accuracy of speculative method solution, the values at the beginning of each subinterval (the choice of the best initial condition) and at the end of subintervals $P_1, P_2, \ldots, P_5$ were compared with the sequential solution. The obtained relative errors are presented in Table 1 and Table 2. The sequential solution as an exact solution, and the speculative solution as an approximate solution were assumed during the determination of relative errors.

Figure 5 presents the value of the estimated speedup. During this estimation, only the number of the Runge-Kutta-Fehlberg method calls was taken into consideration. The time of communication between processors was omitted. For this reason the real speedup is lower

Table 1. Relative errors in the speculative method (at the beginning of subintervals)

	$t_1 = 0.0737\ s$	$t_2 = 0.1562\ s$	$t_3 = 0.2387\ s$	$t_4 = 0.3287\ s$	$t_5 = 0.6087\ s$
	%	%	%	%	%
x_1	0.0052	0.022	0.0443	0.1848	1.3716
x_2	0.0003	0.0019	0.0435	0.0136	0.1417
x_3	0.0109	0.0215	0.0581	0.2009	0.5771
x_4	0.0017	0.0033	0.019	0.0187	0.1522
x_5	0.0025	0.1	0.0982	0.0912	0.0609

Table 2. Relative errors in the speculative method (at the end of subintervals)

	$t_2 = 0.1562\ s$	$t_3 = 0.2387\ s$	$t_4 = 0.3287\ s$	$t_5 = 0.6087\ s$	$t_6 = 1.0\ s$
	%	%	%	%	%
x_1	0.0121	0.057	0.0026	1.4063	convergent
x_2	0.0019	0.0404	0.0183	0.1417	convergent
x_3	0.0114	0.0673	0.0095	0.5906	0.0001
x_4	0.0033	0.0206	0.02	0.1523	0.0003
x_5	0.1109	0.0581	0.092	0.0613	convergent

than the one presented in Figure 5. The number of the Runge-Kutta-Fehlberg method calls means the number of the computations of equations (1), (2) and (3). The present work concerns the exact estimation of the speedup in the speculative method. It should be pointed out that the application of the speculative method requires a different definition of the speedup. The classic definition says that it is a ratio of the total time of computations carried out by means of the sequential implementation of the algorithm measured on a single processor to the total time of computations carried out by a concurrent program activated on n processors. In the case of the speculative method, the time measured on one processor is referred to the time of computations executed by a concurrent program with sectioning the total time of the transient analysis (t_0, t_N) into N sets of parallel processes.

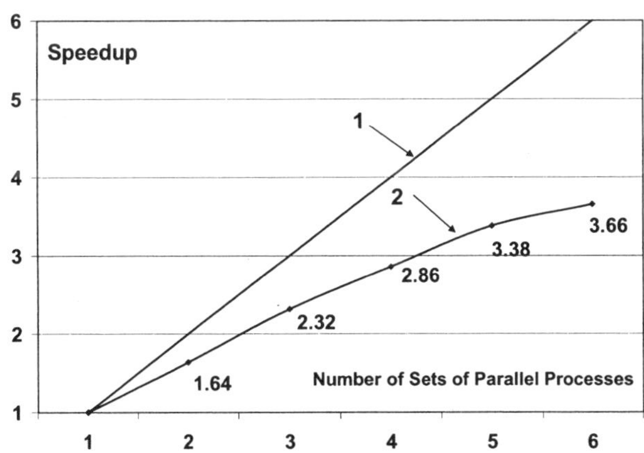

Figure 5. Estimated speedup in the speculative method; 1 - ideal case, 2 - obtained speedup.

5 Conclusions

The application of the speculative method allows us to reduce the time of transient states analysis. This has a particular importance in the case of electrical circuits in which the transient state is described by a very large system of differential equations, and the analysis is not possible with the use of commonly used personal computers. Such a situation takes place in the analysis of short circuits appearing in large electrical power networks and in the research concerning stability of electric power systems. On the basis of the presented example, we can see that the obtained accuracy of computations is high (a maximum relative error not exceed 1.5 %). The accuracy of computations is mainly dependent on the assumed low accuracy of the first computations. The main problem in the speculative method is an appropriate division of the total time of the transient analysis into subintervals so that the same number of the Runge-Kutta-Fehlberg method steps have been executed in each subinterval. This division has a great influence on the value of the speedup.

A drawback of the speculative method is a necessity of the application of computer systems with a large number of computational nodes.

This work was carried out within the frame of the KBN Grant No.: 4T11C 007 22 and internal research grant at PJIIT.

References

[1] J. Machowski, J.W. Bialek and J.R. Bumby, Power System Dynamics and Stability, John Wiley & Sons, New York (1997).

[2] D. Petcu, Parallelism in Solving Ordinary Differential Equations, Mathematical Monographs **64**, Tipografia Universitatii (1998).

[3] J. Forenc, A. Jordan and M. Tudruj, Speculative Parallel Processing Applied to Modelling of Initial Problems in Electrical Circuits, PARELEC'2000 - International Conference on Parallel Computing in Electrical Engineering, Trois-Rivieres, Canada, 2000, IEEE Computer Society, Los Alamitos (2000) 192–196.

[4] J. Forenc and A. Jordan, Speculative Analysis of Transient States, SCI'2001 - World Multiconference on Systemics, Cybernetics and Informatics, Vol.**XV**, Industrial Systems, Orlando (2001) pp. 327–331.

[5] J. Forenc, The Speculative Method of Transient State Analysis with a Variable Integration Step, PARELEC'2002 - International Conference on Parallel Computing in Electrical Engineering, Warsaw, Poland, 2002, IEEE Computer Society, Los Alamitos (2002) 364–368.

[6] J. Forenc, The Application of the Speculative Methods To Transient States Analysis in Transmission Line, 26-th IC-SPETO - International Conference of Fundamentals of Electrotechnics and Circuit Theory, Gliwice-Niedzica, Poland (2003) 431–434.

[7] B. Baron, A. Marcol and S. Pawlikowski, Numerical Methods in Delphi 4, Helion, Gliwice (1999).

[8] A. Krupowicz, Numerical Methods of Initial Problems for the Ordinary Differential Equations, PWN, Warszawa (1986).

[9] WMPI - http://www.criticalsoftware.com/hpc/wmpi.php

[10] Message Passing Interface Forum, MPI: A Message-Passing Interface Standard, Report No. CS-94-230, University of Tennessee, Knoxville (1994).

[11] Z. Fortuna, B. Macukow and J. Wasowski, Numerical Methods, WNT, Warsaw (1998).

Concurrent Information Processing and Computing
D. Grigoras and A. Nicolau (Eds.)
IOS Press, 2005

Block Organization of Parallel Algorithms for Electrostatic and Electromagnetic Fields Analysis

Robert P. Bycul   Andrzej Jordan

Bialystok Technical University, Poland
Wiejska 45 D st., 15-351 Bialystok, Poland
tel. +48 85 7421651, fax +48 85 7421657
rpbyc@vela.pb.bialystok.pl, jordana@pb.bialystok.pl

Abstract. This paper describes a concept and an initial work that has been done towards a creation of a graphical environment for composing parallel algorithms. The algorithms are used for solving a system of algebraic linear equations, which results from applying one of the common methods used in simulations of electrostatic and electromagnetic fields (FEM, FDM, etc. [1]).

Building the algorithms with the use of graphical blocks simplifies the process of defining their parameters, such as a way of the data decomposition in parallel computations etc. The layout of the blocks defines the organization of the algorithm, while the parameters of the blocks define the characteristics of the algorithm.

1   Introduction

A process of a numerical simulation of electromagnetic and electrostatic fields distribution often involves (depending on the method applied for the simulation) solving a system of linear algebraic equations [1]. There are many numerical methods that can be applied to solve the system and the choice of an appropriate method depends mainly, as is known, on the structure and properties of the matrix of coefficients K (Fig. 1). Once the method is chosen, we need to specify additional parameters of it. For instance (for iterative methods),

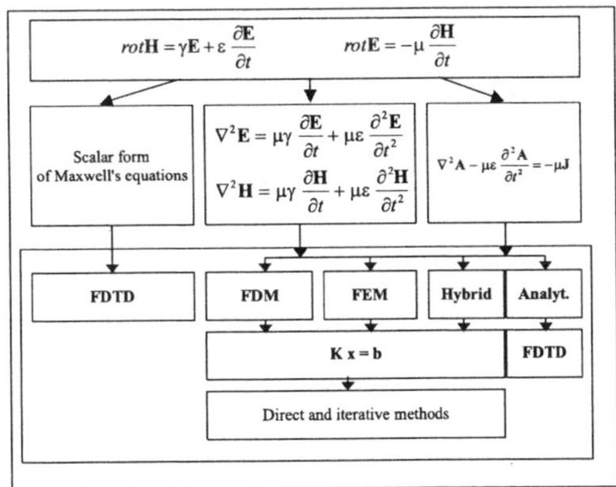

Figure 1. Methods for electromagnetic fields simulation [1].

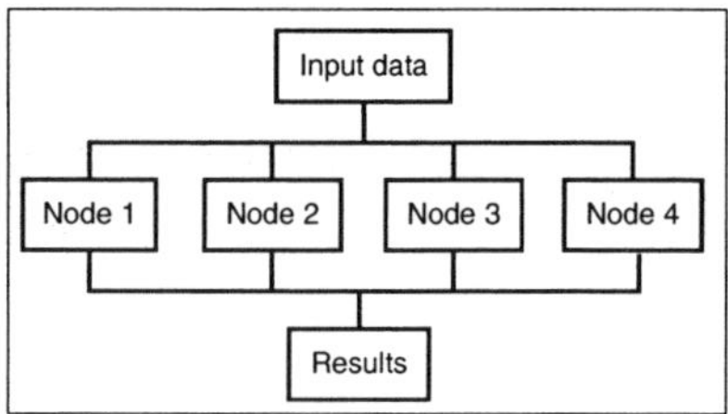

Figure 2. An example of an organization of the parallel conjugate gradient method.

there can be specified a maximal number of iterations, a value of the convergence criterion, a kind of preconditioning and so on.

For parallel implementations of the methods, additional parameters have to be defined: a number of computational nodes, a way of the data decomposition, etc.

The process of fully specifying the method can be complicated. As an aiding tool for accomplishing this task one can use a graphical environment. There are a few graphical environments that can be applied, such as GRADE [2], which is a compound system that can be used during the entire process of a parallel program design.

This paper describes an environment, designed as a parallel solver for the above mentioned system of equations. Its role is to simplify the defining and organizing of solving process by providing a user-friendly graphical interface.

2   Block organization of a parallel algorithm of a conjugate gradient method

As a first numerical method for use with the parallel solver graphical environment (PSGE), a parallel implementation of the conjugate gradient method has been chosen [3]. Fig. 2 shows an example of the computational process outline and Fig. 3 presents a view of the main program window, where a 2-node cluster model has been entered. The PSGE is a Windows$^{\circledR}$ application and it utilizes Windows'$^{\circledR}$ networking mechanisms and WMPI libraries from the Critical Software. With the use of the *System of Equations* block (Fig. 4), the user can define such parameters as the names of the input data files, the properties of the chosen numerical method, etc. The *Results* block gives a possibility of specifying the name of the file where the solution vector is to be stored. The dialog window, where the properties of this block can be entered, has also another application. After the computations are completed, there appears a chart in the window (Fig. 6). The chart represents the values of the solution vector's elements. The *Node* blocks represent computational nodes in a cluster. A node can be defined by the following parameters (Fig. 5): a computer name - this is the network name of the computer on which the process attached to the node is to be run, a location of the solver executable file - the file can be located on either the same computer, or any other computer in the cluster, in a directory that is accessible via the network. The user can also decide whether the computational data partitioning among the nodes should be determined automatically by the program, or entered manually. If it is to be determined automatically, the partitioning is performed by the solver at the beginning of the computations (see [3] for the details). After all the parameters of the blocks are defined properly and the blocks are appropriately connected, the user can start the computations. The PSGE verifies the parameters and if there are no errors in the configuration, the parallel computations in the cluster are started. After

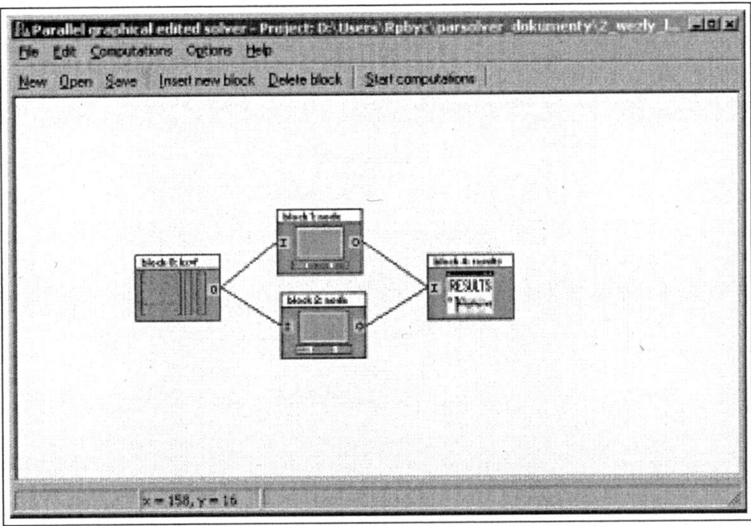

Figure 3. The main window of the PSGE.

Figure 4. The *System of Equations* dialog window.

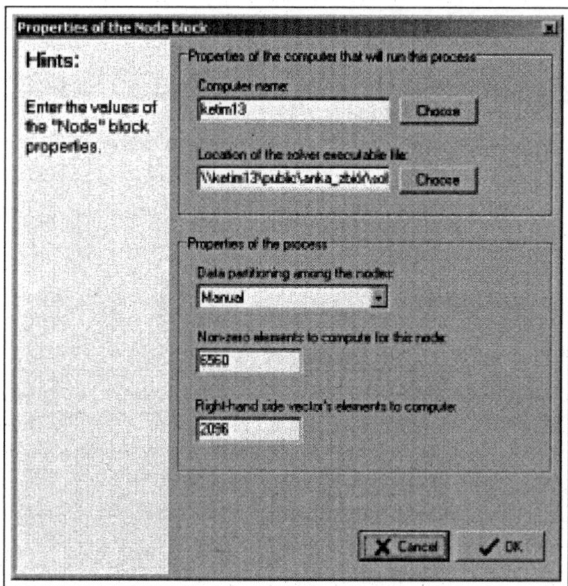

Figure 5. The *Node* dialog window.

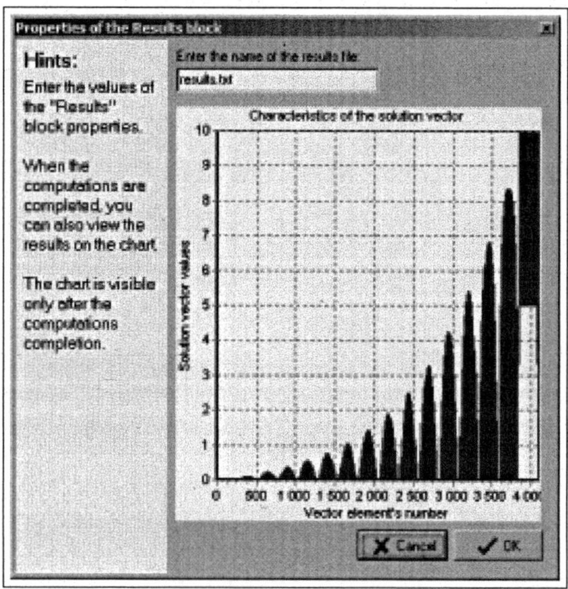

Figure 6. The *Results* dialog window.

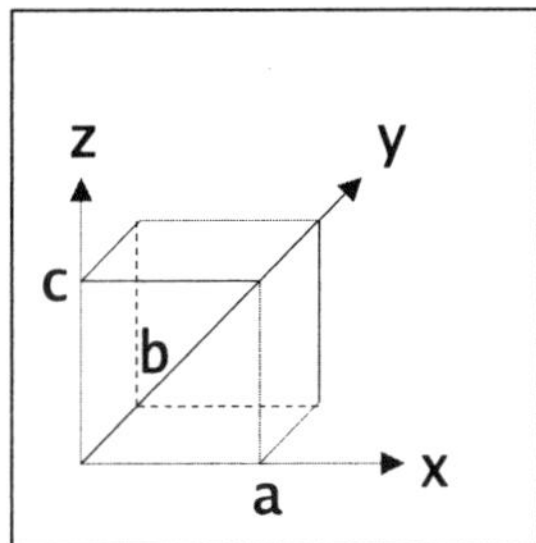

Figure 7. A cubicoid inside of which the distribution of the electrostatic potential is searched.

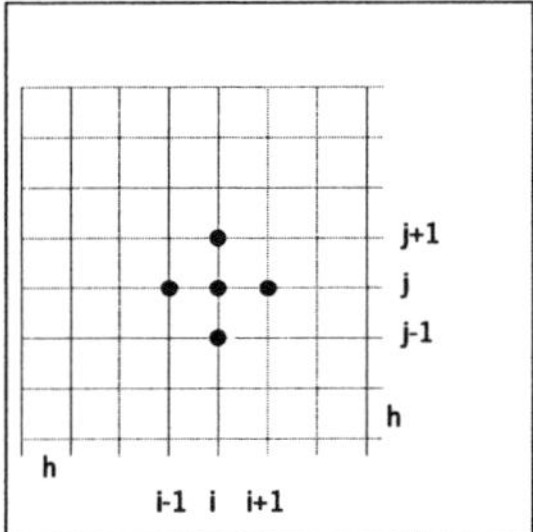

Figure 8. A fragment of the meshed cubicoid.

the computations are finished, the results are written to the previously specified file and the chart presenting the solution vector is invoked.

3 First practical approach: electrostatic potential distribution inside a cubicoid

3.1 Problem description

In the first practical approach, a simple problem with Dirichlet's boundary conditions was chosen for solving (Fig. 7). Having a cubicoid with known values of the electrostatic potential on its walls, we want to determine the function ϕ that describes the potential distribution inside the cubicoid. There are no electrical charges inside, so to solve our problem it is necessary to determine a solution of a 3D Laplace differential equation with Dirichlet's boundary conditions (1).

$$\frac{\partial^2 \phi}{\partial x^2} + \frac{\partial^2 \phi}{\partial y^2} + \frac{\partial^2 \phi}{\partial z^2} = 0 \tag{1}$$

For obtaining the numerical solution of this problem, a finite differences method can be applied. We mesh the cubicoid as is presented in Fig. 8. There is only a 2D cross-section of the cubicoid fragment presented in this figure, but the mesh is 3D (of course, this problem is such a simple one that it can be transformed into a 2D, or even 1D problem, but it was taken only for an illustration of application of the PSGE). Having the meshing performed, we see that the discretization of the Laplace equation (1) can be performed according to formula (2).

$$\frac{\partial^2 \phi}{\partial x^2} \approx \frac{\phi_{i+1,j,k} - 2\phi_{i,j,k} + \phi_{i-1,j,k}}{h^2} \tag{2}$$

Putting (2) into (1) for x, y, z coordinates respectively, we can write the equation describing a value of the electrostatic potential in an i, j, k node of the mesh:

$$\phi_{i,j,k} \approx \frac{\phi_{i+1,j,k} + \phi_{i-1,j,k} + \phi_{i,j+1,k} + \phi_{i,j-1,k} + \phi_{i,j,k+1} + \phi_{i,j,k-1}}{6} \tag{3}$$

Or, putting it another way:

$$\phi_{i+1,j,k} + \phi_{i-1,j,k} + \phi_{i,j+1,k} - 6\phi_{i,j,k} + \phi_{i,j-1,k} + \phi_{i,j,k+1} + \phi_{i,j,k-1} = 0 \tag{4}$$

Writing down the equation (4) for all of the nodes, we have:

$$K * \phi = v \tag{5}$$

where K is a matrix of coefficients of the resulting system of linear algebraic equations, ϕ is a vector of the potential values in the mesh' nodes and v is an excitation vector, here dependent on the boundary conditions.

It is necessary to realize, that putting six different constant values of the electrostatic potential as the boundary conditions on the walls of the cubicoid can lead to discontinuity of the potential value on the corners and on the edges of it. It is caused by the simplicity of the model, but it does no harm here. In a practical application one should assume appropriate functions describing the values of the electrostatic potential on the walls.

3.2 Used algorithms

As it has already been noted, the parallel implementation of the conjugate gradient method was used for solving the system (5). The parallel program has been created with the use of the WMPI libraries from the Critical Software. For now, there is one decomposition method available, so the computational nodes can be connected in one way, as presented in Fig. 2 and Fig. 3. The decomposition method, along with the other details related to the applied algorithm, are described in [4] and [5].

3.3 Obtained results

The program has been implemented on a homogeneous cluster consisting of 5 PCs based on Intel processors, connected via an Ethernet 100Base-T network. Fig. 9 presents obtained speedup for 4 sizes of the problem. There has also been tested the same version of the solver, but without the graphical environment, on the SR-2201 (Hitachi) supercomputer. The speedup obtained from this implementation is presented in Fig. 10.

4 Conclusions

Looking at the obtained speedups, we can see that the speedup in the cluster implementation is below one for all of the analyzed sizes of the problem. It is caused by the large amount of

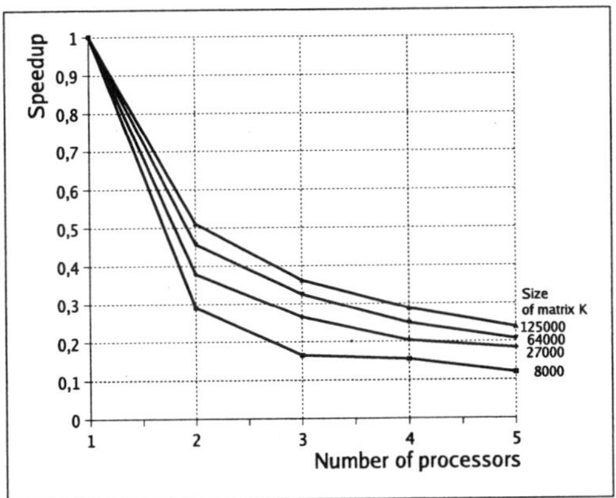

Figure 9. A speedup obtained from the program implementation in a cluster.

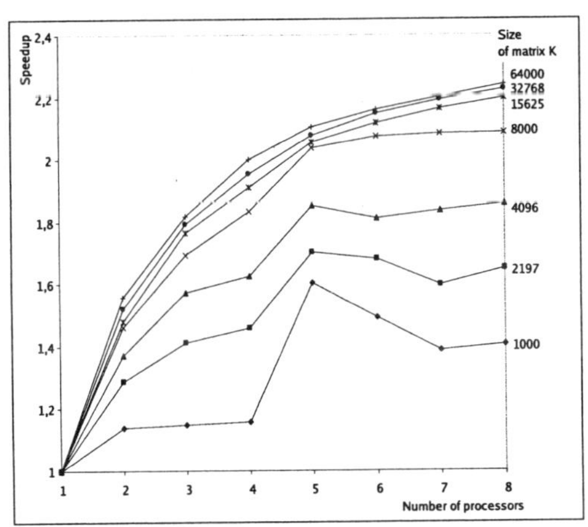

Figure 10. A speedup obtained from the program implementation on the SR-2201 (Hitachi) supercomputer.

data being transmitted between processors during the parallel computations in relation to the amount of computations.

The parallel version of the conjugate gradient method applied here is based on computing in parallel only the most time-consuming operations in the algorithm: a matrix-vector multiplication and a vector inner product [3]. There are only non-zero elements of the matrix K stored in the computers' memory during the process of computations. Knowing this, the processors should only exchange that elements of the vectors (vectors that are used in the matrix-vector multiplication operations), which are not multiplied by zeros from the matrix. It was neglected in this version of the parallel algorithm and this is one of the probable causes of such a low speedup values.

On the other hand, looking at the values of the speedup obtained from the SR-2201 implementation (Fig. 10), we see that for the same program we have better results: all the values are above 1. It only represents known fact that in the case of algorithms that utilize a lot of communication between processors the bandwidth of the network connecting the computational nodes becomes critical. It is, of course, disadvantage of the algorithm presented here, so it will be the first step towards improving it.

Choosing appropriate algorithms for solving particular problems and defining their parameters with the use of graphical blocks (or, generally speaking, a graphical user interface) can simplify the process of building the parallel solver of the system of linear algebraic equations. It lets the users who are not familiar with parallel programming utilize parallel computations in practice. Here the first results of the work have been presented. The main aim of the research is to create a graphical parallel solver environment. The solver is meant to be equipped with a few distinct parallel algorithms for solving the systems of equations, so that the user could choose an appropriate algorithm depending on the structure and properties of the matrix of coefficients.

Although the presented speedup values in the cluster do not encourage applying parallel computations, it needs to be noted that the algorithms can be further optimized towards improving the speedup and that even having the speedup values below one, we can utilize parallel computations for solving huge problems – that would not fit in a single machine's RAM.

This work has been done in the frame of the Bialystok Technical University grant no. S/WE/3/03.

References

[1] A. Jordan, Theoretical background of parallel electromagnetic field computations, International Journal of Applied Electromagnetics and Mechanics **13** (2001/2002) 393–398.

[2] P. Kacsuk, Parallel program development and execution in the grid, Proceedings of the International Conference on Parallel Computing in Electrical Engineering (PARELEC), Warsaw, (2002) 131–138.

[3] R. Bycul, A. Jordan, M. Cichomski, A new version of conjugate gradient method parallel implementation, Proceedings of the International Conference on Parallel Computing in Electrical Engineering (PARELEC), Warsaw, (2002) 318–322.

[4] A. Jordan, R.P. Bycul, The parallel algorithm of conjugate gradient method, NATO Advanced Research Workshop proceedings, Mangalia, Romania, (2001).

[5] Jianming Jin, The finite element method in electromagnetics, John Wiley, New York, (1993).

Concurrent Information Processing and Computing
D. Grigoras and A. Nicolau (Eds.)
IOS Press, 2005

287

Evaluation of the Parallel Algorithms of the FDTD Method with the "Stripes" Decomposition of the Space Domain

Wojciech Walendziuk[1]   Jaroslaw Forenc[1]   Andrzej Jordan[2]

[1]*Bialystok Technical University, Faculty of Electrical Engineering*
Wiejska 45D Street, 15-351 Bialystok, POLAND
tel. +48-85 742-16-51, fax +48-85 742-16-57
{walenw, jarekf}@pb.bialystok.pl
[2]*Polish-Japanese Institute of Information Technology*
Koszykowa 86 Street, 02-008 Warsaw, POLAND
tel. +48-22 621-03-73
jordana@pjwstk.edu.pl

Abstract. The FDTD (*Finite-Difference Time-Domain*) method is often used in the numerical analysis of the high frequency electromagnetic fields. This paper shows parallel algorithms of this method which are based on the "stripes" decomposition of the computation space domain. These algorithms are presented in two ways: a two-dimensional and a three-dimensional one. Other issue discussed in this paper is a description of communications among computation nodes and the efficiency of the parallel algorithms in a cluster of PCs.

1 Introduction

The last decades brought fast development of informational technology which increased interest in numerical simulation methods of physical phenomena. Research concerning the influence of electromagnetic fields of high frequency on living organisms can serve as an example of such computer simulations [1–3]. Among different methods of analysing the propagation of the electromagnetic fields of high frequency, the FDTD (*The Finite-Difference Time-Domain*) method is the most popular one [4–6]. Unfortunately, this method used in cases of complicated numerical models requires large operational memory and, moreover, a fast computational unit. Using parallel algorithms implemented into multiprocessor systems seems to be a good solution to the aforementioned problem. Moreover, this enables us to enlarge the finite differences grid density and increase the accuracy of numerical computations as well as its speedup. This paper presents parallel implementations of the FDTD method with the "stripes" decomposition of the analysed area. The algorithms were created in two versions: a two-dimensional TM (*Transverse Magnetic*) case implemented in a homogenous cluster system, and a three-dimensional case implemented in a heterogeneous cluster system. The presented algorithms were tested in order to examine their efficiency and to check the data exchange among the computational nodes. The obtained speedups of both algorithms, and bandwidths of the networks are presented in this paper.

2 The parallel implementation of the FDTD method

The finite differences method (FDTD) is directly used to calculate the time form of the Maxwell curl equations which provides us with the opportunity to examine the electromagnetic fields varied in time. This method allows these equations to be solved in the time and space domains simultaneously. For an isotropic environment, in which an electromagnetic wave spreads, Maxwell equations take up the following form:

$$\nabla \times \vec{H} = \sigma \vec{E} + \varepsilon \frac{\delta \vec{E}}{\delta t} \qquad \nabla \times \vec{E} = -\mu \frac{\delta \vec{H}}{\delta t} \tag{1}$$

where:
- $\vec{E}$ - vector of the electric field intensity [V/m],
- $\vec{H}$ - vector of the magnetic field intensity [A/m],
- μ - magnetic permeability [H/m],
- σ - electric conductivity [S/m],
- ε - electric permittivity [F/m].

In [4], K.S.Yee proposed an algorithm for numerical realisation of computation. Maxwell equations of the scalar form are then transformed into a differential form according to the Yee cell construction. Particular components of electric $\vec{E}(E_x, E_y, E_z)$ and magnetic $\vec{H}(H_x, H_y,$ field intensity vectors are placed in such cells (Fig.1).

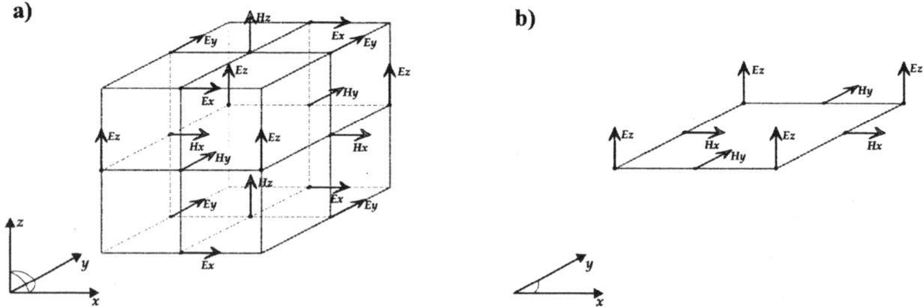

Figure 1. Proper location of the components of the electric and magnetic field intensity vectors in an elementary Yee cell for the three-dimensional case (a) and the two-dimensional TM (*Transverse Magnetic*) case (b).

It is worth stressing that Mur's [7], Mei's [8], PML (*Perfectly Matched Layer*) [9, 10] or other absorbing boundary conditions (ABC) should be applied on the edges of the examined area (in the two-dimensional case) or the surfaces edging this area (in the three-dimensional case).

The parallel algorithms research was conducted in the Master-Slave topology. In such cases the Master computer (e.g. in a cluster) initiates the computation process and the Slave computers take the role of independent computation nodes equipped with the same algorithm. The general course of the computation process may be presented as follows:

1. Master node: sends data to the computation nodes.
2. Slave nodes: receive data initiating computations.
3. Slave nodes: memorize data needed for computations $\vec{E}$ components of the Mur's ABC.
4. Slave nodes: compute the electric intensity components $\vec{E}$.
5. Slave nodes: compute $\vec{E}$ components of the Mur's ABC.
6. Slave nodes: compute the magnetic intensity components $\vec{H}$.
7. Slave nodes: exchange the data between neighbouring computations nodes.
8. Slave nodes: record the obtained results at the end of computations.

In the parallel algorithm the Master node sends the initiation data and a start signal to the Slave nodes (Fig.2). After that it will have a supervisory role. The computation process then consists of two stages: 1) the electric field intensity vector elements $\vec{E}$ are calculated in the even time step and 2) the magnetic field intensity vector elements $\vec{H}$ are calculated in the odd one. Before the electric field $\vec{E}$ components are calculated, there is a need to memorize a part of previous data necessary for establishing Mur's absorbing boundary conditions. Then the data exchange between processors takes place. The computation process stops after N steps, and selected results are later recorded on local Slave hard disks. Note, that the two-dimensional (*Transverse Magnetic*) case computations refer only to the electric field intensity component E_z, and magnetic field intensity components H_x, H_y.

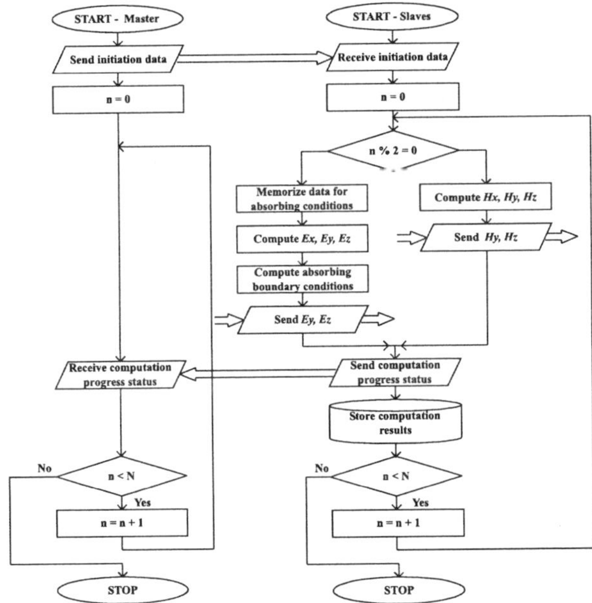

Figure 2. Parallel algorithm of the FDTD method of the three-dimensional case.

2.1 A two-dimensional algorithm of the FDTD TM (Transverse Magnetic case) method in a homogenous cluster system

In a parallel algorithm of the two-dimensional FDTD method the space domain was divided into "stripes" [11,12]. Such decomposition is based on the division of the examined area into smaller parts in which communication takes place only on the parallel edges of the division. Particular nodes conduct parallel computations, and then exchange the data needed to initiate the next computation step. As Fig.3 shows, the magnetic intensity components H_y data exchange (the blue arrows) occurs in the first step, and - the exchange of the electric intensity components E_z (the red arrows) follows. During computations in a homogenous cluster system, the subareas computed in particular nodes are of the same size. Therefore, the quantity of the data exchanged among nodes during their communication is equal (Fig.3).

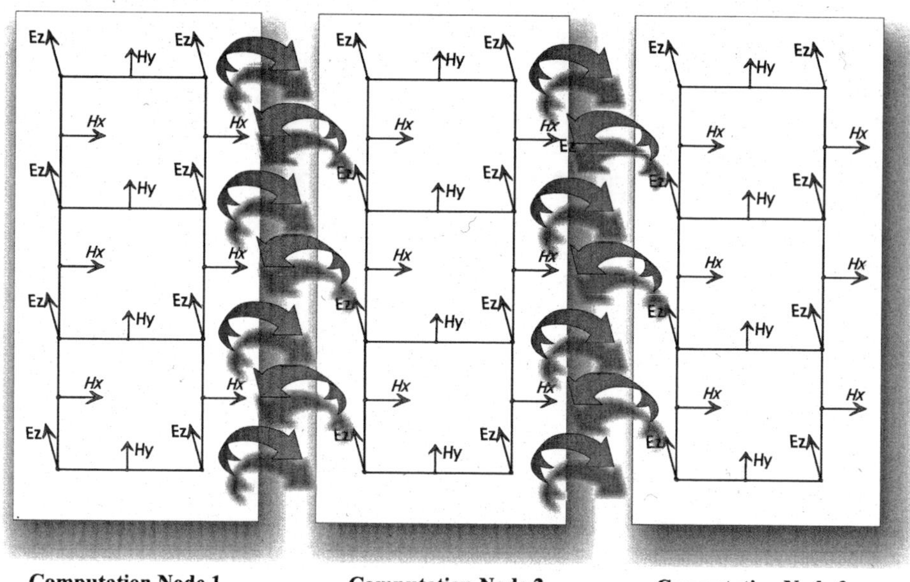

Figure 3. The "stripes" decomposition with the communication data exchange.

Seven identical PC units were used for the computations (six computation nodes + one control unit). Each node was equipped with an Intel Pentium II 866MHz processor and 128MB RAM memory. The computations were conducted in the Microsoft Windows ME operational system with the use of the WMPI 1.2 communication library [13]. The computers used during the research were connected by the Ethernet 10Mbps (the real achieved transfer was 2Mbps). This connection significantly aggravates the efficiency of parallel algorithms' work. However, its application was determined by the fact that for everyday usage those computers constitute the equipment of a didactic laboratory. While evaluating the efficiency of the proposed parallel algorithm it was observed that the speedups, defined as the coefficient of algorithm computation time made on a single sequential machine to the time needed by a multiprocessor system, rises with the increase of the number of the finite differences nodes. With a grid density of 1500x1500 Yee cells, the achieved speedup was 4.8 times for six computation nodes and one control node (Fig.4).

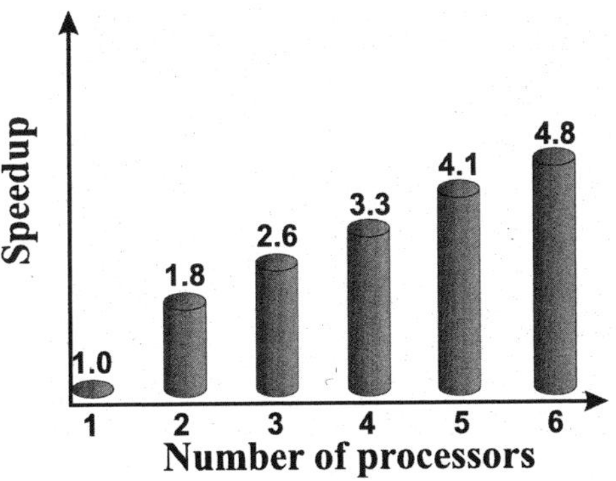

Figure 4. The "stripes" algorithm speedups.

2.2　A three-dimensional algorithm of the FDTD method in a heterogeneous cluster system

The next phase of the research was to create a three-dimensional implementation of the FDTD method shown in Fig.5. In this algorithm the magnetic field intensity components H_y and H_z are sent to the left "neighbour" [14, 15]. During the next time step activity of the algorithm, the electric field intensity components E_y and E_z, which are already calculated, are sent to the right "neighbour". The remaining components - E_x and H_x - do not have to be sent, considering the construction of the K.S.Yee algorithm used in the FDTD method.

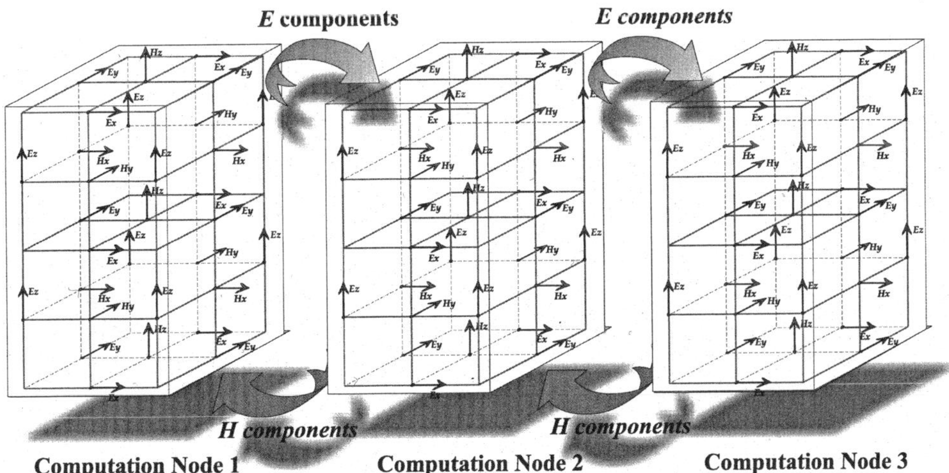

Figure 5. The "slice" decomposition with the data exchange.

Table 1. The basic parameter of the heterogeneous cluster system nodes.

Node type	Processor type	RAM memory
Master	Intel Pentium III 350MHz	128MB
Slave 1	Intel Celeron 400MHz	128MB
Slave 2	Intel Pentium 200MMX	64MB
Slave 3	Intel Pentium III 650MHz	256MB
Slave 4	Intel Pentium III 550MHz	128MB
Slave 5	Intel Pentium III 733MHz	128MB
Slave 6	Intel Pentium III 350MHz	128MB

The research was conducted in a heterogeneous cluster system working under the Microsoft Windows 2000 operational system, consisting of seven PCs (six computation nodes + one control unit). The basic parameters of the cluster nodes are presented in Table1.

The choice of the operational system was determined mainly by the computers assignment - not only are they used for the scientific purpose, but also for the everyday didactic work. The computers were connected with the use of Fast Ethernet 100Mbps by the Intel 520T switch. The maximum bandwidth of the data transmission in this network accounts for about 62Mbps. Therefore, the system is fast enough to conduct numerical computations. Similarly to the previously discussed two-dimensional case, the WMPI communication library was used. The presented algorithm was tested on the system consisting of 216000 Yee cells of the $d_x=d_y=d_z=0.02$m dimension.

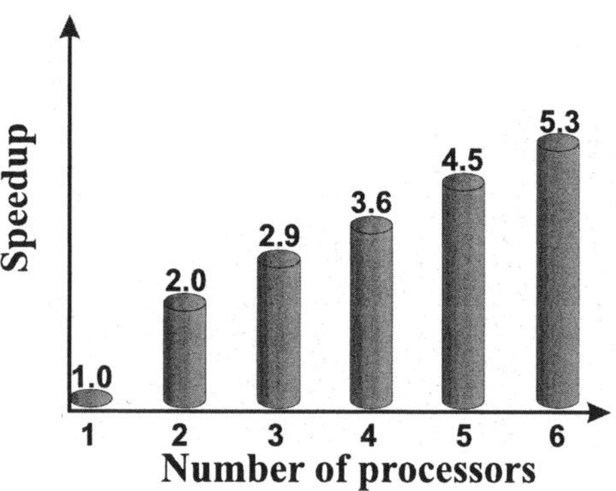

Figure 6. The computation speedups in the three-dimensional FDTD method.

Obviously, it is not the maximum size of a finite differences grid density that can be examined. A selected model was only used for the algorithm efficiency evaluation. Fig.6. shows the achieved speedups. For the six computation processors it accounted for about 5.3.

3 Conclusions

The use of parallel computers or personal computers connected into cluster systems gives the opportunity to accelerate the time of computations. In situation when links among the computation nodes have large bandwidth, great speed is possible. Another important advantage is the possibility to enlarge the examined area, even to the size limited by the capacity of the operational memory of all the nodes working in the cluster. The parallel algorithm examination brought satisfying speedup results. Moreover, the speedups themselves were increasing together with the enlargement of the examined area in particular nodes. It was connected with the fact of sending large amounts of data among the nodes in slow Ethernet systems. Therefore, the coefficient of the computation time to the communication time appears to be significant. As a consequence, better speedup results can be expected in a case when faster cluster system or parallel supercomputer is used.

References

[1] Watanabe S., Taki M., Nojima T., Fujiwara O.: Characteristic of the SAR Distributions in a Head Exposed to Electromagnetic Fields Radiated by a Hand-Held Portable Radio. IEEE Transactions on Microwave Theory and Techniques, Vol. 44, No. 10, October 1996, pp. 1874-1883.

[2] Gandhi O.P., Lazzi G., Furse C.M.: Electromagnetic Absorption in the Human Head and Neck for Mobile Telephones at 835 and 1900 MHz. IEEE Transactions on Microwave Theory and Techniques, Vol. 44, No. 10, October 1996, pp. 1884-1897.

[3] Okoniewski M., Stuchly M.A.: A Study of the Handest Antenna and Human Body Interaction. IEEE Transactions on Microwave Theory and Techniques, Vol. 44, No. 10, October 1996, pp.1855-1864.

[4] Yee K.S.: Numerical Solution of Initial Boundary Value Problems Involving Maxwell's Equations in Isotropic Media, IEEE Transactions on Antennas and Propagation, vol. AP-14, No. 3, 1966, pp. 302-307.

[5] Taflove A., Hagness S. C.: Computational Electrodynamics, The Finite - Difference Time - Domain Method. Boston, Artech House, Inc. 2000.

[6] Kunz K.S., Luebbers R.J.: The Finite Difference Time Domain Method for Electromagnetics, Boca Raton, CRC Press, Inc. 1993.

[7] Mur G.: Absorbing Boundary Conditions for the Finite Difference Approximation of the Time-Domain Electromagnetic-Field Equations, IEEE Transactions on Electromagnetic Compatibility, vol. EMC-23, No. 4, 1981, pp. 377-382.

[8] Mei K.K., Fang J.: Superabsorption - A Method to Improve Absorbing Boundary Conditions. IEEE Transactions on Antennas and Propagation, Vol. 40, No. 9, 1992, pp. 1001-1010.

[9] Berenger J.P.: A perfectly matched layer for the absorption of electromagnetic waves, Journal of Computational Physics, Vol.114, No. 2, 1994, pp. 185-200.

[10] Berenger J.P.: Three-Dimensional Perfectly Matched Layer for the Absorption of Electromagnetic Waves, Journal of Computational Physics, Vol. 127, 1996, pp. 363-379.

[11] Walendziuk W., Forenc J.: Decomposition of the computation area in the parallel implementation of the FDTD algorithm, ISPDC'2002, Informatica Tomul XI, July 17-20, 2002, "Al.I.Cuza" University of Iasi, 2002, pp. 180-192.

[12] Walendziuk W.: SAR and thermal computations with the use of parallel FDTD algorithm, PARELEC'2002, Warsaw, September 22-25, 2002, Polish-Japanese Institute of Information Technology, IEEE, Los Alamitos, 2002, pp. 282-287.

[13] `http://www.criticalsoftware.com/hpc/`

[14] Forenc J., Skorek A.: Analysis of High Frequency Electromagnetic Wave Propagation Using Parallel MIMD Computer and Cluster System, PARELEC'2000 - International Conference on Parallel Computing in Electrical Engineering, Trois-Riveres, Canada, 2000, pp. 176-180.

[15] Walendziuk W., Forenc J.: Application of the Cluster System in the High Frequency Electromagnetic Field Analysis, 8th Scientific-Technical Conference on Computer Application in Electrical Engineering - ZKwE'2001, Poznan/Kiekrz, Poland, April 23-25, 2001, pp. 131-134 (in Polish).

Acknowledgements *The work has been sponsored by KBN grant 4T11C 007 22 and an internal PJIIT research grant.*

Concurrent Information Processing and Computing
D. Grigoras and A. Nicolau (Eds.)
IOS Press, 2005

An $O(n^2)$ Parallel Algorithm for the Maximum Flow Problem

Sabin Tabirca*   Tatiana Tabirca+

** Corresponding Author, + Supported by the Boole Centre for Research in Informatics, UCC*
University College Cork, Department of Computer Science, BCRI
College Road, Cork, Ireland – s.tabirca@cs.ucc.ie

Abstract. The aim of this article is to present a new parallel algorithm for the maximum flow problem. The algorithm is obtained by using the parallel *Divide and Conquer* computation for the *In-Out Rebalancing Flow* method. The complexity of this algorithm is $O(n^2)$ when a PRAM machine with $p = O(m)$ processors is used.

1   Introduction

Network flow problems are major problems in operational research, computer science and engineering. Among these the maximum flow problem is the most important one having several real world and theoretical applications. Since Ford and Fulkerson [5] introduced the maximum flow problem, much work has been done to develop efficient algorithms.

In the following the maximum flow problem is reviewed and some important parallel solutions are outlined. More detailed information about this subject can be found in [1]. Let $R = (G = (V, A), s, t, c)$ be a network where $s, t \in V$ are two special nodes; s is the source node and t is the sink node of the network R. The function $c : A \to (0, \infty)$ is the capacity function, where $c(a)$ is the capacity of the arc a. Let us suppose that $|V| = n$ and $|A| = m$.

Definition 2. *An application $f : A \to [0, \infty)$ is a flow R if the following equations are true:*

$$0 \leq f(a) \leq c(a), \forall a \in A \tag{1}$$

$$\sum_{a \in A^+(i)} f(a) - \sum_{a \in A^-(i)} f(a) = 0, \forall i \in V - \{s, t\} \tag{2}$$

In this case $v(f) = \sum_{a \in A^+(s)} f(a) - \sum_{a \in A^-(s)} f(a)$ is the value of the flow f.

A flow that maximises the value of flow is called a maximal flow, thus f^* is maximal if and only if $max\{v(f) | f \text{ flow in } R\} = v(f^*)$. The maximal flow problem can be formulated as follows:

"**Given a network** $R = (G = (V, A), s, t, c)$ **find the maximum flow** f^*".

From parallel computation point of view, the maximum flow problem belongs to the P-complete class [4]. Although this problem has an inherent sequential character, many parallel algorithms have been developed so far. The first parallel algorithm was proposed by Shiloach and Vishkin [6] and its complexity is $O(n^2 \cdot \log n)$ for $p = O(n)$ processors. This algorithm was based on the Karzanov preflow method and uses the PS-tree structure.

Goldberg [2], [3] has done important work on this direction. He proposed the most efficient parallel algorithms [3] by using the highest labeling distance method. Two algorithms were obtained based on sophisticated data structures. The complexity of these algorithms are $O\left(n^2 \cdot \log\left((2 \cdot \frac{m}{n} + p) \cdot \sqrt{m}\right)\right)$ and $O\left(n^2 \cdot \log\left(n \cdot \frac{\sqrt{m}}{p}\right)\right)$ for a PRAM machine with $p = O(\sqrt{m})$. These results prove that the maximum flow problem can be solved using parallel computation. Another important remark is the complexity of these solutions is around $O(n^2 \cdot \log n)$ for a PRAM machine with $O(n)$.

The *In-Out Rebalancing Flow* method was introduced by Tabirca in [7] and further developed in [8]. Two sequential algorithms were developed to compute the maximum flow based on this method. The first algorithm [7] has the complexity equal to $O(n^2 \cdot m)$. The second algorithm [8] reduces the complexity from $O(n^2 \cdot m)$ to $O(n \cdot m \cdot \log n)$ by using *Divide and Conquer*. These solutions use a sequence of layered networks to compute the maximum flow. For each layered network an admissible flow is found such that there is node, which transports as much flow as it can.

The idea of this method is to set the flow along each arc a equal to the capacity of a and after that to re-balance the flow for all the nodes which do not satisfy Equation (2). The node i is active if $P_{out}(i) = \sum_{a \in A^+(i)} f(a) \neq \sum_{a \in A^-(i)} f(a) = P_{in}(i)$. The rebalancing of flow for the active node i is done by adjusting the biggest flow as follows:

if $P_{out}(i) > P_{in}(i)$ **then**
> **for all** $a \in A^+(i)$ **do** $f(a) := f(a) \cdot \frac{P_{in}(i)}{P_{out}(i)}$;

if $P_{out}(i) < P_{in}(i)$ **then**
> **for all** $a \in A^-(i)$ **do** $f(a) := f(a) \cdot \frac{P_{out}(i)}{P_{in}(i)}$;

Note that the flow along outgoing or incoming arcs is adjusted by multiplying with the same number. Therefore, this adjusting operation can be easely done in parallel.

2 The Parallel Algorithm

In this section, a parallel algorithm for the maximum flow computation is proposed. Let us suppose that a **PRAM** machine with $p = O(m)$ is used. Firstly, we developed a parallel algorithm for computing an admissible flow in a layered network with multiple sources and sinks. Secondly, this algorithm is applied to find the maximum flow in a general network.

2.1 The Parallel Algorithm for a LNMSS

The algorithm uses the parallel *Divide and Conquer* technique for computing the flow in a layered network with multiple sources and sinks (a **LNMSS**). Let $SR = (G = (S_1 \cup S_2 \cup \ldots \cup S_q, E_1 \cup E_2 \cup \ldots \cup E_{q-1}), x, y, c)S$ be a **LNMSS** with q layers. This network has the following elements:

- $G = (S_1 \cup S_2 \cup \ldots \cup S_q, E_1 \cup E_2 \cup \ldots \cup E_{q-1})$ - the support graph for which $E_i \subseteq S_i \cup S_{i+1}$.

- $c : E_1 \cup E_2 \cup \ldots \cup E_{q-1} \to (0, \infty)$ - the capacity function.

- $x : S_1 \to [0, \infty)$ - the source flow potential; $x(s)$ - the potential of the source node $s \in S_1$.

- $y : S_q \rightarrow [0, \infty)$ - the sink flow potential; $y(t)$ - the potential of the sink node $t \in S_q$.

Therefore, **LNMSS** networks represent a generalisation of layered networks such that there are multiple source and sink nodes. A simple layered network

$$R = (G = (S_1 \cup S_2 \cup ... \cup S_q, E_1 \cup E_2 \cup ... \cup E_{q-1}), c)$$

is a **LNMSS** network for which $S_1 = \{s\}$, $S_q = \{t\}$, $x(s) = \sum_{i:a=(s,i)\in E_1} c(a)$ and $y(t) = \sum_{i:a=(i,t)\in E_{q-1}} c(a)$.

Definition 3. *A function $f : E_1 \cup E_2 \cup ... \cup E_{q-1} \rightarrow [0, \infty)$ is named flow in the LNMSS R if*

$$0 \leq f(e) \leq c(e), \forall e \in \cup_{l=1}^{q-1} E_l \tag{3}$$

$$\sum_{j:a=(i,j)\in E_k} f(a) - \sum_{j:a=(j,i)\in E_{k-1}} f(a) = 0, \forall i \in \cup_{l=2}^{q-1} S_l \tag{4}$$

$$\sum_{j:a=(s,j)\in E_1} f(a) \leq x(s), \forall s \in S_1 \tag{5}$$

$$\sum_{i:a=(i,t)\in E_{q-1}} f(a) \leq y(t), \forall t \in S_q \tag{6}$$

For the **LNMSS** network

$$R = (G = (S_1 \cup S_2 \cup ... \cup S_q, E_1 \cup E_2 \cup ... \cup E_{q-1}), x, y, c)$$

we can define the sub-network $R_{l,r}$ as follows:

$$R_{l,r} = (G_{l,r}, PC_{in}(S_l), PC_{out}(S_r), c_{l,r}),$$

which is the **LNMSS** network made with the support graph $G_{l,r} = (S_l \cup ... \cup S_r, E_l \cup ... \cup E_{r-1})$. For this network the functions x, y are given by the in-capacity potentials

$$PC_{in}(i) = \sum_{j:a=(j,i)\in E_{l-1}} c(a), \quad i \in S_l$$

and by the out-capacity potentials

$$PC_{out}(i) = \sum_{j:a=(i,j)\in E_r} c(a), \quad i \in S_r.$$

More information about capacity potentials, flow potentials can be found in [8].

An admissible flow in the **LNMSS** $R_{l,r}$ is found by *Divide and Conquer* as follows:

- If **LNMSS** contains only the layers S_l and S_r then the flow is directly sent along the arcs of the set E_l.

- Find the layer S_{mid} from the middle

- Compute in parallel the admissible flow in the networks $R_{l,mid}$ and $R_{mid+1,r}$.

- Send the flow along the arcs of the set E_{mid}.

- Perform in parallel:

      Rebalance the flow in $S_{mid}, ..., S_l$.

      Rebalance the flow in $S_{mid+1}, ..., S_r$.

The parallel algorithm is detailed in the following.

procedure Flow_Parallel(l, r, c, f);
begin
if $l + 1 = r$ **then begin**
    for all $a \in E_l$ **pardo** $f(a) := c(a)$;
    for all $a = (s, s1) \in E_l$ **pardo**
      if $P_{in}(s) < P_{out}(s)$ **then** $f(a) := f(a)\frac{P_{in}(s)}{P_{out}(s)}$;
    for all $a = (s1, s) \in E_l$ **pardo**
      if $P_{in}(s) > P_{out}(s)$ **then** $f(a) := f(a)\frac{P_{out}(s)}{P_{in}(s)}$;
    for all $a = (s1, s2) \in E_l$ **pardo**
      if $(P_{in}(s1) > P_{out}(s1)) \wedge (P_{in}(s2) < P_{out}(s2)) \wedge (f(a) < c(a))$ **then**
            $f(a) := \min\{P_{in}(s1) - P_{out}(s1),\ P_{out}(s2) - P_{in}(s2), c(a) -$
$f(a)\}$;
  end;
  $mid := (l + r)/2$;
  pardo begin
        Flow_Parallel(l, mid, c, f); Flow_Parallel(mid+1, r, c, f);
  end;
  for all $a \in E_{mid}$ **pardo** $f(a) = c(a)$;
  for all $a = (s, s1) \in E_{mid}$ **pardo**
    if $P_{in}(s) < P_{out}(s)$ **then** $f(a) := f(a)\frac{P_{in}(s)}{P_{out}(s)}$;
  for all $a = (s1, s) \in E_{mid}$ **pardo**
    if $P_{in}(s) > P_{out}(s)$ **then** $f(a) := f(a)\frac{P_{out}(s)}{P_{in}(s)}$;
  for all $a = (s1, s2) \in E_{mid}$ **pardo**
    if $(P_{in}(s1) > P_{out}(s1)) \wedge (P_{in}(s2) < P_{out}(s2)) \wedge (f(a) < c(a))$**then**
        $f(a) := \min\{P_{in}(s1) - P_{out}(s1),\ P_{out}(s2) - P_{in}(s2), c(a) - f(a)\}$;
  pardo begin
    for $j := mid$ **downto** l **do**
      for all $a = (s1, s) \in E_j$ **pardo**
        if $P_{in}(s) > P_{out}(s)$ **then** $f(a) := f(a)\frac{P_{out}(s)}{P_{in}(s)}$;
    for $j := mid$ **to** r **do**
      for all $a = (s1, s) \in E_j$ **pardo**
        if $P_{in}(s) < P_{out}(s)$ **then** $f(a) := f(a)\frac{P_{in}(s)}{P_{out}(s)}$;
  end;
end;
Tabirca [8] proved that the above computation finds an admissible flow in $R_{l,r}$ for which there is a node with the flow potential equal to the capacity potential. This means that the flow passing this node is maximal. Therefore, this node will be removed from the next layered network.

Theorem 5. *The complexity of the Flow_Parallel algorithm is $O(q)$, where q is the number of layers in $R_{r,l}$.*

Proof Let us remark that all the above parallel for loops are execute in $O(1)$ with $p = O(m)$ processors. Thus, the complexity of the algorithm Flow_Parallel does not depend on the number of nodes in each layer nor on the number of arcs between two consecutive layers. This complexity depends on only the number of the network layers.

Let t_i be the computation time of the algorithm Flow_Parallel for a network with i layers. This time satisfies the following equations:

$$t_2 = 1 \tag{7}$$

$$t_i = \max\left\{t_{\left[\frac{i-1}{2}\right]} + 1, t_{\left[\frac{i+1}{2}\right]}\right\} + \max\left\{\left[\frac{i-1}{2}\right] + 1, \left[\frac{i+1}{2}\right]\right\} + 1 \tag{8}$$

Equation (8) is rewritten as follows

$$t_i = t_{\left[\frac{i+1}{2}\right]} + \left[\frac{i+1}{2}\right] + 1.$$

Unfortunately, this equation is not linear and cannot be solved easily. For the particular case $i = 2^k$, this becomes

$$t_{2^k} = t_{2^{k-1}} + 2^{k-1} + 1 \tag{9}$$

and may be solved by using a simple summation. Its solution is given by

$$t_{2^k} = t_2 + \sum_{i=2}^{k}\left(t_{2^i} - t_{2^{i-1}}\right) = 1 + \sum_{i=2}^{k}\left(2^{i-1} + 1\right) = 2^k + k - 2.$$

Based on this formula, the complexity of the algorithm can be assessed. Let $i \in N$ be a natural number so that $2^{i-1} < q \leq 2^i$. Thus, $i = \lceil \log_2 q \rceil$. Provided that the complexity is an increasing function, we find

$$q \leq 2^i \Rightarrow t_q \leq t_{2^i} = 2^{\lceil \log_2 q \rceil} + \lceil \log_2 q \rceil - 2 = O(q).$$

Thus, the complexity of the algorithm Flow_Parallel is equal to $O(q)$.

2.2   The Parallel Algorithm for a General Network

The layered network technique is used to compute the maximum flow in the network $R = (G = (V, A), s, t, c)$. The maximal flow is found by computing an admissible flow for a sequence of layered network. The algorithm repeats the computation of the admissible flow and updates the layered network. This computation is presented in the procedure flow.

```
procedure flow(V, A, s, t, c, f);
begin
for all a ∈ A) pardo f(a) = 0;
repeat
        find the layered network  R_q = (G_q = (S_1 ∪ ... ∪ S_q, E_1 ∪ ... ∪ E_{q-1}), c_q);
        Flow_parallel(1, q, c_1, f_1);
        for all a ∈ A do f(a) := f(a) + f_1(a);
until t is not reached from s;
end.
```

	$p=1$	$p=2$	$p=4$	$p=8$	$p=16$
R_1	10.234	8.935	6.561	5.067	3.81
R_2	15.783	13.345	10.671	8.197	4.943
R_3	25.972	20.753	15.529	11.396	8.164

Table 1. Execution times for R_1, R_2, R_3.

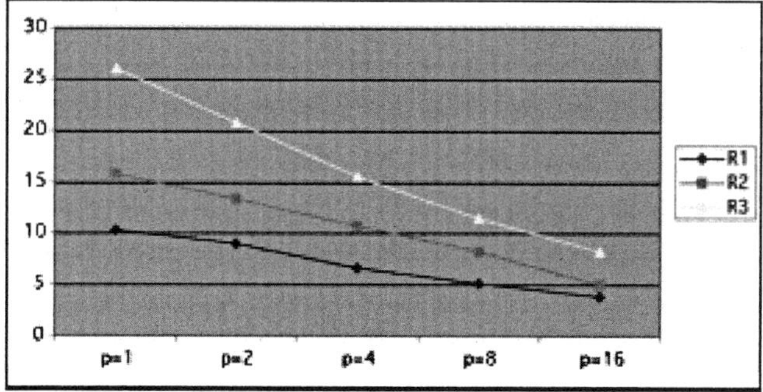

Figure 1. Execution times for R_1, R_2, R_3.

Theorem 6. *If a **PRAM** machine with $p = O(m)$ is used, then the complexity of the procedure flow is $O(n^2)$.*

Proof Suppose that the algorithm gives the sequence of flows f_i, $i = 0, ..., r$. Let q_i be the number of layers in the network $R(f_i)$, $i = 0, ..., r$. The admissible flow in $R(f_i)$ is computed by the algorithm Flow_Parallel in a complexity equal to $O(q_i)$. After that the flow f is increased and the layered network is updated. There is a node for which the admissible flow passing it is equal to its capacity potential. Therefore, that node will be removed from the new layered network $R(f_i)$ which means $q_i \leq |V(R(f_i))| \leq n - i + 1$.

Now, we have

$$\sum_{i=\overline{1,r}} q_i \leq \sum_{i=\overline{1,r}} (n - i + 1) \leq \sum_{i=\overline{1,n}} (n - i + 1) = O(n^2).$$

Thus, the complexity of the procedure flow is $O(n^2)$.

3 Numerical Results and Final Remarks

The execution of the procedure *flow* has been done on a Silicon Graphics Origin 2000 parallel machine with 16 processors (R10000, 195 MHz). It is quite difficult to make comparissons between the parallel algorithm *flow* the preflow methods developed by Goldberg [2], [3] since they use different approches.

We have decided to test the parallel algorithm *flow* on three types of networks. All of them have 1002 nodes that are connected in three different ways. The first network $R_1 = (G = (s \cup V_1 \cup V_2 \cup t, s \times V_1 \cup V_1 \times V_2 \cup V_2 \times t), s, t, c)$ has 2 intermediary layers V_1 and V_2 each of them with 500 nodes. The second network is $R_2 = (G = (s \cup V_1 \cup ... \cup V_{10} \cup t, s \times V_1 \cup V_1 \times V_2 \cup ... \cup V_9 \times V_{10} \cup V_{10} \times t), s, t, c)$ where there are 10 intermediary layers $V_1, ..., V_{10}$ each of them with 100 nodes. The third network is

$R_3 = (G = s \times K_{1000} \times t, s, t, c)$ where K_{1000} is the complete graph with 1000 nodes. The capacities c have been randomly generated between 0 and 100. The execution times on of the parallel algorithm *flow* have been also measured for each network and they are presented in Table 1 and Figure 1.

A few remarks can be made on the execution times. Firstly, the smallest times have been obtained for the network R_1 which has two intermediary layers. Secondly, the biggest execution times have been generated for the network R_3 that has the numerous number of arcs.

The maximum flow problem has been studied intensively for at least thirty years but no many parallel solutions have been proposed so far. Goldberg has done important work in this direction and proposed two efficient parallel algorithms. Unfortunately, both of them are quite complicated and use special data structures. Moreover, the complexity of these solutions was found to be $O(n^2 \cdot \log n)$ for $p = O(n)$ processors.

The algorithm proposed in this article is important from two points of view. Firstly, it is the only parallel solution of the maximum flow problem with the complexity $O(n^2)$. Secondly, this solution has been developed without using sophisticated data structures or special methods.

References

[1] R.K. Ahuja, T.L.Magnati, and J.B.Orlin, Network Flow: Theory, Algorithm and Applications, Prentice-Hall, New Jersey, (1993).

[2] A.V.Goldberg, A New Max Flow Algorithm, Technical Report MIT/LCS/TM-291, MIT, Cambridge, MA, (1985).

[3] A.V.Goldberg, Processor-Efficient Implementation of a Maximum Flow Algorithm, Information Processing Letters, **38**, (1991), 179-185.

[4] L.Goldschlager, L.Shaw and J.Staples, The Maximum Flow Problem is Log-Space Complete for P, Information Processing Letters, **10**, (1982), 105-111.

[5] L.R.Ford, and D.R.Fulkerson, Maximal Flow Through a Network, Canadian Journal of Mathematics, **8**, (1956), 399-404.

[6] Y.Shiloach and U.Vishkin, An $O(n^2 \log n)$ Parallel Max-Flow Algorithm, Journal of Algorithms, **3**, (1982), 128-144.

[7] S.Tabirca, and T.Tabirca, The In-Out Rebalancing Flow Method, Analele Univ. "A.I.Cuza" Iasi, **VIII**, (1998), 135-146.

[8] S.Tabirca, Sequential and Parallel Aspects of the Maximum Flow Problem, PhD Thesis, Brunel University, UK, (1998).

Concurrent Information Processing and Computing
D. Grigoras and A. Nicolau (Eds.)
IOS Press, 2005

Parallel Version of the Global Linearization Method

Andrzej Jordan   Pawel Myszkowski

Bialystok Technical University, Faculty of Electrical Engineering
Wiejska 45D Street, 15-351 Bialystok, POLAND
tel. +48-85 742-16-51, fax +48-85 742-16-57
jordana@pjwstk.edu.pl
pmyszkowski@vela.pb.bialystok.pl

Abstract. In the presented article a multivariable non-linear state equation system $\dot{x} = f(x, u, t)$, $x(0) = x_0$ was solved and a parallel version of the global linearization method was applied. The above method was used for the analysis of the dynamics of a DC drive system supplied by a solar generator with a non-linear characteristics.

1 Introduction

In literature we can find several linearization methods of non-linear state equations:

$$\dot{x} = f(x, u, t), x(0) = x_0 \tag{1}$$

where $x(t) \in R^n$ is the state vector, $u(t) \in R^m$ is the input vector and x_0 represents the vector of the initial conditions. The most commonly used linearization method is a Taylor's series expand $f(x, u, t)$ around the equilibrium point x_{eq}, u_{eq} [1]. For such a case the linear equation is a good approximation of Eq. (1) for small deviations $\Delta x = x - x_{eq}$ and $\Delta u = u - u_{eq}$. Another well-known method is the optimal linearization method [2] that reduces Eq. (1) to a linear equation. The method, however, is costly because it requires computations of optimal coefficients which are the elements of linear system matrix [2].

A less known method, linearizing Eq. (1) in the whole state space, is the global linearization method [4] whose parallel implementation is presented in this article. Global linearization is specified in the whole state space ($x \in R^n, t \rightarrow \infty$). We shall consider the non-linear change of coordinates [4] to obtain a system of linear equations $z(t) = Az(t) + Bv(t)$ with the new excitation $v(t) = u(t) + f(\dot{x})$. The invert transformation $\tilde{x}(t) = \phi^{-1}(z)$ specifies a state vector $\tilde{x}(t)$. This vector transformed by diffeomorphism $\tilde{x}(t) = \phi^{-1}(\phi(x))$ fulfilling a condition $\tilde{x}(t) \cong x(t)$, where $x(t)$ is a solution of the non-linear equation.

It must be noted, that several aspects of parallel analysis of non-linear state equations were presented in studies [5,6].

2   Global linearization of a non-linear model of a DC drive system

In order to practical implement of the global linearization method we use a model of non-linear DC drive system supplied by a solar generator (Fig. 1 and Fig. 2) [2, 3]. This model is described by the equation of three state variables:

$$\dot{x}_1 = -a_1 e^{ax_1} - a_2 x_2 + u$$
$$\dot{x}_2 = a_3 x_1 - a_4 x_2 - a_5 x_3$$
$$\dot{x}_3 = a_6 x_2 - a_7 x_3 \tag{2}$$
$$x_1(0) = V_p, \quad x_2(0) = 0, \quad x_3(0) = 0$$

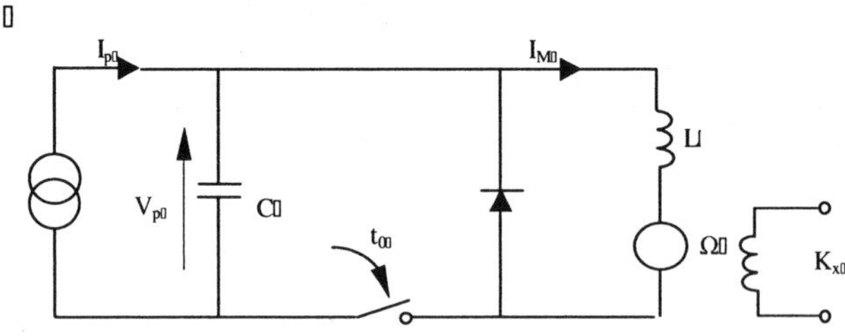

Figure 1. An electric circuit containing a solar generator and a DC motor.

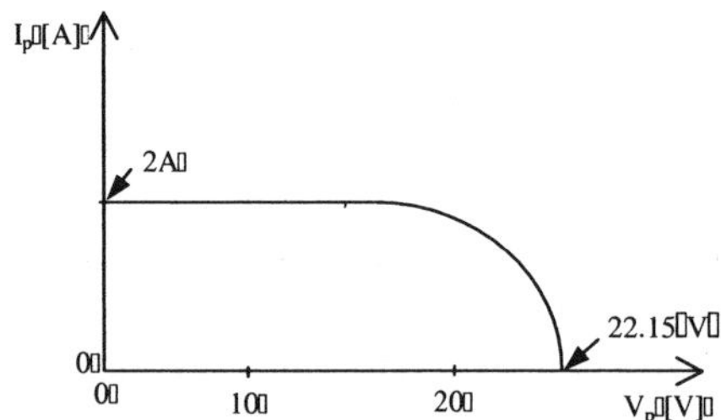

Figure 2. Non-linear characteristics of the solar generator.

where $x_1 = V_p$ is the generator voltage, $x_2 = I_M$ is the rotor current, and $x_3 = \Omega$ is the motor rotational speed and

$$a_1 = \frac{I_s}{C}, \quad a_2 = \frac{1}{C}, \quad a_3 = \frac{1}{L}, \quad a_4 = \frac{R_m}{L}$$
$$a_5 = \frac{K_s}{L}, \quad a_6 = \frac{K_x}{I}, \quad a_7 = \frac{K_R}{I}, \quad u = \frac{I_0 + I_s}{C} \tag{3}$$

Numerical data:

$$I_(0) = 2A, \quad R_M = 12.045\Omega, \quad K_x = 0.5Vs, \quad I_s = 1.28*10^{-5}A,$$
$$L = 0.1H, \quad K_R = 0.1Vs^2, \quad a = 0.54V^{-1}, \quad C = 500\mu F, \tag{4}$$
$$J = 10^{-3}Ws^3, \quad V_{p,0} = 22.15V$$

K_x and K_r are parameters of the DC motor, while "a" is the solar cell parameter, the voltage-current characteristics of which is as follows:

$$I_p = I_0 - I_s(e^{aV_p} - 1). \tag{5}$$

The following replacement of variables $(z = \phi(x))$ is introduced [4]:

$$
\begin{aligned}
z_1 &= x_3 \\
z_2 &= a_6 x_2 - a_7 x_3 \\
z_3 &= a_6 \dot{x}_2 - a_7 \dot{x}_3 = b_1 x_1 - b_2 x_2 - b_3 x_3 \\
z_1(0) &= 0, \quad z_2(0) = 0, \quad z_3(0) = b_1 V_p, 0 \\
b_1 &= a_3 a_6, b_2 = a_4 a_6 + a_2 a_6, b_3 = a_6 a_5 - a_7^2
\end{aligned}
\tag{6}
$$

On making the basic transformations of equation (6) we obtain a system of linear differential equations:

$$
\begin{bmatrix} \dot{z}_1 \\ \dot{z}_2 \\ \dot{z}_3 \end{bmatrix} =
\begin{bmatrix} 0 & 1 & 0 \\ 0 & 0 & 1 \\ k_1 & k_2 & -k_3 \end{bmatrix}
\begin{bmatrix} z_1 \\ z_2 \\ z_3 \end{bmatrix} +
\begin{bmatrix} 0 \\ 0 \\ 1 \end{bmatrix} v
\tag{7}
$$

where

$$
v = b_1 u - c_4 e^{a x_1}
\tag{8}
$$

and

$$
c_4 = b_1 a_1 = a_1 a_3 a_6
\tag{9}
$$

$$
k_1 = -a_2 a_3 a_7, k_2 = -(a_2 a_3 + a_4 a_7 + a_5 a_6), k_3 = a_4 + a + 7
\tag{10}
$$

The original state vector x is determined by means of inverse transformation $x = \phi^{-1}(z)$:

$$
\begin{bmatrix} x_1 \\ x_2 \\ x_3 \end{bmatrix} =
\begin{bmatrix} h_1 z_1 + h_2 z_2 + h_3 z_3 \\ h_4 z_1 + h_5 z_2 \\ z_1 \end{bmatrix}
\tag{11}
$$

where

$$
\begin{aligned}
h_1 &= \frac{b_2 a_7}{a_6 b_1} + \frac{b_3}{b_1} = \frac{a_4 a_7}{a_3 a_6} - \frac{a_5}{a_3}, &
h_2 &= \frac{b_2}{b_1 a_6} = \frac{a_4 + a_7}{a_3 a_6}, &
h_3 &= \frac{1}{b_1} = \frac{1}{a_3 a_6}, \\
h_4 &= \frac{a_7}{a_5}, &
h_5 &= \frac{1}{a_6}
\end{aligned}
\tag{12}
$$

It should be noted, that in the non-linear feedback $v = b_1 u - c_4 e^{a x_1}$ we have the state variable x_1 which is a coordinate of vector x in the non-linear state equation (2). In this case it is an unknown quantity.

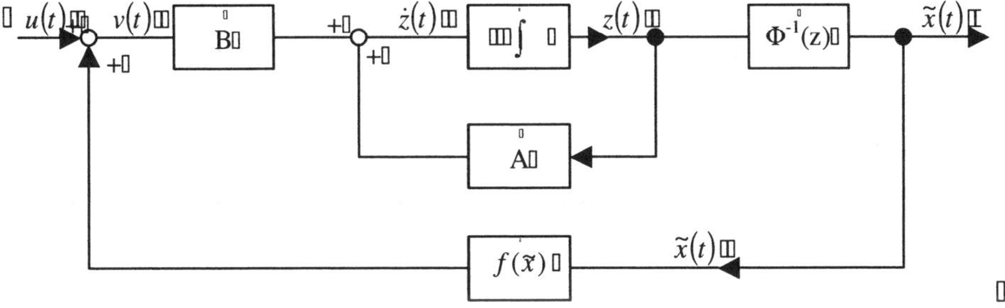

Figure 3. Block diagram of linear system with new input $v = u + f(\tilde{x})$.

For the numerical solution of linear equation (7) the following recurrent model is applied (Fig. 3):

$$v_i = b_1 u_i + f(\tilde{x}_{i-1}), \; i = 1, 2, ..., N \tag{13}$$

$$z_{i+1} = A z_i + B v_i, \; i = 1, 2, ..., N \tag{14}$$

where

$$\begin{bmatrix} \tilde{x}_{1,i} \\ \tilde{x}_{2,i} \\ \tilde{x}_{3,i} \end{bmatrix} = \begin{bmatrix} h_1 z_{1,i} + h_2 z_{2,i} + h_3 z_{3,i} \\ h_4 z_{1,i} + h_5 z_{2,i} \\ z_{1,1} \end{bmatrix}, \; i = 0, 1, ..., N \tag{15}$$

while $\tilde{x}(t) \cong x(t)$, where $x(t)$ is a non-linear solution of equation (2).

The results of the numerical solutions (Runge-Kutta method) are shown in Fig. 4. The curves presented in this figure are an interpretation of the non-linear equation and linear equation (12) solved according to the recurrent equations (13) and (14). We should note here, that in order to calculate a new input $v_i = b_1 u_i + f(\tilde{x}_{i-1})$, $i = 1, 2, ..., N$ in consecutive steps we use the values of the function $f(\tilde{x})$ with $i - 1$ step, which leads to the solution of equation (14) with saticfactory accuracy required for technical reasons (calculating error $\varepsilon_i < 2.6 * 10^{-5}$ for a step of integration $h = 1.0 * 10^{-8}$) [4]. Analytical solution of

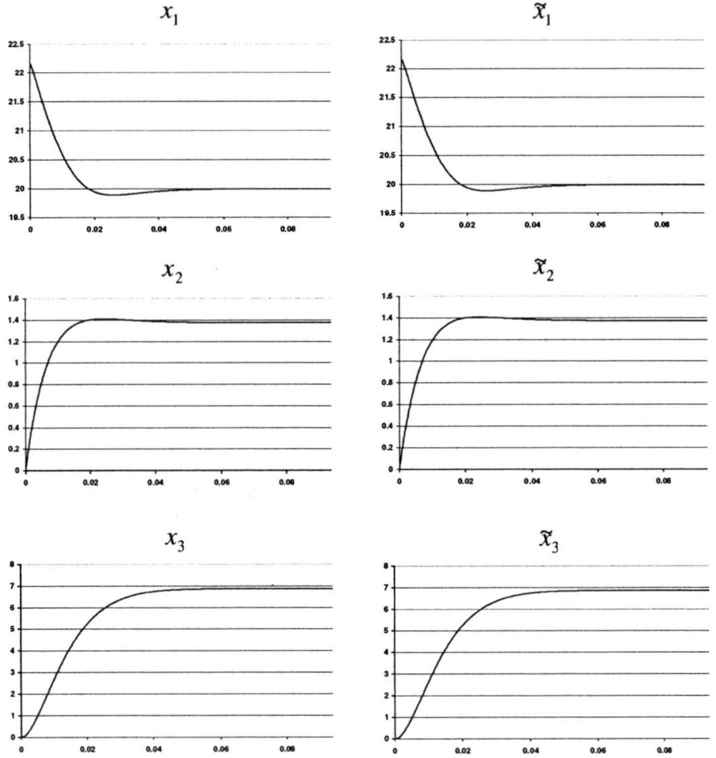

Figure 4. Numerical solution: a) non-linear model (2), b) linear model (13), (14), (15)

equation (7) can be presented as follows [1]:

$$z(t) = e^{A(t-t_0)}z(t_0) + e^{At}\int_{t_0}^{t} e^{-A\tau}Bv(\tau)d\tau \tag{16}$$

This equation is, however, hard to implement using numerical calculations. The exact solution of equation (7) can be obtained using iteration process [7], where $t_0 = kT$ and $t = (k+1)T$, T is a previously specified time interval (eg. $T = 10^{-5}s$):

$$z[(k+1)T] = e^{At}z(kT) + e^{A(k+1)T}\int_{kT}^{(k+1)T} e^{-A\tau}Bv(\tau)d\tau \tag{17}$$

Approximating the input $v(t)$ with the function of constant intervals

$$v(t) = v(kT)\ dla\ kT \leq t \leq (k+1)T,\ k = 0, 1, 2, ... \tag{18}$$

we obtain the solution:

$$z[(k+1)T] = e^{At}z(kT) + (e^{At} - 1)A^{-1}Bv(kT) \tag{19}$$

Substituting the dependences into equation (19):

$$e^{AT} = \sum_{k=0}^{\infty} \frac{(AT)^k}{k!} \tag{20}$$

and:

$$(e^{AT} - 1)A^{-1} = T\sum_{k=0}^{\infty} \frac{(AT)^k}{(k+1)!} \tag{21}$$

we obtain:

$$z[(k+1)T] = \sum_{k=0}^{\infty} \frac{(AT)^k}{k!}z(kT) + T\sum_{k=0}^{\infty} \frac{(AT)^k}{(k+1)!} \tag{22}$$

Using equations

$$A_1 = \sum_{k=0}^{\infty} \frac{(AT)^k}{k!}\ and\ A_2 = T\sum_{k=0}^{\infty} \frac{(AT)^k}{(k+1)!} \tag{23}$$

we calculate the sums of the series according to the convergence criterion:

$$\|S_{k+1}\| - \|S_k\| \leq \varepsilon,\ \varepsilon = 10^{-4} \tag{24}$$

$$\|S\| = max_j \sum_i a_{ij},\ where\ a_{ij}\ are\ elements\ of\ the\ matrix\ A_1\ and\ A_2 \tag{25}$$

Finally, we obtain the following recurrent equation:

$$z(k+1) = A_1 z(k) + A_2 Bv(k) \tag{26}$$

3   Parallel version of the global linearization method

Below we present a parallel computing model for a circuit with a DC motor based on equation implemented on three processors. In this case equation (26) can be presented as follows:

$$\begin{bmatrix} z_1(k+1) \\ z_2(k+1) \\ z_3(k+1) \end{bmatrix} = A_1 \begin{bmatrix} z_1(k) \\ z_2(k) \\ z_3(k) \end{bmatrix} + A_2 B v(k) \tag{27}$$

where:

$$A_1 = \begin{bmatrix} a_{1,11} & a_{1,12} & a_{1,13} \\ a_{1,21} & a_{1,22} & a_{1,23} \\ a_{1,31} & a_{1,32} & a_{1,33} \end{bmatrix}, \ A_1 = \begin{bmatrix} a_{2,11} & a_{2,12} & a_{2,13} \\ a_{2,21} & a_{2,22} & a_{2,23} \\ a_{2,31} & a_{2,32} & a_{2,33} \end{bmatrix}, \ B = \begin{bmatrix} 0 \\ 0 \\ 1 \end{bmatrix} \tag{28}$$

or:

$$z_1(k+1) = a_{1,11} * z_1(k) + a_{1,12} * z_2(k) + a_{1,13} * z_3(k) + a_{2,13} * v(k) \tag{29}$$

$$z_2(k+1) = a_{1,21} * z_1(k) + a_{1,22} * z_2(k) + a_{1,23} * z_3(k) + a_{2,23} * v(k) \tag{30}$$

$$z_3(k+1) = a_{1,31} * z_1(k) + a_{1,32} * z_2(k) + a_{1,33} * z_3(k) + a_{2,33} * v(k) \tag{31}$$

$$k = 0, 1, 2, ..., N$$

We carry out computation in the time interval $[0, 1]$ with a step 10^{-5}.

1. Master processor (which is also one of the computing processors) transfers equations to slave processors: (29) to the P_1 processor, (30) to the P_2 processor and (31) to the P_3 processor.

2. Master processor sends to all slave processors the set of initial conditions $z_1(0)$, $z_2(0)$, $z_3(0)$ and $v(0)$.

3. Slave processors P_1, P_2 and P_3 perform parallel computations for $k = 0$. P_1 processor computes $z_1(1)$, P_2 processor computes $z_2(1)$ and P_3 processor computes $z_3(1)$.

4. P_1 processor stores the result and sends $z_1(1)$ to P_2 and P_3 processors. P_2 processor stores the result and sends $z_2(1)$ to P_1 and P_3 processors. P_3 processor stores the result and sends $z_3(1)$ to P_1 and P_2 processors. Next each of the processors computes the value $v(1)$.

5. Slave processors P_1, P_2 and P_3 perform concurrent computations for $k = 1$. P_1 processor computes $z_1(2)$, P_2 processor computes $z_2(2)$, P_3 processor computes $z_3(2)$ and the procedure is repeated until the predicted end of the time interval is reached.

The algorithm for n equations and N processors is presented as follows:

$$Z = \begin{bmatrix} z_1 \\ z_2 \\ ... \\ z_n \end{bmatrix}, B = \begin{bmatrix} 0 \\ 0 \\ ... \\ 1 \end{bmatrix}, \text{ number of processors } P = N$$

The program works on N processors, everyone gets $\frac{n}{N}$ equations.

1. Master processor sends equations to slave processors.

2. Master processor sends to all slave processors the set of initial conditions $z_1(0)$, $z_2(0)$, $\ldots$, $z_n(0)$ and $v(0)$.

3. Slave processors P_1, P_2, P_3, ..., P_N perform parallel computations for $k = 0$. P_1 processor computes values from $z_1(1)$ to $z_{\frac{n}{N}}(1)$, P_2 processor computes values from $z_{\frac{n}{N}+1}(1)$ to $z_{\frac{2n}{N}}(1)$, P_3 processor computes values from $z_{\frac{2n}{N}+1}(1)$ to $z_{\frac{3n}{N}}(1)$. The last P_N processor computes values from $z_{\frac{(N-1)*n}{N}+1}(1)$ to $z_n(1)$.

4. P_1 processor stores the result and sends values from $z_1(1)$ to $z_{\frac{n}{N}}(1)$ to P_2, P_3,..., P_N processors. P_2 processor stores the result and sends values from $z_{\frac{n}{N}+1}(1)$ to $z_{\frac{2n}{N}}(1)$ to P_1, P_3,..., P_N processors. P_3 processor stores the result and sends values from $z_{\frac{2n}{N}+1}(1)$ to $z_{\frac{3n}{N}}(1)$ to P_1, P_2,..., P_N processors. The last P_N processor stores the result and sends values from $z_{\frac{(N-1)*n}{N}+1}(1)$ to $z_n(1)$ to P_1, P_2,..., P_{N-1} processors. Next each of the processors computes the value $v(1)$.

5. Slave processors P_1, P_2, P_3, ..., P_N perform parallel computations for $k = 1$. P_1 processor computes values from $z_1(2)$ to $z_{\frac{n}{N}}(2)$, P_2 processor computes values from $z_{\frac{n}{N}+1}(2)$ to $z_{\frac{2n}{N}}(2)$, P_3 processor computes values from $z_{\frac{2n}{N}+1}(2)$ to $z_{\frac{3n}{N}}(2)$. The last P_N processor computes values from $z_{\frac{(N-1)*n}{N}+1}(2)$ to $z_n(2)$ and the procedure is repeated until the predicted end of the time interval is reached.

4 Conclusions

The considerations presented in sections 2 and 3 allow us to make the following conclusions:

- numerical solution of the linear model remains in good agreement with the numerical solution of the non-linear model in the whole state space,

- analysis of linear equation can be used to formulate conclusions concerning the uniqueness of the non-linear model and its stability.

The parallel version of this algorithm makes it possible to keep both of the above features, in this way speeding up the computing process. Although the acceleration cannot be observed in this case of three state variables due to a considerable dominance of messages (i.e. data transfer between slave processors) over the number of computations, but for a higher number of state variables used, for instance, in the analysis of power systems or wave phenomena in transmission lines, the speed up of the computation process should be satisfactory.

Acknowledgements: *This project has been carried out within the teamwork no. W/WE/2/03.*

References

[1] T. Kaczorek, *Linear Control Systems*, vol. 1 and 2, J. Wiley, 1993

[2] A. Jordan et al., *Optimal Linearization of Non-linear State Equations*, Rairo - Automatique, Systems Analysis and Control (1987), 263–271

[3] M. Barland et al., *Commende optimal d'un systeme generateur photovoltaique convertisseur statique - recepteur*, Revue Phys. Appl. 19, Commision des Publications, Francaises de Physique, Paris, 905–915

[4] Kaczorek T., Jordan A., Forenc J.: *Global linearization of a Non-linear model of a DC Drive System*, The Second Grant Conference - "Numerical methods in the electrical devices computations" , pp. 7-16, PJIIT, Warsaw, 2002

[5] Stahir P., Rendzinyak S., Krupskyy B.: *Parallelization of Diacopbic Methods for Multiprocessor Computing System*, accepted for the Bulletin of the Polish Academy of Sciences

[6] Petcu D.: *Parallelism in solving ordinary differential equations*, Timisoara University Press, Romania, 1998

[7] Baron B et al.: *Numerical methods in Delphi 4 (in Polish)*, pp. 381-391, 1999

[8] Baron B., Krych J.: *The application of finited differences method and Fehlberg method to transient states analysis in transmission line (in Polish)*, ZkwE 2001, pp. 29-32

[9] Forenc J.: *The Application of the Speculative Methods To Transient States Analysis in Transmission Line*, 26-th IC-SPETO International Conference of Fundamentals of Electrotechnics and Circuit Theory, Gliwice-Niedzica, Poland, 2003, pp. 431-434

Concurrent Information Processing and Computing
D. Grigoras and A. Nicolau (Eds.)
IOS Press, 2005

309

CFDA : A CCA-based Component Framework for Distributed Applications

Iyad Alshabani   Bernard Toursel*

Laboratoire D'Informatique Fondamentale de Lille (LIFL) - USTL
UMR CNRS 8022
59655 Villeneuve d'Ascq Cedex – France
Tel: 33 (0)3 20 43 45 39 - Fax: 33 (0)3 20 43 65 66
**Ecole Polytechnique Universitaire de Lille (Polytech'Lille)*
{alshaban,toursel}@lifl.fr

Abstract. Nowadays one of the important issues of software engineering is the component-based development. But existing component models like JavaBeans/Enterprise JavaBeans [11], CORBA [9] or COM [8] are not adapted to parallel and distributed computing. Then we take care of the building of a framework for distributed computing. In this context, we present here our needs and works on components, by implementing some services like event services, demand and data driven operating modes,and introducing concepts like super-component. We use the CCA (Common Component Architecture model) [4] for our developments.

1 Introduction

The rapid deployment of computer networks and Internet and the emergence of new programming technologies have introduced the new age of programming paradigm. Component-based development is one of the new technologies that becomes nowadays an important issue in software engineering. At the same time, these technologies are being used to develop infrastructures for distributed computing and the grid structure [6]. The co-operation between different applications of computing over a network or a grid is one of the necessities that faces scientists. This involves the possibility of coupling multiple codes of scientific computing. Component technology appears as a solution to the problems encountered in the development and the deployment of such programs over a computing network. The common existing component models like JavaBeans/ Enterprise JavaBeans [11], CORBA [9] or COM [8] address sequential components. Some works on component architecture for parallel computing are presented by the Common Component Architecture (*CCA*) Forum [4] Other works [10] extends an existing commercial model like CCM for parallel components. The contributions of our work consists of extending the CCA component model and implementing it through a framework in which we can have the necessary control and basic parallel components. Through our work CFDA(*CCA-based Framework for Distributed Application*), we aim to give a framework that provides a minimum of services that ensure the creation, instantiation, inter-connection between components and component activation and to treat with some aspects of composition and component granularity.

The paper is structured as follows. Section 2 is a state of the art about existing component architectures and their loose for high performance issues. Section 3 is an overview of the CCA component model on which depends our work and our motivations behind CCA. We present in section 4 our actual works and experiments, and in section 5 our future works.

2   Related Works

Industrial corporations have defined and implemented component architecture standards such as JavaBeans/Enterprise JavaBeans [11], CORBA [9] and COM [8]. These computing environments are distributed object computing systems that extend object-oriented programming systems

Industrial standards do not address the needs for high performance computing because they do not support efficient parallel component abstraction and related communication and interaction between parallel components. In this section, we review these industrial standards and explain their limitations for high performance computing needs.

2.1   Sun's JavaBeans and Enterprise JavaBeans

JavaBeans and Enterprise JavaBeans(EJB) [11] are component architectures that are based on Java programming language. The JavaBeans specifications define a Bean as a reusable component that can be manipulated visually in a builder tool. It is clear that a Bean is a graphical component as any Java object that have an interface class. Enterprise JavaBeans model represents a groundwork of components servers still called business components to design transaction-oriented distributed applications and to support the design of implementing reusable components.

Despite of their technology because of business aspects of these models they don't address the distributed and parallel computing and high performance aspects.

2.2   CORBA Components

CORBA is a distributed object specification supported by the OMG (Object Management Group). CORBA supports the interaction of complex objects written in different languages distributed across a network of computers running with different operating systems. The OMG defined the CORBA Component Model (CCM) [7], a model of distributed software components based on a technology of containers similar to those of EJBs.

The CCM extends the CORBA IDL to make the Component Implementation Definition Language (CIDL) with new keywords to define ports, attributes and interactions between CCM components.

Some researches [10] are in progress to make extension of the CCM model for parallel components. But CCM model stills a heavy one that addresses business logic needs.

2.3   Common Component Architecture

The *Common Component Architecture* (CCA) is a project raised by the Department Of Energy (DOE) in the USA. The objective of the CCA Forum [4] is to define a minimal set of standard features that a high-performance component framework has to provide, or can expect, in order to be able to use components developed within different frameworks. Such standard will promote interoperability between components developed by different teams across different institutions. This direction is not taken in account in other component models which make of it a good choice for people who are working in distributed and parallel computing. In the next section we present more precisely the CCA architecture.

3   Overview of the CCA Architecture

We present here an overview of the CCA components model and specifications [2]. The Common Component Architecture consists of two types of entities: components and frameworks which we present in the following sections.

3.1   Components and Ports

Components are the basic units that are composed to form an application. Components could be simple, "computation code", or composed "multiple encapsulated components". They also may be an application or a service of the framework. Components cannot be accessed directly but using interfaces and services of the framework. In CCA, the interfaces that components offer are called *ports*. These ports are of two types: *provides* ports and *uses* ports.

Provides ports are the set of public interfaces, implemented by the component, which can be referenced and used by other components. A component can have zero or more *provides* ports. A *provides* port could also be thought as a service that is provided to other components or to the framework. The member functions of a *provides* port may be thought as a handler functions that are executed by the component on behalf of the component's users.

Uses port can be viewed as a connection point on the surface of the component where the framework can connect references to *provides* port provided by other components or by the containing framework itself. Viewed from the inside of the component, a *uses* port is an object that implements the capability the component needs to use. The component makes calls on a *uses* port reference to use the provided capabilities. A component may have zero or more *uses* ports. Depending on the framework, one or more *provides* ports may be connected to a single *uses* port and a *provides* port may be provided to one or more *uses* ports. In general, if the capability needed by a *uses* port returns a value, the number of *provides* ports connected to it may be restricted to be one. Frameworks supporting *direct connects* (one-to-one connections) may actually supply the *provides* port object reference directly as the connected *uses* port. In these cases there is only one function call between a user and a provider, affording the least amount of overhead possible.

3.2   Frameworks

A component framework is said to be CCA compliant if it conforms to the specifications i.e. it provides a minimum of necessary services and implements the required CCA interfaces. Through services one can access the component, connect two or more components, run a computational component and exposes the services provided by a component to other frameworks. There exists some CCA compliant framework like CCAT [3] or the CCAFFEINE [1] each of them is an application-specific framework but they could have a kind of collaboration between them. The CFDA project is a framework that is CCA-compliant.

3.3   Component interaction

As we have seen above, CCA ports are the communications end points that define the connection model for component interaction. The *provides/uses* approach enables connections that do not impede inter-component performance, yet allows a framework to create distributed connections when desired. Connections are of two types: Direct and collective.

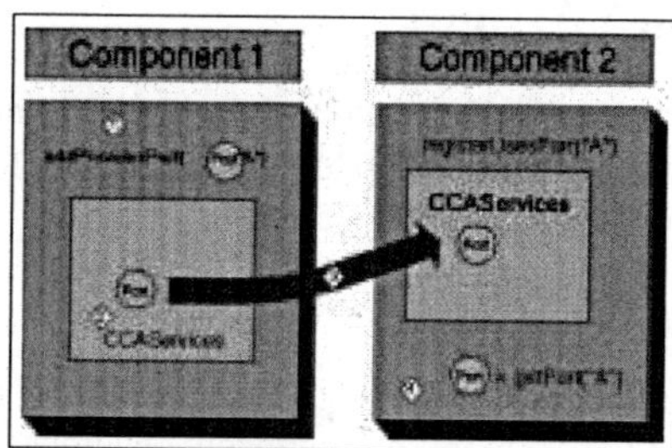

Figure 1. Component direct-connection mechanism

- *Direct connection.* This type of connection (Figure 1), makes the most sense when the component instances exist in the same address space. The simplest way for making such a connection is to create an object that exports a *DirectConnectPort* interface subclassing both the *UsesPort* and *ProvidesPort* interfaces. By this way, the framework gets a *provides* interface from one component and gives that same interface directly to a connecting component as a *uses* interface. With this approach the framework still retains full control over the connection between components.

- *Collective ports.* They are a type of ports, introduced by CCA forum, for parallel interactions and parallel data redistribution between components, but they don't have yet any model for this type of ports.

3.4 Scientific Interface Definition Language (SIDL)

The CCA forum has introduced an IDL language for high performance needs :the *Scientific IDL*. It provides language interoperability that hides language dependencies to simplify the interoperability of components written in different programming languages, with the proliferation of languages used for numerical simulation.

An implementation of SIDL specifications is the *Babel* [5] SIDL. The goal of such SIDL is to support complex numbers and dynamic multi-dimensional arrays as well as parallel communication directives that are required for parallel distributed components.

In our work we make no use or implementation of SIDL. The CFDA is implemented in the Java programming language which is a good solution for heterogeneity and distribution issues. Moreover, Java presents an interface model that is similar to that of IDL in addition to exception handling.

4 CFDA implementation details

We aim through our work CFDA *CCA-based Framework for Distributed Application* to build a framework for parallel and distributed applications. We are specially interested in components and tools required for parallel executions and more specially for the optimization problems, like the flow-shop problem [12].

We need components running on different computers and communications in the context of a high performance environment. So we choose to develop our framework according to CCA specifications, since the CCA is oriented for parallel and distributed computing.

4.1　Needs and motivations

We try, through our work to answer some questions like how a component can be activated ? what type of method invocation we may use? How data can be delivered from component to another ?

4.1.1　Component activations

Components are CCA compliant. This means that they implement one interface which is the *Component* described by the CCA model. A component developer is a person who creates a component class by implementing the *Component* interface and define the internal operation of this component. A component can have one or more methods that represent operations or computations with inputs and outputs. Components may be activated by the framework through a method invocation which is one of the following cases:

- Single activation: it is impossible to have any other activations on the same method,

- Single activation with the possibility to have successive activations in a queue,

- Multiple activations which is the case of parallel threads.

Components may have no state so each activation of the component is independent or they may have some states so each activation depends on the precedent one.

As it has been introduced in section 3.1 a component must provide a port to allow some other components execute what its offer. So if the framework wants to activate a components and execute it, it needs to invoke a method in a provides port that is declared by this component. We make use of special port introduced by some CCA compliant frameworks it's the *GoPort*

```
public interface GoPort extends Port {
  public void go();
}
```

which is declared by the component as a provides port. The framework activates the component by using the *GoPort* and invoking it's method *go()*. In the application it's necessary that we have at least one component that implement the *go()* method to start the whole application and consequently it make a successive invocations through *uses-provides* connections.

4.1.2　Method invocations

In CCA architecture, methods of a component are treated through ports. So a port is supposed to have a service (method) and a method invocation could be:

- Blocked with result return,

- Non blocked with result return,

- Blocked or non blocked without result return (*sequential chaining*),

- Iterated in which a thread is created in the first invocation and stay in queue for following invocations.

4.1.3 Data exchange

Data transmission between components is strictly made through port interfaces, and their implementation decide the functionality of this exchange. For that we consider two types of port *GetPort* and *SetPort* with getObject and setObject methods.

```
public interface GetPort extends Port {
  public Object getObject();
}

public interface SetPort extends Port {
  public void setObject(Object obj);
}
```

Let us suppose that we want send data from a component *C1* to a component *C2*. This could be done (Figure 2):

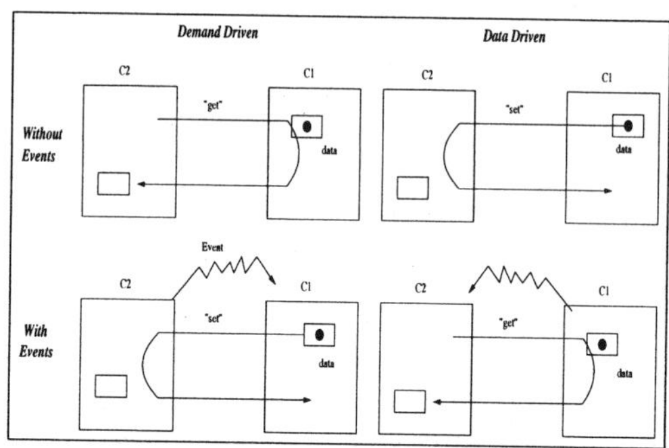

Figure 2. The four possibilities of data transmission

- **Without event notification.** In this case, methods are blocked and we can do this by two possibilities:

    - *Demand Driven:* Component *C2* requires a data of *C1* by calling "get" on *C1*.
    - *Data Driven:* Component *C1* transmits his data to *C2* by calling "set" on *C2*.

- **With event notification.** In this case, we try to make non-blocked method calls and we can do this by two possibilities:

    - *Demand Driven:* Component *C2* requires a data of *C1* by notifying *C1* about its need. Then *C1* calls a "set" on *C2* when it has a data.
    - *Data Driven:* Component *C1* informs *C2* that it has a data for it by notifying *C2* about the availability of a data. Then *C2* calls a "get" on *C1* when it becomes itself available.

4.1.4 Framework services

Components are instantiated and connected to each other through the framework services. The framework contains all meta-information concerning components, their instances,ports, types of ports and connections. The services that the CFDA implements are the instantiation, connection and event services.

An **Instantiation services** is simply a service that uses a Java Class loader. As a result of instantiation some information are kept by the framework about these instances and ports it uses or provides. In another word the framework execute the method implemented by each component *setServices*

```
public class myComp implements Component {
  ...
  public void setServices(Services svc) {
    ...
  }
}
```

The implementation of such a method uses an instance of the services. So it exposes the *provides* ports that the component has and registers the *uses* ports of the component.

A **Connection Service** is used to connect a component that has a *Provides* port and another that have a *Uses* one. It needs the port's name and component's name for the two components that are connected. If there is a type mismatch then a connection exception is thrown. We consider dynamic and static connections. When connection is established, a *connection event* is generated to inform the framework about it. An **Event service** is used in framework in addition to components. Event services are: *Connection events,Component Change Events* and *Component events*. For example, a component that releases a port fires an event to the framework about this change. Or if a connection has been established then a connection event is fired.

4.1.5 Composition

One of the important issue in component-based programming is to be able to create new components from other ones. This super-component is a kind of container that can compose some internal components with more fine granularity. Consequently we call a super-component developer is the person who create a super-component through the assembly of other ones and defines its operating aspect. On figure 3,the two components *C1* and *C2* are encapsulated in a super-component called *SC*. A super-component developer needs to have the compo-

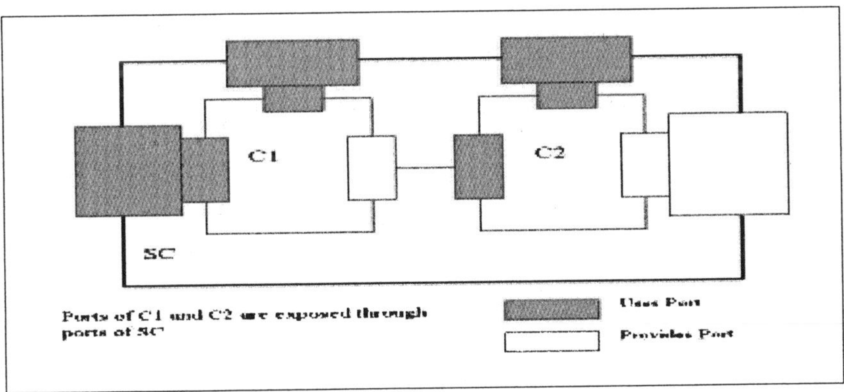

Figure 3. Super-component of two components

nent classes with meta-informations about ports that are exposed. As the framework does with components the super-component is using a service instance to get information from internal-components, but as in the internal-components the internal data are encapsulated and hidden to other components. The super-component developer is able to hide or to exposes ports of the internal ones to the outside world. We use a mechanism, illustrated in the figure 4, to connect the internal component to the external world. We distinguish two cases:

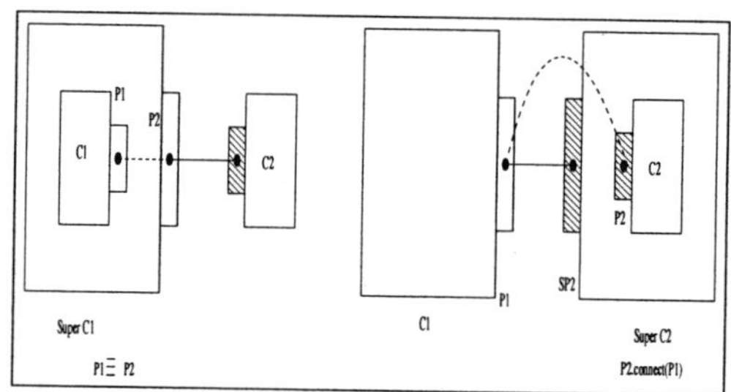

Figure 4. Mechanism of connecting internal components to the outside world

- The super-component has a *provides* port (*P2*): In this case we make a simple mapping to say that the P2 is equivalent to port of the component (*P1*). This can be done in CCA using a *getPort()* method when developing the super-component. So a component that have a *uses* port can connect to the super-component such that this connection be direct to the internal component but this connections is hidden to the outside world.

- The super-component has a *uses* port(*SP2*): In this case by using the framework services, after connections have been established between a super component and others components, the super component can obtain dynamically the services it needs by the method *getConnections()* of *uses* ports(*SP2*). So it obtains a reference to *provides* port(*P1*) which is connected to the *SP2*, then it uses a dynamic connection between *P2 Uses* port and the *P1 Provides* port using the method *connect(ProvidesPort)*.

4.2   Example: A pipeline

In order to help and illustrate, we built a pipeline adapted to parallel and distributed treatments. Through such a pipeline we can be able to create an assembly of generic components that will be the stages of a pipeline. Data is transmitted in a pipeline fashion between computing phases which are represented by components connected to the stages of the pipeline.

The pipeline (Figure 5)is made of a variable number of stages, each stage being connected to a computing component. It is also connected to a data source component and data consumer component. Components and operating mode of this pipeline are presented in the following sections.

4.2.1   Description of Components

- **Stages:** Each one is connected to a precedent stage component or a data source, to a following stage component or a data consumer, and to a computing component, so it needs three ports :

    - A *provides* port that provides data to the next stage in the pipeline,

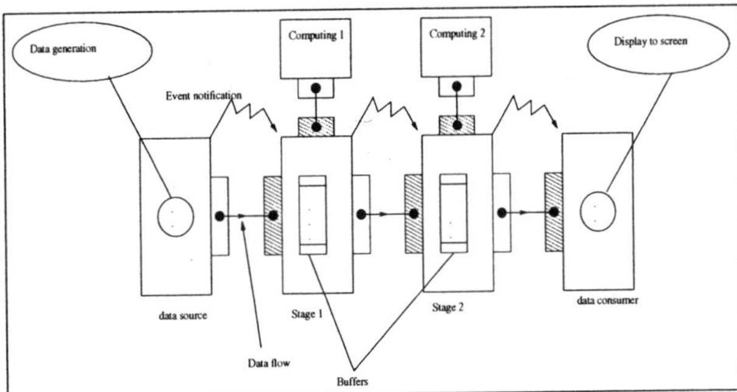

Figure 5. The Pipeline with its components

- A *uses* port that uses data given by the precedent stage in the pipeline, and

- A *uses* port that uses data given as a result of a computing operation given by the computing component.

In addition to ports each stage has a *buffer* that represents its internal state.

- **Computing components:** Each one is connected to a stage of the pipeline through its *provides* ports. Each one provides a service in the form of a computing result on data given by the stage of the pipeline.

- **Data source:** It simulates a source of data which generates data and delivers them to the first stage of the pipeline through its *provides* port.

- **Data consumer:** It consumes data delivered by the last stage of the pipeline. For example the consumption is made by displaying data on screen.

4.2.2   Operating mode

We consider that each stage of the pipeline as well as data source and data consumer are running in a thread in its own, so method calls between these components depend on wait-notify mechanism. In the other hand, method calls between stages and computing components are blocked ones.

When the pipeline is built and all connection are established between the different components the successive operations in the mode *data driven* are the following:

The data source generates a data (it simulates a data flow) so it sends a notification event to the first stage of the pipeline. If the buffer of this first stage is available so the data can be transmitted by the data source. During this time the computing component is doing its computing work on the data previously in the buffer. If the computing has finished and returned its result to first stage, this last one will notifies the next stage about the availability of a data. The same process is repeated on each stage of the pipeline.

Activating stages is done one time and it's made by the framework that call the *go()* method of the interface *GoPort*

5 Future works

We aim to test our framework on a case study. While writing this paper we try to apply an application of multi-objective optimization problem, the *flow shop* problem. Components of different granularities will be implemented and run over different computers using the Java RMI technology with the CCA specifications. But firstly we try to provide parallel components that depends on the CCA-Forum collective ports and components. Data exchange between components will be reached as well as distributed services which will need some deployment capabilities. In addition to make our framework, we plan to make it inter-operable with other CCA frameworks using the SIDL.

References

[1] B. Allan, R.Armstrong, A. Wolfe, J. Ray, D. Bernholdt and J. Kohl. The CCA Specification In a Distributed Memory SPMD Framework. *Concurrency: Practice and Experience* vol 14, N.5, 25 April 2002.

[2] R. Armstrong, D. Gannon, A. Geist, K. Keahy, S. Khon, L. McInnes, S. Parker and B. Smolenski. Toward a Common Component Architecture for High-Performance Scientific Computing. In *Proceedings of the 8th IEEE International Symposium on High Performance Distributed Computing*, August 1999.

[3] R. Bramley, K. Chiu, S. Diwan, D. Gannon, M. Govindaraju, N. Mukhi, B. Temko and M. Yechuri. A Component Based Services Architecture for Building Distributed Applications. In *Proceedings of the 9th IEEE International Symposium on High Performance Distributed Computing*, August 2000.

[4] CCA Forum web page: *http://www.cca-forum.org*.

[5] A. Cleary, S. Kohn, S. Smith, and B. Smolinski. Language interoperability mechanisms for high-performance scientific computing. In *Proceedings of the SIAM Workshop on Object-Oriented Methods for Inter-Operable Scientific and Engineering Computing*, October 1998.

[6] I. Foster and C. Kesselman. The Grid: BluePrint for New Computing Infrastructures. *Morgan Kaufmann Publishers Inc.* 1998.

[7] R. Marvie and P. Merle. Vers un modèle de composants pour CESURE - le CORBA Component Model. *Technical Report 3*, Projet RNRT 98 CESURE, 2000.

[8] Microsoft's COM web page: *http://www.microsoft.com/COM*

[9] OMG. CORBA components. *Technical Report*, 1999.

[10] Christian Pérez and André Ribes. Vers des composants parallèles. *Journ ées composants: Flexibilité du Système au langage*, Besançon 2001.

[11] Sun's java products web page: *http://java.sun.com/products/*.

[12] E. G. Talbi, M. Rahoual, M. H. Mabed and C. Dhaenens. A Hybrid Evolutionary Approach for Multi-criteria Optimization Problems: Application to the Flow Shop. In E. Zitzler et al., editors, *Evolutionary Multi-Criterion Optimization*, volume 1993 of LNCS, pages 416-428, Springer-Verlag, 2001.

Author Index